AF361339

Developing Systemic Functional Linguistics

Developing Systemic Functional Linguistics:

Theory and Application

Edited by Fang Yan and Jonathan J. Webster

SHEFFIELD UK   BRISTOL CT

Published by Equinox Publishing Ltd.

UK: Unit S3, Kelham House, 3 Lancaster Street, Sheffield, S3 8AF
USA: ISD, 70 Enterprise Drive, Bristol, CT 06010

www.equinoxpub.com

First published 2014

ISBN 978-1-84553-995-5 (hardback)

British Library Cataloguing-in-Publication Data

A catalogue record for this book is available from the British Library.

Library of Congress Cataloging-in-Publication Data
Developing systemic functional linguistics : theory and application / Edited by Fang Yan and Jonathan J. Webster.
    pages cm
Includes bibliographical references and index.
ISBN 978-1-84553-995-5 (hb)
1. Functionalism (Linguistics) 2. Systemic grammar. I. Yan, Zhong, 1934- editor of compilation. II. Webster, Jonathan, 1955- editor of compilation.
P147.D48 2013
410.1'8--dc23
                                    2012046463

Typeset by CA Typesetting Ltd, Sheffield, www.sheffieldtypesetting.com
Printed and bound in Great Britain by Lightning Source UK Ltd., Milton Keynes and Lightning Source Inc., La Vergne, TN

Contents

Preface

The aim of *Developing Systemic Functional Linguistics* is to present a collection of chapters which explore recent developments in Systemic Functional Linguistics (SFL) in theory and application. Although the majority of the papers included here were presented at the 36th ISFC held in Beijing, co-hosted by Tsinghua University and City University of Hong Kong in 2009, some have been especially prepared for this volume. The leading chapter by M. A. K. Halliday is based on his plenary talk presented at the 37th ISFC (International Systemic Functional Congress) hosted by University of British Columbia, Vancouver in 2010. Ruqaiya Hasan's chapter is adapted from her plenary speech at the 10th China Functional Conference held at Jiangxi Normal University, Nanchang, China in 2007. Yang Xueyan's chapter is from her book *Modelling Text As Process – A Dynamic Approach to EFL Classroom Discourse* published by Continuum in 2010; the chapter by Yang Guowen is a brief summary of her PhD dissertation published by Peter Lang in 2007. Finally, Mick O'Donnell was especially invited to contribute an original piece on applying Corpus Linguistics as a tool in SFL research.

This book consists of three parts. The first part 'Theoretical issues in description' addresses the advancement of various theoretical aspects of SFL in recent years. In the first chapter entitled 'Some systemic functional reflections on the history of meaning', M. A. K. Halliday discusses the history of meaning as it relates to 'the meaning potential that characterizes a language as a whole'. The second chapter, co-authored by J. Martin *et al.*, elaborates on the subject of 'Choice and consequence in youth justice conferencing'. The remaining chapters in this first part are contributed by scholars in China. Zhang Delu discusses the similarities and differences between the theoretical notions of 'syntax' among scholars within SFL; Yan Shiqing compares SFL with Lev Vygotsky's constructivist view on language; and Yang Guowen develops a system network of 'aspect' for the Chinese language.

Part Two 'Theory and its applications' focuses on attempts at applying SFL in different fields. The leading chapter 'Linguistic sign and the science of linguistics: The foundations of applicability', written by Ruqaiya Hasan, looks at Saussure's concept of 'linguistic sign' in relation to Halliday's notion of 'appliable linguistics'. In *Appliable Discourse*

Analysis, Christian Matthiessen notes that to be truly effective Applicable Discourse Analysis (ADA) needs to be not only comprehensive in its coverage of languages and other semiotic systems but also explicit enough to support automated analysis leading ultimately to both high-volume and high level automated analysis. The next four chapters discuss the application of SFL in discourse analysis and translation. Chapter 8 by Geoff Thompson presents a contrastive study of interpersonal 'discourse acts' and their functions in two registers – academic writing and personal blogs. Yang Xueyan models and analyses the phenomenon of ellipsis in classroom discourse in teaching English as a foreign language. Li Zhanzi, in Chapter 10, presents a detailed analysis of a Chinese classical literary work using genre and appraisal theories. Research on translation is covered in Chapter 11 by Huang Guowen, who discusses the analysis of the reporting clause in translating Confucius's *Lun Yu* (論語 or *The Analects*) into English.

Part Three looks at 'Developing directions' in the years to come. In Chapter 12, O'Halloran and her team discuss their software *Semiomix* and its application for future studies of multimodal and multisemiotic texts. Chapter 13, written by David G. Butt and his team, introduces the cross-disciplinary efforts of both linguists and psychotherapists. Chapter 14 is contributed by Heidi Byrnes, who considers SFL to be 'an education-friendly theory', as evident from their efforts at Georgetown University to develop 'an integrated four-year undergraduate curriculum that puts major tenets of SFL into educational practice in foreign language teaching and learning'. In the next chapter Mick O'Donnell elaborates on the application of Systemic Functional Linguistics to Corpus Linguistics'. He envisages a tool based on corpus linguistics so that 'the ideal system would allow the linguist to present the tool with a hypothesis, and be given in return the evidence (instances and statistics) for or against the hypothesis'. The last chapter by Eija Ventola calls for a greater presence for SFL on the internet or 'cyberspace', including setting up an online university, all of which may provide greater access to global SFL resources and unify 'SF-teaching and research' worldwide so as 'to meet the challenges, possibilities, and responsibilities to and of SF-community in the twenty-first century in Cyberspace'.

We owe our thanks to the many contributors to this book, in particular M. A. K. Halliday and Ruqaiya Hasan. We also wish to express our thanks to Kim Wong from the Halliday Centre for Intelligent Applications of Language Studies at City University of Hong Kong for her help with the preparation of this volume for publication.

Acknowledgement

'Language evolving: Some systemic functional reflections on the history of meaning', from *The Collected Works of M. A. K. Halliday Volume 11 Halliday in the 21st Century*, Bloomsbury, 2013, pages 237–254. Reprinted with the permission of Bloomsbury Publishing.

1 Language evolving: Some Systemic Functional reflexions on the history of meaning

M. A. K. Halliday[*]

1.1

Languages change; they are changing all the time, even as we speak them. This was already known to linguists of the ancient world – such as the phonologists of the period before the Tang dynasty in China, who recognized that the sound patterns of the Chinese syllable were significantly different from what they had been at an earlier time. We usually think of linguistic change first of all in terms of the changing sounds of speech; or, if we consider change in meaning, then it is in terms of the meaning of single words, or small clusters of words that are related. We do not usually think in terms of the meaning potential that characterizes a language as a whole.

Language, and every particular language, has a history. It is helpful, I think, to recognize three distinct dimensions of time along which changes take place. There is the history of language as system – its phylogenesis; there is the history of the individual speaker – their ontogenesis; and there is the history of each instance of language – of the text, for which I suggested the term 'logogenesis', using logos in its original sense of 'discourse'. And these follow three different trajectories. The text **unfolds** in time; it may head for a target, or it may meander (most texts are a mixture of both), but meaning accumulates as each moment in the text reshapes the context for what is to come.

The language of the individual speaker follows the course of their life: it **develops** from base zero, grows to maturity, and eventually dies, perhaps with an intervening period of decline. Only the language system **evolves,** persisting through constant change in interaction with its environment. The

---

* M. A. K. Halliday is Emeritus Professor of Linguistics, University of Sydney. First published in M. A. K. Halliday, *The Collected Works of M. A. K. Halliday Volume 11 Halliday in the 21st Century*, ed. Jonathan J. Webster (London: Bloomsbury, 2013).

early comparative philologists took Darwin's evolutionary theory as their model, which was fine, although they had a rather restricted view of what constituted the relevant environment, their focus being on the phonetics of the syllable or the semantics of the lexical item. Any given instance of language use is the product of these three histories – language as evolving, language as developing, language as unfolding.

I want to keep these three histories in mind, while at the same time keeping 'evolving' in the foreground; so let me come back to this formulation, which I gained many years ago from discussion with Jay Lemke: that the **system** is maintained in being through constant change in interaction with its environment. I shall assume, with Terrence Deacon (and now I think many others), that in the past, at least, human language has co-evolved along with the human brain. The immediate environment of language is the brain itself, as modelled for linguists by Sydney Lamb in his relational network theory. The brain, in this case, is being seen as the interface between language and the two 'poles' of the material environment. At the **expression** pole are the physiological systems (articulation and auditory perception) that are involved in the production and reception of speech; at the **content** pole are the phenomena that we model as 'context' (context of culture, instantiated as contexts of situation) and to which we extend the privilege of being treated as a stratum of language (this being an important proviso of an 'appliable' linguistics).

So when we talk about language evolving in interaction with its environment, we are referring to both these aspects: one, the 'signifying body', as described by Paul Thibault – the biological evolution of the articulatory organs under the general pressure to mean (and presumably the organs of hearing as well, otherwise the quickness of the tongue would deceive the ear); two, the 'eco-social context', the increasing complexity of the physical and social processes that shape and define the conditions of human life. The evolution of the **meaning potential** of the human species involved both these factors simultaneously: the human body as signifier (the 'expression') and human eco-social experience as signified (the 'content'). The early philologists were not wrong in adopting an evolutionary perspective on language. Their limitation was in treating single features, especially speech sounds and lexical items, in isolation, or at most in a rather localized monostratal environment.

If I may digress for a moment, let me briefly revisit the old issue of the uniqueness or otherwise of the human capacity for language. Probably all warm-blooded species exchange meanings; and some, such as the bonobo, can play the human game of using conventional symbols, and even hearing human sounds apart. But it is doubtful whether any other species fully severs the bond between content and expression, achieving a 'duality of patterning' which requires an openended articulatory or other symbol-generating system. Unless you evolve a truly 'arbitrary' sign system, decoupling the expression from the content, you cannot refer, and without reference you cannot construe your experience as meaning. The semioticizing of the whole of experience does appear to be a uniquely human attribute, part of the history of meaning that is specific to the human species.

So this rather peripatetic paper is organized around that topic: the history of meaning as a distinctively human semiotic. When we think of language evolving, we usually think either of sound systems or of rather specific features of the lexicogrammar – lexicosemantic fields, or grammatical systems that can be formally identified and defined. I am asking whether we can consider the evolution of the **meaning potential** of languages, and if so, what are the relevant contextual factors that might make this something sensible, and useful, to explore.

1.2

If we switch to the ontogenetic perspective for a moment: we can track the outline history of meaning in children as their language develops. Children progress from a non-referring **protolanguage** to a referential **language** – that is, to language in its adult (i.e. post-infancy) sense. Almost at once they progress from **proper** to **common** reference (individual to class referents), then from **concrete** to **abstract** reference (sensible to imaginable referents), then from **congruent** to **metaphorical** reference (actual to virtual referents). This series of developmental steps – referring, then generalizing, then abstracting, then metaphorizing – is roughly matched in the progression of the contexts in which meanings are exchanged: first the home and the neighbourhood, then the primary school, then the secondary school. This of course is no coincidence, since these contexts are the social institutions that have evolved to exploit the developmental sequence in the child's potential to mean.

We can also think of these stages in terms of the ongoing development of **knowledge.** There are no generally agreed terms for this, but I have usually talked about the **commonsense** knowledge of home and neighbourhood, the **educational** knowledge of the primary school, and the **technical** knowledge of the secondary school. If you will accept that 'knowledge' begins at (or before) birth, then we can perhaps distinguish a pre-commonsense phase of 'personalized', or self-aware, knowledge in the home, associated with pre- and proto-language, from the commonsense knowledge of the neighbourhood, beginning with the transition from protolanguage to mother tongue; but that would need separate discussion. The point to be emphasized here is that, whatever phases we identify, each one encompasses all those that have gone before. (Yes: some earlier particulars may be lost, as with the development of the body as a whole; but that does not invalidate the total picture.) Knowledge accumulates, and this process subsumes those cases where something already learnt gets reorganized at the next stage, as happens when the child studies something like the conservation of matter in primary school, bringing to conscious awareness a principle that they have already mastered in their experience of daily life.

But there is a problem with this conceptualization: what I am calling 'knowledge' is being assumed to be only ideational knowledge – and I have just described the developmental history of meaning as a history of ways of referring, which likewise focuses uniquely on the ideational. But meaning, along whatever dimension of its history, covers all the metafunctions of language; and the history of meaning includes enacting as well as construing – the interpersonal as well as the ideational. We could bring the interpersonal in under 'knowledge' in the sense of 'knowing how to ...', where the ideational is 'knowing that ...'; but this suggests something like 'knowhow', in the sense of technical or managerial skills, whereas interpersonal meaning is still linguistic meaning but it is language enacting social and personal relationships. Knowing how language does this, and being able to refer to interpersonal meaning, is of course ideational knowledge; but that is different from engaging in acts of meaning, where every act of meaning embodies an interpersonal as well as an ideational component. This is why I have always tried to talk about meaning as something you do – like saying rather than like knowing – for example in calling my earlier book ***Learning How to Mean***. People were often unhappy about this, especially my translators; I had to point out to them that I had had to tweak the English language to make it mean this, so why shouldn't they tweak their own languages in an analogous way?

But wait – is this telling us something about the nature and the history of knowledge itself? Let me come back to the perspective of evolution, but within a historical time depth. The history of meaning has been driven by – or rather, it has been a part of – changes in the nature of the speech fellowship (I use Firth's term, in preference to the more usual 'speech community', to suggest something more in the nature of a community of shared meanings): the speech fellowship evolved from nomadic to agricultural/pastoral, and then to industrial (for the moment I am leaving out the late industrial, digital/electronic; I'll come back to this below). For those of us whose forebears followed this route, our meaning potential has a history of the exchange of meanings in forest, in farm and in factory; and in the course of this progression the outward face of language has also evolved. It has gone from speech to writing, and from writing to printing: from text as process addressed by speaker to listener, to text as entity manoeuvred from writer to reader, then text as self-replicating entity, with multiple copies out there for access by a 'readership', a set of receivers unknown by, and unknown to, the originator of the text. And again, of course, all of this history is with us in the present: most adolescents and adults in our culture engage with all of these modes of discourse every day of their lives.

If the outward face of language has evolved in such a fashion, what about its inner essence, the underlying characteristics of language as a semiotic system? Does that evolve at the same time, as part of the same historical progression? It seems that it does. If we want to maintain a matching sequence of terms, we can enumerate the series **spoken language, written language, standard language**; these were the terms I used at the Kachru Symposium in the context of 'World Englishes', and there I added as a fourth term **global language**, as this has been used in reference to the status of English today. Up till now, in this chapter, I have been ignoring the most recent stage of history, the digital/electronic stage of mass communication and multimedia; so let me say a few words on this topic now. We need a more general term which would cover the kinds of text that are associated with these multiple modalities and are indifferent to political boundaries, from the appropriately named Fox News, to the internet and the worldwide web, to the daily messaging that socializes each new generation of our children. These can take place, in principle, in any language or language mix, although the more affluent languages are inevitably playing the most significant part.

There have been and continue to be many studies of 21st century patterns of language use – of blogging, twittering, facebook conversations and the like. We can read about innovations in writing practices: about rebus writing, emoticons and so on; about code switching and code mixing; about multimodal and multimedia discourses – all of which goes to build up our picture of this fourth stage, multiple aspect language. But I don't know how much has been described of its semantic properties: as Christian Matthiessen has said, it is not so much multi-modal as multi-semiotic, with new ways of meaning and of combining the meaning potential of different semiotic systems. Even within one language we can see new patterns in the integration of the metafunctions, with meaning now often packaged as a succession of bite-sized chunks to accommodate the reduced space on a small screen and the reduced time scale of much of today's interaction, and perhaps the reduced attention span of the interactants. Here, both interpersonal and textual meanings take on a new prominence, though for different reasons: the textual is **integrating** the various semiotic strands, with the interesting consequence that it becomes **less** explicit in the text, rather like the subtitles in a foreign language movie; the interpersonal on the other hand becoming **more** explicit as the exchange of meaning becomes increasingly individualized and personalized (we are rarely shown parliamentary debates on our television screens, only the ranting and swapping of abuses that are thought to make 'good television').

Here you can hear the interpersonal element intruding into my own text, since it is clear that I don't like to find so much of meaning reduced to a series of bite-sized chunks, and I don't like the way any thoughtful discourse by those we have elected to govern us is overtaken by verbal brawling – and I blame the media for it: that explains the scare quotes just now when I referred to 'good television'. This is just one small symptom, not in itself important (but then symptoms never are); but symptomatic of a process that I have talked about as the **destruction of knowledge**, which as an old-fashioned socialist and lifelong marxist I see as part of the death throes of what is now corporate capitalism. Capitalism is a sociopolitical structure that was spectacularly successful when it first evolved (because its controls evolved along with it), but has now passed its use-by date – it has moved on, as most structures do, from being **enabling** to being **constraining,** and will destroy anything in its ruthless determination to survive.

But what is happening to knowledge is perhaps not so much its destruction, in absolute terms, but its polarization; the increasing gap in our societies between the knows and the don't-knows (replacing the haves and the have-nots, which has become a world-wide phenomenon, inter- rather than intra-societal). Either way, of course, it is destructive. But let me return to history, and to my various schemata of periodization, and ask how knowledge has been **construed** in language at different periods of our history – when, as I put it just now, our living space was defined first by forest, then by farm and then by factory. (I haven't got a fourth term for that series, which also ought to begin with f – perhaps **fantasyland** might be an appropriate name?)

1.3

I have been criticized, reasonably enough, for being too fond of grand generalizations. My defence is that I find such general patterns very useful to think with; they can be exemplified, tested, and modified or else abandoned. So I am tempted to try to map the construal of knowledge into the schemata outlined so far. But I won't – not because there are no patterns there (I am sure there are), but because I don't know enough about the subject, and I haven't read enough of recent work. So I will just say a little about some different ways of knowing – of codifying and transmitting knowledge – that have evolved in different contexts over the course of human history.

One genre that has played an important part in the evolution of knowledge is **narrative**, in which preserved accounts of past (or imaginary) events are rehearsed, in a more or less stylized and ritualized form, events which encapsulate the accumulated experience of the community. This mode of knowing was illustrated in a nice episode of the *Star Trek* TV series ("Darmok"), where Captain Picard's universal translator seemed to him to be totally malfunctioning, because when he asked the inhabitants of this particular planet, who were technologically rather sophisticated, to explain how they had arrived at some problem-solving strategy – I forget now what exactly it was – the response always came in the form of a story, a narrative of some particular past event. In the end, Picard got the message: the narrated events embodied significant moments of collective experience, from which the receiver would distil the relevant principle that had to be applied – the same as we do when reading a scientific paper.

Such narratives are instantial: they have particular protagonists (who have proper names) along with their own particular doings. Alongside such narratives, we find generalized propositions and proposals, telling what happens, or may happen, if …, or what should or should not be done. These are not stories; they are adages, and may be familiar to us in the form of **proverbs**. Proverbs are often in archaic and/or phonologically memorable language, perhaps with a touch of what Malinowski called the 'coefficient of weirdness'; but their essential feature is that they construe knowledge as generalization: the grammar detaches them from particular persons and events, making it clear that they contain a principle that is generally appliable. Proverbs were the traditional repository of common-sense knowledge in the situations of daily life; where I come from in the north of England they survived into my childhood – my grandmother was one of the last generation who used proverbs unselfconsciously; with my mother they had already become quaint and were played with as semiotic toys.

But proverbs construe knowledge in small isolated doses; they do not combine to build up any larger patterns. Narrative can do this, and the story can have a place in a broader compendium of knowledge-oriented texts. Unlike the forest, the farm produces surplus wealth; this gives rise to townships ('cities', or even 'city states'), where a division of labour evolves: the esoteric knowledge of the priests is matched by the technical knowledge of the craftsmen, and perhaps by more abstract forms of knowledge among 'philosophers' – those who have the leisure, or are directed, to pursue it. Story evolves into history, and acquires a written form.

Let me glance at two ancient centres of knowledge, which we call 'classical' for that very reason: Greece, and China. New ways of meaning were evolving in the discourses of knowledge construction – in cosmology, in mathematics, in medicine; and history was among them. Kappagoda looked at the language of two grand narratives of ancient Greece, the *Iliad* of Homer, and Thucydides' *History of the Peloponnesian War*, composed roughly six hundred years apart; and in a detailed grammatical analysis of portions of these two texts he examined how they construed history as knowledge. Homer, around 1000 years BCE, made extensive use of **simile**: this event, or this protagonist, was like some other phenomenon, and therefore served to exemplify some general pattern or principle; the likeness might be with some higher realm, such as the gods, or the forces of nature. By the time of Thucydides there had been two or three centuries of enquiry; there were texts in cosmology, geometry and medicine, with some foundation in mathematics, Thucydides sought explanations in terms of cause-&-effect, construed as clause complexes and with abstract nouns for processes and qualities – terms evolving by grammatical metaphor with the transcategorization of adjectives and verbs. In this process systematic knowledge had evolved alongside the knowledge of commonsense. Its channel was not speech but writing; its lexicogrammar still further removed from the particular.

A parallel evolution was taking place, under similar conditions, in the 'Warring States' of ancient China; these were united into the Han empire, during the same epoch as when the Romans were taking over Greece and the eastern Mediterranean; and the languages, 'classical' Chinese and Latin, became the vehicles of systematic knowledge for most of the next two millennia. Their semantic systems continued to evolve; we can't measure this, of course, but my impression is that there was about the same difference between Han and Song Chinese as there was between classical and medieval Latin over roughly the same period. I don't know how to describe the difference – it needs investigating properly; but the language of abstract learning is not insulated from other discourses: it would interact both with the language of technology (especially in China, where technology was on the whole more advanced) and with the language of commonsense (especially in Europe, where the scholars spoke a wide variety of vernaculars before taking up Latin as their second language, and these other tongues increasingly took over as the media of learned discourse). Remember also that contact between Europe and China, while frequently disrupted, was never completely lost; it was mediated by a succession of peoples who had, or soon acquired, similar semantic resources: the Byzantines and Persians, then the Arabs, and finally the Mongols who opened up the whole Eurasian continent and so helped pave the way for one further phase in the linguistic construal of knowledge – the one we're in now, in fact.

1.4

The semantic signature of our present phase of knowledge construal is **metaphor**; more specifically **grammatical metaphor**, which creates a parallel semiotic universe of virtual things, especially virtual entities and virtual processes, all of which are good for thinking with. Knowledge now takes the form of theories, which are explanatory, predictive, and generate hypotheses; these can be tested, allowing the theory to be validated and improved. In terms of the development of the individual, this level of specialized, technical knowledge is reached in the secondary school – single abstractions like *speed, product, bisect* can be coped with in the primary school, but the fully metaphoric mode of meaning is largely inaccessible to children before they reach the age of puberty.

I would like to emphasize that all these different ways of knowing are part of our semiotic make-up; the later mode does not drive the earlier ones out of the picture. Our meaning potential evolved along with our bodies and brains, and with the emergence of *homo sapiens* the human brain had evolved to where it is today. I am not talking about our ancestors previous to *homo sapiens*. The meanings of what I called the forest are the semantic resources that supported the lives of many of the first nations in North America, the Aboriginal peoples of Australia and New Guinea, the first inhabitants of South Africa, South America and the Arctic, whether they lived in forest, savannah, prairie, desert or icefield. Probably none of their representatives today, or perhaps only a very few isolated groups, have entirely retained their inherited patterns of knowledge. Much of the details of that knowledge must have been lost; you cannot transmit what you know of the medicinal properties of hundreds of plants if they have all disappeared from the scene with the coming of the farms and the factories. But the ways of meaning that supported this knowledge have become part – the foundational part – of the human experience; we see them in the patterns of our lexicogrammar, and in the way we build semiotic models of our eco-social environment – of the social groups in which we interact, and our own place within them; and also of the significant features of the situations in which we live, and of our abilities (successes and failures) when we try to manage them.

But if we are suggesting that the meaning potential has been expanding throughout these phases of knowing, we need to specify in what senses – on which of the dimensions of history – this is to be understood. To start with the brain: the brain's capacity to mean – what we ought to call its meaning potential **potential** – is common to all the human species, and while it is obviously finite, there is no reason to think it is anywhere near to being exhausted. The meaning potential of the individual expands as they learn their first language, throughout childhood and adolescence; it also expands if they learn one or more other languages, something our educators do not seem to be aware of. But what about the meaning potential of the system? Is this a meaningful concept, or just a fancy?

I think the meaning potential of the system is a meaningful concept. We should not be fooled by those who say there is no such thing as a language, or indeed as language; they are simply refusing to move to the level of theory, of thinking in terms of systems and populations. Take some arbitrary location in space-time as a starting-point – say, the kingdom of Mercia, or middle England after the Anglo-Saxon invasions, around 600 CE (because this happens to be where I come from). The inhabitants spoke a variety of Saxon: call it Mercian – which was probably not written when they first arrived, but soon afterwards started to be written down. Did writing increase its meaning potential? Let us think about this. If we isolate the act of writing from its contexts of use, the answer is no; in and of itself, writing does not affect the meaning potential of a language. But of course it does not happen like that: writing is not a decontextualized process, and writing together with the contexts in which it evolves and is transmitted certainly does increase the meaning potential, whether in trading relations and commodity exchange, in codifying laws, in developing technology, or in simply keeping records of any kind – all those contexts where meaning arises from reflecting and building on shared knowledge and shared text. In terms of our third, **logogenetic** dimension of history, writing made possible new forms of discourse with new relations to the context.

Several hundred years later, one form of Mercian evolved to become the **standard** language of England as an emerging nation state, backed up by the technology of **printing**, which arrived from Germany though having originated some time earlier in China. Did this increase the meaning potential of the language? – again, what was effective was the combination of the new medium, the printed text, with the contexts of language use, in this case the expansion of English to become the language of commerce, administration and the law. And where writing had disseminated religious knowledge, printing promoted technical and scientific knowledge. The printed text is directed at 'others', large numbers of people that the writer doesn't know, doesn't even know the existence of; it creates its own new meaning group, a speech fellowship linked by shared knowledge in some increasingly specialized domain. From now on no single individual will achieve the meaning potential of the whole system (if indeed they ever did); but the history of education suggests that even at the level of the individual the meaning potential generally tended to increase.

Just as every individual has their own story, so every language has its own story, though with many features shared across a common culture band – as for example, in most of the language communities of Europe, in the late Middle Ages, much of the meaning potential was encoded in Latin. In China too the pattern was diglossic, though with less of a gap between the two codes (written and spoken Chinese); and there were differences between China and Europe in their socio-political evolution: Chinese feudalism was more centralized and bureaucratized, less rigidly stratified, than that of Europe. But Chinese historians have worked out that the rate of turnover of landowning families was about 5% per century, and 1 would guess that that wasn't very different at the European end of the continent; 1 wonder whether such a low rate of social mobility would constrain the growth of meaning potential? – since it implies that there was relatively little exchange of meanings between the landlord and the peasant households. But that's just a fleeting thought.

1.5

There is a lot of guesswork here, though I think the basic proposition makes sense: that the meaning potential of a language does, at least under certain conditions, tend to increase. In any case we can't measure it, neither in the species (the potential potential) nor in the speech fellowship nor in the individual; we can only try to compare one stage, or one state, with another. I should point out, though, that the account carries no prosody of evaluation; we have to clear the air by detaching notions of value from evolutionary processes. You may have your personal preferences – no doubt every one of us has. (I grew up in FactoryLand, but spent a lot of my childhood in FarmLand; I like the physical environment of FarmLand and I like the interpersonal environment of FactoryLand. But I like the professional environment of whatever land we live in now, especially the doctors and the dentists). It is hard not to be bemused by the fact that evolutionary processes are ordered in time; what came later must be better (or, for some people, must be worse) than what went before it. But that is no part of the evolutionary story.

But one question of **value** does arise, in the sense not of evaluation but of effect on the overall system: namely, whether some acts of meaning, or some individuals, do carry special weight in expanding the meaning potential of a language. In the past I have called this the **Hamlet factor**, since an obvious candidate for such special effects in English would be Shakespeare, and above all perhaps the text of *Hamlet*. Other possible candidates would be the King James Bible, Milton, Jonathan Swift, Francis Bacon and Isaac Newton; and, more particularly for British English, Jane Austen, Dickens, Darwin, Lewis Carroll and Beatrix Potter. However, what spring to mind are particular pieces of wording, such as you might find in the *Oxford Dictionary of Quotations*; whereas what really counts is whether these writers, through the impact of their works as a whole, enlarged or in some way reshaped the meaning potential of the language. The example often cited in modern China is the writer Lu Xun, from the first part of the twentieth century, although his impact may have come more from the social message he was putting over than from his own rather idiosyntactic way of writing. His work is perhaps a manifesto rather a model; in this way he figures both as writer and as reformer, alongside those who have established new 'national languages' in countries such as Norway, or what is now the Czech Republic; or even reforming statesmen such as Kemel Ataturk, who succeed in releasing large amounts of semiotic energy among their citizens.

But there is no act of meaning that leaves a language exactly as it was before. Every act of meaning perturbs, however minutely, the probabilities of the language system, and so contributes to its ongoing evolution. The meaning potential is statistically modulated; that is how it is transmitted from one generation to the next. A grammatical system that is on its way out will be destabilized, one of its terms becoming less and less frequent until it disappears altogether – as has happened with one of the systems of English modality within my adult lifetime. New systems may arise, perhaps by grammaticalization like the distinction between what are now the two derivational suffixes *–less* and *–free*, as subtypes of 'privatory' with different interpersonal loading: these can now appear with the same lexical item (e.g. *valueless/valuefree,* on the model of *careless/carefree*). Such minor quantitative effects accumulate as the speakers ongoingly interact with their eco-social environment.

1.6

It is a habit of human beings to intervene in processes of evolution – to try to improve on them by introducing design. We now call this **language planning**. There is no clear line between planning and evolution – even the invention of writing could be regarded as an instance of intervention by design; but some activities are clearly designed so as to speed up, or deflect, or even to inhibit the evolution of a language. In the ancient world some texts were singled out as canonical, even sacred, and were required to be preserved and transmitted intact; while others, or the same ones at another time, were felt to threaten some new or existing order, and so had to be destroyed (the 'burning of the books'). Many societies have exercised forms of language control: some rulers have told their minorities 'your language is forbidden; you must use this one'; others, like the Nazis in Germany, have engineered a language to support their own ideology. Nowadays those who control information technology set limits on what we can mean: not only do they dictate our spelling and put restraints on our range of vocabulary, they go as far as checking our grammar to ensure that it matches their picture of 'correctness' (that it conforms to a set of arbitrary rules invented some time in the past). Presumably those who impose these constraints do not realize that the lexicogrammar is where meaning is made – or it may be, on the other hand, that they do.

Does this mean that language planning never serves to increase the meaning potential of a language? No, I don't think so; I think there are certain occasions where it clearly does. The seventeenth century language planners in England and France, like Wilkins, Dalgarno and Mersenne, set out with the intention of shaping a new form of language for construing scientific knowledge. What was needed, they reckoned, was to systematize the vocabulary so that all words were clearly and logically interrelated. They saw no need to reform the grammar; what little they said about grammar was largely within the mainstream European tradition. Their specific proposals for constructing words were never taken up; but the principle of taxonomic organization was. This principle is of course already embodied in the vocabulary of the everyday language; but the language planners brought it into prominence, and their ideas about how to make the taxonomic organization fully explicit were followed in later chemical and biological terminology.

We can see now that the most significant innovation was actually taking place in the **grammar**, without any attention from the language planners at all; this was the extension of grammatical metaphor throughout the discourse, creating a parallel universe of virtual entities and virtual processes which made it possible to construct elaborate scientific theories and develop chains of rational argument. There can be no doubt that the total effect of these extensions to the lexicogrammar of the major European standard languages – in which the language planners played their part – did expand their overall powers of meaning.

Nowadays, 'language planning' suggests committees of specialists creating lists of new terminology for a newly emerging national language. This has sometimes been derided, because such terms tend to be selected on grounds of linguistic purism – as if borrowing sounds was somehow less respectable than borrowing wordings (calquing). I remember reading about an early example from modern Greece: when the streetcar was first introduced, the Greeks were urged to refer to it as <u>o aftosiderodromos</u> ('self iron runner') rather than by the general European term <u>to tram</u>. To the extent that such coinages, whatever their origin, were construing new meanings, they were of course adding to the meaning potential of the language. Adding new words is a significant factor; it is simply not the whole story.

One group of people whose role in the history of meaning is easily overlooked is that of translators. Translators provide a simulation of multilingualism, by introducing into their target language discourses, and discourse patterns, of the other languages that they use as sources for their texts. Let me come back once more to the Chinese experience. When the Ming rulers defeated the Mongolian forces late in the fourteenth century, they reacted strongly against Mongolian internationalism; they closed the country to outsiders and outside institutions, and forbade their own citizens to travel overseas. At the time of the Yuan (Mongol) dynasty, Chinese scientists were at least on a par with their European colleagues; according to the historian Mark Elvin, they had evolved all but one of the distinctive meaning styles that proved critical to the evolution of modern science in the west. Their literary language included a large number of abstract terms powered by grammatical metaphor. But it had not developed the elaborated metaphoric mode of discourse that was evolving in Europe at the time of Galileo and Newton. This had to wait until the end of the nineteenth century, when Chinese translators, using English and German sources, often via the intermediary of translation into Japanese, made extensive texts of European scholarship available. Within a few decades, which included the move from classical to modern Chinese beginning in the 1920s (the 'May 4th movement'), Chinese had evolved patterns of discourse that are no less driven by grammatical metaphor than those of English and German. Was this a case of linguistic 'borrowing'? I would think of it rather as a process of evolution in Chinese, that was triggered off by the work of the translators. It was brought about by the changing context of China in the modern world – and also, of course, it helped to bring that changing context about.

1.7

The problem is that, while for the particular subset of the total meaning potential that is constituted by systematic institutionalized **knowledge** we can track the course of its evolution, because it was written down and a significant amount of it has survived, we have practically no evidence for the evolution of the meaning potential of the daily lives of the population as a whole. We can assume that people have always talked about the technical resources they were using, and keeping under repair, in farmlands, workshops and kitchens, naming their parts and the processes and qualities associated with their use. At the least, vocabulary would tend to grow as **things** became more varied and more complex – but, as I keep saying, it would be wrong to measure meaning potential simply by size of vocabulary.

In a few cases we can look at meaning potential as a function of what people were able to understand, because we have drama: the plays from the Mongol dynasty in China, and the miracle and mystery plays from the same period in England. The audiences were town-dwellers, or at least frequenters of the market; mainly but not entirely adult males, of whom quite a number would have been literate; in any case the themes and the stories would have been very largely familiar. But what about Shakespeare and Marlowe, whose plots would surely not have been known in advance? Two thousand years earlier, the Athenians had listened to performances of intricate tragic dramas in equally intricate language; again the stories were drawn from familiar epics and legends – but not those of the comedies of Aristophanes, or of the plays of the Roman playwrights Plautus and Terence? It seems likely that city-dwellers at any rate were operating at a level of linguistic understanding that would not have been noticeably different from today.

Country dwellers of farm and forest, with no written forms of their languages, were often thought to be just linguistic simpletons; there used to be stories about them having 'no more than a few hundred words', and these are still around in some popular accounts of language. As I keep saying, counting words tells us little about total meaning potential (remember that Ogden and Richards' *Basic English* was reckoned to have only 18 verbs); but in fact the reality is rather different. Many components go to make up the meaning potential of a speech community. In the first place, there are prodigious resources for construing complex areas of experience like the calendar, and sources of food and medication – and for both construing and enacting highly complex social structures and kinship systems. Second, people without writing often memorize and transmit large quantities of coherent text, including long and complicated narratives and rituals. And third, though this is more true of forest dwellers than farm dwellers, they often speak three, four or five different tongues – different languages, or quite divergent varieties of their own. It is surprising how little is known, or has been recorded, of their true discursive abilities.

We ought not to get too distracted by questions of size. It may be that languages tend to get bigger in the course of long-term history, in the number of options available to their speakers; but we can't measure this – even if we could count all the options, they wouldn't all carry the same value. What we can try to observe – and what is relevant to an **appliable** kind of linguistics – is how the meaning potential changes over time; or rather, how it **varies**, both diachronically and diatopically. In other words, we try to observe and explain **semantic variation**, exactly as Ruqaiya Hasan has defined it. Hasan showed how semantic variation can be studied, by observing and analysing large-scale quantitative patterns of natural linguistic interaction in clearly delimited populations of speakers; her work provides a model of scientific research wherever sufficient data can become accessible. Then, if we ever can combine this with some measure of the size of a language, we might get a sense of meaning potential as **semiotic power**. I am not sure whether semiotic power, as the full meaning potential of the individual, the speech fellowship or the language, is or is not something that can usefully be explored. But I think it ought to be.

References

Chang, Ha-joon (2010) *23 Things They Don't Tell You About Capitalism.* London: Allen Lane (Penguin Books).

Halliday, M. A. K. (2003) Written language, standard language, global language. In B. B. Kachru, Y. Kachru and C. L. Nelson (eds) *The Handbook of World Englishes* 349–365.

Halliday, M. A. K. and Martin, J. R. (1993) *Writing Science: Literacy and Discursive Power.* London: Falmer.

Hasan, R. (2009) Semantic variation: meaning in society and in sociolinguistics. In J. Webster (ed.) *Collected Works of Ruqaiya Hasan* (Vol. 2). London: Equinox.

Kappagoda, A. (2005) What do people do to know? In R. Hasan, C. M. I. M. Matthiessen and J. Webster (eds) *Continuing Discourse on Language* (Vol. 1). London: Equinox.

Klemperer, V. (2000) *The Language of the Third Reich (LTI – Lingua Tertii Imperii): A Philologist-notebook* (trans. Martin Brady). London: The Athlone Press. (Original German edition *LTI Notizbuch eines Philologen.* Halle: Max Niemeyer Verlag, 1957.)

Lamb, S. M. (1999) *Pathways of the Brain: The Neurocognitive Basis of Language.* Amsterdam: Benjamins.

Lemke, J. L. (1993) Discourse, dynamics, and social change. *Cultural Dynamics* 6 (1): 1–2.

Malinowski, B. (1935) *Coral Gardens and Their Magic* (Vol. 2). London: American Book Co.

Matthiessen, C. M. I. M. (2009) Ideas and new directions. In M. A. K. Halliday and J. Webster (eds) *Companion to Systemic Functional Linguistics.* London: Continuum.

Thibault, P. J. (2004) *Brain, Mind and the Signifying Body: An Ecosocial Semiotic Theory.* London: Continuum.

Weatherford, J. (2004) *Genghis Khan and the Making of the Modern World.* New York: Three Rivers Press.

Appendix

Some temporal sequences relevant to the histories of meaning

Modes of language	Modes of construing knowledge	Workplace	Speech community	Modes of knowing	Modes of reference	Education
spoken +written +printed (+electronic)	narrative +proverb +principle +theory	forest farm factory (office)	clan region nation (globe)	common sense +educational +technical- scientific	(proper) +common +abstract +metaphorical	(family) +neighbourhood/ pre-school +primary +secondary

2 Beyond redemption: Choice and consequence in youth justice conferencing

J. R. Martin, Michele Zappavigna and Paul Dwyer[*]

2.1 Teenage identity in youth justice conferencing

The question of teenage identity has become an important issue in our work on restorative justice in relation to youth justice conferencing in Australia. As part of this research we are studying the ways in which conferences are organized to reintegrate adolescent offenders into the community (Martin *et al.*, 2007, 2008, 2009, in press; Zappavigna *et al.*, 2008, 2009, in press). A typical conference canonically includes the stages listed below and ideally involves the Young Person (YP), and their support person (typically their mother), the Victim (or their representative) and their support person, an arresting officer, a police Youth Liaison Officer (YLO), and where appropriate an Ethic Community Liaison Officer (ELO) and Translator. The conference is coordinated by a Convenor, who is a lay person especially trained for this process; there may be some variation in staging depending on the convenor. The result of a successful conference normally involves an agreed upon community service plan for the YP. Overall the conference has been designed as a restorative justice alternative to retributive justice – i.e. going to court and receiving punishment from a magistrate, possibly involving juvenile detention.

[*] J. R. Martin is Professor of Linguistics at the University of Sydney. Michele Zappavigna is a lecturer in the School of Arts and Media at the University of New South Wales. Paul Dwyer is a Senior Lecturer in the Department of Performance Studies at the University of Sydney.

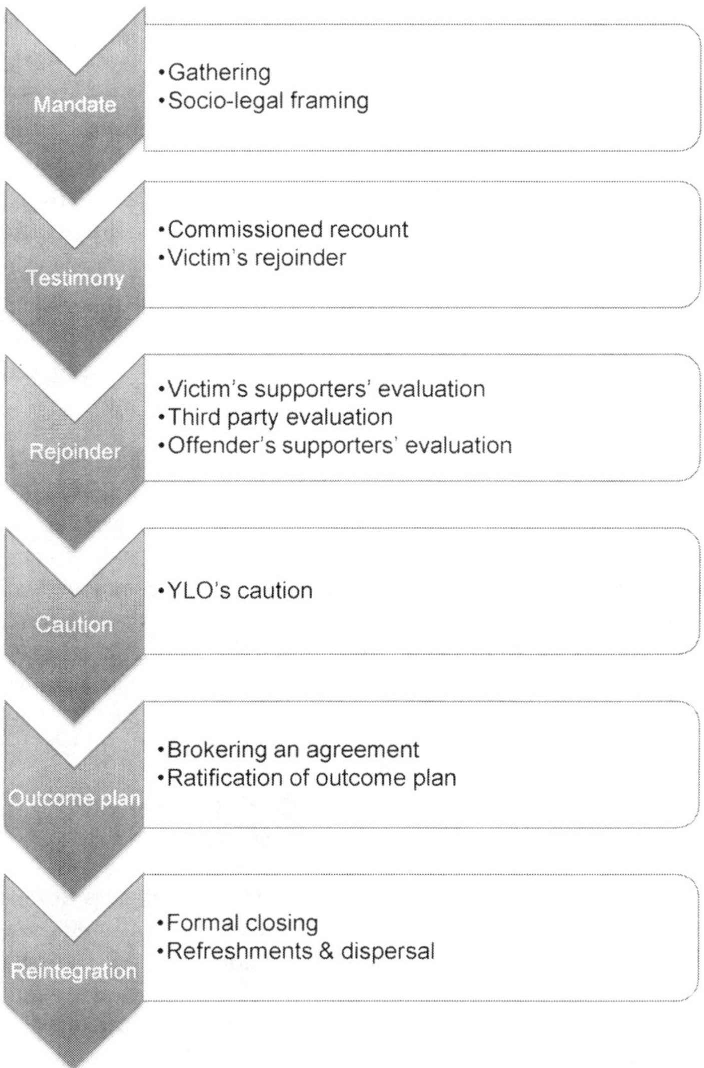

Conference macro-genre and staging

In our work on the Commissioned Recount genre in this macro-genre, which has the structure (Orientation) ^ Record of events ^ (Re-Orientation) ^ (Extension) ^ Interpretation^ Ramifications, we found that the YP generally offered a relatively succinct retelling of the events of the offence, which often needed to be extended into a fuller account through questioning by the Convenor; in addition the YP generally provided very little evaluation of these events, except when prompted to do so by the Convenor. As has already been reported in our publications, in the conferences we have considered to date, there is also a highly visible regulative discourse (Bernstein, 1975; Martin *et al.*, 2009), with the Convenor controlling the interaction. This is understandable since this is a legal process and an unfamiliar genre for several participants (the YP, Victim or Victim representative, and their supporters). Following on from this point, the Convenor initiates almost all exchanges with the YP, typically with questions. And interpretation of the recount is jointly constructed with the Convenor introducing virtually all evaluation (with respect to both emotion and values) and YP responding a word or phrase at a time.

Advocates of restorative justice ceremonies of this kind admit that conferences may well get off to a slow start, but suggest that they transform into a 'passion play' of shame, remorse and forgiveness later on:

> In a reintegrative family group conference ... the initial response of the perpetrator is often indifferent and unconcerned ... Yet as the conference runs on and both family groups began to speak about their estrangement from the perpetrator, that individual comes swiftly to learn that the love of the community is a deeply missed and quite important part of his or her world. **With such recognition comes an avalanche of shame, after which the individual is likely to express remorse, accept the forgiveness of all concerned**, and sign a document pledging to work in some way to repair or undo the damage produced by the antisocial act. (Nathanson, 1997: 25)

The Australian designers of the New South Wales Youth Justice Conferences we are considering make observations of a similar kind:

> Braithwaite's predictions about the collective willingness to forgive but not forget, and about the collective concern to achieve social reintegration, were proving to be highly accurate. But neither he nor we could account for the emotional power of conferences. We could not well explain **the regular tangible, visible progression through clearly marked stages of tension, anger, shame, remorse, apology, forgiveness, relief, and cooperation.** (Moore and O'Connell, 1994: 70)

In our observations and data analysis to date, however, we have found that interactions between the YP and other conference participants continue throughout the conference to unfold very much along the lines described above. We have seen only glimpses of remorse and apology, and in most cases these had to be elicited by the Convenor or YLO/ELO involved. In NSW it has been reported to us that about 50% of conferences take place without a Victim present, that some of the 'Victims' are actually police (who may have been attacked and abused making the arrest), and that several conferences include a Victim representative from a retail organization rather than the employee directly affected by the crime. The absence of a 'real' victim may be influencing the presence or not of the envisaged passion play.[1] In general, however, YPs and Victims (when present) report satisfaction with these and related restorative justice procedures (Trimboli, 2000). Elsewhere we have explored this disjunction in relation to a Turner-inspired notion of 'ritualised redressive action' (Martin *et al.*, 2009); our concern here is to focus on how young offenders may or may not live up to designers' expectations, and how this impacts on the way we model users of language in systemic functional linguistic (SFL) research.

2.2   Realization, instantiation and individuation

SFL has had a long-standing concern with users and uses of language (e.g. Halliday *et al.*, 1964: Chapter 4). That said, the primary focus of its research effort over the past six decades has been on language systems, organized by strata, rank and metafunction on a hierarchy referred to as realization (as schematized in Figure 2.1). For state of the art perspectives on this trajectory see Hasan *et al.* (2005, 2007); Webster (2008); Halliday and Webster (2009); and Matthiessen and Halliday (2009). Exemplary work on English is consolidated in Halliday and Greaves (2008) (phonology), Halliday and Matthiessen (2004) (lexicogrammar) and Martin and Rose (2007) (discourse semantics); for other languages see Caffarel *et al.* (2003).

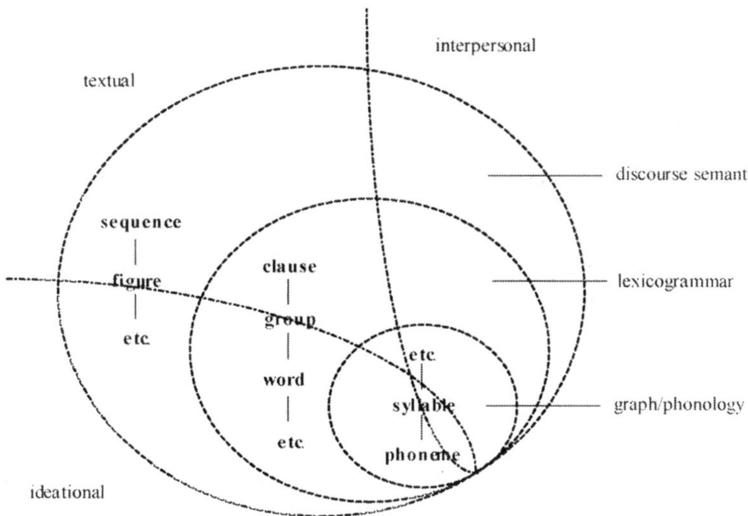

Figure 2.1: Realization (strata, rank and metafunction)

For the most part SFL has brought users and uses of language into this picture by further stratifying language in relation to social context. This has meant adding on an additional stratum to model social context as field, tenor and mode (sometimes called register – e.g. Martin, 1992), and for some systemicists (e.g. Martin and Rose, 2008) one more stratum to re-contextualize these as genre (see Figure 2.2). In a realization hierarchy of this kind, strata are related through metaredundancy – as patterns of patterns; the realization hierarchy is thus formulated as a hierarchy of abstraction, beginning with phonological or graphological patterns and ultimately pushing through to genre.

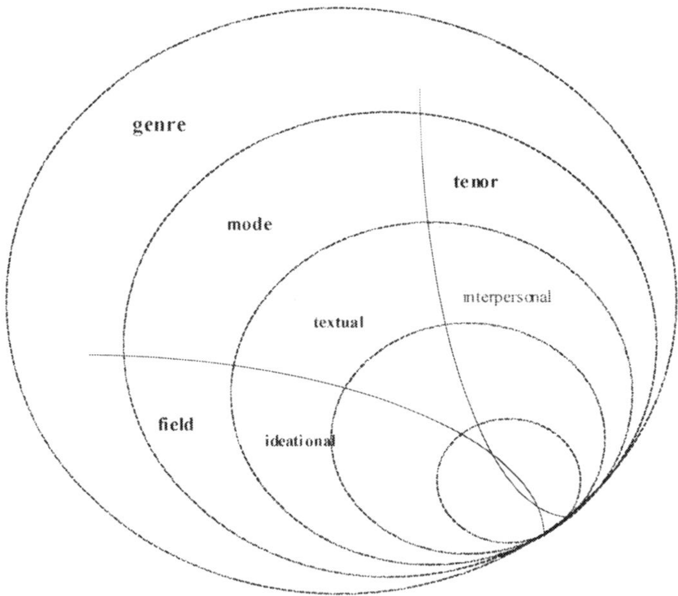

Figure 2.2: Realization (language, register and genre)

This is not of course to argue that alternative perspectives on uses and users have not been proposed. Halliday (e.g. 2005: 254) regularly acknowledges the presence of an additional hierarchy oriented to language use, referred to as instantiation (see Table 2.1). His cline of instantiation has language and cultural systems at one end, generalizing long term patterns, and texts in particular situations at the other, specifying instances of language use; in between he places his notions of register/text type for language and institution/situation type for context. Be that as it may, SFL contributions to the vertical axis in Table 2.1 (realization), along the system column of instantiation far and away outstrip contributions to the horizontal axis, along the system via sub-system/instance type to instance rows. Numerous descriptions of specific instances of use have of course been published, but these have by and large not been generalized up the instantiation cline – primarily because of the difficulty of computing meaning and the time consuming task of manual analysis given the rich realisation apparatus discussed above.

Table 2.1: Halliday's instantiation/stratification matrix

STRATI-FICATION \ INSTANTIATION	system	sub-system / instance system	instance
context	culture	institution / situation type	situations
semantics	semantic system	register / text type	[text as] meanings
lexico-grammar	grammatical system	register / text type	[text as] wordings

Martin (e.g. 2006, 2008a, 2008b, 2009) elaborates the instantiation hierarchy by adding genre/register and text type as stepped degrees of generality on the ladder, and adding reading as a sub-potentialization of text to allow for different users' uptake of meaning in socially subjective ways (Figure 2.3). Compared with realization, which is a hierarchy of abstraction, instantiation is a hierarchy of generalization. It is this difference that lies behind the different position of genre on the two hierarchies. As a recurrent configuration of field, mode and tenor patterns, genre sits on top the realization hierarchy, as the highest level pattern of patterns. But since each genre constitutes a subpotential of the meaning potential of the system as a whole, it sits one rung down on the instantiation hierarchy, on the way from system to reading. Genre and register are positioned at the same level of generality in Figure 2.3 because they constitute the same degree of sub-potentialization (since genre coordinates and phases relationships among a culture's recurrent field, tenor and mode configurations as unfolding discourse; Martin, 1999, 2001).

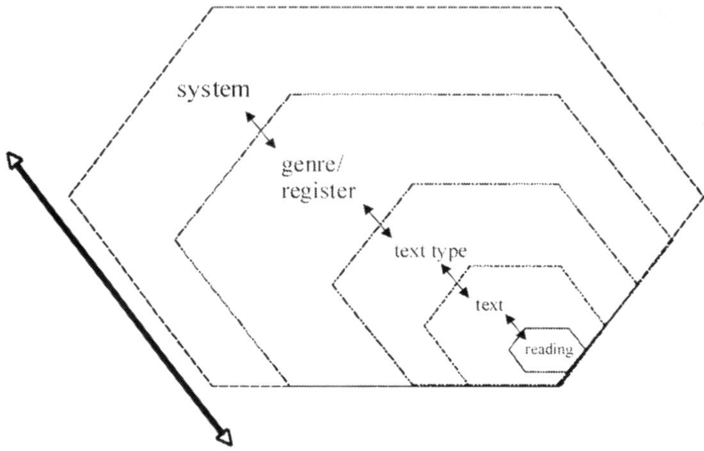

Figure 2.3: Instantiation as a hierarchy of generalization

Recently SFL (e.g. Bednarek and Martin, 2010) has begun to supplement work on realization and instantiation with work on a third hierarchy, individuation. Individuation brings a focus on users of language into the picture alongside uses. To date, SFL researchers have explored two complementary ways of thinking about individuation. One, inspired by Hasan's work on semantic variation (Hasan, 2005, 2009; Williams, 2005), interprets individuation as a hierarchy of allocation whereby semiotic resources are differentially distributed amongst users – both in terms of which options are available and of those available, which are likely to be taken up in specific contexts of instantiation. Bernstein uses the metaphor of reservoir and repertoire to describe the semiotic affordances of – users in relation to their communities as a whole along these lines:

> I shall use the term repertoire to refer to the set of strategies and their analogic potential possessed by any one individual and the term reservoir to refer to the total of sets and its potential of the community as a whole. Thus the repertoire of each member of the community will have both a common nucleus but there will be differences between the repertoires. There will be differences between the repertoires because of the differences between members arising out of differences in members context and activities and their associated issues. (Bernstein, 2000: 157)

One thing we have to guard against here as functional linguists is a neuro/biological interpretation of individuals and communities instead of a social semiotic one. As Firth warns, it is not psycho-biological entities we are exploring, but rather the bundles of personae embodied in such entities and how these personae engender speech fellowships. We're not, in other words, looking at individuals interacting in groups but rather at persons and personalities communing in discourse.

> The unique object of Saussurian linguistics is '*la langue*', which exists only in the *collectivité*. Now at this point I wish to stress the importance of the study of persons, even one at a time, and of introducing the notions of personality and language as in some sense vectors of the continuity of repetitions in the social process, and the persistence of personal forces. (Firth, 1957a: 183)

> if we take a sociological view of the *personae* or parts we are called upon to play in the routine of life. Every social person is a bundle of *personae*, a bundle of parts, each part having its lines. If you do not know your lines, you are no use in the play. It is very good for you and society if you are cast for your parts and remember your lines. (Firth, 1957a: 184)

> A speech fellowship sees itself and hears itself as different from those who do not belong. Such speech, besides being a bond among fellows, is a bar to the outsider ... within such speech fellowships a speaker is phonetically and verbally content because when he speaks to one of his fellows he is also speaking to himself. (Firth, 1957a: 186)

> My intention is to link language studies with social human nature, to think of persons rather than individuals. Linguistics may learn something from the sciences which treat human beings as separate natural entities in their psycho-biological characters, but it is mainly interested in persons and personalities as active participators in the creation and maintenance of cultural values, among which languages are its main concern. (Firth, 1957a: 186)

This brings us to a second, complementary perspective on individuation which looks at how personae mobilize social semiotic resources to affiliate with one another – how they share attitude and ideation couplings,[2] in Knight's (2009) terms, to form bonds, and how these bonds then cluster as belongings of different orders (including relatively 'local' familial, collegial, professional and leisure/recreational affiliations and more 'general' fellowships reflecting 'master identities' including social class, gender, generation, ethnicity and dis/ability). As with realization and instantiation, it is difficult to find a neutral term which privileges neither a top-down nor a bottom-up perspective. We'll adopt the term individuation for this hierarchy here, keeping in mind that it is concerned with both how semiotic resources are distributed among users (allocation) and how these resources are deployed to commune (affiliation). An outline of this user oriented hierarchy is presented as Figure 2.4.

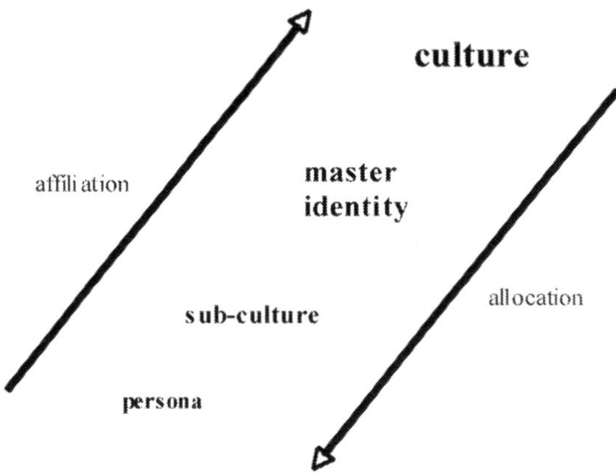

Figure 2.4: Individuation as a hierarchy of affiliation and allocation

The different orientations to meaning implicated by an individuation perspective on semantic variation have repercussions for instantiation, since they condition both recognition and realization rules (Bernstein, 2000: 104f). Recognition rules allow speakers to identify the specificity or similarity of contexts, and thus orient to what is expected or legitimate in that context; realization rules enable speakers to produce culturally specific texts and practices. As Bernstein comments 'one may be able to recognise that one is in a sociology class but not able to produce the texts and context-specific practices. In order to produce the legitimate text it is necessary to acquire the realisation rule' (2000: 105).

As with instantiation, we need to keep in mind that as far as realization is concerned, all strata individuate (Figure 2.9). As Firth (1957b: 191–192) once quipped in relation to phonology and accent, 'It is part of the meaning of an American to sound like one', and similarly so for every higher level of language and social context – i.e. lexicogrammar, discourse semantics, register and genre. Taking all three hierarchies into account is a challenging task; but as social semioticians we have to keep in mind that speakers always already individuate **as** they instantiate **as** they re/deploy the realization resources of their culture.

2.3   Adolescent identity in youth justice conferencing

From the perspective of instantiation, we can ask questions about the social function of different phases of a youth justice conference. The first part of a conference features the commissioned recount noted above in which the YP gives their version of events as far as the offence they have admitted is concerned. From the perspective of individuation, we can ask how different YPs perform this task – what kind of persona do they project in taking on this role? For example, in this situation many YPs retell the bare bones of what went on, generally prompting the Convenor to extract further detail. Here's an example of this kind of minimalist admission:

[Mobile phone]

YP: Yeah, I was, I was walking to a mate's house. This guy just came up to me and goes 'Do you want to buy a phone?' and I go 'No' and I go 'Do you want to swap?' [inaudible] want to swap with my phone and he looked at my phone and he goes 'Yeah' and we swap and I went and stayed at my mate's house and when it came to night time I was going back home, and he was walking, was walking up the road and the police just came and got us.

Convenor: … [convenor nodding expectantly]

YP: That's it.

This unforthcoming persona contrasts with one which we occasionally find, in which a much fuller account is offered:

[Train tracks]

YP: Well um I was just staying at [suburb], staying at a friend's place, [name], and um, and her mum's and she had her own flat-mates so I … (and mum had her own) and I was staying at theirs ( ) so I could get back ( ). And um, well, we had ( ), y'know, we was just sitting around, chuffing on so um … we just started taking drugs and um (mainly we) um, got some, um, acid trips. And we got on top of some, yeah. I was under the influence of drugs at the time. We were just walking around ( ) with nothing else to do and (saw some) shops down the road so (I had, sort of like) had the munchies so I started to go down the road, and um, steal a packet of chips and yeah. Well first, we stood out the front, like y'know, really suss, and talkin' about it and then we all walked into the store and stood around and (just laughing and) next thing you know, sort of like, walked down there and went (out) and back up to the front and um, and then ( ) yeah, went back in and grabbed a bag of chips and then we started running down the road and we came across one of the other people (that were) at the shop, so we kept running (to about) down to the train station, and we already gone to [place] to come back at that time and um, we were sitting at the train station back down [place] and um well I was sittin' there ( ) in my hand and chips in the other and um, yeah I was (saw) the copper walkin' down and um … well I, I freaked out and thought 'oh shit (I should) run'. And um so (he made [name of friend]) sitting next to me, she told me to sit down and I said no it's like ( ) (I'm not getting caught on somethin'). So I started running down the tracks and um, threw my chips at the train, started running, and then, like, got down to the bridge and I watched the copper, [name] and that walk up to the thing (sort of ( ) what he was saying to me) and um as I was climbing up ( ) just leave the train station and then I ran all the way, like, back up to the flats I was staying at. And, yeah, went back up to the flats and I was sitting inside (with the mum) and just asked her not to tell the copper I was there but the coppers knocked on the door, and ( ). Knocked on the door and um, asked if I was there and [name]'s gone yeah and plus I left the door at the back ( ) so she had to go out anyway, so I just walked out anyway and stood up (near the stairs) and one of the officers told me not to run, so the (first thing I did) was run ( ) down the road and then finally one of the (young) officers got me just down the road and um, yeah. He got me and I just kept, y'know, swearing at him and just wouldn't stay still and um yeah I got taken back to the cop station and then, taken to the hospital. ( ) That's what happened.

In Maton's (2000, 2007, 2010, to appear; Moore and Maton, 2001) terms what we are considering here is an epistemic relation between the YPs performance and what actually went on when the offence occurred; we're asking how forthcoming the YP is about the events.

Returning to instantiation, we can also ask how evaluative resources give significance to the commissioned recount. And from the individuation perspective we can ask how different YPs perform this task. Typically, as with the minimalist 'Mobile phone' record of events above, the YP does not evaluate what happened during his testimony. Rather, evaluation has to be extracted by the Convenor:

[Mobile phone]

Convenor: And what did dad say when he got here?

YP: He (was) just asking why am I here?

And the police told him.

Convenor: And was he happy? Did he say anything to you?

YP: Don't go anywhere.

Convenor: As is when you get home you've got to stay home? Do you think your father was disappointed in you?

YP: Yep.

...

Convenor: Do you think you deserved the lecture? Why did you deserve the lecture?

YP: Because I did something wrong.

...

Convenor: Do you think that mum and dad were disappointed in you?

Were you disappointed in yourself? Or Not? Or you don't care?

YP: Yeah.

Convenor: Yeah or you don't care?

YP: Disappointed in myself.

This reluctantly contrite persona contrasts with one we occasionally find, in which the YP is more of a self-starter as far as remorse and apology are concerned:

[Train tracks]

Convenor: So what have you thought about since, um, since this incident?

YP: How stupid I was. I was just, y'know, I dunno, I was just stupid, I think, at that time. I'll think twice next time (before I do something like that again).

...

Convenor: So how long after the incident did you have a chance to sort of reflect back on it and think about what happened.

YP: Pretty much that day (I called home and I was describing to my mum) that doing that stupid incident that night because that

> day I (wanted to) go back and apologise cause ( ) I always go there
> and I felt so bad cause um, they're always nice to us and we went
> and done stupid things ( ). Yeah, I was stupid.

In Maton's terms what we are looking at here is the social relation between the YP and what went on, where this social relation involves an explicit axiological orientation to the offence.

This means that as far as epistemic relations are concerned we are dealing in this context with an axis of admission (how forthcoming a persona the YP performs) and as far as social relations are concerned we are dealing with an axis of contrition (how remorseful a persona the YP performs). A topology of the personae positioned by these axes is outlined in Figure 2.5. The upper right hand quadrant represents the 'redeemed' (forthcoming, contrite) persona youth justice conference theorists, designers and practitioners celebrate as far as the performance of restorative justice ideals are concerned. The lower left hand quadrant represents what we have more commonly experienced as the mundane 'small target' reality, namely an 'accused' (unforthcoming, reluctantly remorseful) YP. The topology also includes the possibility of two further personae we have observed – a forthcoming but unremorseful YP ('guilty' as charged, but inclined to blame others for what went wrong), and a remorseful but unforthcoming 'prodigal' YP (common enough where the YP is sorry but was too intoxicated by drugs or alcohol for example to remember much of what went on).

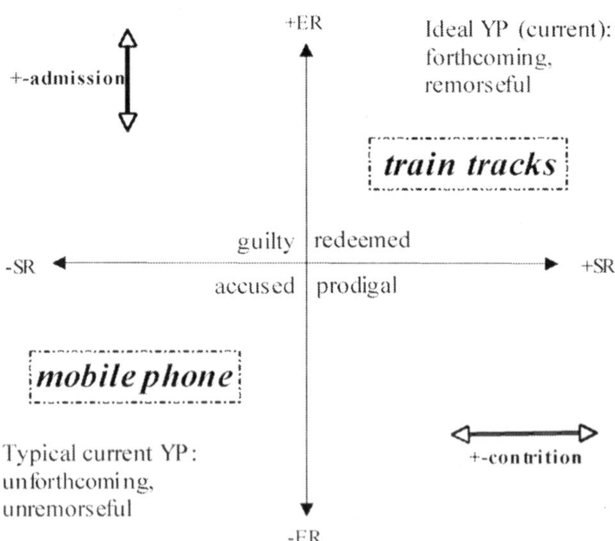

Figure 2.5: YP personae topology for the commissioned recount genre

As noted above, our work topologizing performed identities in youth justice conferencing draws on work by Maton, his Legitimation Code Theory in particular (Maton, 2007, 2008, 2010, in press, to appear). Like Bernstein, Maton is a sociologist of education; he extends Bernstein's late work on knowledge structure (Bernstein, 2000) by also focusing on knowers. Of special relevance here is his work on Specialization, or what makes something different, special and worthy of attention. His model begins from the premise that every practice, belief or knowledge claim is about or oriented towards something and is by someone, and so sets up epistemic relations to the object and social relations to the subject respectively. Addressing educational contexts, his epistemic relations (ER) refer to relations between educational knowledge and its proclaimed object of study (school physics and the material world for example); his social relations (SR) refer to relations between educational knowledge and the author or actor making the knowledge claims. Each relation may be more strongly (+) or weakly (-) emphasized in practices and beliefs, along continua, and these axes simultaneously position educational identities as outlined in Figure 2.6 (Maton, 2007: 97). For Maton this gives four principal codes: for the 'knowledge' code (upper left quadrant) it matters more what you know and how, and less who you are (e.g. anyone can learn chemistry); for the 'knower' code (lower right quadrant) it matters less what you know and how, more who you are (e.g. you need the right 'cultivated gaze' to do literary criticism); for the 'relativist' code, neither what you know nor who you are is emphasized (everyone's perspective is equally valid); and for the 'elite' code it matters both what you know and who you are (in nineteenth century England for example, Darwin, the wealthy gentleman biologist, was in a much stronger position to propose evolutionary theory than Wallace, whose humbler social position afforded him a smaller supporting role as far as promoting the ideas he had independently conceived was concerned).

As we have argued elsewhere (Martin *et al.*, 2009), youth justice conferences can be treated as a kind of pedagogic discourse, with a regulative discourse projecting an instructional one. They are designed in other words to 'educate' YPs by repositioning them in relation to the offence committed and their future behaviour. Since Maton's model is concerned with different knower identities in education, we were able to adapt it to think about YP roles in conferencing. His epistemic relation refers in Figure 2.5 to the relation between the YP's recount and what actually went on as far as the offence is concerned (how forthcoming or not); here we are concerned with the specificity of the YP's commitment of ideational meaning in relation to how much the Convenor wants replayed. And Maton's social relation refers in Figure 2.5 to the relation of the YP to that offence (how remorseful or not); critical there is the YP's axiological orientation to what s/he has done wrong.

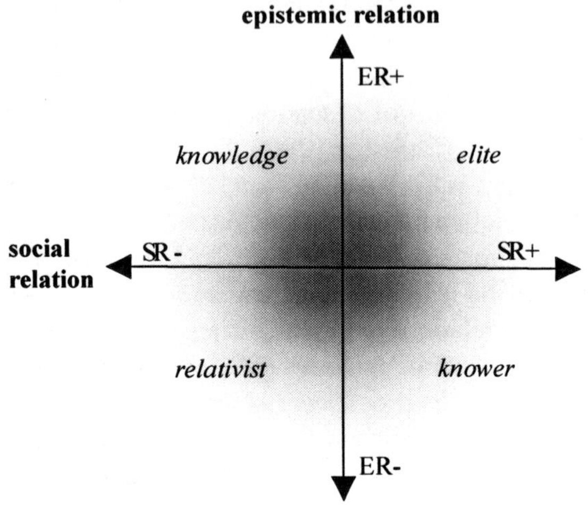

Figure 2.6: Maton's 2007 topology of specialization codes in educational contexts

2.4   Youth Liaison Officer (YLO) interventions

The New South Wales Young Offenders Act was designed to provide alternative processes to courtroom proceedings and apply the least restrictive form of sanction against a young person alleged to have committed an offence. It involves a hierarchy of warning, caution, conference and court procedures. Warnings involve an on-the-spot reprimand by police. Cautions are formal admonishments, managed by Youth Liaison Officers, who prepare a record of the caution; cautions require an admission of guilt and are delivered in a meeting at the police station including the YP, a support person and the administering YLO. Conferences, described above, are used for more serious offences and repeat offenders (no more than three cautions are allowed). Finally there is court. In addition to managing cautions, YLOs regularly attend conferences. In some of our data, they take an active role, warning YPs about the consequences of bad behaviour and encouraging them to reintegrate into the community. It has been suggested to us that YLOs are in fact using the conference to 'caution' YPs, something not envisaged by restorative justice conference designers. It has also been suggested to us that because of the discretion police have about recommending either a caution or a conference the line between cautions and conferences is becoming somewhat blurred. The offence related in the mobile phone recount above for example is arguably something that could have been dealt with through a caution.

Be that as it may, it does appear that some conferences shift from a retrospective account of the offence and its evaluation to prospective consideration of how the YP should behave in future. We'll consider data from two such interventions here (for fuller transcripts see Appendices 2.1 and 2.2). One rhetorical motif pursued by YLOs has to do with getting YPs to think about the consequences of their actions. The idea here seems to be that obeying the law because the police might nick you is not enough. YPs are admonished to discipline themselves by thinking through how what they do might harm or negatively influence someone else.

['shopping trolley']

YLO: Um, I just want to, um, (…?) X is – you were saying before about how you were worried about committing an offence and, because it was illegal, OK. As X was saying, I'd really like you to start looking at it in the sense of the consequences, OK? Not so much the fact that there's that chance that the police may be hiding in the bushes to collect you, alright. I'd really like you to look at it in the sense, as X was saying, a train may be derailed, um, whatever may happen. And with any crime, you know, a lot of people, whether they're talking on their mobile phones while they're driving, they're, um, they've had six beers or whatever it may be and jump in their car, OK, a lot of that mentality may be, you know, OK, they advertise, every cop car can pull you over and breath test you and you may get caught, how about we look at it in the sense where, if we're on our phones, um, you have (momentary?) trouble, lose our concentration and we run over a poor lady that's crossing the road, OK. Um, so I'd really like you to look at this, um, as far as, not getting caught, OK, because they're illegal, but how about, 'I'm not going to throw that trolley because someone maybe lose a leg, or, whatever the case may be'. (YP: Yep) OK, um, … I think that mentality more than anything would be – you know, something that would – in the future, you know …

['mobile phone']

YLO: It also has consequences with your family. You have younger brothers and sisters? (Young person: (…) older brother) Older? Yeah? Have your older brothers and sisters, or older brothers been in trouble? … No? (Young Person: (I don't know)) Cause what happens is, especially when you've got younger brothers and sisters, or little cousins, … you you set an example for them. And a lot of the times, because they idolise their big brother, or their cousin, or whatever, they look at them and they – they love them you know? And they tend to copy the behaviour and then they end up doing it. And we see it time and time again where the – where the older brothers have been in trouble and then the younger brothers just keep coming through and they do the same because they're influenced by the older people. Same as you could be influencing I mean your – your cousin. He's sitting here listening to this. You know, this influences them, they see what happens and – you know, in either a positive or a negative way, … but it influences them.

This negative consequences motif is complemented by another which focuses on positive outcomes – if the right choices are made. The main idea here seems to be is that life offers range of opportunities to YPs, and that this 'big wide world out there' is something they are in danger of throwing away.

['mobile phone']

YLO: And as a Youth Liaison Officer, I want to see you do that – I want to see yous have – you know, have all the opportunities that you can to be the person that you want to be, you know. … Um. That's about all I wanted to – you probably – you've covered everything that I've said anyway, but as a mother I just had to nag that one in anyway. … But, yeah, only you can choose which way you are going to be. Seriously look at your friends. Cause you are at a really influential point now where you can go that way, or you can go that way. You know that don't you. … Yep.

['shopping trolley']

YLO: … we're here to, you know, discuss what's happened and hopefully steer you on a path where you go 'Alright, I've learnt from this experience, I was only a kid', um, you know, go ahead with your apprenticeship, you know, you never know, it may lead to bigger and better things. You get contacts, get to know people, get some numbers, go and work for, you know you could – if (…?) been a butcher, you could end up overseas mate and work. You know, you've got a whole lot ahead of you. You got so much to experience and learn, you don't want to end up in Juvy and getting to know other kids who, um, don't have parents that you have, OK, (…?) lucky (…?) got support there. Alright, there's a lot of kids that don't have that support and I think that has a lot to do with it also. You can see by their attitude (…?), you don't want to end up down that path. Look it as, OK, 'As a kid, I made mistakes, everyone does, unfortunately I got caught', OK, but take away

> from this that, you know, you've got a job, hopefully you've got
> new mates, um, you know, you've got a big opportunity now with
> this skill, um, you know, you can, even interstate, you know, you
> might go to Perth, or, you know, a butcher, it's one of those things
> that you can pretty much – well you can, take anyway. Um, you
> know, it's a big wide world out there and it's not all about X Rail-
> way Station, OK, so.

Significantly, the YLOs are not foregrounding proposals in their advice.
They're not, in other words, telling the YP what they should or shouldn't do.
So there are very few imperatives (*Don't do this / do this*), modulated commands (*You shouldn't do this / you should do this*) or wishes (*I'd like you to do
this / I'd prefer you not to do this*). Neither are the YLOs foregrounding rules;
their counsel is not about spelling out the law as something to be obeyed.

Rather, as illustrated above, the YLOs are more concerned with propositions dealing with the consequences of an offence. Instead of explicit
proposals they favour propositional contingency. So a proposal like '*You
should not take the wrong fork in the road*' is reconstrued as '*You can go this
way or you can go this way*' or '*If you go X way then Y will happen*'. Here
are some examples, relating to various outcomes:

– adulthood

> But what we're creating now, is your – we're creating a, um,
> what do you call it, a pattern of how you're going to be when
> you turn eighteen, and **if you continue this pattern now**, it
> will go on into your adult lifehood, and that will make a huge
> difference to you.

– mates

> **… if he's going to continue going down that track**, do you
> want to go down that track too?

> **… if he is doing stuff and you're with him**, you'll get into the
> same sort of trouble.

> So, **if he is one of your really good friends** and I'd really –
> you need to really start to question what you are going to do
> and how you are going to end up, because he will get you into
> some big trouble.

– employment

> **If you work for a bank,** and a lot of people now, even do it
> for retail, just working in being a checkout person. They will

ask as part of their criteria to have a criminal history check, and you will have to provide that for them **if you want to go for that job**.

If you had a robbery offence on your record and you went – do you think – how easy do you think you would get into a trade?

– feelings

if your mum or sister was on that train, how would you feel, knowing that you were responsible for what had happened?

because, **if you'd ever been robbed**, you would know, especially when somebody's made you give something over, you'd know how horrific that can be, and how – how largely that can affect that person that was robbed.

I can only imagine how I would feel if somebody grabbed me and threw me in the back of the wagon. But then I guess it depends whether you've done something wrong or not. If you haven't done anything wrong, then that would be even worse. But, when you know you've done something wrong, and you're in the back of the wagon and you think 'Oh ()', cause, you know, well 'This is what I get for doing the wrong thing'. It's it's how it goes. ...

Contingency is also explored in terms of what could have happened but didn't (the clear implication being that if the offence happens again, 'could haves' can become 'will haves'):

'You must have known that there is the possibility it **could** have gone a bit further, god forbid.'

'I understand what you're saying. That you purposefully didn't throw it on the tracks, but somebody else **could**.'

'And, you **might** not of even known, thrown it over, **could** have hit somebody in the head. Somebody **could** have been drunk and stumbled over the train tracks.'

'... it's not one of the most serious offences we've ever seen, no way, () really huge, but at the end of the day it's what **could** happen, that's all I'm sort of saying, like – it's what **could** happen. It's not what did happen, it's what **can** happen.'

The metalinguistic term YLOs use to focus on these contingent outcomes is *consequences*:

['mobile phone']

'Um, I guess a lot of the things have already been spoken about, like the **consequences** and all that sort of thing.'

Um, you've already spoken about the **consequences** obviously, you know. This can have major **consequences** for you, let alone the rest of your family.

But now you'll start to learn about **consequences**, and if you choose to keep staying with him then you're choosing to be in the – in the eye of the police … and looking at trouble.

['shopping trolley']

I'd really like you to start looking at it in the sense of the **consequences**, OK?

However, as I was getting back to, you've got those **consequences** there, where someone's life and their family and their friends are suffering, OK.

Balancing this bad consequences motif is the notion of possibilities later in life, referred to variously as choices, options and opportunities:

The Young Offenders Act allows us to be able to deal with you alternatively, rather than just throwing you in the court system, OK, because the court system doesn't really solve any of the issues as to why you're here to start with. It just sets the punishment of what happens after. Once you turn eighteen you don't have those **options** anymore. You understand that?

And as a Youth Liaison Officer, I want to see you do that – I want to see yous have – you know, have all the **opportunities** that you can to be the person that you want to be, you know.

You don't have a good job, you have no money, you have … no **choices**. But you have money, you have **choices**.

OK, but take away from this that, you know, you've got a job, hopefully you've got new mates, um, you know, you've got a big **opportunity** now with this skill,

The future is also explored through modalizations of possibility …

Good things **may** happen in the future if you change your behaviour

You **might** go to Perth …

You know, you **could** if () been a butcher, you **could** end up overseas mate and work.

… and also in terms of modulations of ability shading into inclination:

And as a Youth Liaison Officer, I want to see you do that – I want to see yous have – you know, have all the opportunities that you **can** be the person that you want to be, you know …

Cause you are at a really influential point now where you **can** go that way, or you **can** go that way.

But, yeah, only you **can** choose which way you are going to be.

and only you **can** learn. You **can** – you **can** either … go, you know, take what we're saying and take it on, or you **can** ignore it, but – and we'll see you again later. But it's up to you.

The overall message is that YPs should avoid bad consequences and not foreclose choices. The YLOs' negative axiological charging of consequences are outlined in Figure 2.7, including possible problems relating to detention, unemployment, mates, education, family, isolation, affect and injury.

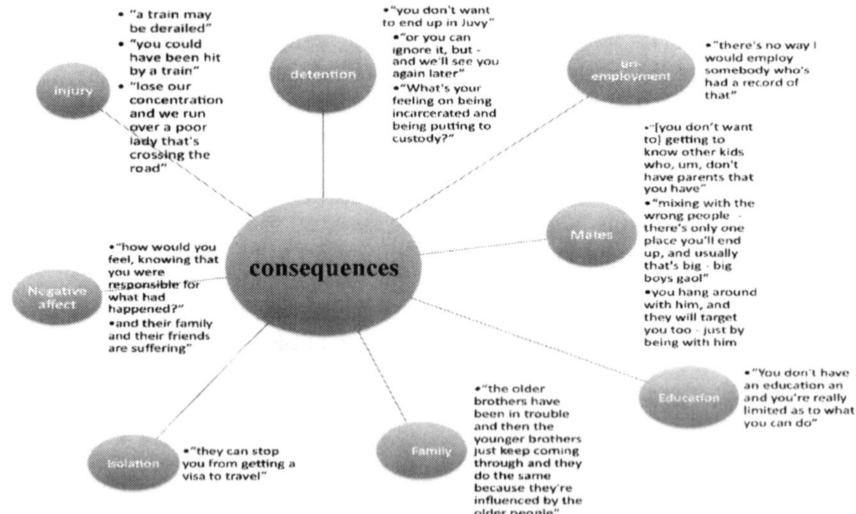

Figure 2.7: Constellation of negatively charged consequences

Their positive charging of choices is summarized in Figure 2.8, including desirable outcomes having to do with employment, education, travel and self-esteem.

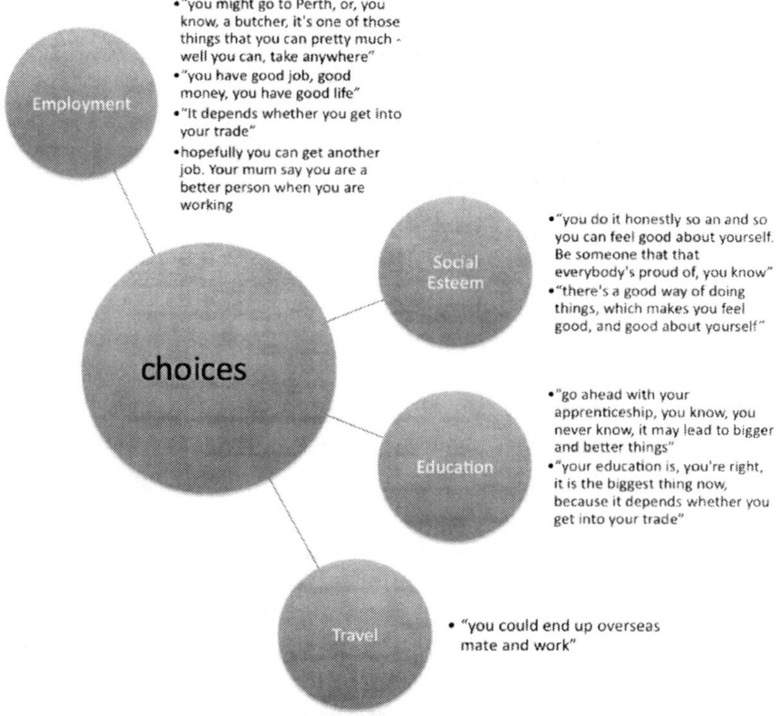

Figure 2.8: Constellation of positively charged choices

As we reviewed above in relation to Maton's work, 'intellectual fields are not only structures of knowledge, they also comprise actors with passions, hopes, desires, EMOTIONS ...' (Maton, 2008, to appear). And in Bourdieu's terms, they comprise actors with taste (1984). As Maton continues, just as taste in film, furniture or clothes says something about you, so

> choice of concepts, terms, theories, approach, writing style, referencing style, figures, use of quotes, etc. tell others something about what kind of person you are. They show whether your heart is in the right place and so whether you are one of us or one of them. (Maton, 2008)

Developing these ideas he introduces his notion of cosmology of intellectual fields:

> I shall highlight a feature of intellectual fields I shall call their ***cosmology***. Ernest Gellner described an 'ideology' as 'a system of ideas with a powerful sex appeal' (p. 2). A 'cosmology' is what makes some ideas sexy and others not so hot. Every field has a cosmology. In fields like the natural sciences, they tend to be primarily epistemological in nature and the sex appeal of theories is related to their comparative explanatory power. In fields like sociology and Education, they tend to be less epistemological and more axiological; i.e. a moral ordering which works to allocate ideas and authors to different poles of field, as either on side of good or evil. To understand what happens in fields ... we need to understand how such an ***axiological cosmology*** works. (Maton, 2008)

According to Maton a cosmology works by means of the 'creation of ***constellations*** of positions through a process of association whereby ideas, practices and beliefs are grouped together and contrasted to other groups.' Analogizing again from his concerns to our conferencing data, we can ask about the kind of cosmology the YLOs are advocating for young offenders. And the provisional answer would seem to be one involving the competing constellations of consequence and choice outlined above.

In relation to these constellations the YLOs' prospective positioning of YPs complements the retrospective positioning scaffolded earlier by the convenor. As far as personae to be performed, the relevant axes this time round are rationality and affiliation. As far as epistemic relations are concerned, the YLO is pushing for a rational YP who makes decisions in terms of consequences. As far as social relations are concerned, what the YLO wants is a YP who leaves the bad influence of mates behind and re-integrates with family and community (as kin, kith, student, citizen and employee).

The ideal YP would now perform a rational, re-affiliating persona, embodying 'reintegration'. Less desirable personae involve a hardened criminal YP who is rational but prefers to hang with his mates and has plans to further offend, a law-abiding YP who leaves mates behind and stays out of trouble for fear of being caught, and a delinquent YP who gets inadvertently caught up in illegal behaviour as a result of the mates he keeps as friends.

As Karl Maton has pointed out (personal communication), the ideal retrospective YP for the convenor and ideal prospective YP for the YLO perform comparable personae – both embody a persona capable of displaying publicly that they are self-disciplining social subjects that have internalized the power that will ensure they maintain ways of acting, thinking and being appropriate to a citizen (after Foucault, 1977). The YLOs' re-instatement of this idealized identity is outlined in Figure 2.10.

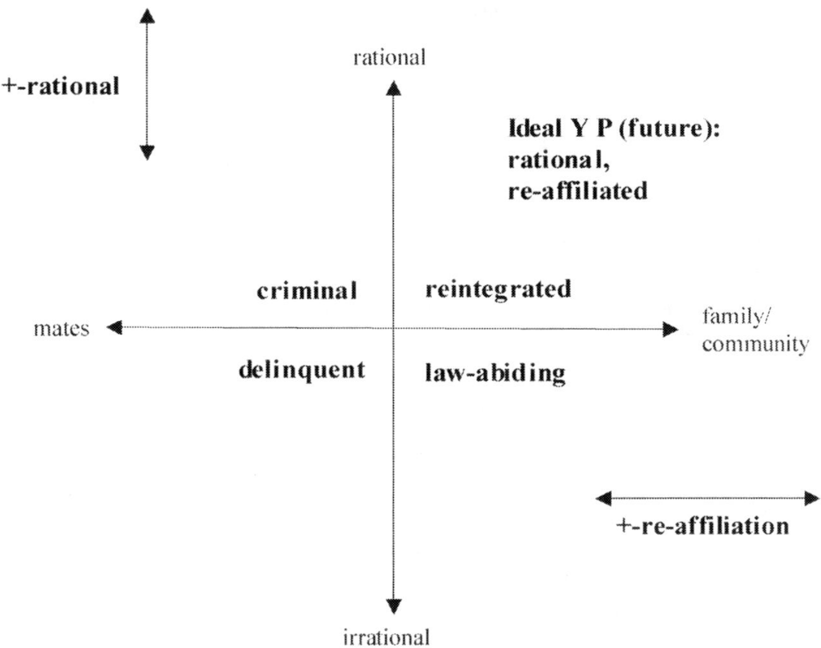

Figure 2.9: YP personae topology for the YLO conference 'caution'

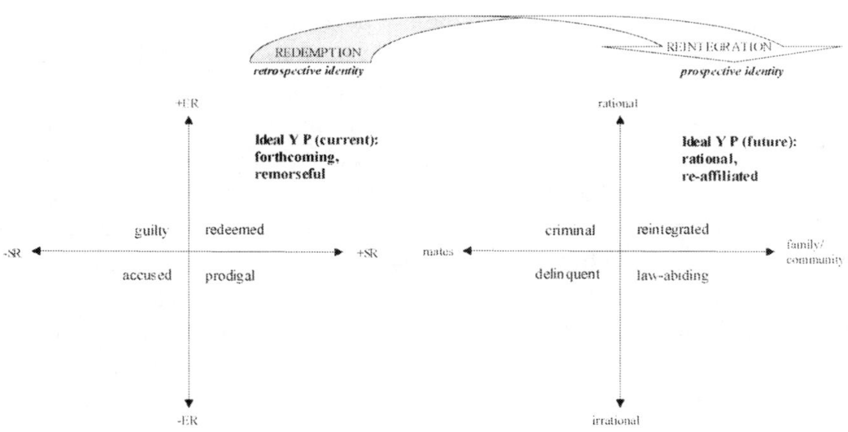

Figure 2.10: Retrospective and prospective identities in Youth Justice Conferencing

2.5 Identity and Community

In this chapter we have explored the question of teenage identity in youth justice conferencing and mapped out the personae that young offenders perform in two phases of the conference – the commissioned recount and the YLO's conference caution. Drawing on Maton, his Legitimation Code Theory and notion of axiological cosmology in particular, we have proposed identity topologies for these phases, involving both epistemic and social relations. The epistemic axes involved a cline of admission and rationality, respectively, and the social axes clines of contrition and re-affiliation. Ideally YPs assume a forthcoming contrite identity in the recount phase and a rational, re-affiliated identity in the caution. But the public display of ethical self-governance required to assume these roles is not something that comes easily to most of the YP we have observed. Their age, ethnicity and social class have allocated them few resources for either recognizing what is expected of them or enacting such even if they do. Only a few, for reasons that bear consideration in further research, can affiliate in the genre in the ways its apologists, designers and practitioners apparently expect them to.

Perhaps the metaphor of fashion can be helpfully pressed into service here. Out of the reservoir of clothing in the culture our YPs have been allocated specific semiotic wardrobes. From this repertoire they have to choose clothes to conference in – the right outfit for the occasion. If they don't have the right clothes, or don't choose the right clothes, or don't wear them properly, they won't be able to perform the expected restorative justice role. In Firth's terms they aren't lucky enough to have been cast for their part and given lines they can remember. They don't have the right clothes and they don't know what to wear. And so they don't fit in.

Taking this into account, at this point in time SFL doesn't really have the right clothes either. And progress developing models of individuation, from the perspectives of both allocation and affiliation, is probably going to be as slow for this hierarchy as it has been for work on instantiation. For one thing, SFL's main tool for modelling meaning, the system network, is a synoptic one; it crystalizes snapshots of semiotic valeur at particular points in time. The animated representations needed to interpret meaning unfolding through time, whether logogenetic, ontogenetic or phylogenetic are still under development. And then there is the difficulty of computing meaning, once we move from parsing texts as bags of words to treating them as phonological, lexicogrammatical and discourse semantic textures, through which meanings accumulate as texts unfold. The low level counting which technology currently affords is too shallow as far as meaning is concerned; and the rich manual analysis SFL currently enables is too limited as far as data is concerned. We're next to blind, groping towards a model of users and uses, in spite of, and in fact because of, our establishment of the richest realizational apparatus so far designed.

That said the challenge of modelling identity is not going to go away. Given its appliable linguistics mandate, there are too many interventions where a theory of users of language, alongside uses, matters. And to this we need to add the challenge of change, since as we have seen, users may adopt different persona from one stage of a genre to the next, and adjust their repertoire of personae throughout life, just as a culture evolves its reservoir of identities – in ever more interesting affinities it might be said in the global warming hot house of our post-colonial world. An outline of these challenges in presented in Figure 2.11, mapping the three hierarchies touched on in this chapter (realization, instantiation and individuation) in relation to realms of time (logogenesis for unfolding discourse, ontogenesis for developing individuals and phylogenesis for evolving culture). A cartographic reminder of the work that lies ahead.

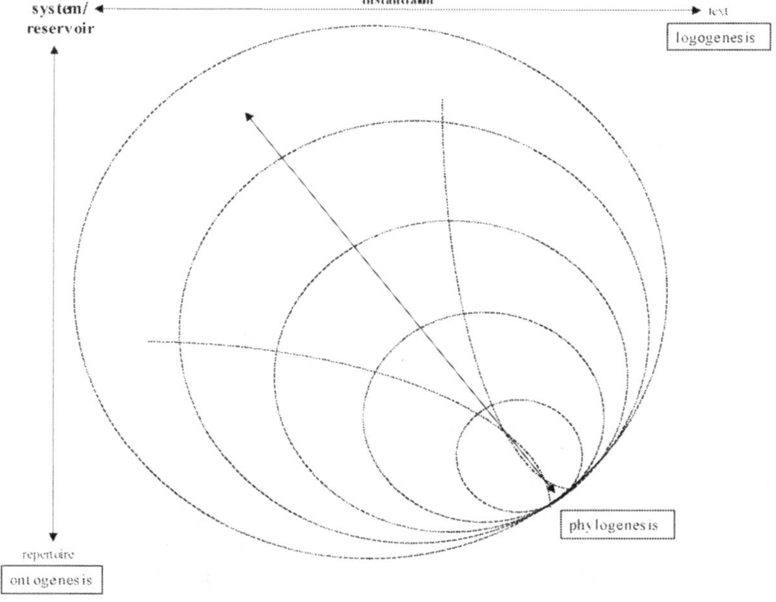

Figure 2.11: Realization, instantiation and individuation in relation to genesis

Acknowledgements

The authors acknowledge the support of the Australian Research Council for a Discovery Project grant supporting this restorative justice research.

Notes

1.   One exception in our data to the general pattern we are describing here involved theft from a blind woman, who was present at the conference, a young offender whose grandmother and carer had died since the time of the offence, and several significant support persons for the young offender (mother, step-grandfather, girlfriend, girlfriend's mother); a remorse-apology-forgiveness 'passion play' was in fact facilitated by the convenor at this conference.
2.   For notes on coupling in relation to instantiation see Martin (2008a, 2009).

References

Bednarek, M. and Martin, J. R. (eds) (2010) *New Discourse on Language: Functional Perspectives on Multimodality, Identity and Affiliation*. London: Continuum.

Bernstein, B. (1975) *Class, Codes and Control 3: Towards a Theory of Educational Transmissions*. London: Routledge & Kegan Paul (Primary Socialisation, Language and Education).

Bernstein, B. (2000) *Pedagogy, Symbolic Control and Identity: Theory, Research, Critique*. London: Taylor & Francis. [Revised Edition].

Bourdieu, P. (1984) *Distinction: A Social Critique of the Judgement of Taste*. Cambridge, MA: Harvard University Press.

Braithwaite, J. (1989) *Crime, Shame and Reintegration*. Cambridge: Cambridge University Press.

Caffarel, A., Martin, J. R. and Matthiessen, C. M. I. M. (eds) (2004) *Language Typology: A Functional Perspective*. Amsterdam: Benjamins

Caldwell, D. (2009) Meaking metre mean: identity and affiliation in the rap music of Kanye West. In M. Bednarek and J. R. Martin (eds) (2010) *New Discourse on Language: Functional Perspectives on Multimodality, Identity and Affiliation*, 59–79. London: Continuum.

Christie, F. and Martin, J. R. (2007) *Language, Knowledge and Pedagogy: Functional Linguistic and Sociological Perspectives*. London: Continuum.

Firth, J. R. (1957a) Personality and language in society. *Papers in Linguistics 1934–1951*, 177–189. Oxford: Oxford University Press.

Firth, J. R. (1957b) *Papers in linguistics 1934–1951*. London: Oxford University Press.

Foucault, M. (1977) *Discipline and Punish: The Birth of the Prison*. London: Allan Lane.

Halliday, M. A. K. (2005) Computing meanings: Some reflections on part experience and present prospects. *Computational and Quantitative Studies* (Volume 6 in *Collected Works of M. A. K. Halliday*, J. J. Webster (ed.)), 239–267. London: Continuum.

Halliday, M. A. K. (2008) *Complementarities in Language*. Beijing: The Commercial Press.

Halliday, M. A. K. and Matthiessen, C. M. I. M. (2004) *An Introduction to Functional Grammar* (3rd edn). London: Arnold.

Halliday, M. A. K., McIntosh, A. and Strevens, P. (1964) *The Linguistic Sciences and Language Teaching*. London: Longmans.

Halliday, M. A. K. and Webster, J. (eds) (2009) *Continuum Companion to Systemic Functional Linguistics*. London: Continuum.

Hasan, R. (2005) *Language, Society and Consciousness*. London: Equinox (*The Collected Works of Ruqaiya Hasan* edited by J. Webster, Vol. 1).

Hasan, R. (2009) *Semantic Variation: Meaning in Society and Sociolinguistics*. London: Equinox (*The Collected Works of Ruqaiya Hasan*, edited by J. Webster).

Hasan, R., Matthiessen, C. M. I. M. and Webster, J. (eds) (2005) *Continuing Discourse on Language: A Functional Perspective* (Vol. 1). London: Equinox.

Hasan, R., Matthiessen, C. M. I. M. and Webster, J. (eds) (2007) *Continuing Discourse on Language: A Functional Perspective* (Vol. 2). London: Equinox.

Knight, N. (2010) Wrinkling complexity: Concepts of identity and affiliation in humour. In M. Bednarek and J. R. Martin (eds) (2010) *New Discourse on Language: Functional Perspectives on Multimodality, Identity and Affiliation*, 35–58. London: Continuum.

Martin, J. R. (1992) *English Text: System and Structure*. Amsterdam: Benjamins.

Martin, J. R. (1999) Modelling context: The crooked path of progress in contextual linguistics (Sydney SFL). In M. Ghadessy (ed.) *Text and Context in Functional Linguistics*, 25–61. Amsterdam: Benjamins (CILT Series IV).

Martin, J. R. (2001) A context for genre: Modelling social processes in functional linguistics. In J. Devilliers and R. Stainton (eds) *Communication in Linguistics: Papers in Honour of Michael Gregory*, 287–328. Toronto: GREF (Theoria Series 10).

Martin, J. R. (2006) Genre, ideology and intertextuality: A systemic functional perspective. *Linguistics and the Human Sciences* (Special Issue on Genre edited by J. Bateman) 2 (2): 275–298.

Martin, J. R. (2008a) Tenderness: Realisation and instantiation in a Botswanan town. *Odense Working Papers in Language and Communication* (Special Issue of Papers from 34th International Systemic Functional Congress, edited by Nina Nørgaard), 30–62.

Martin, J. R. (2008b) Innocence: Realisation, instantiation and individuation in a Botswanan town. In N. Knight and A. Mahboob (eds) *Questioning Linguistics*, 27–54. Cambridge: Cambridge Scholars Publishing.

Martin, J. R. (2009a) Realisation, instantiation and individuation: Some thoughts on identity in youth justice conferencing. *DELTA – Documentação de Estudos em Linguistica Teorica e Aplicada* 25: 549–583.

Martin, J. R. (2009b) Semantic variation: Modelling system, text and affiliation in social semiosis. In M. Bednarek and J. R. Martin (eds) *New Discourse on Language: Functional Perspectives on Multimodality, Identity and Affiliation*, 1–34. London: Continuum.

Martin, J. R. and Rose, D. (2003) *Working with Discourse: Meaning Beyond the Clause* (2nd Revised Edition 2007). London: Continuum.

Martin, J. R. and Rose, D. (2008) *Genre Relations: Mapping Culture*. London: Equinox.

Martin, J. R. and White, P. R. R. (2005) *The Language of Evaluation: Appraisal in English*. London: Palgrave.

Martin, J. R., Zappavigna, M. and Dwyer, P. (2007) Negotiating narrative: Story structure and identity in youth justice conferencing. *Linguistics and Human Communication* 3 (2): 221–253.

Martin, J. R., Zappavigna, M. and Dwyer, P. (2008) Syndromes of meaning: Exploring patterned coupling in a NSW Youth Justice Conference. In A. Mahboob and N. Knight (eds) *Questioning Linguistics,* 103–117. Newcastle: Cambridge Scholars Publishing.

Martin, J. R., Zappavigna, M. and Dwyer, P. (2009) Negotiating shame: Exchange and genre structure in youth justice conferencing. In C. Lipovsky and A. Mahboob (eds) *Studies in Applied Linguistics and Language Learning,* 41–73. Newcastle upon Tyne: Cambridge Scholars Press.

Martin, J. R., Zappavigna, M. and Dwyer, P. (in press) Negotiating evaluation: Story structure and appraisal in youth justice conferencing. In A. Mahboob and N. Knight (eds) *Appliable Linguistics: Texts, Contexts, and Meanings.* London: Continuum.

Maton, K. (2000) Recovering pedagogic discourse: A Bernsteinian approach to the sociology of educational knowledge. *Linguistics & Education* 11 (1): 79–98.

Maton K. (2007) Knowledge-knower structures in intellectual and educational fields. In F. Christie and J. R. Martin *Language, Knowledge and Pedagogy: Functional Linguistic and Sociological Perspectives,* 87–108. London: Continuum.

Maton, K. (2008) *Knowledge-building: How can we create powerful and influential ideas?* Paper presented at Disciplinarity, Knowledge & Language: an international symposium. University of Sydney. December.

Maton, K. (2010) Progress and canons in the arts and humanities: Knowers and gazes. In K. Maton and R. Moore (eds) *Social Realism, Knowledge and the Sociology of Education: Coalitions of the Mind,* 154–178. London: Continuum.

Maton, K. (in press) Knowledge-building: analysing the cumulative development of ideas. In G. Ivison, B. Davies and J. Fitz (eds) *Bernstein's Sociology of Knowledge.* London: Routledge.

Maton, K. (to appear) *Knowledge and Knowers: Towards a Realist Sociology of Education.* London: Routledge.

Maton, K. and Moore, R. (eds) (2010) *Social Realism, Knowledge and the Sociology of Education: Coalitions of the Mind.* London: Continuum.

Maton, K. and Muller, J. (2007) A sociology for the transmission of knowledges. In F. Christie and J. R. Martin (eds) *Language, Knowledge and Pedagogy: Functional Linguistic and Sociological Perspectives,* 14–33. London: Continuum.

Matthiessen, C. M. I. M. and Halliday, M. A. K. (2009) *Systemic Functional Grammar: A First Step into the Theory.* Beijing: Higher Education Press.

Moore, R. and Maton, K. (2001) Founding the sociology of knowledge: Basil Bernstein, intellectual fields and the epistemic device. In A. Morais, I. Neves, B. Davies and H. Daniels (eds) *Towards a Sociology of Pedagogy: The Contribution of Basil Bernstein to research,* 153–182. New York: Peter Lang.

Moore, D. B. and O'Connell, T. (1994) Family conferencing in Wagga Wagga: A communitarian model of justice. In C. Alder and J. Wundersitz (eds) *Family Conferencing and Juvenile Justice: The Way Forward or Misplaced Optimism?* 15–44. Canberra: Australian Institute of Criminology.

Nathanson, D. L. (1997) From empathy to community'. *The Annual of Psychoanalysis* 25: 125–143.

Tann, K. (2009) Imagining communities: A multifunctional approach to identity management in texts. In M. Bednarek and J. R. Martin (eds) *New Discourse on Language: Functional Perspectives on Multimodality, Identity and Affiliation,* 163–194. London: Continuum.

Trimboli, L. (2000) *An Evaluation of the NSW Youth Justice Conferencing Scheme.* Sydney: NSW Bureau of Crime Statistics and Research.

Webster, J. (ed.) (2008) *Meaning in Context: Strategies for Implementing Intelligent Applications of Language Studies.* London: Continuum.

Williams, G. (2005) Semantic variation. In R. Hasan, C. M. I. M. Matthiessen and J. Webster. (eds) (2005) *Continuing Discourse on Language: A Functional Perspective* (Vol. 1), 457–480. London: Equinox.

Zappavigna, M, Dwyer, P. and Martin, J. R. (2008) 'Just like sort of guilty kind of': The rhetoric of tempered admission in Youth Justice Conferencing. In M. Zappavigna (ed.) *ASFLA 2007 Proceedings.* Australian Systemic Functional Linguistics Association. http://www.asfla.org.au/2008/07/31/the-rhetoric-of-tempered-admission-in-youth-justice-conferencing/

Zappavigna, M., Dwyer, P. and Martin, J. R. (in press) Visualising Appraisal Prosody. In A. Mahboob and N. Knight (eds) *Appliable Linguistics: Texts, Contexts, and Meanings.* London: Continuum.

Zappavigna, M., Cleirigh, C., Dwyer, P. and Martin, J. R. (2009) Multimodal Coupling in Youth Justice Conferencing. In M. Bednarek and J. R. Martin (eds) *New Discourse on Language: Functional Perspectives on Multimodality, Identity and Affiliation,* 219–236. London: Continuum.

3 The meaning of function: Syntax in Systemic Functional Linguistics

ZHANG Delu*

3.1 Introduction

In systemic functional linguistics (henceforth termed as SFL), the term 'syntax' seems to be avoided as much as possible, since the pioneer of this theory, Michael A. K. Halliday, rarely uses the term, and his preferred term is 'grammar'. The reasons for him to reject the term are twofold. First, it only refers to one part of grammar, which consists of syntax, vocabulary and morphology; syntax is too narrow a term for the areas of research of systemic functional grammar (henceforth called SFG). Second, as Halliday says:

> The term (syntax) suggests proceeding in a particular direction, such that a language is interpreted as a system of forms, to which meanings are then attached. In functional grammar, on the other hand, the direction is reversed. A language is interpreted as system of meanings, accompanied by forms through which the meanings can be realized. (Halliday, 1994: xiv)

However, some scholars within SFL, such as Morley (2000, 2004) and Fawcett (2000, 2008, 2011), have used the term for the formal aspect of grammar. So in this chapter, 'syntax' is used in the same sense as grammar with an emphasis on its upper ranks, the group, the clause and the sentence, including both functional syntax and formal syntax.

SFL focuses on the functions of language, so it will put emphasis on the functional aspect of syntax. In his *Introduction to Functional Grammar* (1985, 1994, with Matthiessen, 2004, 2013) and some of his earlier works, Halliday has developed a theory of SFG which is pushed 'fairly far' in the direction of the semantics (Halliday, 1994: xix). At the same time,

*   Zhang Delu is Professor of Linguistics at the School of Foreign Languages, Tongji University, Shanghai, China.

Fawcett (2000, 2008) and Morley (2000, 2004) begin to study the formal aspects of the grammar in terms of both form and function. Then the related questions are: (1) What is the relationship between functional syntax and formal syntax? (2) Whether functional grammar should be only function-oriented or both form-oriented and function-oriented, that is, whether functional grammar should be entirely based on function or on both form (taking form as a criterion for the discussion of functional structures) and function? (3) What constitutes the semantic level? The present chapter is intended to explore the areas concerned with these questions, to give a clearer picture of the relations between the different areas and models, and suggest tentatively the directions to be pursued in future research.

3.2   Models of syntax in Systemic Functional Linguistics

The development of SFL is gradual and continuous, and two models stand out: (1) SFG developed by Halliday and his colleagues; and (2) Cardiff Grammar (henceforth called CG) developed by Fawcett and his colleagues. In this section, we will give a brief survey of both the theories.

3.2.1 Systemic Functional Grammar

Halliday's SFG has been developed in two stages: Scale and Category Grammar (henceforth called SCG)[1] and SFG. The SCG was developed at the latter part of the 1950s and the beginning of the 1960s represented by his seminal article 'Categories of the theory of grammar' (Halliday, 1961). In this article, 'he focuses on "grammar", roughly equivalent to a combination of the traditional senses of the terms "syntax" and "morphology"' (Fawcett, 2000). In the latter part of the 1960s and the early part of the 1970s, Halliday began to focus on the functions of language (Halliday, 1967–1968, 1970a, 1970b, 1971–1973, 1973). As a result, he began to privilege two categories in his 'SCG', that is, structure and system, particularly system, so that he developed his Systemic Grammar (henceforth called SG) and Functional Grammar (henceforth called FG). Systemic grammatical theory was introduced in articles and book chapters (Halliday, 1970a, 1970b, 1971, 1973, 1978, 1982). Halliday's functional grammar was first published in 1985, the revised version republished in 1994 and further revised versions in 2004 and 2013 in collaboration with Christian Matthiessen. Syntactically, it seems that he narrows his scope of investigation from all the four categories to two, but it is actually a change of priority or focus. As he moves from a somewhat formal theory to a largely functional theory, the change is inevitable.

3.2.1.1 Systemic grammar

By prioritizing the functions of language, Halliday gives primary privilege to the system of language, so his theory came to be called 'systemic grammar' in the 1970s and the 1980s. Today, the standard term for this school of linguistics is SFL as it consists of two parts: systemic linguistics and functional linguistics. In grammar, therefore, we have SG and FG.

The theory is largely based on Firth's system and structure theory, and derives many abstract principles from the European functional tradition, such as Hjelmslev (the Copenhagen School), and the Prague School. The main concept of the theory is System, which is used in the Firthian sense of functional paradigm, but developed into the formal construct of a system network. A system network is a network of systems of language which defines the theory of language as choice. It means that language, or any part of language, serves as a resource for making meaning by making choices from the system networks.

A system network can be very complex, but it generally consists of a small number of rudimentary types. The terms chosen from a system network are called 'selection expression', and they are to be realized in grammatical structures, actual words and expressions, referred to as 'realization statements.' (Halliday, 1993: 4505)

3.2.1.2 Functional Grammar

Following Halliday's paper 'Notes on Transitivity and Theme in British English' (1967–1968), FG has been developed for more than forty years. Its formal appearance was marked by the publication of *An Introduction to Functional Grammar* (1985), and its three revised versions (see 3.1 above).

A language is interpreted as a system of meanings, and a FG is concerned with how these meanings are realized functionally. And according to Halliday, language is functional in three senses: (1) in its interpretation of the text, that is, how language is used in the context; (2) in its interpretation of the system, that is, how it realizes the ideational or reflective, interpersonal or active, and textual meanings; (3) in its interpretation of the elements of structure, that is, how the elements are related to their functions in the total linguistic system. 'But meanings are realized through wordings; and without a theory of wordings – that is, a grammar – there is no way of making explicit one's interpretation of the meaning of a text' (Halliday, 1985: xvii).

Here, a question arises concerning how the wordings and meanings are dealt with in a FG. In FG, the general idea of their relation is clear and consistent: the wordings are presented as a special kind of constituent structure: the ranked constituent structure, the formal syntax of FG, which presents less syntactic differentiations, but is based on the functions of the constituents (or elements) of the structure in realizing meaning. Then on the basis of the constituent structure, there are several functional structures related to the three metafunctions of language: transitivity structure and the complex structures at different ranks for the **ideational** metafunction; mood structure for the **interpersonal** metafunction, and Thematic Structure for the **textual** metafunction.

The constituent structure is based on rank. **The Ranked Constituent Analysis** is also called '**minimal bracketing**', that is, 'put a bracket only where you have to', in contrast to '**maximal bracketing**' or **Immediate Constituent Analysis**, which puts 'a bracket everywhere you can' (Halliday, 1985: 22).

On the basis of the ranked constituent analysis, functional structures are set up, that is, each constituent[2] in the structure is liable to have one or more functions in particular functional structures for realizing particular components of meaning.

The clause is taken as the basic unit of grammar, so functional structures are developed on the basis of the clause. First, 'clause as message' deals with how the meanings are organized in terms of Theme and Rheme. It realizes the textual metafunction. Second, 'clause as exchange' is concerned with the clause in its function as an interactive event involving speaker, or writer, and audience. It realizes the interpersonal metafunction by the Mood structure, which consists of Mood and Residue. Third, 'clause as representation' is concerned with the clause in its function of representing the patterns of our experiences as processes, which refer to going-ons, happenings, feelings and beings, etc. The system here is Transitivity, which 'specifies the different types of process that are recognized in the language, and the structures by which they are expressed' (Halliday, 1985: 101). A process consists potentially of three components: (1) the process itself; (2) participants in the process; and (3) circumstances associated with the process. Based on the patterns of human experience, processes are classified into six types: three major ones and three minor ones. The major processes are the Material process, the Mental process, and the Relational process. The minor processes are the Behavioural process, the Verbal process, and the Existential process. There are a certain number of participants in each process; some are obligatory and some optional.

Then after presenting the functional structures of the clause, the rank scale moves first downward to the group and phrase (prepositional phrase) structures with their complex structures for realizing ideational, interpersonal and textual metafunctions, and then it moves upward to the sentence rank, dealing with the clause complex in terms of Interdependency relation and Logicosemantic relations, which is mainly concerned with the realization of **logical** and textual meanings.

Besides the clause, rhythm and intonation are studied for their realization of textual and interpersonal functions. The information structure realizes the textual meaning, and is based on rhythm and stress, with the New information highlighted by the tonic element.

Then around the clause, Cohesion is brought in as devices for text formation. It realizes the textual metafunction. There are four of these devices: Reference, Substitution and Ellipsis, Conjunction and Lexical Cohesion.

Finally, FG is concerned with the interpretation of incongruent clause structures with the patterns of transitivity, mood and modality, and the phenomenon is called 'Grammatical Metaphor', which refers to any structure departing from its congruent one. In such a structure, a process may be encoded as a Thing, termed as ideational metaphor, and a modal element typically expressed by a word may be conveyed as a clause, termed as interpersonal metaphor.

On the basis of one constituent structure, there are several functional structures for the realization of different strands of meaning (see Figure 3.1):

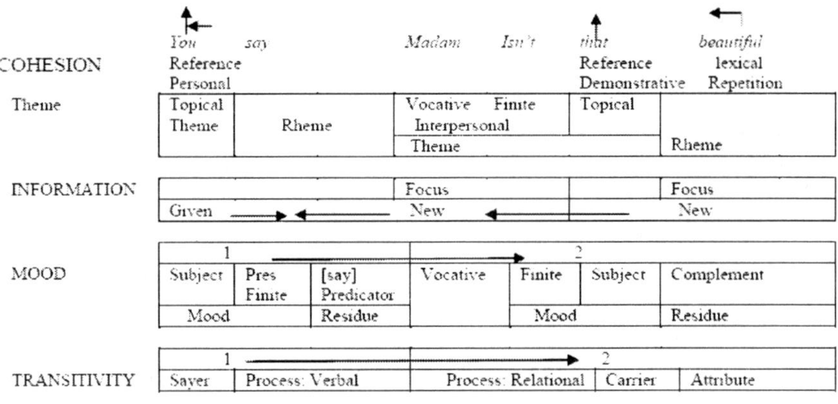

Figure 3.1: An integrated analysis of the functional structures of a clause complex

As the grammar is more and more pushed in the direction of semantics, the focus has shifted to meaning and functions although Halliday claims that it will 'not lose contact with the ground (Halliday, 1994: xix)'. Figure 3.1 identifies all the functional structures for realizing the ideational, interpersonal and textual meanings, but no ranked constituent structure is represented. The gap left here is filled by Morley's work on functional syntax (Morley, 2000, 2004), in which he presents a descriptive syntactic framework in the light of functional dimensions.

3.2.2 The Cardiff Grammar

The CG has been principally developed by Robin Fawcett, Gordon Tucker and a number of other linguists working at (or otherwise associated with) Cardiff University. The CG is not a different kind of grammar from SFG (or Sydney Grammar, as is called for differentiating it from the CG). They have a common ground: both have been developed from Halliday's SFL, especially Halliday's earlier works in the 1960s and 1970s, such as the SCG. Both are intended to interpret language from a functional point of view; both regard language as a system; and both hold that 'every clause serves several different functions at the same time' (Fawcett, 2008: 44).

However, there are also significant differences between the two so that they can be considered different models of the same theory. In the following, we will briefly introduce the theory, and compare it with that of Halliday's SFG at the same time.

Fawcett gives eight reasons for the development of the CG, but the important overtone is that in a SFG, both form and meaning should be taken into consideration, and both form and meaning have potential systems and actual instances, and this results in the theoretical model, as shown in Figure 3.2.

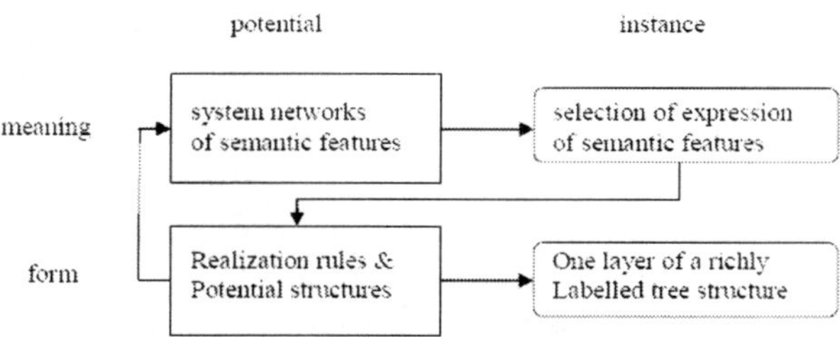

Figure 3.2: The components and their outputs in a CG (Fawcett, 2008: 41)

Meaning potential is represented in this model as a system network of semantic features, which is instanced by the selection expression of semantic features, and the potential is realized by form as realization rules and potential structures, which is instanced by one layer of a richly labelled tree structure.

Syntactically, the CG is mainly concerned with realization rules and potential structures in terms of form potential and the one layer of a richly labelled tree structure as instance. The two are integrated into a whole, and are not separate from each other. The system networks in the meaning potential are represented in the same way as Halliday's SFG (see Figure 3.3).

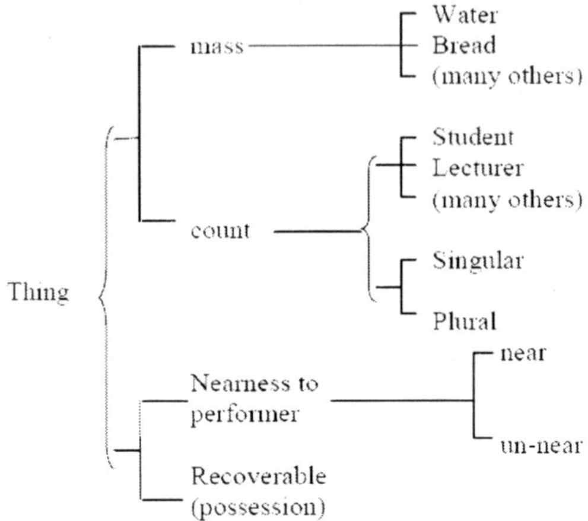

Figure 3.3: A highly simplified system network for the 'thing' in English

The realization rules are greatly improved and adapted to the new model, but are formulated in a similar way as Halliday's.

One of the striking characteristics of the CG is the unified syntactic structure, that is, all the functions are unified into one syntactic structure, which differs from Halliday's FG, in which almost all the elements of the structure have functions in realizing the ideational, interpersonal and textual meanings, and so there are several functional structures on the basis of one ranked constituent structure, such as the transitivity structure, the mood structure, and the theme structure.

As a result, another feature stands out: in the CG, not all the elements of the structure function to realize all types of meaning, but a certain element or a set of elements of the structure realize a particular type of meaning, as shown in Figure 3.4.

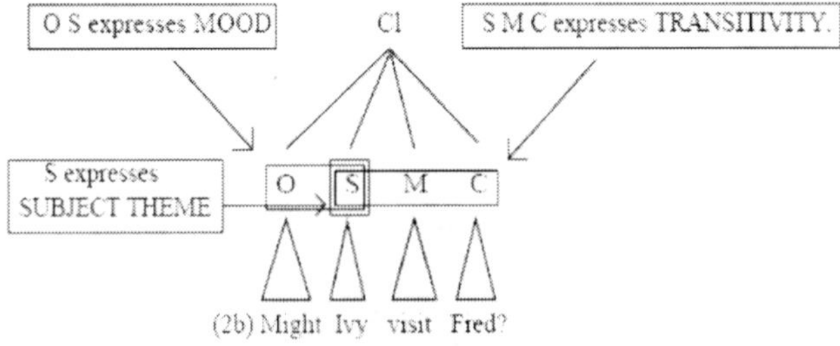

Key: O = Operator S = Subject M = Main Verb C = Complement

Figure 3.4: Transitivity, Mood and Theme in a simple clause (Fawcett, 2008: 113)

There are four elements: O, S, M, and C, in this unified structure. The Theme is realized by S (the Subject Theme), the Mood by O and S, and the Transitivity by S, M and C. In contrast, in Halliday's SFG, the formal syntactic structure is the ranked constituent structure with the elements marked by class labels, and several functional structures go side by side on the basis of the constituent structure with one or more elements realizing a particular function in a functional structure (see above Section 3.2.1.2).

The third striking feature of the CG is that the **functional structures** in Halliday's SFG are interpreted as **semantic structures** in the CG, and, there are also substantial differences in both structure and element analysis in the two models of grammar. For example, the six types of processes in transitivity in the CG are Action, Relational, Mental, Environmental, Influential and Event-Relating with their own different participant roles; and the mood system consists of two choices: 'Information' and 'Proposal for Action'; within 'Information', there is a subsystem with 'Giver', 'Seeker', 'Confirmation Seeker', 'Exclamation' and 'Others' as choices, and 'proposal for action' can be made by 'Addressee', 'Self', 'Addressee and Self', and 'Others'. In the Theme system, there are principally three types of themes: the Subject Theme, the thematized elements, and the different types of Enhanced Theme. The syntactic structure and the semantic components it realizes in the CG can be shown in Figure 3.5.

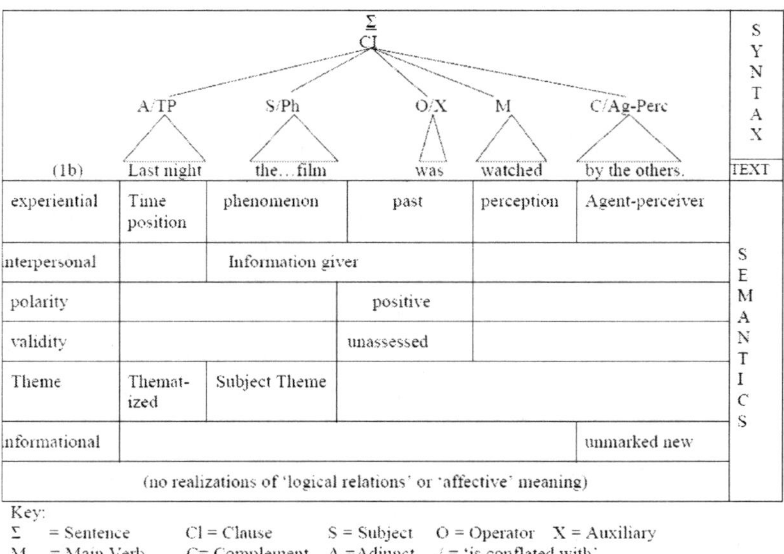

Key:
Σ   = Sentence   Cl = Clause   S = Subject   O = Operator   X = Auxiliary
M   = Main Verb   C = Complement   A = Adjunct   / = 'is conflated with'
TP = Time Position Ph = Phenomenon   Ag-Perc = Agent-Perceiver

Figure 3.5: The syntactic and semantic representations of a clause (Fawcett, 2008: 242)

Here, the different strands of meaning are realized by a certain element or a set of elements in the same syntactic structure manifested as 'A/TP ^ S/ PH ^ O/X ^ M ^ C/Ag-Perc'.

The last prominent feature of CG is that more attention is paid to the procedures and methodology in analysis. It provides guidelines and test methods for text analysis, in which procedures and steps are indicated for the analysis and the test of a particular type of meaning or structure.

The differences between SFG and CG are not accidental, but based on their differences in perspective and focus, which will be discussed below.

3.3   The meaning of function

We have briefly outlined the two models of grammar within SFL: Halliday's SFG and the CG. Associated with these two grammars, there arise several questions for further study in relation to syntax in SFL: (1) whether the grammar is at the level of form or at the level of meaning; (2) whether we should take both constituent structure and functional structure into consideration, or only functional structure; and (3) whether metafunction is defined only from the higher level, the context, or from both the context and the lower level, the grammar.

3.3.1 Form or meaning

In regards to the first question, Halliday describes a FG as 'one that is pushed in the direction of the semantics'. And later he states, 'the higher-rank choices in the grammar can be essentially choices in meaning without the grammar thereby losing contact with the ground' (Halliday, 1994: xix), which shows how far the grammar has been pushed towards meaning. From these quotations, we can be quite sure that Halliday holds that a FG is still at the level of form, that is, lexicogrammar. No matter how far it is pushed, it is not yet meaning proper, but only pushed closer to it. Indeed, this conviction is supported by what he says in the latter part of the same section from which the above quotations are taken:

> The fact that this is a 'functional' grammar means that it is based on meaning: but the fact that it is a 'grammar' means that it is an interpretation of linguistic forms. Every distinction that is recognized in the grammar – every set of options, or 'system' in systemic terms – makes some contribution to the form of the wording. (Halliday, 1994: xx)

It is clear that what Halliday means is that a FG is not a grammar of semantics, but a grammar in which formal categories are interpreted in terms of meaning. The relation between form and meaning is that of realization, that is, the grammar realizes or encodes the meaning. In this sense, a FG is not a functional semantic theory. Therefore we need a higher level of semantics.

However, this position is questioned by Fawcett:

> Halliday is clearly saying that he does not think that his system networks for TRANSITIVITY, MOOD and THEME have NOT been pushed as far as the semantics, and that they constitute a layer of 'meaning potential' that lies somehow WITHIN the same general level as the output from the lexicogrammar ... On the other hand, his networks are clearly well above the level of form itself, because, as we have just noted, Halliday himself says, his grammar has been 'pushed fairly far' towards the semantics. (Fawcett, 2008: 43)

Then, he further questions:

> What is now clear, however, is that Halliday assumes that there is in fact a need for a higher layer of system networks, i.e. ANOTHER level of 'meaning potential', and that this constitutes the 'true' semantics (Halliday 1994: xx). And Halliday considers that 'at the present state of our knowledge we cannot yet describe the semantic system of a language.' (Fawcett, 2008: 43).

Here, we can see that the difference between Halliday and Fawcett lies in view of the role of the concept of function in a linguistic theory. For Halliday, there are actually two levels of functions: **macrofunction** or metafunction, and **micro-function**. In terms of macrofunction or metafunction, function equals meaning (Halliday, 1973: 38–39), as function here refers to the function of language as a whole, such as ideational function, interpersonal function and textual function. In terms of micro-function, function refers to the function of an element in the structure, such as Actor, Goal, Theme and Rheme. So the grammar is used for the interpretation of form in relation to meaning. In this sense, it is clear that function is the intermediate factor relating meaning with form as form is interpreted in relation to meaning in a functional theory. Indeed, this idea is supported by Dik (1989) and Hjelmslev (1954) (see Johansen, 1996: 333), who consider function to be a relational notion. For Dik, 'In the fabric of FG pride of place is given to functional or relational as opposed to categorical notions' (Dik, 1989: 23), where function refers to a relation between an element and the structure in which it occurs, such as that between the subject and the rest of the clause.

However, for Hjelmslev, function is the relation between levels (Johansen, 1996: 333), that is, the element that **relates** expression form and the content form.

From Halliday's theory of functions and Hjelmslev's sign theory, we can see that the function of an element in the structure is that it can realize an element in the structure of the upper level, and when we study the function of a formal element in the structure, we actually study how it realizes meaning. For example, in 'Mary sailed the boat', there are three groups: two nominal groups and one verbal group in the clause. They are related to each other by their functional roles to each other: 'Actor–Material Process–Goal', and their capacity of realizing a particular kind of experience: 'a female human being called Mary made a boat move on the surface of water, or Person moved Thing' (see Table 3.1).

Table 3.1: Function as a relation between form and meaning

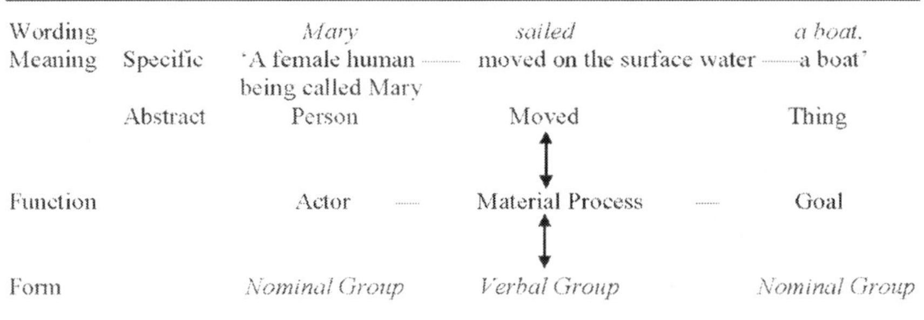

Wording		*Mary*	*sailed*	*a boat.*
Meaning	Specific	'A female human being called Mary	moved on the surface water	a boat'
	Abstract	Person	Moved	Thing
Function		Actor	Material Process	Goal
Form		*Nominal Group*	*Verbal Group*	*Nominal Group*

If we accept this role of function, and regards function as a relational notion, then it is easy to interpret Halliday's notion of FG. As a functional structure is a relation between formal structure and semantic structure, it is intermediate between form and meaning. However, its intermediate position is not fixed exactly in the middle, but may go up and down the scale according to the nature of the functional theory. If it is, as Halliday states, pushed fairly far towards semantics, it is close to meaning and far away from form; and if it remains close to form, it is far away from semantics (see Figure 3.6).

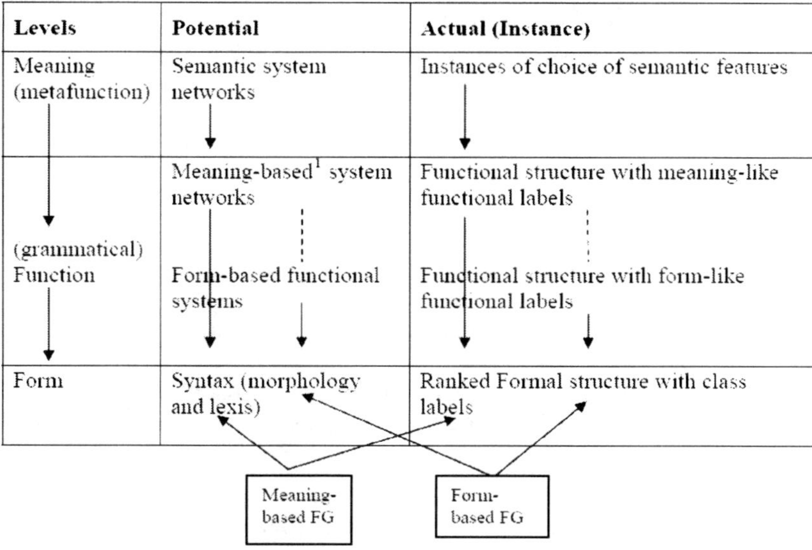

Levels	Potential	Actual (Instance)
Meaning (metafunction)	Semantic system networks	Instances of choice of semantic features
(grammatical) Function	Meaning-based[1] system networks Form-based functional systems	Functional structure with meaning-like functional labels Functional structure with form-like functional labels
Form	Syntax (morphology and lexis)	Ranked Formal structure with class labels

Figure 3.6: A comparison among meaning-based FG, form-based FG and formal grammar.[3, 4]

For a meaning-based FG, like Halliday's SFG, it will be necessary to have a higher level semantics to capture the system of meaning proper. At the level of semantics, meaning is closely related to use, or a realization of the communicative function of language in social interactions. Here, the meaning is not only realized by human language, but can also be realized by any other semiotic systems, such as gestures, music, dance, Morse Code, traffic code system, architecture, etc. Such a FG is always ready to go upward for the realization of meaning and also the communicative purpose in a sociocultural environment at its upper end.

The meaning that language expresses will be realized by form through the functions of the elements in the structure. So the semantic networks at this level are purely meaning features, which accept realization rules from different semiotic systems. If it is realized by language, it is realized first through the functional grammatical system networks, which relates the semantic features with the formal features in the form of language, that is, lexis and grammar. The features in this system are like the semantic features, but they are based on form, keeping contact with the 'ground'.

For a form-based FG, the grammatical function is defined only in relation to other elements in the same structure, and not directly related to the meaning in the upper level. But this grammar is designed in such a way that it is easy to be endowed with upper level functions that are directly associated with meaning, such as the CG in terms of functional syntax. Such a grammar will also be organized in terms of rank scale for the elements to be ready for their functions in realizing upper level meaning.[5]

As said above, because it is form-based, and the form specifically refers to language form, the meaning it realizes will not be expected to exceed that realized by language. So it is not necessary to have an upper level semantics (see Figure 3.5).

3.3.2 Constituent structure and functional structure

From above, we can see that, when a text is analysed in terms of FG, the focus is on the functional structure of the clause, and its constituent structure is rarely analysed. But in the CG, the constituent structure is analysed in a great detail, and endowed with grammatical functions based on form, such as Subject, Operator, Main Verb, Complement, etc.

The reason for this seems obvious. As Halliday's SFG is 'pushed fairly far in the direction of the semantics', it gives priority to meaning instead of form, and the purpose of that analysis is to see how form realizes meaning, not how form is constructed by the aid of meaning, so the focus will be on meaning. The final result of the analysis is the meaning of the text as a whole in social communication. The form will be made explicit when it is necessary; for example, when we try to find what meaning is realized in what element or elements of the constituent structure, so that the grammar will not lose contact with the 'ground'. In this sense, we can say that it is not always necessary to have the constituent structure made explicit in the functional analysis of a text.

However, in a form-based FG, the constituent structure constitutes the form itself, so it must be made explicit in the analysis though it is not necessarily in the form of formal constituent structure. In such a grammar, the formal constituent structure is analysed in terms of the grammatical functions, so that it is ready for use in a higher level analysis. In this sense, we can say that it is based on a solid ground. But at this stage, it is only the ground yet, with no 'superstructure' constructed.

3.3.3 Macro-function and micro-function

As is said above, Halliday (1973: 104) recognizes two types of functions: micro-function and macro-function (1973, 1978, 1985a; with Hasan, 1989). Halliday's macro-functions or metafunctions are 'highly abstract linguistic reflexes of the multiplicity of social uses of language' (1973: 36). They are the abstractions from the numerous concrete uses of language, and are defined in terms of the most essential factors involved in communication: the activity that takes place, the participants involved and the media or channel of the communication. The functions of language that realize the three aspects of the situation are the ideational, the interpersonal and the textual metafunctions respectively. So they are made as abstract and general as possible, and not in terms of specific aspects of meaning, such as affect, attitude, polarity, etc. We can say here that the metafunctions are defined from higher levels: the situational and cultural levels irrespective of the characteristics of language form. The model of semantics developed by Halliday is more characteristic of a meaning-based FG. However, Fawcett (2008: 56) concludes, 'Thus Halliday presents his model of language as having **four** strands of meaning, whereas in the CG we find it valuable to distinguish **eight** (experiential, logical relations, interpersonal, negativity, validity, affective, thematic and informational).'

The difference here is not just a difference in the recognition of the number of meanings, but a difference in the ideology and perspective of approaching language functions. As a form-based FG, Fawcett tries to match his functions closely with his functional syntax. When there is a negative marker, there should be a function of polarity; and when there is an affective element in the grammar, then there should be an affective function, etc. In this sense, the eight functions are still general. In my view, the eight functions can all be subsumed into Halliday's three metafunctions (see Table 3.2), although there are disagreements as both Validity and Polarity can be either ideational or interpersonal.

Table 3.2: A comparison of the components of functions between Halliday's SFG and the CG

Model	Function							
Halliday	Ideational		Interpersonal				Textual	
Fawcett	experiential	logical	interpersonal	polarity	validity	affective	thematic	informational

3.4 Discussion

Although the term 'syntax' is not used in Halliday's works so as to avoid the suggested overtone that 'a language is interpreted as a system of forms, to which meanings are then attached' (Halliday, 1994: xiv), it is used here to show that both form and meaning are taken into focus in the present chapter. And syntax here means both formal syntax and functional syntax, and it is the aim of this chapter to show their relations in the different models of FG in SFL.

First, for Halliday's SFG, the formal syntax is the ranked constituent structure that is chosen from the formal system with ranked class labels for their constituents, and the functional syntax is the FG that is pushed 'fairly far in the direction of the semantics'. As it focuses on how meaning is realized, it is mainly concerned with the functional structures that are close to semantics, and leaves the constituent structure in the background, rarely analysed in text analysis.

For the CG, a formal syntax is embodied in its form-based functional syntax. At the lexicogrammatical level, that is what it is mainly concerned with, and for the sake of bringing out the implicit participant roles, the formal functional roles at the clause rank are also accompanied by the participant roles of the transitivity structure (which is considered semantic structure by the CG.)

This difference also results in another difference in the orientation of analysis. For Halliday's SFG, as the focus is on meaning, the formal characteristics will be kept to a minimum (that is what it means by 'minimal bracketing' (Halliday, 1994: 20–28). Although it is totally accountable in terms of the structures of lower rank units (for example, the detailed structure of a participant role in the clause can be made explicit by analysing the structure of the group or phrase that realizes it), the lower rank structures are rarely made explicit in actual text analysis. However, for the CG, it is mandatory to assign a functional label for all the elements at different ranks except those at the morphemic rank as morphology is not included in syntax, and the functional label will usually be accompanied by a class label under it so that both class labelling and formal functional labelling are given to the syntactic elements concerned.

Second, the 'function' in functional syntax is understood as a relational term as Hjelmslev envisaged it (Hjelmslev, 1954). So grammatical functions in FG, such as Actor, Goal, Subject, etc. are also relations between formal constituents and the semantic elements the formal constituents realize. As a form-based FG ready for accommodating the functional structures, the CG focuses on the syntactic functions and their structures, with a view that the functional structures can be readily accommodated. And the functional structures here are the semantic structures, and so it is not necessary to have a higher level semantics. Therefore, the functional structures in Halliday's SFG are taken as semantic structures in the CG, and no higher level semantics is necessary.

However, whether there should be a higher level semantics or not is not a right or wrong issue, but a difference in perspective and scope of the research.

Halliday's SFG studies language from a social-semiotic or sociocultural perspective, and from this perspective, the meanings that grammar realizes should be meaningful in a sociocultural context, therefore they will be directly associated with the wider context of culture and the context of situation. Also the meanings in the wider contexts of culture and situation are not restricted to language, that is, they are not only realized by language, but are also realized by other semiotic systems. That is why a higher level semantics is necessary for the wider concept of meaning. So the scope of analysis for Halliday's SFG extends well beyond the boundary of language into other semiotic systems, and the theory can be readily employed for multimodal discourse analysis (Kress and van Leeuwen, 2001; O'Halloran, 2006; Royce and Bowcher, 2007) and critical discourse analysis (Fairclough, 1995; Weiss and Wodak, 2003; Young and Harrison, 2004).

The CG studies language from a cognitive-interactive perspective, a perspective in which the performer plans and reasons his interaction with others in a belief system. So the approach is both interactional and individual. It is also called a consulting model as the performer is 'to consult widely, to weigh the evidence, and to reach a decision as to which feature in a system should be chosen' (Fawcett, 2014: forthcoming). As a consultation model, the choices will be made not in a one-way direction from the sociocultural to the form, but bidirectional, with meaning closely related to form, the 'richly labelled tree structure'. As a bidirectional model, the meanings are not made before considering the choices in form, but simultaneously, so that the meanings are in conformity to form and vice versa. In this sense, the semantic field of the CG will be confined to that capable of being handled by form in the lexicogrammar. That also shows why it is not necessary to have a higher level semantics.

Metafunctions are at a level higher than the micro-functions of the elements of the structure, and they are meanings that language is supposed to realize together with other semiotic systems. It is at this level that Halliday equates function with meaning (Halliday, 1973: 104–106, 1985: xiii). At the same time, they are also relations, not the relations between form and meaning, but the relations between language as a whole and the sociocultural contexts and the communication purpose and needs. The function or meaning at this level is defined extrinsically by reference to the notion that language plays some part in human life just as Halliday says (1973: 15), 'People do different things with their language; that is, they expect to achieve by talking and writing, and by listening and reading, a large number of different aims and different purposes.'

It is at this level that we can say that language shares the same semantic system with many other semiotic systems. From this point of view, meaning can be independent of the linguistic form, so we need a separate level for semantics. However, function here does not equal use because it is interpreted not just as the use of language, but as a fundamental property of language, something that is basic to the evolution of the semantic system of language (Halliday, 1989: 17). The functional variation of language is interpreted as something that is built into language as the very foundation of language itself, and particularly to the organization of the semantic system. From this point of view, the language system and structure are determined and shaped by the semantic system.

Finally, we come to the relation between the two models of SFG. They are complementary and overlapping in many areas, but there are also significant differences in perspective, focus and scope of study.

They are complementary because a functional theory needs to be built both close to semantics to capture its characteristics of serving certain universal human demand for achieving a large number of different aims and purposes, and on a solid ground to make every functional category have repercussion in form. Halliday's SFG satisfies the first demand as a FG and the CG does the second. The latter brings the grammar down to earth, so to speak, placing it on a solid ground, not just 'without losing contact with the ground'. The same purpose is also fulfilled by Morley's work.

The two models overlap in many areas of SFL, such as genre and register studies, semantics (system networks and their realization), lexicogrammar (especially syntax) and phonology (especially intonation) with minor differences in focus, point of view and methodology (see Figure 3.7).

3.5   Conclusion

The above studies show that the two models of SFL, although sharing common ground, have their own focus, scope of research, perspective and characteristics. They are also developed for different purposes. They are complementary and overlapping in many aspects, but there are also substantial differences between them. The differences between the two models mainly lie in their different views of the function of language in grammatical studies. For FG, the micro-function is the relation between form and meaning, and the meta-function is the relation between language as a whole and the sociocultural contexts and the communication purpose and needs. For CG, function is meaning that can be realized by the linguistic form, so both micro-function and meta-function are at the level of meaning.

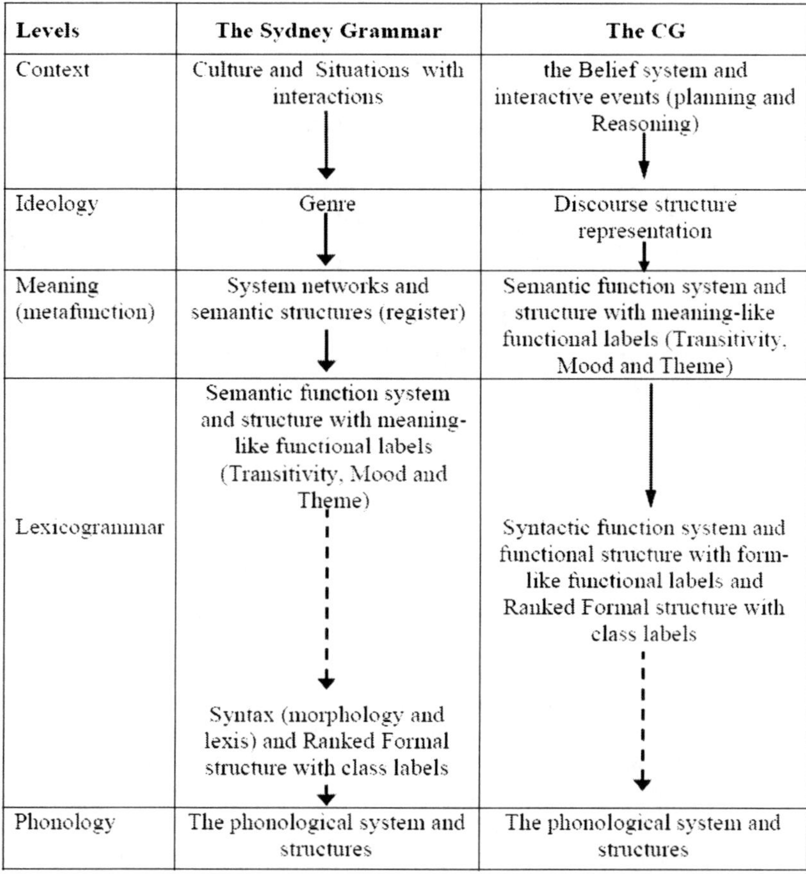

Levels	The Sydney Grammar	The CG
Context	Culture and Situations with interactions	the Belief system and interactive events (planning and Reasoning)
Ideology	Genre	Discourse structure representation
Meaning (metafunction)	System networks and semantic structures (register)	Semantic function system and structure with meaning-like functional labels (Transitivity, Mood and Theme)
Lexicogrammar	Semantic function system and structure with meaning-like functional labels (Transitivity, Mood and Theme) … Syntax (morphology and lexis) and Ranked Formal structure with class labels	Syntactic function system and functional structure with form-like functional labels and Ranked Formal structure with class labels
Phonology	The phonological system and structures	The phonological system and structures

Figure 3.7: A comparison between SFG and CG.[6]

While the present study is mainly qualitative in nature, it could be useful to carry out a comparative study of texts analysed on the basis of the two theories. We expect that such studies emerge soon and hope that we can develop more models of similar kind for other purposes, such as theoretical explorations, translation studies, corpus studies, etc.

Notes

1.　Halliday's Scale and Category Grammar can be presented succinctly as 'four categories and three scales'. The four categories are unit, structure, class and system, and the three scales are rank, delicacy and exponence.

2.   A constituent in a structure may realize a particular function in a functional structure, but may also realize part of a functional element or have no function in a particular functional structure.
3.   A downward arrow here means 'be realized by'.
4.   A bold line here means that what it points to is the focus of research of the theory.
5.   The upper level meaning here means the semantic features the grammar is supposed to realize, such as experiential, interpersonal, thematic, polarity, etc., which includes both the functional features in Halliday's functional grammar and the semantic features in his semantics.
6.   The difference between Halliday's SFG and the CG is that in the CG, the elements of the verbal group are elevated to the clause rank as elements of the clause.

References

Dik, S. C. (1989) *The Theory of FG: Part I: The Structure of the Clause*. Dordrecht: Foris Publications.

Fairclough, N. (1995) *Critical Discourse Analysis: The Critical Study of Language*. London: Longman.

Fawcett, R. P. (1980) *Cognitive Linguistics and Social Interaction: Towards an Integrated Model of a Systemic Functional Grammar and the Other Components of an Interacting Mind*. Heidelberg: Julius Groos and Exeter University.

Fawcett, R. P. (2000) *A Theory of Syntax for Systemic Functional Linguistics. Current Issues in Linguistic Theory*. Amsterdam: John Benjamins.

Fawcett, R. P. (2008) *Invitation to Systemic Functional Linguistics through the Cardiff Grammar: An Extension and Simplification of Halliday's Systemic Functional Grammar* (Third Edition). London: Equinox.

Fawcett, R. P., Tucker, G. H. and Lin, Y. (1993) How a Systemic Functional Grammar works: The role of realization in realization. In H. Horacek and M. Zock (eds) *New Concepts in Natural Language Generation*, 114–186. London: Pinter.

Fawcett, R. P. (2013) (forthcoming). *Functional Syntax Handbook: Analyzing English at the Level of Form*. London: Equinox.

Halliday, M. A. K. (1961) Categories of the theory of grammar. *Word* 17(3): 241–292.

Halliday, M. A. K. (1967-1968) Notes on transitivity and theme in British English. *Journal of Linguistics* 3 and 4: 1–3.

Halliday, M. A. K. (1970a) Language structure and language function. In J. Lyons (ed.) *New Horizons in Linguistics*, 140–165. Harmondsworth: Penguin.

Halliday, M. A. K. (1970b) *A Course in Spoken English: Intonation*. Oxford: Oxford University Press.

Halliday, M. A. K. (1971–1973) Linguistic function and literary style: An inquiry into the language of William Golding's *The Inheritors*. In M. A. K. Halliday *Explorations in the Functions of Language*, 103–143. London: Arnold.

Halliday, M. A. K. (1978) *Language as Social Semiotic: The Social Interpretation of Language and Meaning*. London: Arnold.

Halliday, M. A. K. (1982) Text semantics and clause grammar: How is a text like a clause? In S. Allén, (ed.) *Text Processing: Text Analysis and Generation, Text Typology and Attrition* (Proceedings of Nobel Symposium 51: 209–247. Stockholm: Almqvist and Wiksell.

Halliday, M. A. K. (1985*) An Introduction to Functional Grammar*. London: Arnold.

Halliday, M. A. K. and Hasan, R. (1989) *Language, Context, and Text: Aspects of Language in a Social-semiotic Perspective*. Oxford: Oxford University Press.

Halliday, M. A. K. (1993) Systemic theory. In R. E. Asher (ed.). *Encyclopaedia of Languages and Linguistics*, 4905–4908. Oxford: Pergamon Press.

Halliday, M. A. K. (1994) *An Introduction to Functional Grammar* (2nd edition). London: Arnold.

Halliday, M. A. K. (2002) On grammar. In J. J. Webster (ed.) *The Collected Works of M. A. K. Halliday* Vol. 1. London: Continuum.

Halliday, M. A. K. and Matthiessen, C. M. I. M. (2004) *An Introduction to Functional Grammar* (3rd edition). London: Arnold.

Halliday, M. A. K. and Matthiessen, C. M. I. M. (2013) *Halliday's Introduction to Functional Grammar* (4th edition). London: Hodder Education.

Johansen, J. D. (1996) Sign structure and sign event in Saussure, Hjelmslev, and Peirce. In V. M. Colapietro and T. M. Olshewsky (eds) *Peirce's Doctrine of Signs: Theory, Applications, and Connections*, 329–338. Berlin and New York: Mouton de Gruyter.

Kress, G. (ed.) (1976) *Halliday: System and Function in Language*. London: Oxford University Press.

Kress, G. and van Leeuwen, T. (2001) *Multimodal Discourse: The Modes and Media of Contemporary Communication*. London: Arnold.

Morley, D. (2000) *Syntax in Functional Grammar: An iIntroduction to Lexicogrammar in Systemic Linguistics*. London: Continuum.

Morley, D. (2004) *Explorations in Functional Syntax: A New Framework for Lexicogrammatical Analysis*. London: Equinox.

O'Halloran, K. (ed.) (2006) *Multimodal Discourse Analysis: Systemic-Functional Perspectives*. London: Continuum.

Royce, T. D. and Bowcher, W. L. (eds) (2007) *New Directions in the Analysis of Multimodal Discourse*. Mahwah. NJ: Lawrence Erlbaum Associates.

Weiss, G. and Wodak R. (eds) (2003) *Critical Discourse Analysis: Theory and Interdisciplinarity*. Basingstoke: Palgrave Macmillan.

Young, L. and Harrison, C. (eds) (2004) S*ystemic Functional Linguistics and Critical Discourse Analysis*. London: Continuum.

4 Systemic linguistic interpretation of constructivism

YAN Shiqing*

4.1 Introduction

The relationship between systemic linguistics and constructivism is briefly mentioned in the book *Construing Human Experience*, in which Halliday and Matthiessen remind readers to guard against the misconception that systemic linguistics adopts an 'essentialist' or correspondence approach to grammar and meaning, according to which 'meaning' preexists the forms in which it is 'encoded' (1999: 17). After briefly explaining the essentialist view on meaning, they declare that they adopt a constructivist view: 'According to this view, it is the grammar itself that construes experience, that constructs for us our world of events and objects' (Halliday and Matthiessen, 1999: 17). In this chapter, we shall try to show the isomorphism between constructivism and systemic linguistics, with special emphasis on exploring the philosophical implications of the evolutionary theory of meaning, grammatical metaphor theory and textual metafunction.

4.2 A historical account of constructivism

Though constructivism seems more closely related to Jean Piaget's developmental epistemology (Piaget, 1978) and Lev Vygotsky's social constructivism (Vygotsky, 1978, 1986), it is deeply rooted in western culture and has become a philosophical trend of thinking in the modern times. In the following historical account of world views on epistemology, we shall demonstrate that the constructivist view originates from philosophers' quest for the accessibility of reality and truth (Wilson, 1998).

* Yan Shiqing is Professor of English Linguistics at Suzhou University, and Vice Chairman of China Functional Linguistics Association.

Indeed, interest in constructivism has grown as a result of the contrast between the Chomskyan and Piagetian ideologies on language and language acquisition or development (Yan, 2000). However, little attention has been paid to the philosophical implications of the constructivist approach to reality and truth. Part of the reason for this negligence may be attributed to this generation's pervasive respect for science. Just as Andrew Ortony (1993) points out:

> A central presupposition of our culture is that the description and explanation of physical reality is a respectable and worthwhile enterprise – an enterprise that we call 'science'. Science is supposed to be characterized by precision and the absence of ambiguity, and the language of science is assumed to be correspondingly precise and unambiguous – in short literal. … This belief reached a peak in the doctrine of logical positivism, so pervasive amongst philosophers and scientists sixty years ago. A basic notion of positivism was that reality could be precisely described through the medium of language in a manner that was clear, unambiguous, and, in principle, testable – reality could, and should, be literally describable. (Ortony, 1993: 1)

However, a constructivist approach to epistemology offers a different picture of reality, or perhaps a hypothetical vision of reality, since reality to constructivists is inaccessible. Quoting Ortony:

> The central idea of this approach is that cognition is the result of mental *construction*. Knowledge of reality, whether occasioned by perception, language, or memory, necessitates going beyond the information given. It arises through the interaction of that information with the context in which it is presented and with the knower's preexisting knowledge. This general orientation is the hallmark of the relativist view that the objective world is not directly accessible but is constructed on the basis of the constraining influences of human knowledge and language. (Ortony, 1993: 1–2; original italicization)

Ortony's remark makes explicit the connection between constructivism and logical relativism.

4.2.1   The evolution of world views

The fundamental issues arising in connection with the term constructivism are universal to human cultures, be they oriental, occidental, or aboriginal. The issues include: How do we come to know what we know? What is knowledge? What is truth? What is reality? They are important not only for epistemologists or philosophers who study knowledge, but, also for those interested in science, language, values, educational psychology, and even for computer scientists developing artificial intelligence.

In Wilson's (1998) description of the evolution of world views, he identified four stages: Ancient times, the period of Renaissance, Modern (after Kant), and postmodern. In Ancient times, it is argued that people believed only God could provide glimpses of the real world. Mathematics and logic had an important role to play in making this knowledge manifest. During the Renaissance, the scientific method evolved as the generally recognized method for uncovering truth. Kant, however, denied this possibility of arriving at a precise grasp of absolute knowledge. It was the postmodernists who preferred to reject the idealized view of truth inherited from the ancients and replace it with a dynamic, changing truth bounded by time, space and perspective.

Wilson's study clearly illustrates how world views have evolved from a static view of knowledge towards a more adaptive and active view. The kind of view held by the ancients, later inherited by logical positivists, and now pervasive is said to be passive and static, because it considers knowledge to be the awareness of objects that exist independent of any subject. Such a view is termed by Wilson as objectivism, according to which objects have intrinsic meaning, and knowledge is a reflection of a correspondence to reality. In other words, knowledge should represent a real world that is thought of as existing, separate and independent of the knower; and this knowledge should be considered true only if it correctly reflects that independent world. Interestingly, Halliday and Matthiessen (1999) also touches on objectivism, though in a slightly ironical tone:

> This approach to meaning is objectivist: (extensional) meanings are phenomena existing in the world. There are no meaners construing meanings, and there is no perceptual system mediating between semiotic expressions and their extensions. Truth is a matter of correspondence, not (as it is in everyday discourse) a question of consensus among people. (Halliday and Matthiessen, 1999: 421)

There are two points worth noting here: On the one hand, Halliday and Matthiessen put the essentialist approach to meaning under the category of the objectivist approach since both adopt a correspondence view of truth or meaning. On the other hand, Halliday and Matthiessen criticize the mistaken view that there could be truth or meaning whatsoever without the existence of meaners (that is, human kind) or perceptual system (that is, human thought).

In contrast, the constructivist view argues that knowledge and reality do not have an objective or absolute value or, at the very least, we have no way of knowing this reality. Von Glasersfeld (1995), for example, holds the view that the knower interprets and constructs a reality based on his experiences and interactions with his environment. Rather than thinking in terms of *truth*, von Glasersfeld focuses instead on the notion of *viability*, such that concepts, models, theories, and so on are viable if they prove adequate in the contexts in which they were created.

Wilson's study seems to hint that objectivism or logical positivism whatsoever has always been the orthodox ideology in the mainstream western intellectual arena. However, since Kant, constructivist ideology has become the central notion of postmodernists. The questions that Thomas Kuhn poses to argue for the constructivist view on epistemology are highly representative:

> What is the world, I ask, if it does not include most of the sorts of things to which the actual language spoken at a given time refers? Was the earth really a planet in the world of pre-Copernican astronomers who spoke a language in which the features salient to the referent of the term 'planet' excluded its attachment to the earth? Does it obviously make better sense to speak of accommodating language than of accommodating the world to language? Or is the way of talking which creates that distinction itself illusory? Is what we refer to as 'the world' perhaps a product of a mutual accommodation between experience and language? (Kuhn, 1993 in Ortony, 1993: 541–542)

4.2.2   Piaget's contribution to constructivism

Formalization of the theory of constructivism is generally attributed to Piaget who proposed mechanisms by which knowledge is internalized by learners (Yan, 2000). Piaget (1978) suggested that through processes of accommodation and assimilation, individuals construct new knowledge from their experiences. Piaget, whose ideas are classified under the category of cognitive constructivism, was chiefly concerned with constructing a model simulating the child epistemological development. In addition to accommodation and assimilation, Piaget (1978) further attests that a child's cognitive structure increases in sophistication with development, moving from a few innate reflexes such as crying and sucking to highly complex mental activities. The Stages are classified into four: (1) Sensorimotor stage (birth–2 years old); (2) Preoperational stage (ages 2–7); (3) Concrete operations (ages 7–11); and (4) Formal operations (beginning at ages 11–15).

Besides psychology, Piaget's influence can be seen in a number of disciplines including philosophy, education, linguistics, artificial intelligence and pedagogy.

4.2.3   Lev Vygotsky and social constructivism

There is a great deal of overlap between cognitive constructivism and Vygotsky's social constructivist theory (Wertsch, 1997). However, according to Vygotsky, it is culture that gives the child the cognitive tools needed for development. The type and quality of those tools determines the pattern and rate of development, to a much greater extent than they do in Piaget's theory (Wertsch, 1997). Parents and teachers are conduits for the tools of the culture, including cultural history, social context, and language.

Although most of Vygotsky's publications did not appear in English until after 1960, there are a growing number of applications of social constructivism in the area of educational technology. He is of vital importance to us not only because of his basic notions concerning the influence of culture on language and learning and the importance of the social context for cognitive development are shared by systemic linguists, but also because some of the latest developments in systemic linguistics seem to show much isomorphism with Vygotsky's view.

In order to gain an understanding of Vygotsky's theories on cognitive development, one must understand two of the main principles of Vygotsky's work: the More Knowledgeable Other (MKO) and the Zone of Proximal Development (ZPD) (Vygotsky, 1978, 1986). The MKO is somewhat self-explanatory; referring to someone who has a better understanding or a higher ability level than the learner, with respect to a particular task, process, or concept. Although the implication is that the MKO is a teacher or an older adult, this is not always the case. Often, a child's peers or an adult may be the individuals with more knowledge or experience.

In fact, the MKO need not be a person at all. Some companies, to support employees in their learning process, are now using electronic performance support systems. Electronic tutors have also been used in educational settings to facilitate and guide students through the learning process. The key to MKOs is that they must have (or be programmed with) more knowledge about the topic being learned than the learner does.

The concept of the More Knowledgeable Other is related to the second important principle of Vygotsky's work, the Zone of Proximal Development (ZPD). Taken together, the MKO and the ZPD form the basis of the scaffolding component of the cognitive apprenticeship model of instruction. Vygotsky (1978) defines the ZPD as the distance between the 'actual developmental level as determined by independent problem solving and the level of potential development as determined through problem solving under adult guidance or in collaboration with more capable peers' (1978: 86). Vygotsky believed that when a student is at the ZPD for a particular task, providing the appropriate assistance (scaffolding) will give the student enough of a 'boost' to achieve the task. Once the student, with the benefit of scaffolding, masters the task, the scaffolding can then be removed and the student will then be able to complete the task again on his own.

In addition to the two terms mentioned above, we consider Vygotsky's concern with the developmental nature of human epistemology and fascination with the study of the so-called higher-ordered thinking in human beings to be of equal importance. In *Thought and Language* (also known as *Thinking and Speaking*), originally published in 1934, Vygotsky presents his belief that although the development of thought and that of language are similar processes, they are independent of one another and develop separately. Vygotsky reached his conclusions regarding thought and language development by observing and studying the behaviour of apes, specifically chimpanzees. Vygotsky considered the behaviour of children in the early stages of development to be similar to the behaviour of chimpanzees. Initially, children learn the names of objects because they are instructed by an authority figure to do so. Eventually, they develop an independent curiosity about objects and want to know what they are called. This curiosity leads to a significant increase in vocabulary. When children have developed the desire to learn language on their own and begin to experience success, the processes of thought and language acquisition become integrated.

As regards higher-ordered thinking in human beings, Vygotsky makes a distinction between primate and human child development by noting that children engage in egocentric speech to help solve a problem as well as using tools to complete tasks. This combination of using tools and speech to address problems is regarded as of primary importance by Vygotsky. He sees humans as distinct from animals because they engage in a dialectical, adaptive form of development, thus rejecting a behaviourist or Piagetian view of human intellectual development. Vygotsky sees intellectual development as both an internal and a social process that is complex and interwoven. When children are left alone, their speech moves from the social to the egocentric and becomes internalized; they look to their environment – which could include signs, tools, or peers – to help them solve problems.

Vygotsky also notes that human beings have the ability – in contrast to animals – to perceive 'real objects' – objects that have a sense and a meaning beyond shapes and colours – that they can understand and describe through external or internal speech in our environment. As children gain in their use of speech and visual perception, they begin to synthesize 'elements of past experience with the present', reconstructing their memory into a mediating influence between them and their environment.

Indeed, it is precisely these two aspects that define Vygotsky as a social constructivist and differentiate him from Piaget. On the one hand, the distinction between thought and language does not suggest sympathy with the traditional objectivist view on knowledge but instead allows room for the influence of social context. On the other hand, the recognition of the higher-ordered thinking in human children paves the way for his assumption that synthesizing ability (namely, the power of abstraction) has its origin in social processes. Thus, the key notes of Vygotsky contain three core themes: (1) a reliance on a genetic or developmental method, arguing that human epistemology demonstrates both ontogenetic and phylogenetic features; (2) the claim that higher mental processes have origin in social processes including language; and (3) the claim that mental processes can be understood only if we understand the tools and signs that mediate them (semiotic mediation).

4.2.4   The metaphor mania and constructivism

A direct impact of constructivism on the discipline of linguistics is perhaps the onset of metaphor mania. Beginning with Max Black (1962), linguists have approached metaphor from different perspectives depending on their respective theoretical stance. Indeed, views on metaphor have been proposed from a variety of disciplines, leading to an abundance of theories on metaphor. One thought provoking way of classifying twentieth-century theories on metaphor is that adopted by Ortony (1993), who notes the opposition between constructivism and non-constructivism.

The non-constructivist metaphor school includes the comparison/substitution theory and TG views. The former is largely proposed within the framework of stylistics or rhetoric. The nature of metaphor is seen as an implied comparison (thus the term comparison view). The TG view on metaphor was initiated by Chomsky's treatment of deviant expressions in an effort to show how deviant expressions can be related to the categories and rules of the grammar and thus to the grammar's regular output. Followers of Chomsky have come up with other solutions for excluding deviant sentences to avoid the output of nonsensical sentences (Katz, 1972; Levin, 1977).

The constructivist view of metaphor, on the other hand, is marked by the postulation of the relativity of meaning and interpretation, from which we can easily see traces of influence from the constructivist view on the nature of truth, knowledge and reality. Although Black (1962) is generally recognized as the pioneer of the twentieth-century metaphor mania, we have to start our introduction to the twentieth-century constructivist metaphor theory with I. A. Richards, one of the leading figures of New Criticism, who based his discussions of metaphor on the interactive property of meaning, arguing that meaning is not meant by the linguistic expressions but are universally relative, only appropriate to and valid in the cultural context in which they occur (Richards, 1936). Richards' interaction view was inherited by Black, whose approach to the study of metaphor prompted widespread interest in the study of metaphor among linguists and scholars of other disciplines. A symposium on metaphor and thought was held at Illinois University in 1977, at which Black and other renowned scholars like J. Searle, T. Kuhn, D. Rumelhart, S. Levin, R. Boyd, B. Fraser, G. Miller, T. Sticht and G. Lakoff participated. Their papers presented at the symposium were edited by A. Ortony and published in 1979 and later revised and republished as the second edition in 1993. Grammatical metaphor theory proposed by systemic linguists, as we shall see in the following discussions, fits very well into the constructivist school of metaphor theory.

4.3   Isomorphism between systemic linguistics and constructivism

Since 1990s Halliday has been more concerned with the theoretical or even philosophical considerations of linguistic issues. Though Halliday himself cautiously denies being a philosopher, his work over the past two decades expounded grammatical metaphor theory, established the evolutionary theory of meaning and emphasized the second order nature of the textual metafunction. It is precisely in these three perspectives that we can easily identify the isomorphism between systemic linguistics and constructivism and that systemic linguistics contributes much to the general edifice of constructivism.

4.3.1   Grammatical metaphor theory

Although the theory was put forward more systematically in 1985, the term grammatical metaphor appeared in some of Halliday's earlier papers. Halliday (1978) pointed out that the word *language* is a grammatical metaphor and in the strict sense we should say *languaging*, arguing to the effect that language exists in the form of human interaction. When Halliday put forward the grammatical metaphor theory, he classified metaphor into ideational metaphor and interpersonal metaphor. By ideational metaphor he meant the variation taking place in the terms of choices in the transitivity system of a language, including the selection of process type, of transitivity functions and of sequence of group/phrase classes. Interpersonal metaphors are further classified into metaphors of modality and those of mood. Another important notion is textual metaphor as proposed by Martin (1992), though it has not gained much recognition in the systemic linguistic circle.

In his later treatment of grammatical metaphor, Halliday attempts to redefine the term, elaborating on the mechanism of grammatical metaphor, exploring the discursive function of grammatical metaphor and above all emphasizing the metatheoretical function of language in reshaping human experience by means of grammatical metaphor (Halliday, 1995, 1996, 1999). In his re-definition, grammatical metaphor is said to differ from lexical metaphor such that 'the same signified with different signifier' versus 'the same signifier with different signified'. As far as the mechanism and function of grammatical metaphor are concerned, Halliday associates it with rank shifting, such that grammatical metaphor involves a downward rank shift, employing forms of lower rank to represent meanings of higher rank. In addition, Halliday puts forward the term syndrome of metaphor to refer to expressions that undergo various types of rank shift and 13 kinds of grammatical metaphor transformation are identified. The discursive function of grammatical metaphor is indicated not only by the fact that a grammatical metaphor, especially one that takes the form of nominalization, can perform the function of a token to which predication and modification can be ascribed, but also that it can help to facilitate information flow. What is of particular interest to us, however, is the metatheoretical function of language in reshaping human experience especially by way of grammatical metaphor, which can be seen from the following perspectives: (1) grammatical metaphor performs the function of taxonomization by means of mechanisms like distilling and filtering so that the terms produced will gradually come to be recognized as the purely objective scientific taxonomy; (2) the evolution of modern scientific discourse genre is marked by the tendency towards the abundant and systematic use of grammatical metaphor; (3) a dynamic approach to the nature of metaphor is adopted: 'Much of the history of every language is a history of demetaphorization: Of expressions which began as metaphors gradually losing their metaphorical character' (Halliday, 1985: 327); (4) the study of language development shows that grammatical metaphor only appears in adult language.

The above introduction shows that grammatical metaphor theory can very well be subsumed under the constructivist school. In adopting what Halliday terms the evolutionary approach to metaphor, systemic linguistics not only presupposes a constructivist view on knowledge, but also shows how language represents human knowledge in a constructive way in the metatheoretical sense, which is assumed to be involved in a move towards 'thingness', that is, a move towards the concrete, with nouns, typically as the names of participants as the terminal point. Furthermore, the analyses of the evolution of taxonomy indicate that so-called scientific terms are also the product of such a demetaphorizing process, so that the truth that scientists endeavour to investigate or ascertain are relative by necessity. Therefore, to a large extent, studies of grammatical metaphor by systemic linguists help to illustrate the validity of constructivism.

4.3.2 The evolutionary theory of meaning

The evolutionary theory of meaning was initially put forward in a paper by Halliday in 1992 and further elaborated on in 1999 by Halliday and Matthiessen to show how grammar (or lexicogrammar) construes human experience and constructs a world of events and objects. Three time frames are identified to account for historical evolution:

1. the evolution of human language, i.e. the phylogenetic time frame;
2. the development of the individual speaker, i.e. the ontogenetic time frame; and
3. the unfolding of the act of meaning itself or the instantial construction of meaning in the form of a text, i.e. the logogenetic time frame.

These three time frames represent the major processes of semohistory, by which meanings are continually created, transmitted, recreated, extended and changed. The relationship between these processes consists in that each provides the environment within which the next process in the sequence we listed above; and conversely, each process provides the material out of which the previous one is constructed. The following figure quoted from Halliday and Matthiessen (1999: 18) illustrates this relationship:

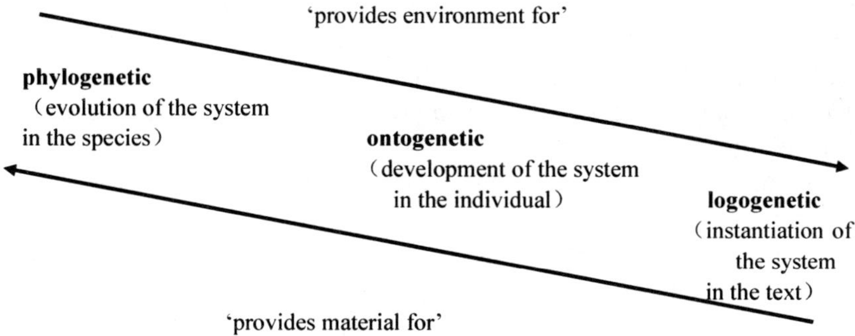

Figure 4.1: The Three Semohistories Related

In explaining the phylogenetic frame of evolution, Halliday calls attention to the distinction between mammalian experience and human experience. The mammalian experience is marked by the construers' (or the experiencers') dependence on the immediate situation of experience. Or to put it in simple words, construers at this stage can only react or reflect on the experience that they encounter on the spot, and the plane of expression employed to realize such experiences can only be said to be forms of protolanguage. Obviously, such a kind of experience or protolanguage is not unique to man but shared by many other mammals. Indeed, the forms of communication other than those among human beings identified by modern linguists all fall into this category, including bees' dancing, ants' language, courting cries of cats, etc. It is with the successful evolution of the lexicogrammatical stratum as the elastic interface between the expression plane and the content plane that man is finally freed from the immediate situation and can construe and reshape his experience, for the simple reason that the world that man experiences seemingly adopts a feature of the otherness with the now independent man being the observer, although such a notion of the world is illusive in nature according to the constructivists (Ortony, 1993). The whole process of phylogenetic evolution is slow and long, and it has taken perhaps millions of years. Many terms are borrowed from biology to account for the evolutionary process and we are not to go into details about these terms.

Since the phylogenetic frame of evolution is largely hypothetical, Halliday (1992) emphasizes the analogy between phylogenetic and ontogenetic frame. The kind of language in the early stage of child language development is also termed the protolanguage, which is marked by the absence of grammatical metaphor. Another interesting aspect of analogy between protolanguage of the phylogenetic process and child protolanguage consists in their both being dependent on the immediate situation of experience. For a child, protolanguage is marked by his employing expressions of all kinds to perform what Halliday terms microfunctions. The ontogenetic development of a child's language ability is associated with the child's developing into a social man, so that the seven microfunctions that protolanguage performs evolve into three metafunctions. It is important to emphasize that the evolution from microfunctions to metafunctions is not a mere reduction in number but a huge stride from childish reliance on the adult world to the recognition by society of an independent individual with unique ability to construe experience.

In terms of time length for the evolution of each process, the phylogenetic frame obviously has taken the greatest length of time, and the known human history takes up perhaps less than 0.1% of the total human history (Halliday and Matthiessen, 1999). For the ontogenetic process, it takes 2 to 3 years. The evolution of the logogenetic frame, on the other hand, takes the shortest time, but investigation into this frame can show clearly how a language speaker draws upon the lexicogrammatical system to construct a linguistic world of its own. Another important aspect of the logogenetic evolution largely neglected is that systemic linguists also emphasize the evolutionary process of certain discourse genres, scientific genre in particular. The kind of generic features shared by scientific publications has actually undergone several centuries' development, beginning from the age of Renaissance, starting from Isaac Newton in the English language. The evolution of the scientific genre indicates not only from a new perspective the difficulty that the phylogenetic evolution experiences but also points to the developing nature of language as a whole (Halliday, 1999).

All these three frames of evolution, furthermore, represent the semogenetic process of language use. In other words, language use is by nature a matter of meaning creation, rather than the expression of meaning or referring or denoting or describing whatsoever. The relationship between the signifier and the signified proposed by Saussure is replaced by systemic linguists with the familiar Chinese figure yin and yang (Halliday and Matthiessen, 1999), because the content plane and the expression plane (meaning and wording) emerge together and systemic linguists deny existence of any pre-existing meaning.

The relationship between meaning and wording is said to be one of realization (non-arbitrary) forming a potential that can be used to create meaning. Interestingly, the potential itself can also expand along certain aspects. First, we can create new wordings to construe newly found participants. Second, the potential can be expanded by increasing the semantic delicacy. Third, the expansion can take the form of deconstructing the two components and it is here that grammatical metaphor plays an important role in driving the expansion.

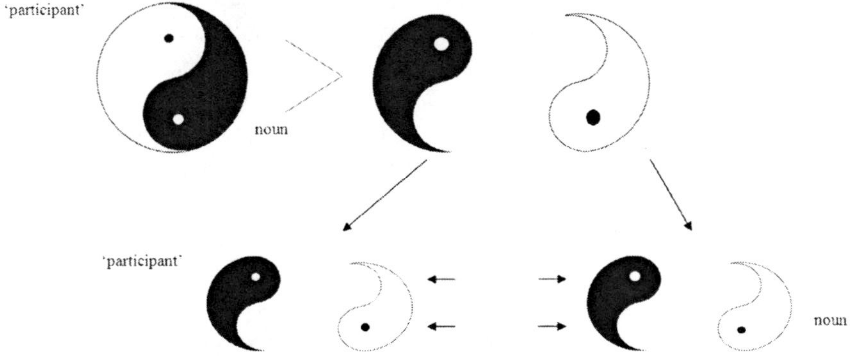

Figure 4.2: The Semogenic Process Arising from the Sign itself (Halliday and Matthiessen, 1999: 21)

From Figure 4.2, we can easily perceive the permutation between the signifier (noun) and the signified (participant), a view that challenges the traditional idea of the arbitrariness of the relationship between the signifier and the signified. Obviously, the relationship is no longer seen as arbitrary now that they can permute into each other. What is of special interest to us is that the mutation from the signified to the signified has been well illustrated by the so-called naming function of grammatical metaphor, defined as a kind of downward rank shift by Halliday (1995, 1996, 1999), but the mutation from the signifier to the signified as shown in the picture also suggests an upward rank shift. Thus, the picture hints at a change of stance on the nature of grammatical metaphor. Furthermore, in borrowing the yin and yang ideology from the Chinese culture, Halliday and Matthiessen (1999) clearly abandon the Saussurean coin analogy and suggest that the signifier and the signified are simply one thing that can permute in-between because they are both the product of the human consciousness, a view echoing the constructivist view that language is an instrument not for representing but constructing or constituting reality.

The preceding discussions suggest some further impact of constructivism (especially that of Vygotsky's theory) on systemic linguistics: (1) In a casual dialogue between Halliday and the author of this chapter, Halliday pointed out that the terms phylogenetic and ontogenetic aspects of evolution are borrowed from biology, but it is certainly not mere coincidence that both Halliday and Vygotsky employ the same terms to account for the developmental nature of language and cognition. The coincidence is largely due to the similar theoretical stance that both adopt, that is, a sociological stance. The ingenuity of both theorists consists in that they not only recognize the interactive and constructive nature of language communication or epistemology, but also attempt to account for the evolutionary processes of language and cognition. Both their studies show adequately that the constructive nature of truth is not only a plausible but also a necessary outcome of human evolution as a species. (2) Vygotsky's emphasis on the importance of social processes rather than on mental processes is echoed in Halliday and Matthiessen's argument for the importance of the reuse of wordings for creating new meaning potential. From another perspective, we can very well argue that discussions about the sociological aspect of communication actually illustrate the conventionalizational process of semiotic signs, which challenges the traditional view of the arbitrary nature of linguistic sign. (3) Vygotsky's study of the distinction between chimpanzees and the so-called higher-ordered thinking in human beings seems to be captured by the distinction between mammalian experience and human experience in systemic linguistics. (4) Systemic linguists are perhaps more radical constructivists because they not only illustrate by a diachronic approach that human language evolves from primitive forms of communication but also point out the evolutionary nature of child language development and textual metafunction, without acknowledging any pre-existing priority of language ability. To systemic linguists, a child is not born with the ability to learn or acquire a language, but to create some kind of protolanguage of his own, which gives way to the adult language in the process of language development. The constructive nature of language in construing experience is thus more explicitly explicated. (5) The logogenetic frame of evolution seems to be the creation by systemic linguists but this aspect is again closely related to the constructivist view on knowledge and truth. Vygotsky's recognition of man's unique ability to perceive the real objects is similar in essence to the logogenetic aspect of language evolution, because the so called ability to perceive real objects in Vygotsky's theory is actually a kind of ability of abstraction, a detachment from the immediate situation and the ability to perceive order out of chaos, which will eventually be realized in the form of a text. We shall come back to it in the following discussions of the second order nature of textual metafunction. (6) In arguing that the expansion of the expression plane and that of the content plane can both produce new pairs of expression and content, systemic linguists not only further reinforce their notion of the merging of form and meaning, but also suggest that linguistic reality thus constructed comes to adopt some mechanism of its own development, which is the unique production of mankind. Being chiefly linguists or grammarians in their own term, systemic linguists mainly focus on the study of the evolution of some discourse genres, but such a view is also imbued with philosophical implications. If the so-called objective world in the objectivist myth is largely illusive, linguistic considerations can shed new light on man's search for truth, though the truth is no longer absolute but relative in nature.

4.3.3 The second order nature of text metafunction

Matthiessen (1992) emphasizes the second order nature of text metafunction, which represents systemic linguists' direct commitment to the constructive stand. The basic assumption is that text does not correspond to the primary form of existence directly but to a result of construction and social interaction. It can be delineated in the following aspects:

1. A text is dynamic by nature. To systemic linguists, text itself is a social act, subject to the interaction between language speaker and the changing social context. In other words, text is a means of social interaction rather than a static product.

2. The constructivist denial of objective reality and absolute truth is acknowledged. Matthiessen (1992) borrows from physics the theory of field to represent the relationship between language and reality: Language is Field and Reality is Wave. The interaction between them is subject to distraction or reflection. Textual function is the enacting function because it helps construct a reality that is rational and coherent so as to impart ideology.

3. The mere focus on the study of cohesive devices, thematic progression, etc. as interpreted by scholars of other schools seems to be misleading (Butler, 1985; van Dijk, 2008). They dwell upon the trifling details without concern for the more important metatheoretical function of constructing social reality. Indeed, coherence and rationality are the features of semiotic reality constructed by language, while the actual world is chaotic and illogical. Thus too much emphasis on the study of the linguistic features of a text will blur our consciousness of the ideology imparted. Furthermore, there are also some aspects that are largely neglected, for example, the idea of textual wave proposed by Matthiessen (1992). What Matthiessen attempts to explore by his textual wave theory is largely the organic mechanism of textual development and thus is worthy of special attention.

4. Grammatical metaphor theory provides evidence for the view that text is constructed and thus secondary rather than innate and primary. The study of functions of grammatical metaphors in discourse genre indicates not only that the so-called objectiveness marking scientific texts is a mere result of abundant use of grammatical metaphor of different degrees but also that many scientific terms are the result of grammatical metaphorization and demetaphorization. In this sense, grammatical metaphor is both a key feature of scientific texts and promotes scientific development in its own way. In adopting an evolutionary approach to the linguistic features of discourse genres, systemic linguists often endeavour to unpack the information or ideology deeply rooted in these texts, we can thus argue that they not only fit well into the constructivist school but can be called deconstructivists.

4.4 Conclusions

The conclusions we attempt to draw include the following: (1) systemic linguistics is compatible with the constructivist view on language in that both schools hold that language is a product of human construction rather than anything innate; (2) the evolutionary theory of meaning proposed by Halliday (1992) explores the mystery of meaning construction and relativity of truth; (3) the grammatical metaphor theory provides a dynamic approach to the logogenetic frame of language evolution, and the second order nature of textual metafunction thus recognized is the systemic version of constructivism; (4) Halliday's evolutionary theory of meaning is isomorphic with Vygosky's theory that emphasizes the social constructive perspective of language Halliday and his followers have come to draw on constructivist theory to reinforce the sociological approach to language, a stand that characterizes the systemic school; (5) considering the recent development of systemic linguistics, we can well argue that systemic linguists not only draw on constructivism but contribute vigorously to it in the sense that they provide both philosophical and linguistic evidence for constructivist ideas; (6) by admitting that they adopt a constructivist perspective on meaning construction, systemic linguists adequately contribute to the linguistic circle with their unique research approach and practice, a kind of dynamic deconstructivist approach to issues linguistic or philosophical; (7) though Halliday and his followers claim that they are grammarians rather than philosophers, their notions on the relationship between language and world touch upon the nature of meaning, an issue fundamental to philosophy. We conclude therefore that the hegemony of science can and should be rejected so as to achieve a better understanding of truths of the universe, which are, to be sure, relative and constructive in nature.

References

Black, M. (1962) *Models and Metaphors*. Ithaca, NY: Cornell University Press.

Halliday, M. A. K. (1978) *Language as Social Semiotic: The Social Interpretation of Language and Meaning* . London: Edward Anold.

Halliday, M. A. K. (1985) *An Introduction to Functional Grammar*. London: Edward and Arnold.

Halliday, M.A.K. (1992) How do you mean? In M. Davies and L. Ravelli (eds) *Advances in Systemic Linguistics: Recent Theory and Practice*, 20–35. London and New York: Pinter Publishers.

Halliday, M. A. K. (1995) Language and the reshaping of human experience. In B. Dendrinos (ed.) *Proceedings of the Fourth International Symposium on Critical Discourse Analysis*. Athens: University of Athens Press.

Halliday, M. A. K. (1996) Things and relations: Regrammatizing experience as technical knowledge. In J. R. Martin and R. Veel (eds). *Reading Science: Critical and Functional Perspectives on Discourses of Science*. London: Edward Arnold.

Halliday, M. A. K. (1999) The grammatical construction of scientific knowledge: The framing of the English clause. In R. Rossini, G. Sandri and R. Scazzieri (eds) *Incommensurability and Translation*. Cheltenham: Elgar.

Halliday, M. A. K. and C. M. I. M. Matthiessen (1999) *Construing Experience through Meaning: A Languange-based Approach to Cognition.* London and New York: Continuum.

Katz, J. J. (1972) *Semantic Theory.* New York: Harper & Row.

Levin, S. R. (1977) *The Semantics of Metaphor.* Baltimore, MD: Johns Hopkins University Press.

Martin, J. R. (1992) *English Text.* Philadelphia, PA: John Benjamins Publishing Company.

Matthiessen, C. (1992) Interpreting the textual metafunction. In M. Davies and L. Ravelli (eds) *Advances in Systemic Linguistics: Recent Theory and Practice,* 37–81. London and New York: Pinter Publishers.

Ortony, A. (ed.) (1993) *Metaphor and Thought* (2nd edition). Cambridge: Cambridge University Press.

Piaget, J. (1978) *Success and Understanding.* Cambridge, MA: Harvard University Press.

Richards, I. A. (1936) *The Philosophy of Rhetoric.* Oxford: Oxford University Press.

von Glasersfeld, E. (1995) *Radical Constructivism: A Way of Knowing and Learning.* London and Washington, DC: The Falmer Press.

Vygotsky, L. S. (1978) *Mind in society: The Development of Higher Mental Processes.* Cambridge, MA: Harvard University Press.

Vygotsky, L. S. (1986) *Thought and Language (Newly revised and edited by Alex Kozulin).* Cambridge, MA: The MIT Press.

Wertsch, J. V. (1997) *Vygotsky and the Formation of the Mind.* Cambridge, MA: Harvard University Press.

Wilson, E. O. (1998) *Consilience: The Unity of Knowledge.* New York: Alfred Knopf.

Yan, Shiqing (2000) *Metaphor, Metaphorization and Demetaphorization.* Suzhou: Suzhou University Press.

5 The system network for generating expressions of Chinese aspect

YANG Guowen*

5.1 Introduction

What will be presented in this chapter is part of our work on theoretical descriptions and the computational implementation of the semantics of Chinese aspect. The system network of Chinese aspect is based on the theory of Systemic Functional Linguistics (SFL) (Halliday, 1976, 2004/2008) and implemented with the multilingual generator KPML (Komet Penman Multilingual) – a system for developing and maintaining multilingual systemic functional descriptions, and for using the resources for text generation (Bateman, 1997a, 1997b). It is believed that the computational implementation of theoretical descriptions may benefit studies of language comparison, language teaching, and grammar verification.

According to the theory of SFL, language is a system of choice of meaning, and the three kinds of metafunction of language, i.e. the ideational, the interpersonal, and the textual, along with the lexicon, can be represented by hierarchical system networks (Halliday, 2004/2008). Grammatical similarities and distinctions of different languages can be shown in system networks constructed from the paradigmatic organization of meaning alternatives and syntagmatic ordering of categorical functions. Studies have shown that most of the ideational descriptions of English, including the classification and the frameworks of roles of processes, are applicable to Chinese (Halliday and Matthiessen, 1999/2008: 303–304; Yang, 2001b, 2002, 2004); however, the descriptions relevant to inflectional changes of English may need to be adapted for Chinese grammar due to the fact that Chinese lacks inflectional changes: aspect is one such area of this kind.

Aspect is different from tense; they are two distinct conceptual categories. Tense relates situation time to a deictic centre. Aspect involves differ-

* Yang Guowen is Associate Professor at the Institute of Linguistics of Chinese Academy of Social Sciences.

ent ways of viewing the states of a situation with respect to the situation's internal temporal constituency (Comrie, 1976; Yang, 2007). Aspect is determined by situation type and viewpoints which construct specific temporal relations between the view point and the internal temporal constituency of the situation, and which reflect what the speaker focuses on when s/he views situation. This distinction can be well illustrated by Comrie's example as shown below:

> The difference between *John was singing* and *John is singing*
> in English is one of tense, namely a location before the present
> moment versus a location including the present moment; while
> the difference between *John was singing* and *John sang* is one of
> aspect. (Comrie, 1985: 6)

In traditional studies of western languages, tense and aspect are rarely studied separately. As Comrie (1985: 6–7) has pointed out, 'the reader should, however, beware that in many linguistic works, especially traditional grammars, the term tense is rather misleadingly used to cover both tense and aspect'.

The ways of realizing aspect in English and Chinese are different. In English, aspect expressions are regularly constructed from the finite element and the verb, and are recursively involved in tense with the inflectional changes of the finite and the verb. In Chinese, aspect is realized by auxiliary morphemes and some temporal adverbs; and the constructions of complex aspect are both grammatically and semantically restricted.

From a morphological point of view, Chinese does not have compulsory grammatical means for expressing tense like that in English (e.g. *is making* and *was making, have made* and *had made*). Nevertheless, this does not mean that Chinese does not have its own way to express time and temporal relations (e.g. Gong, 1995; Li, 1998; Peng, 2011). In Chinese the sense of time is realized by temporal nouns, adverbs, phrases, clauses, and sometimes by contextual inferences from joint influences of situation and aspect, as Comrie (1985) states, in conjunction with knowledge of the world. If an English boy says to his mother '*I am having my breakfast when she came this morning*', he will be corrected because he has used 'am' rather than 'was' for the past tense; but it is believed that in this case the mother could still understand what the boy meant. In contrast to English, what the boy said would be valid in Chinese grammar. The Chinese counterpart of the above sentence with the focalized progressive aspect 正在+V (Zhèngzài+V) (cf. Yang, 2007, 2010) can be naturally uttered for the situation of any time: past, present, and future, e.g. 早上她来时我正在吃早饭 (zǎoshàng tā lái shí wǒ zhèngzài chī zǎofàn, *I was having my breakfast when she came this morn-*

ing), 我现在正在吃早饭 (wǒ xiànzài zhèngzài chī zǎofàn, *I am having my breakfast now*), 明天早上她来时我 (可能) 正在吃早饭 (míngtiān zǎoshàng tā lái shí wǒ (kěnéng) zhèngzài chī zǎofàn, *I will (probably) be having my breakfast when she comes tomorrow morning*). Because of the distinctions, it is necessary for us to design a system network for Chinese aspect in the grammar network.

Chinese is rich in aspect expressions, including both *simple aspect* and *complex aspect*. A simple aspect is realized by one aspect marker; a complex aspect is realized by more than one aspect marker. Working within the theoretical framework of SFL, we organized simple expressions and 26 complex expressions of aspect into a single hierarchical grammar network. In the present study some grammatical expressions like verb reduplication and resultative verb complements are not taken as aspect forms because both of the expressions construct only two kinds of situations in lexical and grammatical ways and neither of them can express specific aspectual meanings alone (Yang, 2007, 2011). With the network we have constructed, 40 different aspect forms have all been correctly generated in sentences. This chapter will focus on elaborating the principles applied to constructing the system network to ensure well produced expressions of complex aspect. The work will be described in the following respects: the classification of Chinese aspect, the development of the primary systems, the selection order principle, and the reasons for rejecting the parallel derivation in the network drawing. A sample network of durative aspect will also be presented.

5.2   The forms of Chinese aspect

5.2.1   The forms of simple aspect

Like other linguistic categories, aspect has both a semantic level and a surface realization. To some extent, aspect may have cross-linguistic features at the semantic level, including the definitions of aspect itself, and of the basic types of aspect such as the perfective and the imperfective (Comrie, 1976). However, the ways of realizing aspect are language specific. Compared with Chinese, the basic simple aspect forms of English are structurally more consistent. Generally speaking, there are three basic forms of aspect in English, i.e. 'have+V-ed participle' (perfect), 'be+V-ing' (progressive), and 'be going to' (imminent) (Klein, 1994). In contrast, the scope of simple aspect in Chinese is not so clear and definite as that of English. In the field of Chinese aspect research it is difficult to find a consistent classification of aspect expressions (e.g. Lü, 1953; Chao, 1968; Li and Thompson, 1981; Wang, 1985; Smith, 1997; Gong, 1995; Dai, 1997).

Based on a rather thorough investigation into the state of affairs with Chinese aspect study, we think that taking only fully grammaticalized auxiliary morphemes as aspect expressions is insufficient to cover all the aspectual phenomena in Chinese due to the fact that Chinese lacks morphological changes. Hence, the method of taking both auxiliary morphemes and temporal adverbs as aspect markers has been adopted in the present research. Given the fact that the progressive aspect marker 在 (zài) is also a temporal adverb, this method has already been widely used in previous studies (e.g. Fan, 1984; Huang and Davis, 1989; Gong, 1995; Klein *et al.*, 2000; and many others). According to this criterion, 14 simple aspect forms have been included in the present system. The 14 expressions of simple aspect have been classified into three types: the perfective, the imperfective, and the imminent.

Perfective aspect includes the realized aspect V+了 (V+le) / 已经 +V+(了) (yǐjing+V+(le)), the experiential aspect V+过 (V+guo) / 曾经 +V+(过) (céngjīng+V+(guo)), and the recent past aspect V+(NP)+来着 (V+(NP)+láizhe), all of which show the property of viewing the states of a situation from outside of the situation structure. In the present research the reference time is defined as the time from which the state of a situation with respect to the situation's internal temporal constituency is contextually examined. The reference time of perfective aspect is either to the same as or subsequent to the termination time of the situation.

Imperfective aspect includes the unmarked durative aspect V+着 (V+zhe), the durative progressive aspect 在+V (zài+V), the long durative aspect 一直+V (yīzhí+V), the focalized progressive aspect 正在+V (zhèngzài+V) / 正+(PP)+V (zhèng+(PP)+V) ('PP' is the abbreviation of 'Prepositional Phrase'), the inceptive aspect V+起+(N)+来 (V+qi+(N)+lai), and the continual aspect V+下去 (V+xiaqu), all of which show the property of viewing the states of a situation from inside of the situation structure. The reference time of imperfective aspect is located in between the initial time and the termination time of the situation.

Imminent aspect includes 即将(jíjiāng)/将要 (jiāngyào)/就要 (jiùyào)/快要 (kuàiyào)/快 (kuài)/要 (yào)+V, which, similar to perfective aspect, shows the property of viewing the states of a situation from outside of the situation structure; however, the reference time of imminent aspect is shortly before the initial time of the situation, emphasizing the imminent occurrence and change of state of the situation. The expressions 即将 (jíjiāng)/将要 (jiāngyào) +V are the markers of imminent aspect in the written style, while the expressions 就要 (jiùyào)/快要 (kuàiyào)/快 (kuài)/要 (yào)+V occur in the spoken style.

As a revision of Yang (2001a) and Yang and Bateman (2002), the expression 将+V (jiāng+V) is not considered an aspect marker in the present research for the following reasons: (a) the expression将+V (jiāng+V) does not have imminent meaning, and does not focus on the change of state of the situation either; (b) as a modal verb, it is common to see that 将 (jiāng) shows either the intention of the participant or the prediction of the speaker rather than the objective aspect meaning; (c) in a specific context, the expression 将+V (jiāng+V) may have the similar function with 'will/shall' in English, providing a clue as to the future situation. Further discussion on excluding the expression 将+V (jiāng+V) from the aspect system is presented in Yang (2012).

The abbreviations of the names of the 14 simple expressions of aspect are as follows (in alphabetical order):

CTN: continual aspect V+下去 (V+xiaqu)
DPG: durative progressive aspect 在+V (zài+V)
ICP: inceptive aspect V+起+(N)+来 (V+qi+(N)+lai)
LDR: long durative aspect 一直+V (yīzhí+V)
MEX: marked experiential aspect 曾经+V+ (过) (céngjīng+V+(guo))
MFPG: marked focalized progressive aspect 正+(PP)+V (zhèng+(PP)+V)
PEF: perfect aspect 已经+V+(了) (yǐjing+V+(le))
REP: recent past aspect V+(NP)+来着 (V+(NP)+láizhe)
SIM: spoken imminent aspect 就要/快要/快/要+V (jiùyào/ kuàiyào/kuài/yào+V)
UDR: unmarked durative aspect V+着 (V+zhe)
UEX: unmarked experiential aspect V+过 (V+guo)
UFPG: unmarked focalized progressive aspect 正在+V (zhèngzài+V)
URE: unmarked realized aspect V+了 (V+le)
WIM: written imminent aspect 即将/将要+V (jíjiāng/ jiāngyào+V)

Given the classification of aspect above, we can further explain the fact that Chinese aspect expressions are more finely classified compared with those of English. A single aspect form of English, e.g. 'have+V-ed participle' (perfect), covers several different aspectual meanings. The form *have been* can express the meaning of result perfect (Comrie, 1976), as in *He has been here* (*already*), and the meaning of experiential perfect (Comrie, 1976: 56–60), as in *He has been here before*. However, in Chinese, the meaning of 'result perfect' and the meaning of 'experiential perfect' can respectively be expressed with the realized aspect V+了 (V+le) / 已经+V+(了) (yǐjing+V+(le)) as in example (1) and the experiential aspect V+过 (V+guo) / 曾经+V+(过) (céngjīng+V+(guo)) as in example (2).

(1) 他   （已经）   来   了。
     tā   yǐjing   lái   le
     he   PEF   come   PEF / URE
     (He has been here (already)).)

(2) 他   （以前）   来   过。
     tā   yǐqián   lái   guo
     he   before   come   UEX
     (He has been here before.)

The present and active participle be+V-ing in English can also be taken as an example to illustrate this point. The form of be+V-ing in English can indicate both stative states and the progression of action, as in the sentences *A picture is hanging on the wall* and *He is hanging a picture*. The term 'stative state' here refers to a durative unchanging situation associated with the activity meaning of an activity verb (Li and Thompson, 1981). Different from English, stative states and the progression of actions can be expressed with distinct aspect forms in Chinese. Stative states can be expressed with the unmarked durative aspect V+着 (V+zhe) as in example (3); while the progression of actions can be expressed with either the focalized progressive aspect 正在+V (zhèngzài+V) / 正+(PP)+V (zhèng+(PP)+V) as in example (4a) and (4b), or the durative progressive aspect 在+V (zài+V) as in example (4c).

(3)   墙   上   挂   着   一   幅   画。
      qiáng shàng   guà   zhe   yī   fú   huà
      wall on   hang UDR   one   CL   picture
      (A picture is hanging on the wall.)

(4) (a) 他   正在   挂   一   幅   画。
        tā   zhèngzài guà   yī   fú   huà
        he   UFPG   hang one   CL   picture
        (He is hanging a picture.)

    (b) 他   正   往   墙   上   挂
        tā   zhèng   wǎng   qiáng   shàng   guà
        he   MFPG   towards wall   on   hang

        一   幅   画。
        yī   fú   huà
        one   CL   picture
        (He is hanging a picture on the wall.)

    (c) 他   在   挂   一   幅   画。
        tā   zài   guà   yī   fú   huà
        he   DPG   hang one   CL   picture
        (He is hanging a picture.)

In the present research, a temporal adverb, such as 已经 (yǐjing), 在 (zài), and 即将 (jíjiāng), is taken as an aspect marker if it can uniquely determine a viewpoint in context (i.e., the reference time), which has specific temporal relations with the internal temporal constituency of the situation.

5.2.2 The forms of complex aspect

Complex aspect shows a combined aspectual meaning composed of the meanings of more than one expression of aspect. Ways for constructing complex aspect are language specific. One of the most delicately elaborated accounts is the English tense (tense + aspect) presented by Halliday (Halliday, 1976, 2004/2008). Halliday presents all of the possible grammatical expressions of tense and elaborates the regular ways in which the corresponding complex verbal groups are constructed. It is clear that in English tense is mixed with aspect and is symbolized by morphological changes of the finite element and verb (cf. Comrie, 1985) as seen in the pairs of *is taking* and *was taking*, *have taken* and *had taken*, *take* and *took*. Because the focus of the present research is on aspect, we discuss only the aspect related descriptions involved in Halliday's tense model. Halliday (1976) presents several English verbal variants according to their morphological changes. As he writes (Halliday, 1976: 139):

> English verbs display a 'scatter' of from three to five variants – or, in the case of the verb *be*, eight. From the point of view of their function in the verbal group, these variants need to be grouped into four distinct forms (one of which is then subdivided) which can be specified as follows, where x stands for any verb:

> (a) x^0 – base form ('zero' form, 'infinitive', 'dictionary form')
> (b) x^f – finite form, subdivided into:
> x^s ('present tense')
> x^d ('past tense')
> (c) x^n – nonfinite, present/active form ('present or active participle')
> (d) x^n – nonfinite, past/present form ('past or passive participle')

Another two forms added by Halliday to this group are:

> (e) $will^f$ – will/shall/would/should; or any modal
> (f) $will^g$ – going to/about to

We retain $will^g$ and exclude $will^f$ from our discussion because $will^f$ is related to modality and tense, whereas $will^g$ has, in certain contexts, imminent meaning. The aspect related simple forms can be combined to construct aspect complexes in a regular way. Halliday (1976: 154) presents a list of tense combinations in English; we now ignore the forms of tense changes, and present only the forms of aspect combinations in the present tense as shown in Figure 5.1, where x^f, $x^{ŋ}$, x^n, and will^{ŋ} are referred to as f, ŋ, n, and ŋ-o respectively.

Expressions of Complex Aspects	Types of Individual Aspects
1 takes/does take	f
2 has taken	f n
3 is taking	f ŋ
4 is going to take	f ŋ-o
5 is going to have taken	f ŋ-o n
6 has been taking	f n ŋ
7 is going to be taking	f ŋ-o ŋ
8 has been going to take	f n ŋ-o
9 has been going to have taken	f n ŋ-o n
10 is going to have been taking	f ŋ-o n ŋ
11 has been going to be taking	f n ŋ-o ŋ
12 has been going to have been taking	f n ŋ-o n ŋ

Figure 5.1: The list of aspect combinations of English

We can consider the forms of 'f n', 'f ŋ', and 'f ŋ-o' in Figure 5.1 to refer to three simple expressions of aspect 'have+V-ed participle' (perfect), 'be+V-ing', and 'be going to' respectively. Hence, expressions 1, 2, 3, and 4 in Figure 5.1 illustrates simple aspect; 5, 6, 7, and 8 are examples of complex aspect with two simple expressions of aspect; and 9, 10, and 11 are complex expressions of aspect with three simple expressions of aspect; the last expression 12 is a complex expression with four simple expressions of aspect. All the expressions in the list are grammatically acceptable.

Unlike complex aspect in English, the construction of complex aspect in Chinese shows far fewer regularities; and it is semantically restricted by the functions and temporal structures involved. Some simple expressions of aspect, e.g. the unmarked durative aspect (UDR) V+着 (V+zhe), show a higher combination potential compared with other types of aspect. Focalized progressive aspect 正+(PP)+V (zhèng+(PP)+V) / 正在 +V (zhèngzài+V), however, shows a lower combination potential. From a semantic point of view, the combinations of aspect of similar types result in an emphatic effect; the combinations of aspect of different types result in a complementary effect. Based on the analysis of our data, we formulate the following two conditions of aspect combination, abbreviated as CBCs:

CBC (1) Shared and compatible semantic features of individual expression of aspect will be inherited, while contradictions of semantic features are not allowed.

CBC (2) Complex expression of aspect has a proper temporal structure with specific range or location(s) for the reference time(s).

The CBC (1) means that the expressions of individual aspect involved should share certain semantic features. In other words, the two expressions of aspect have some overlapping properties. The features shared mostly are *dynamic* versus *stative*, and *durative* versus *punctual*. The shared features of an individual expression of aspect will be inherited by the complex expression of aspect. Meanwhile, there might be some features which are not shared, but compatible with another expression of aspect; it means that the features associated with one can be accepted by another so long as it does not have any specific restrictions in the corresponding respect. These features will also be inherited by the constructed complex aspect. This usually happens to the features *far precede* and *shortly precede* which indicate qualitative distance between time points.

The features associated with the two expressions of individual aspect should not, moreover, cause semantic contradictions. For instance, the ICP aspect V+起+(N)+来 (V+qi+(N)+lai) requires that the situation referred to shows a change of state; therefore, it cannot be used together with the UDR aspect V+着 (V+zhe) which requires just the opposite, i.e. the situation referred to does not show a change of state. Semantic contradictions also exist between the LDR aspect 一直+V (yīzhí+V) and the focalized progressive aspect 正+(PP)+V (zhèng+(PP)+V) /正在+V (zhèngzài+V). The LDR aspect requires that the time interval over which the situation holds is relatively long. In contrast, the focalized progressive aspect require that the time interval over which the situation holds is relatively short. Hence, these both kinds of aspect do not combine.

The CBC (2) also plays a significant role in constructing complex aspect. It says that the complex aspect constructed should have a proper temporal structure built by combining the temporal structures of the individual expression of aspect. Before two expressions of simple aspect combine, each of them has its own reference time. If the reference times of the two compatible expressions of aspect are located differently, the newly constructed complex aspect should have a dominant reference time which is consistent with the reference time of either one. The reference time of another participating aspect will be taken as nondominant reference time showing a complementary aspectual function of the combined aspect. The dominant reference time has more potential to be taken as the viewpoint of the combined aspect in context than the nondominant reference time (Yang, 2007, 2009).

In order to produce the correct forms of complex aspect, a strategically designed system network is required. We will elaborate this in detail in the next section.

5.3   The design of the system network

According to the theory of SFL, language has three strata: semantics, lexicogrammar, and phonology. Semantics is the resource for meaning corresponding to three kinds of metafunction. Lexicogrammar is the resource for wording the meaning into linguistic structures by choices of features in the grammatical network. Semantics and lexicogrammar together build the component of content. Phonology is the resource for sounding by phonetics and intonation (Matthiessen and Bateman, 1991; Halliday, 2004/2008). Hence, drawing system networks is one of the most important tasks for language generation.

System is a fundamental concept in systemic linguistics. Halliday (1976: 3–4) defines *system* in the following words:

> A system is a set of options with an entry condition: that is to say, a set of things of which one must be chosen, together with a statement of conditions under which the choice is available. ... The system network specifies what are the possible combinations of choices that could be made; each permitted path through the network is thus the description of a class of linguistic items. Thus the description of a linguistic item is the set of features selected in that item from the total available. (Halliday, 1976: 3–4)

Hence, '[a]ny set of alternatives, together with its condition of entry, constitutes a system in this technical sense' (Halliday, 2004/2008: 22). The nodes in a system network represent grammatical features, i.e. meaning alternatives. A feature can be the output of a system and, at the same time, the input of another system. According to the theory of SFL, the grammar of any language can be represented by a large system network, i.e. an arrangement of options in paradigmatic and hierarchical relationships (Halliday, 1976, 2004/2008). A set of features selected can be used to compose entry conditions for a specific system. A system network is composed of grammar and realization rules, including the lexicon of the resource. The process of language generation is then realized by traversing system networks step by step, i.e. following the choices of grammatical features made during the traversal. Different generation results can be achieved by different combinations of feature selections. Realization rules attached to the features in the network serve to add new elements to the generated structure, arrange the order of constituents, select items from the lexicon, and so on (Halliday, 1976, 2004/2008; Fawcett, 1987; Matthiessen and Bateman, 1991; Bateman, 1997a).

5.3.1 The system development from the primary aspect

In the present research, a system containing only simple expressions of aspect is called a *primary system*; simple expression of aspect is also called *primary aspect*. Two simple expressions of aspect can combine to construct a *secondary aspect*. A secondary aspect plus a simple aspect can construct a *tertiary aspect*. None of quaternary aspect forms, i.e. the form constructed from four simple expressions of aspect, was found in our data. A primary system can be developed further when the simple expressions of aspect of the system show secondary aspect; similarly, a system of secondary aspect can be further developed when its forms have tertiary aspect forms. Figures 5.2 and 5.3 show examples of secondary aspect and tertiary aspect respectively (the realization rules are left out), which are developed from the unmarked durative (UDR) aspect V+着 (V+zhe) in the network.

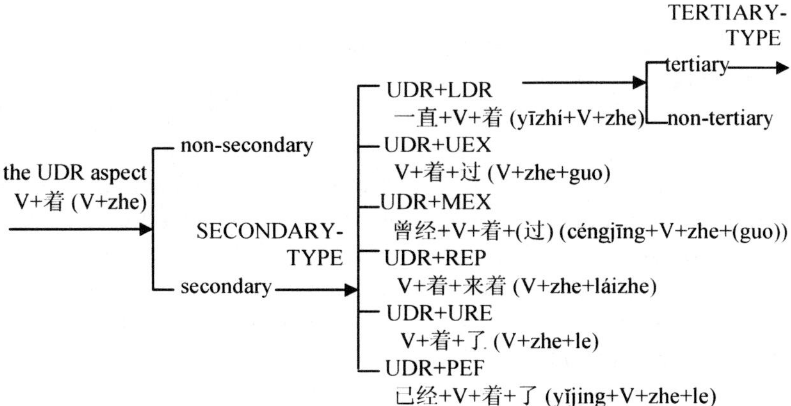

Figure 5.2: Expressions of secondary aspect of the UDR aspect V+着 (V+zhe)

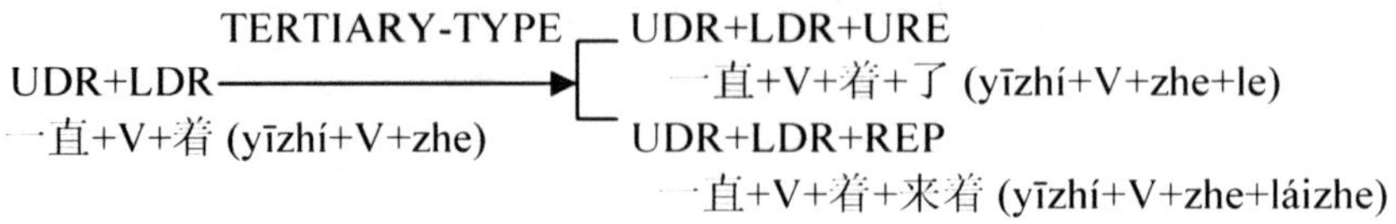

TERTIARY-TYPE ⌐ UDR+LDR+URE

UDR+LDR ————————————▶ [一直+V+着+了 (yīzhí+V+zhe+le)

一直+V+着 (yīzhí+V+zhe)   UDR+LDR+REP

一直+V+着+来着 (yīzhí+V+zhe+láizhe)

Figure 5.3: Expressions of tertiary aspect of the UDR+LDR aspect 一直+V+着 (yīzhí+V+zhe)

As shown in Figure 5.2, the UDR aspect V+着 (V+zhe) has the broad potential to combine with other simple expressions of aspect to construct secondary aspect. Among the expressions of secondary aspect constructed, the UDR+LDR aspect 一直+V+着 (yīzhí+V+zhe) can combine with the REP aspect V+(NP)+来着 (V+(NP)+láizhe) and the URE aspect V+了 (V+le) to further construct the UDR+LDR+URE aspect 一直+V+着+来着 (yīzhí+V+zhe+láizhe) and the UDR+LDR+URE aspect 一直+V+着+了 (yīzhí+V+zhe+le) as shown in Figure 5.3.

In the process of producing the complex aspect, the order of aspect selection, i.e. the decision as to which simple aspect is selected (generated) first, also influences the constructed result. In the next section, we will present a selection order principle applied to the development of the grammatical network, and explain the reason why we reject the parallel way of deriving secondary aspect in the system network drawing.

5.3.2 The principles of developing the aspect network

There are formally several ways in which the selection of the complex aspect forms might be captured in a system network. Suppose that we want to construct a secondary aspect composed of the LDR aspect 一直+V (yīzhí+V) and the UDR aspect V+着 (V+zhe), both of which have imperfective properties, should we attach the secondary aspect to the LDR aspect or to the UDR aspect; or to both? We can consider the motivations for one choice rather than another as follows. There are theoretically four options concerning which simple aspect should be taken as the basic aspect selected first in system traversal and to which the complex aspect should be attached. The four options are shown in Figure 5.4.

We analyse the four networks in Figure 5.4 as follows. Attaching the secondary aspect either to both of the expressions of simple aspect (graph (c) of Figure 5.4) or to the LDR aspect 一直+V (yīzhí+V) (graph (b) of Figure 5.4) is not safe. By being 'safe', I mean that the generated aspect form can be guaranteed to be correct. It follows that the extended system can be connected to just one simple aspect. Then which simple aspect should be selected to take this role?

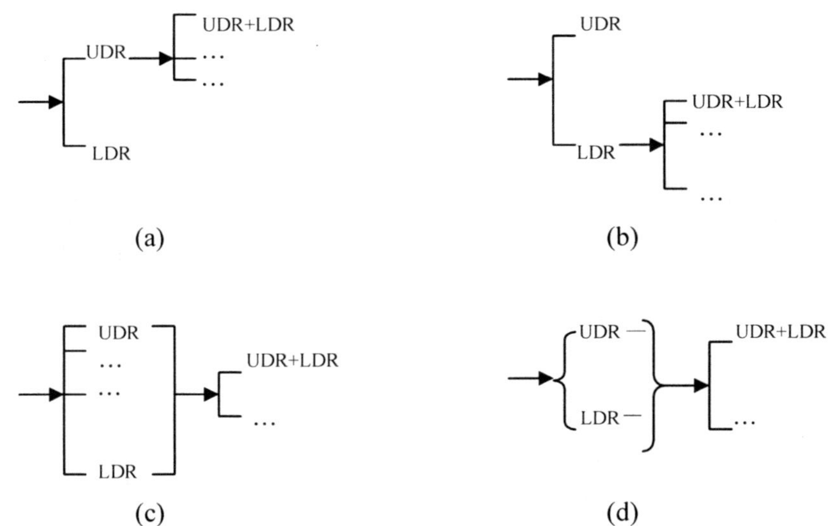

Figure 5.4: Four possible alternatives to derive the UDR+LDR aspect

In our present case, compared with the LDR aspect一直+V (yīzhí+V), which serves to indicate that the situation exists continuously over a relatively long time period (Lü *et al.*, 1999), the UDR aspect V+着 (V+zhe) has more restricted requirements in its usage. It serves to indicate an either dynamic or stative state holding over an open time period, but cannot be used for intensive relational processes associated with relational verbs such as, 是 (shì, be) and 等于 (děngyú, equal) (cf. Meng *et al.*, 1999), and so, the secondary aspect constructed from these two aspect expressions cannot be used for processes of intensive relational type either, even though the LDR aspect一直+V (yīzhí+V) can. To guarantee that the process expressed in the UDR+LDR aspect 一直+V+着 (yīzhí+V+zhe) is not of an intensive relational type, we can base the secondary system on the UDR aspect V+ 着 (V+zhe) (graph (a) in Figure 5.4). In other words, the requirements of the UDR aspect V+着 (V+zhe) should be met first in generation. Reversing the dependency in the network would not guarantee the correctness of the constructed secondary aspect. For example, suppose that an intensive relational process 是 (shì, be) is expressed in the LDR aspect in the form 一直+是 (yīzhí+shì). Then, if the secondary aspect UDR+LDR 一直+V+ 着 (yīzhí+V+zhe) is attached to the LDR aspect (graph (b) in Figure 5.4), the constructed complex aspect will be 一直+是+着 (yīzhí+shì+zhe) — but this is an unacceptable expression because it involves the relational verb是 (shì), which inappropriately takes the UDR aspect V+着 (V+zhe). This is the reason why the secondary aspect UDR+LDR 一直+V+着 (yīzhí+V+zhe) is attached to the UDR aspect V+着 (V+zhe) as shown in Figure 5.2, but not to the LDR aspect 一直+V (yīzhí+V).

Thus, because the simple aspect forms differ in terms of how restricted they are in their usage with particular situation types or process types, the criterion for choosing the first selected aspect that we adopt is based on the degree of both semantic and grammatical restriction shown by the expressions of aspect in their usages. The aspect which is more semantically and grammatically restricted in usage is taken as the basic aspect in constructing a secondary aspect. The less restricted aspect is made dependent on the first selected aspect and the secondary aspect is attached to the first selected aspect. We call this the Selection Order Principle (SOP); which is determined by the applicability conditions of aspect.

The network of (d) in Figure 5.4 is a parallel way of deriving the secondary aspect: it is constructed with conjunctions over the grammatical features. In this case, both the UDR aspect V+着 (V+zhe) and the LDR aspect一直+ V (yīzhí+V) are theoretically selected at the same time to construct the secondary aspect. This method is rejected by the present study for the following reason. The parallel entries fail to distinguish different semantic functions of simple aspect. It is true that the semantic functions of some simple expressions of aspect overlap with each other, but when used in context, speakers always have their aspectual focus on the situations referred to, and the properties of focus associated with different expressions of aspect are not the same. Different expressions of aspect, no matter how similar their functions are, have distinctions, although the distinctions are sometimes subtle. One of the goals of the present research is to discover these distinctions and their corresponding surface realizations. In the present account, each individual expression of aspect in the Chinese aspect system has its own applicability conditions and selecting more than one simple aspect at the same time is not possible. Based on this analysis, the parallel derivation of aspect in the system networks is rejected in the present research; instead, the expressions of secondary aspect are all attached to one simple aspect according to the SOP defined above.

A tertiary aspect of the system is similarly developed from the aspect, which is most semantically and grammatically restricted among the three expressions of simple aspect; in other words, the first selected aspect is the one that is most restricted in usage. The selection order of the other two is basically also determined by the restriction degrees in their usage.

One point needs to be clarified here. According to the theory of delicacy of systemic linguistics, less delicate decision points generally correspond to less finely specified semantics and dominate more delicate decision points in system networks (Halliday, 1976, 2004/2008). The way of designing the grammar network in the present research is not contradictory to this principle. In our system, 40 aspect expressions are hierarchically organized: from simple aspect to secondary aspect, and to tertiary aspect. From the semantic point of view, the system is developed in the direction of more finely specified aspect choices. In Mandarin Chinese, the frequency of appearance of complex aspect is much lower than that of simple aspect. In the corpus of 415,000 Chinese characters (Yang, 1999, 2001a), examples of complex aspect appeared only 134 times. This is because the construction of complex aspect, as elaborated already in the above text, is semantically restricted, so their usage is limited. The application of the SOP in the present research does not exert any negative impact on the theory of delicacy because the SOP acts on the parallel, rather than consecutive, features of the network. In other words, the aspect selections made according to the SOP are at the same level; and compared with simple aspect, the semantics of combined aspect can only be more finely specified.

5.4   A sample network of Chinese aspect

The Chinese aspect system of the present research includes 14 expressions of primary simple aspect, 21 secondary, and five tertiary. All of the expressions of aspect are organized into the network as subsystems; and each path through the network from the root to an end node corresponds to a specific language expression. In this section, we present a sample network of durative aspect in concert with the elaborations given in previous sections. All expressions of aspect presented in the network are denoted by their abbreviated names; and the realization rules applied to constructing the corresponding grammatical structures are presented in boxes under the name of each aspect. In the realization statements, aspect markers are denoted by functions PAM1/2, SAM1/2 and TAM1/2, which are abbreviations for 'primary marker1/2', 'secondary marker1/2' and 'tertiary marker1/2' respectively. The aspect markers numbered with 1 occur before the verb; the markers numbered with 2 occur after the verb.

All the functions associated with the aspect markers are uniformly inserted during network traversal. For example, when the aspect selected is among the URE aspect V+le, the UEX aspect V+guo, and the UDR aspect V+zhe, PAM2, which corresponds to a primary aspect marker located after the verb, will be inserted. Hence, the realization statement (Insert FUNC-

TION) is not present in the system network. Other realization statements cannot be generalized in the same way and have to be applied separately when the relevant expressions of aspect are selected. The realization statements used in the system network include the following (Bateman, 1997b):

> (a) (**Order** Function1 Function2) – This operation orders Function1 immediately to the left of Function2. The statement is notated as 'Function1 ^ Function2'.

> (b) (**Partition** Function1 Function2) – The operation orders Function1 anywhere to the left of Function2. The statement is notated as 'Function1 ... Function2'.

> (c) (**OrderAtEnd** Function) – The operation orders the Function as the rightmost constituent of the level of structure to which the Function most immediately belongs. The statement is notated as 'Function ^ #'.

> (d) (**Lexify** Function Word) – the operation realizes Function as the particular lexical item Word. The statement is notated as 'Function ! LEXEME'.

(Bateman, 1997b)

Because of the limitation of input associated with relevant files in the implementation, we use numbers 1, 2, 3, and 4 to refer to the four tones of Chinese characters in all the realization statements. For instance, *wang1*, *wang2*, *wang3* and *wang4* refer to *wāng*, *wáng*, *wǎng* and *wàng* respectively. The neutral tone is not marked by numbers. Hence, in corresponding realization statements, the aspect markers, e.g. *yīzhí*, *láizhe* and *yǐjing*, are written in the forms *yi1zhi2*, *lai2zhe* and *yi3jing*. The sentences generated in the implementation are in both Chinese phonetic alphabets and Chinese characters.

In the whole grammatical network the system IMPERFECTIVE-PRIMARY-TYPE has four subsystems: durative, focalized progressive, the ICP aspect, and the CTN aspect. The complete network description of the system DURA-TYPE (durative type) is presented in Figure 5.5. The system is constructed from three kinds of durative aspect: the LDR aspect 一直+V (yīzhí+V), the DPG aspect 在+V (zài+V), and the UDR aspect V+着 (V+zhe). The DPG aspect在+V (zài+V) is attached by two expressions of secondary aspect: the DPG+LDR aspect 一直+在+V (yīzhí+zài+V) and the DPG+UDR aspect 在+V+着 (zài+V+zhe). The LDR aspect一直+V (yīzhí+V) has two expressions of secondary aspect: the LDR+URE aspect一直+V+了 (yīzhí+V+le) and the LDR+REP aspect一直+V+来着 (yīzhí+V+láizhe). The UDR aspect V+着 (V+zhe) has six secondary expressions of aspect: the UDR+LDR aspect 一直+V+着 (yīzhí+V+zhe), the UDR+UEX aspect V+着+过 (V+zhe+guo), the UDR+MEX aspect 曾经+V+着+(过) (céngjíng+V+zhe+(guo)), the UDR+REP aspect V+着+(NP)+来着 (V+zhe+(NP)+láizhe), the UDR+URE aspect V+着+了 (V+zhe+le) and the UDR+PEF aspect 已经+V+着+(了) (yǐjing+V+zhe+(le)). Among the six expressions of secondary aspect, the UDR+LDR aspect 一直+V+着 (yīzhí+V+zhe) has two expressions of tertiary aspect: the UDR+LDR+REP aspect 一直+V+着+来着 (yīzhí+V+zhe+láizhe) and the UDR+LDR+URE aspect 一直+V+着+了 (yīzhí+V+zhe+le).

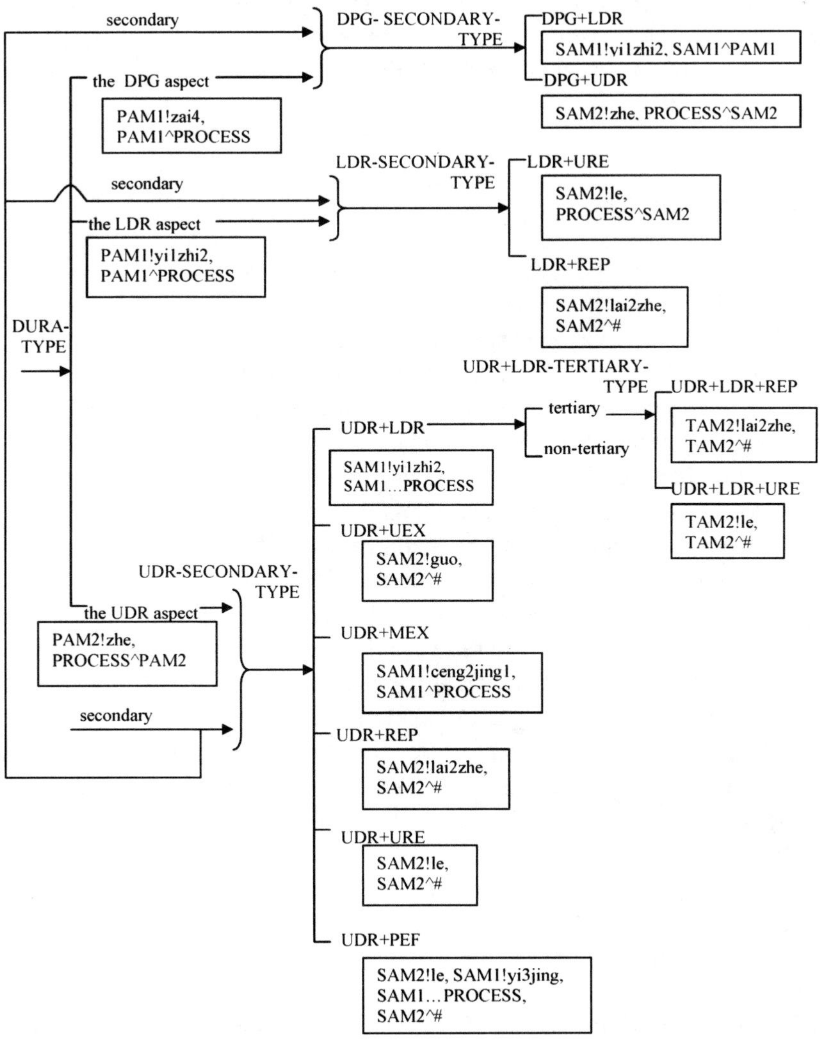

Figure 5.5: The system of DURA-TYPE (DURATIVE-TYPE)

Generally speaking, imperfective aspect is more semantically restricted than perfective aspect because the situations expressed by imperfective aspect are all required to be durative. Following the SOP, all expressions of secondary aspect constructed from these two kinds of aspect are dependent on, i.e., are attached to, imperfective aspect (see Figure 5.5). Hence, imperfective aspect involved in the combination will be taken as the basic aspect and selected first in the system traversal.

Because all the expressions of aspect are organized according to the SOP in the system networks, the key to correctly generating a complex aspect in the implementation is to provide system traversal with the guidance through the network for appropriately selecting the basic aspect from which the complex aspect to be generated is derived (Yang, 2007; Yang and Bateman, 2009).

5.5   Conclusion

This chapter presents a description of the Chinese aspect system, concerned mainly with its components and organization, with a special emphasis on the generation of complex aspect in this language. It is hoped that it may contribute to the study of Chinese linguistics. We find that compared with English, the combinations of aspect in Chinese are more restricted in both semantic and grammatical respects. Different expressions of simple aspect differ in their potential to combine with other types of aspect. Under the principal conditions, both expressions of individual aspect should share some aspectual features, and be compatible to build a proper temporal structure with specific range or location(s) of the reference time(s).

Complex aspect is developed from the primary aspect systems in the grammar network; this is related to the selection order of the individual aspect during the system traversal. The order of the aspect selections in the generation of complex aspect is determined by the SOP. The SOP indicates that the aspect which is more or most semantically restricted in usage is taken as the basic aspect and is selected first, and the other expression(s) of aspect will then be made dependent on the basic aspect in the grammar network.

Systemic grammar networks capture a functionally oriented organization, in which different kinds of grammatical expressions are arranged according to their semantic functions. Grammatical features associated with the semantic functions of language expressions make connections between paths and provide choices for system traversal. While going along a specific path, the traversal carries out a process of generating a specific language expression from the semantics to the surface realization.

The correctness and effectiveness of the grammatical organization of the aspect functions in the whole system network have been computationally verified. The complete system files and the sentences generated are available on the website http://www.fb10.uni-bremen.de/anglistik/langpro/kpml/genbank/chinese.htm.

Acknowledgements

I am very grateful to Professor John A. Bateman of the University of Bremen for his technical advice and financial support for this study. I thank Peter Lang Publisher for allowing me to use the relevant content of my book (Yang, 2007) in this chapter. I would like to thank Professor Fang Yan for her carefully reading the manuscript of the chapter and giving detailed suggestions for the revision. I also thank the reviewers of the revised version of the chapter for correcting my English.

References

Bateman, J. A. (1997a) Enabling technology for multilingual natural language generation: The KPML development. *Natural Language Engineering* 3 (1): 15–55.

Bateman, J. A. (1997b) *KPML Development Environment: Multilingual Linguistic Resource Development and Sentence Generation.* (Release 1.1). GMD – Studie Number 304. Sankt Augustin: German National Center for Information Technology (GMD).

Chao, Yuen Ren [赵元任] (1968) *A Grammar of Spoken Chinese.* Berkeley and Los Angeles, CA: University of California Press.

Comrie, B. (1976) *Aspect.* Cambridge: Cambridge University Press.

Comrie, B. (1985) *Tense.* Cambridge: Cambridge University Press.

Dai, Yaojing [戴耀晶] (1997) 《现代汉语时体系统研究》 [Xiàndài Hànyǔ Shítǐ Xìtǒng Yánjiū, *The Study of Chinese Aspect System*]. Hangzhou: 浙江教育出版社 [Zhéjiāng Jiàoyù Chūbǎnshè].

Fan, Kaitai [范开泰] (1984) 汉语'态'的语义分析 [hànyǔ tài de yǔyì fēnxī, Semantic analysis of Chinese aspect]. *Journal of Chinese Language Teachers Association* 19: 85–105.

Fawcett, R. P. (1987) System networks in the lexicalgrammar. In M. A. K. Halliday and R. P. Fawcett (eds) *New Developments in Systemic Linguistics Vol 1: Theory and Description,* 130–183. London: Pinter.

Gong, Qianyan [龚千炎] (1995) 《汉语的时相 时制 时态》 [Hànyǔ De Shíxiàng Shízhì Shítài, *Situation Type, Tense, and Aspect in Chinese*]. Beijing: 商务印书馆 [Shāngwù Yìnshūguǎn].

Halliday, M. A. K. (1976) The English verbal group. In G. R. Kress (ed.) *Halliday: System and Function in Language.* London: Oxford University Press.

Halliday, M. A. K (Revised by Christian Matthiessen) (2004/2008) [the third edition] *An Introduction to Functional Grammar*. London: Hodder Arnold/Beijing: Foreign Language Teaching and Research Press.

Halliday, M. A. K. and Matthiessen, C. M. I. M. (1999/2008) *Construing Experience through Meaning*. London: Cassell/Beijing: 世界图书出版公司 [Shìjiè Túshū Chūbǎn Gōngsī].

Huang, L. M. and Davis, P. W. (1989) An aspectual system in Mandarin Chinese. *Journal of Chinese Linguistics* 17: 128–166.

Klein, W. (1994) *Time in Language*. London: Routledge.

Klein, W., Li, P. and Hendriks, H. (2000) Aspect and assertion in Mandarin Chinese. *Natural Language and Linguistic Theory* 18: 723–770.

Li, Xiangnong [李向农] (1998) 《现代汉语时点时段研究》 [Xiàndài Hànyǔ Shídiǎn Shíduàn Yánjiū, *The Study of Time Point and Time Duration in Chinese*]. Wuhan: 华中师范大学出版社 [Huázhōng Shīfàn Dàxué Chūbǎnshè].

Li, C. N. and Thompson, S. A. (1981) *Mandarin Chinese*: *A Functional Reference Grammar*. Berkeley, CA: University of California Press.

Lü, Shuxiang [吕叔湘] (1953) 《中国文法要略》 [Zhōngguó Wénfǎ Yàoluè, *An Outline of Chinese Grammar*]. Shanghai: 商务印书馆 [Shāngwù Yìnshūguǎn].

Lü, Shuxiang [吕叔湘] *et al.* (eds) (1999) [the revised edition of 1980] 《现代汉语八百词》 [Xiàndài Hànyǔ Bābǎi Cí, *Eight Hundred Words in Modern Chinese*]. Beijing: 商务印书馆 [Shāngwù Yìnshūguǎn].

Matthiessen, C. M. I. M. and Bateman, J. A. (1991) *Text Generation and Systemic Functional Linguistics*. London: Pinter Publishers.

Meng, Cong [孟琮] *et al.* (eds) (1999) 《汉语动词用法词典》 [Hànyǔ Dòngcí Yòngfǎ Cídiǎn, *Dictionary of Chinese Verb Usage*]. Beijing: 商务印书馆 [Shāngwù Yìnshūguǎn].

Peng, Xuanwei [彭宣维] (2011) 《语言与语言学概论 — 汉语系统功能语法》 [Yǔyán Yǔ Yǔyánxué Gàilùn — Hànyǔ Xìtǒng Gōngnéng Yǔfǎ, *An Introduction to Language and Linguistics — Chinese Systemic Functional Grammar*]. Beijing: Peking University Press.

Smith, C. S. (1997) [second edition of 1991] *The Parameter of Aspect*. Dordrecht: Kluwer Academic Publishers.

Wang, Li [王力] (1985) [a bound volume of 1943 and 1944] 《中国现代语法》 [Zhōngguó Xiàndài Yǔfǎ, *Modern Chinese Grammar*]. Beijing: 商务印书馆 [Shāngwù Yìnshūguǎn].

Yang, Guowen [杨国文] (1999) 汉语复合态的语义关系类型及其生成的有向性 [hànyǔ fùhé tài de yǔyì guānxì lèixíng jíqí shēngchéng de yǒuxiàngxìng, The semantic properties of complex aspect and the ordering requirements in the generation]. *Proceedings of the 5th Chinese Conference on Computational Linguistics*, 21–26. Beijing: Tsinghua University Press.

Yang, Guowen [杨国文] (2001a) 汉语态制中复合态的生成 [hànyǔ tàizhì zhōng fùhé tài de shēngchéng, The generation of aspect complex in Chinese aspect system]. 中国语文 [*Zhōngguó Yǔwén*] 284(5): 418–427.

Yang, Guowen [杨国文] (2001b) 汉语物质过程中 '范围' 成分与 '目标' 成分的区别 [hàyǔ wùzhì guòchéng zhōng 'fànwéi' chéngfèn yǔ 'mùbiāo' chéngfèn de qūbié, Differences between Range and Goal of material processes in Chinese]. 语言研究 [*Yǔyán Yánjiū*] 45(4): 8–17.

Yang, Guowen [杨国文] (2002) 汉语 '被' 字式在不同种类的过程中的使用情况考察 [hànyǔ 'bèi' zìshì zài bùtóng zhǒnglèi de guòchéng zhōng de shǐyòng qíngkuàng kǎochá, An investigation of the usage of the *bei4* construction in different process types in Chinese]. 当代语言学 [*Dāngdài Yǔyánxué*] 4(1): 13–24.

Yang, Guowen [杨国文] (2004) The systemic theory of process types applied to the *bǎ* construction in Chinese. *Journal of Chinese Language Teachers Association* 39(2): 49–84.

Yang, Guowen [杨国文] (2007) *The Semantics of Chinese Aspects – Theoretical Descriptions and a Computational Implementation.* Frankfurt am Main: Peter Lang.

Yang, Guowen [杨国文] (2009) The semantics of complex aspects constructed from two imperfective simple aspects in Chinese. *Journal of Chinese Linguistics* 37(2): 297–359.

Yang, Guowen [杨国文] (2010) 焦点进行时态 '正在+V'/'正+(PP)+V' 功能辨析 [jiāodiǎn jìnxíng shítài 'zhèngzài+V'/ 'zhèng+(PP)+V' gōngnéng biànxī, The functional discrimination of the focalized progressive aspect 'zhèngzài+V'/ 'zhèng+(PP)+V']. In 中国语文杂志社 [Journal of Zhōngguó Yǔwén] (ed.) 《语法研究和探索》 [Yǔfǎ Yánjiū Hé Tànsuǒ, *The Study and Exploration of Grammar*] (15) 108–119. Beijing: 商务印书馆 [Shāngwù Yìnshūguǎn].

Yang, Guowen [杨国文] (2011) '动词+结果补语'和'动词重叠式'的非时态性质 ['dòngcí+jiéguǒ bǔyǔ' hé 'dòngcí chóngdiéshì' de fēishítài xìngzhì, The nonaspectual properties of resultative verbal complements and verb reduplication]. 当代语言学 [*Dāngdài Yǔyánxué*] 13(3): 217–225.

Yang, Guowen [杨国文] (2012) 汉语的即行时态及其与完全时态的区别和关联 [hànyǔ de jìxíng shítài jíqí yǔ wánquán shítài de qūbié hé guānlián, The distinctions and connections between imminent aspect and perfective aspect in Chinese]. In 中国语文杂志社 [Journal of Zhōngguó Yǔwén] (ed.) 《语法研究和探索》 [Yǔfǎ Yánjiū Hé Tànsuǒ, *The Study and Exploration of Grammar*] (16): 254–275. Beijing: 商务印书馆 [Shāngwù Yìnshūguǎn].

Yang, Guowen [杨国文] and Bateman, J. A. (2002) The Chinese aspect system and its semantic interpretation. *Proceedings of the 19th International Conference on Computational Linguistics* 1128–1134. Taipei: Morgan Kaufmann Publisher.

Yang, Guowen [杨国文] and Bateman, J. A. (2009) The Chinese aspect generation based on aspect selection functions. *Proceedings of the 47th Annual Meeting of the ACL and the 4th IJCNLP of the AFNLP,* 629–637. Singapore: World Scientific Publishing Co. Pte Ltd.

6 Linguistic sign and the science of linguistics:[1] The foundations of appliability

Ruqaiya Hasan*

> ...we boldly submit that discussion is in vain unless you know what you are discussing...
>
> (Ferdinand de Saussure, 2006: 166)

6.1 Introduction

Systemic functional linguistics, especially the variety associated with the name of Halliday,[2] has been perhaps unique in explicitly and defiantly celebrating the inherent relations of theory and practice from its earliest stages (e.g. Halliday, 1960). The actual range of purposes for which SFL has been used is indeed remarkable (Appendix A; Halliday, 2008: 190ff; Hasan *et al.*, 2005, 2007). But my aim here is not to join in praise or denigration; I wish instead to raise a basic question: *what enables a linguistic theory to become appliable*? Why do some theories such as SFL or Prague School linguistics become widely appliable?[3] Why do other models, some with claims of elevated intellectual pedigree, remain above or below human use?

It occurs to me after some reflection that the property of appliability in a linguistic theory is simply a by-product: the features that facilitate applications are not found there *because* someone remembered to insert them specially as additional elements. Rather, the power of appliability in a linguistic theory has its origins in ideas about language, which is what gives the theory its identity.

---

* Ruqaiya Hasan is an Emeritus Professor (Linguistics) at Macquarie University, Australia.

6.1.1 The essence of language

The acknowledged complexity of language has led to much debate about the nature of linguistics. The founder of modern linguistics, Ferdinand de Saussure, clearly identified what *he* thought to be central to linguistics: it is clear from both the earlier *Course* (1966) and the more recent *Writings in General Linguistics* (2006; henceforth *Writings*), that the first step in finding the 'truth in linguistics' is to successfully identify the nature of the linguistic sign: thereafter its exploration will lead the theory to everything that is important to understanding language. The impact of Saussure's theory of the linguistic sign has been such that modern linguists and their theories have since been positioned by reference to him: they are known as pre-Saussurean, Saussurean, anti-Saussurean, post-Saussurean or non-Saussurean (cf. Firth, 1957: 179). SFL is post-Saussurean: its point of departure is Saussurean; it accepts his concept of sign and agrees with much he has to say about the linguistic sign system, but goes beyond Saussure in developing his position and elaborating many of his theoretical concepts (section 6.4.3, below). This leads me to hypothesize that *the primary foundation for the appliability of a linguistic theory resides in a faithful description of the nature of sign and what follows from that description*: Halliday's SFL is such a theory.

6.1.2 Theorizing the Concept of language as langue

I will begin this chapter by assuming with Saussure that the prime object of study for linguistics is the 'interplay of signs, called LANGUE' (Saussure, 2006: 21), that 'language is a system of signs that express ideas' and as a theory of signs, 'linguistics is only a branch of the science of semiology' (Saussure, 1966: 16). This means establishing Saussure's views about the nature of sign and its attributes (section 6.2); in section 6.3, the linguistic sign will be compared with other, non-linguistic sign types, in order to examine the validity of Saussure's claim. This will form the foundation for drawing attention, in section 6.4, to relevant implications of adopting the Saussurean positions. I will indicate, this time with an eye to the theory as developed in SFL, some characteristics of language, which although deemed external to langue by Saussure, *have to be* considered essential to a theoretically valid description of the linguistic sign system. I will argue that, judged by standards of inferential thinking set by Saussure himself, the working of langue as the nub of the semiotic system can neither be validated nor be represented explicitly without close attention to these so-called 'langue-external' issues chief amongst which is PAROLE. If the aim of linguistics is to *account for all those phenomena concerning langue which*

Saussure takes to be central for discovering the truth of language, then the object of enquiry for linguistics has to be SFL's elaborated conception of language: from this wider perspective, Saussure's 'langue' would be simply one aspect of the object of enquiry for an explanatory linguistics (Hasan, 2013). Granted, langue is central to viable linguistics: it captures the basic semiotic properties which 'enable' the language system to work the way it does in the community; but, without the extensions and elaborations undertaken by SFL, the concept of langue itself will remain jejune. Attention to the systemic nature of language use, i.e., PAROLE, is essential if linguistics is to explain the working of langue in the community's social life.

6.2   Sign: The basic unit of language

In the *Course* (1966), Saussure's discourse on linguistics commences with the linguistic sign and concludes with the possibility of the science of semiology.[4] The clarification of the complex relations of SIGNIFIED and SIGNIFIER deeply occupied Saussure's attention in the earlier chapters of the book. Beginning with a rather simplified account where he said that 'the linguistic sign unites not a thing and a name, but a concept and a sound image' (1966: 66), Saussure moved to the complexities of these terms. The sign, Janus-like, presents two faces in one unit: the signifier refers to the sign's material expressive aspect and the signified to its abstract semantic VALUE on which SIGNIFICATION, the act of referring to the extra-linguistic world, depends. Saussure was at pains to show that, in isolation from each other, neither face of the linguistic sign could be recognized as a 'signing' entity. In and of themselves, neither had any semiotic status, and in this sense their materiality as well as their abstractness are less noteworthy than their sign-constituting function (2006). Today with the added evidence of his *Writings* (2006: 15ff) it is obvious that Saussure was caught between the need both to affirm the sign as one unit and to confirm that the sign's material manifestation and its 'psychological' import are phenomena of distinct orders: in unity alone can they present both the meaning-evoking and the evoked meaning aspects of the sign.

The sign's make up is the primary theoretical axiom for Saussure's linguistics of langue: thinking inferentially from this axiom, he came to a number of rich concepts that pertain to the linguistics of langue, such as the sign's SYSTEMICITY, its VALUE and IDENTITY; ASSOCIATIVE and SYNTAGMATIC relations, STRUCTURE as a 'template' as opposed to the material continuity of sign, which forms the outer face of parole. Saussure (1966: 67) assigned 'two primordial characteristics' to the linguistic sign: (i) ARBITRARINESS; and (ii) LINEARITY.

6.2.1 Characteristics of the linguistic sign: (i) arbitrariness

The term 'arbitrary' applies to only one relation in Saussurean linguistics, namely, that which unites the signifier and the signified: everything in his linguistics flows *logically* from the sign's nature. He carefully spelt out the meaning of this term:

> The word 'arbitrary' … should not imply that the choice of the signifier is left entirely to the speaker; … I mean that it [i.e, the choice of the signifier, RH] is unmotivated, i.e., *arbitrary in that it actually has no natural connection with the signified.* (Saussure, 1966: 68–69, *emphasis added*, RH)

Saussure points out that even though speakers of English will normally take a given phonic form such as /sistə/ as evoking the meaning 'sister', no reason exists for seeing this association except the *communal conventions of a language* whereby this 'acoustic image' becomes associated with that particular value/meaning:

> Even if people were more conscious of language than they are, they would still not know how to discuss it. The reason is simply that any subject in order to be discussed must have a reasonable basis. It is possible for instance to discuss whether the monogamous form of marriage is more reasonable than the polygamous form and to advance arguments to support either side. … ; but language is a system of arbitrary signs and lacks the necessary basis, the solid ground for discussion. (Saussure, 1966: 73, *original emphasis*, RH)

As Halliday (1999, 2005) says the sign's substance belongs to the realm of the material; its meaning to that of the semiotic, created by 'the interplay of signs called langue' (Saussure 2006: 21). So the secret of the acceptance of a particular signifier evoking a particular meaning has its foundation in social convention, i.e., in the regular practice of using that 'sound image' with that 'sign value'.

6.2.2 Characteristics of the linguistic sign: (ii) linearity

The second attribute, linearity, inheres in the material nature of the sign's 'form', i.e., the signifier: whether encountered as speech or as writing, language use can only run along the single dimension of space-time. By default, the elements 'form a chain' (Saussure, 1966: 70). To those not familiar with the language in question, the chain of speech does not offer any obvious principles for identifying the boundaries of individual signs as the phones/graphs occur one after the other in parole: the identity of a particular signifier or signified is not 'within' a particular sign. Speakers of a language easily 'locate' individual signs and make sense of them due to the robust communal conventions whereby they have grown up hearing and later speaking the language of their speech community. However, it is not in social conventions that the identity and the value of signs have their foundations: as Saussure points out 'a' particular sign works because 'all' signs in a language work together, e.g.

> The ultimate law of language is … that nothing can ever be said to exist in *one* term (since quite simply linguistic symbols have no link with what they are meant to refer to), *a* cannot refer to anything without the help of *b*, and the same goes about this term without the help of *a*; either both are validated by their reciprocal *differences*, or neither is valid. (Saussure, 2006: 153)

6.2.3 Characteristics of the linguistic sign: (iii) systemicity

Both arbitrariness and linearity arise from the internal make up of the linguistic sign, while the systemic nature of the sign may be seen as rooted in the sign's arbitrariness. A linguistic sign in itself can have neither an identity nor a value: the signified has no 'logical' link with what it actually refers to, and the signifier has no natural reason for being associated with a particular signified; 'man' is as good a sign for referring to a 'human adult male' as the Urdu sign /admɪ/ or the French 'homme'.

This negative character of the linguistic sign is counteracted in two ways: first, members of a speech community use linguistic signs in their parole, thus reinforcing the association of the signified and signifier of a particular sign. But more importantly, underlying this 'typically reinforced association' is the 'interplay of signs', i.e., the mutual relationship of signs, which fixes their value and identity. The relationships are of two kinds: (a) SYNTAGMATIC and (b) ASSOCIATIVE; Saussure characterized them as '*in praesentia*' and '*in absentia*', respectively. These relations are analogous to the axes of CHAIN and CHOICE in SFL (Halliday, 1963).

The axis of chain i.e., syntagm is a property of language use, i.e. parole. Their spatio-temporal patterns of contiguity become indicative of 'syntagmatic relations', contributing to the 'determination' of mutual values, as evident from examples 1–3:

1. On Saturday the bank closes at 1 o'clock.
2. The bank is being shored up to contain the huge overflow of water.
3. Every page of that article contained at least one figure or a table.

As exemplified by the above, on the syntagmatic axis all the interacting signs are present on 'the scene', i.e., they are 'in praesentia'. Firth's COL-LOCATION would most probably have been regarded as an 'in praesentia' relationship, though Saussure's own examples better fit Firth's concept of COLLIGATION.

The associative relation differs in this respect; here interaction between signs occurs through remembered relations though the signs themselves are absent from 'the scene', i.e., they are 'in absentia'. The associative axis is concerned with choice from a range of inter-related signs such that only one sign will be present from among all those that 'qualify' as members of the same 'associative range' (i.e., PARADIGM); the bond is there by virtue of the speaking person's familiarity with the paradigm: it depends on a mental recognition of the paradigm. Thus when the syntagm justifies seeing the sign /beə/ (written as 'bear') as in associative relation with 'tolerate' or 'reject', it will have a different value from that /beə/ ('bear') which is in associative relation with 'bearing, bore, born, birth'; each of these /beə/ differs in value from /beə/ ('bare') that is in the same paradigm as 'bares', 'bared', 'naked', 'clothed', 'dress'; and all the foregoing differ from /beə/ as in 'polar bear', 'grisly bear'; and so on. Because each sign in a syntagm carries both its syntagmatic 'in praesentia' relations and also the penumbra of its associative 'in absentia' relations, the acculturated brain familiar with the speech conventions of the community readily identifies a given sign as a particular sign, different from all the others, and yet similar in behaviour to some of them. These two relations represent the major modes of the sign's interplay.

It is not the shape/form of the 'acoustic image' that 'produces' the sign's meaning: the meaning (the signified) is 'in' the morphology, i.e., created by the relations of all the signifieds in a given language. This account of its production foreshadows the independent status of linguistic meaning, which is not constrained by the 'real' world of objects or the 'mental' world of thoughts and ideas: according to Saussure (1966: 112): 'There are no pre-existing ideas, and nothing is distinct before the appearance of language.'

6.3   The semiological nature of signs: Some implications

In this section, using insights from Firth, Halliday and, to a lesser extent from Hjelmslev, I will attempt to elaborate some details pertaining to the concept of semiology/semiotic as introduced in section 6.2.

6.3.1 The linguistic sign in the context of other sign types

Saussure set great store by assigning to the basic unit of language the status of sign. The *raison d'être* of a sign is that it brings meaning into being. Thus every category of sign may be said to 'have' a signified/meaning which is 'brought to notice' by something that is experienced bodily, i.e., every sign 'has' a part analogous to a signifier. The signifier is *always* fashioned 'materially'; and as such, in terms of Russell, it is SENS-IBLE. By contrast, the signified is purely 'INTELLIG-IBLE': its interpretation depends on the acculturated brain, i.e., 'the mind'. This is one *crucial* respect in which all signs are alike, although the terms as applied to the linguistic sign are remarkably different from the others as the brief comparison of the sign types would show.

The nature of sign types has been much discussed for many decades; nonetheless, the accounts are neither exhaustive nor is there terminological consistency across different approaches. The sketch of the world of signs shown in Figure 6.1 has benefited from the work of many other scholars including Aarsleff (1982), Saussure (1966, 2006), Wittgenstein (1953), Peirce (1955), Firth (1957), and Halliday (1992, 1993, 1999), the final responsibility is mine. The various signing phenomena usually discussed as MULTIMODALITY in SFL have been ignored for lack of space.

For lack of space the sign types and their properties have been tabulated. Some of the properties of the non-linguistic signs are mentioned to highlight how they contrast with the linguistic ones.

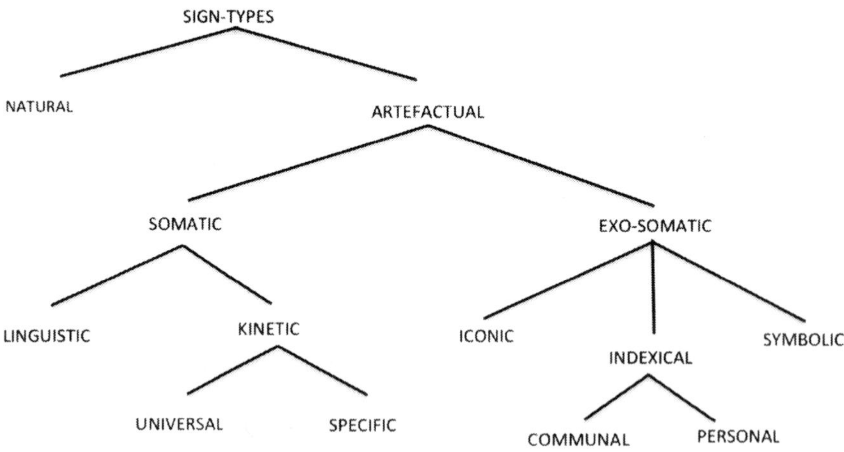

Figure 6.1: The world of signs: A tentative account

Table 6.1: Sign types and their properties

s-type	s-maker	s-medium	user-volition	sd/sr-relation	systemic	example
natural	nature	natural force	none	physical logic	no	dark clouds→ rain
artefactual	human	material	–	–	–	[general category; various]
somatic	”	user body	–	–	–	[” ” ”]
kinetic	”	”	uncertain	uncertain	not inherent	[” ” ”]
universal	”	”	”	”	”	Smile → happy
specific	”	”	”	”	”	[culturally variable gesture]
linguistic	”	”	yes	arbitrary	inherent	'go away!' → order to leave
exo-somatic	”	matter	”	–	no	[general category; various]
indexical	”	”	”	arbitrary	”	[see next two entries]
communal	”	”	”	”	”	school bell→play time
personal	”	”	”	”	”	front door bell → visitor
iconic	”	”	”	similarity	”	✂ → 'cut here'
symbolic	”	”	”	similarity+	”	scales → justice

LEGEND: S= sign; sd= signified; sr= signifier

6.3.2 The linguistics sign viewed as a sign amongst signs

It will be useful to position Saussure's conception of the linguistic sign *vis-á-vis* the non-linguistic ones by revisiting its characteristics in terms of the features by which other sign types have been identified in Figure 6.1 and Table 1. I will also highlight some implications of Saussure's claims.

Like most of the other signs, the linguistic sign too is ARTEFACTUAL, which implies that users are able to control the production and use of the sign; they can consciously decide whether to speak, what to say, and how to say it. Yet Saussure's claim that in parole, the speaker is 'the master' must be questioned: speaking *is* using the semiotic system of language, but the reason for using language is not inside the semiotic system: the process is socially 'regulated', and this regulation extends beyond the instance to the system through its role in the genesis of linguistic variation (6.4.2 below). An important implications is that the degree of conscious management of parole varies according to what the social context requires (Hasan, 1989). Later I will argue that sign morphology á la Saussure is impossible without consulting the systemic patterns of parole, which is also central for providing an explanatory account of the SEMOGENIC processes of language (Halliday and Matthiessen, 1999).

6.3.2.1 The sign's value, reality and reference

Like the kinetic sign types, the linguistic sign is SOMATIC, so its production and use require nothing else than the user's body and an acculturated brain; but unlike the universal kinetic sign, the 'signifier-signified' pairing of *particular linguistic signs is never universal, although the sign's basic design and attributes including its systemicity are universal.* Due to the 'wholly arbitrary' relation of the signifier and signified, the felicitous use of this sign type depends on acculturation. The internal logic of language makes even onomatopoeia sound 'unfamiliar': in Urdu the rooster goes /kʊkRõkũ/; in English /kɔkədudldu/, in French /kokoriko/, and so on. Saussure doubted that intuition or common sense would help one understand the nature of language as a sign system; in fact intuition could be quite misleading by encouraging the belief that a sign's meaning 'is' actually a particular concrete object in the world. For example, it might appear justified to an English speaker to imagine that the referent of the word 'sun' 'is' actually that shining orb in the sky. To counteract this, Saussure reminds the reader of languages 'in which' one 'cannot sit *in* the sun'. Urdu, happens to be one such: as a speaker of that language what I see shining in the sky is called /surədz/ but I cannot sit *in* / surədz/; what I sit in is /dhup/, the bright warmth shed by /surədz/. Common sense, supported by sensuous experience, might lead the Urdu speaker to believe that the 'division' of the referential domain in his language is really real, that the English sign 'sun' is 'lacking in specificity'; it neither refers to the orb up there in the sky, nor to the warm light shed by it on the earth; it simply 'confuses' the two. Common sense would be mistaken in both cases: the simple fact is that ordinary speakers of any language are unable to 'see through' the linguistic system without a painstaking 'scientific' analysis. What this discussion highlights is the *fundamental independence of the linguistic sign from the so-called 'real world'*: languages place different grids on the world of reality, thus shaping 'the real' in human experience.

6.3.2.2 The inherent systemicity of the linguistic sign

The INHERENTLY SYSTEMIC nature of the linguistic sign compensates for its 'wholly arbitrary' quality. This too has some serious implications as evident from closer examination of the discussion of 'sun' v. /surədz/, /dhup/.

As Saussure pointed out repeatedly, no linguistic sign, in itself, can be said to 'have' a meaning or even an expression form that is *its own*; the identity and value of the linguistic sign inheres in its relation with other signs: simplifying, if Urdu had only one sign to refer to that domain, no matter whether /surədz/ or /dhup/, the difference between that sign and 'sun' would be hardly noticeable. The linguistic signs are quite different in the intensity of their mutual relationships compared to all other sign types, whose categories typically represent a collection of individuals, so the life of one sign bears no consequence for that of any other. The *unequivocally robust individual systems* of the linguistic signs can be easily integrated into larger system networks following principles that inhere in the nature of the language (Hasan, 1987). As Firth (1957) suggested, language is a system of systems.

The 'wholly arbitrary' and systemic nature of the linguistic sign as described here frees the signified from being bound by any pre-existing phenomena: the fact that the object sun exists and is sensed by all human beings as a shining orb in the sky is not a binding fact for linguistic sign; it creates a parallel universe in a complex relation to objects, and their specific qualities, or space-time location in the sensuous world. This is part of the secret of the SEMIOTIC POWER of language: instead of signs being modelled on pre-existing things or events whether in nature or in culture (e.g. saturated clouds bringing rain, the scissors indicating 'cut here', or the evenly balanced scales as symbolic of justice), language sets its own parameters for the referents of its signs. It can create what has never been, what cannot be sensed, and what exists only virtually: it is this quality of the linguistic sign that enables it to 'create' frameworks of concepts which may correspond to invisible existents, to work out their interactions which may not be sens-ible, and thus 'build' theoretical structures, the proof of whose existence lies in their efficacy in action rather than in being visible. The valued human social institutions such as those producing knowledge and technology, law and medicine, religions and aesthetic artefacts, owe their existence largely to this source of the sign's semiotic power. This, in turn, implies that a linguistic theory able to tap into the semiotic power of language would have a better likelihood of being appliable.

6.3.2.3 Speech and writing: Two ways of accessing language

A characteristic of the linguistic sign that Figure 6.1 fails to show is the emergence of an additional 'mode of discourse': the primary mode for the expression of the linguistic sign had been exclusively ORAL-AURAL. However, with the arrival of writing, language acquired a secondary mode, GRAPHIC-VISUAL. In the world of signs represented in Figure 6.1, this 'bi-modality' is unique to language: the first technology to engage with language, writing became another mode of communication. What is notable is the non-random division of labour between the use of spoken and written modes: the choice became a resource opening up a path for the evolution of language into distinct varieties. Whatever the virtue of an oral culture, it is unquestionable that writing is an additional resource that changes human cultures (Goody, 1968, 1977; Hasan, in press).

6.3.3 The place of linguistics in the science of semiology

Now that we have a fair idea of how the various sign types in Figure 6.1 are positioned in relation to each other, we may ask: is linguistics *a branch of semiology,* 'a science that studies the life of signs within society'?

First, if semiology is a science that studies the life of signs within society, it would need to use language for the purpose because no other sign system is capable of performing this activity: they do not have the affordance. Second, it is far from clear that sign types other than the linguistic ones are capable of being *scientifically* studied, if the term means more than simply describing the empirically observed phenomena objectively: an observationally correct account of an arbitrary inventory of signs such as the exosomatic ones is feasible, including information about how they operate in society and the history of their evolution. But how would this measure up to the *science of the linguistics of langue* such as Saussure envisaged? None of the non-linguistic sign types have so far got to what Saussure called 'the first principles' in linguistic research: their description is presented largely as an inventory of 'isolated individuals'. Is the point of departure for their discussion amenable to scientific study? Strange as it may sound, Saussure would share the doubts expressed here: commenting on the significance of the 'wholly arbitrary' nature of the linguistic sign, he had concluded:

> Signs that are wholly arbitrary realize better than the others the ideal of the semiological process; that is why language, the most complex and universal of all systems of expression, is also the most characteristic; *in this sense linguistics can become the master-pattern for all branches* of semiology although language is only one particular semiological system. (Saussure, 1966: 68, *emphasis introduced,* RH)

As emphasized throughout this chapter, the consequences of the sign's primordial attributes are incalculable: 'arbitrariness' is a case in point. All sign types, including the linguistic ones, are encountered by individuals as social conventions; few are created anew.[5] In this sense they are all conventional; but while the massive materiality of other sign types modifies their conventionality (scissors are used for cutting; so a scissor ready to cut 'says' *cut here*), the behaviour of the 'wholly arbitrary' linguistic sign is intensely systemic; without its systemic relations the linguistic sign would not be a sign of anything.

6.4   Language use in community and the linguistic system

While accepting Saussure's impressive ideas on the linguistic sign, this section will follow the directions implicit in that description, thus elaborating the likely shape of a more developed Saussurean linguistics. The heart of Saussure's projected linguistic theory consists of the study of the 'interplay of signs called langue'; to achieve this Saussure identified certain aspects of language which he deemed either as *external* or *internal* to that linguistics. This led to certain contradictions, which were perceived as 'Saussurean paradoxes'. I will argue that SFL's development of theoretical concepts since the early 1960s are compatible with Saussure's view of sign and that they have made it possible to re-evaluate most of the so-called Saussurean paradoxes. In following faithfully where the nature of Saussure's view of the sign leads, SFL goes BEYOND Saussure's professed notions. The justification for these departures and modifications is very simple: they are necessary because *without these departures* neither the nature of the sign nor its impressive systemicity as evident in the 'interplay of signs' can be fully investigated; in short, *Saussure's linguistics of langue cannot be achieved*. Phenomena that Saussure had considered *the heart of the study of langue* cannot proceed beyond an abstract principle without extensions and modifications. To my mind this is justification enough for injecting new ideas into it.

The move outlined above is relevant to the validation of the claim (6.1.1 above) that *the primary foundation for the appliability of linguistics resides in a faithful description of the nature of sign and the pursuit of what follows from that description*: if SFL is such a linguistic theory, and SFL is also recognized as appliable, there is a *prima facie* case for maintaining that appliability is a by-product of the linguist's conceptualization of language.

6.4.1 The linguistic sign: Implications of its essential duality

The first Saussurean paradox lies in the *essential duality of the sign* as discussed earlier. Common sense would reject the Saussurean view as self-contradictory, but a semiological theory of language must agree that Saussure is right on both counts.

However, problems have arisen in the presentation of the sign's essential duality. One way of resolving such problems is to theorize, as SFL does, the relations of signified-signifier by using the concept of STRATI-FICATION *á la* Hjelmslev (1961): something stratified can be viewed analytically as two (or more) separate orders of abstraction, with the unity of the stratified object implicit in the metaphor of stratification: this solidary relation inheres in the stratified object. To refer to that particular kind of solidary relation whereby two distinct orders of abstraction are related to each other, SFL has borrowed Hjelmslev's term (1961: 40) REALIZATION.[6] Figure 6.2 shows this stratification of the sign, identifying strata within each part.

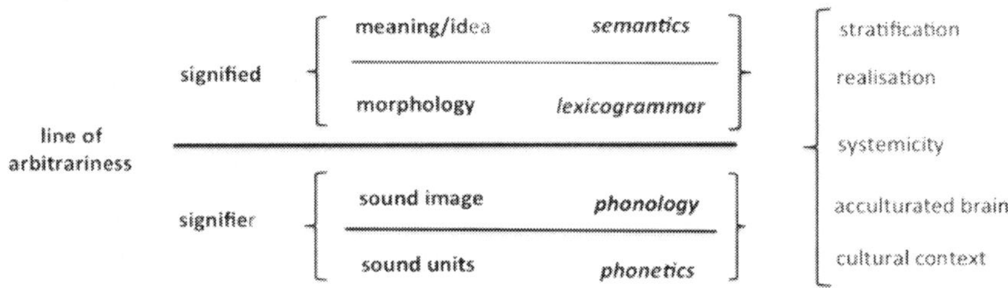

Figure 6.2: The dual essence of language: An elaboration

In Figure 6.2, the line of arbitrariness runs between signified and signifier forming the primary strata. Saussure's terminology for further stratification of the strata is shown in ordinary script, the current SFL terms which 'translate' them are in italics. The big open brace lists the main implications of viewing the linguistic sign through the mediation of these concepts, some of which have been adumbrated in sections 6.2 and 6.3. Instead of methodically following this listed order of implications, the sections below discuss them under two general headings: both relate ultimately to Saussure's conception of sign, and both demonstrate, though in different ways, why following the sign faithfully where its nature leads is a critical factor in creating an appliable linguistic theory.

(1) the sign, its user and the users' community (6.4.2 and subsections)
(2) the sign, its morphology, and templates (6.4.3 and subsections)

The central feature of Saussurean linguistics is its commitment to the systemic aspects of language; it ignores the accidental as irrelevant to linguistics. So, the systemic nature of the linguistic phenomena will be emphasized below, especially where SFL has been led to depart from, add to or modify Saussure's ideas.

6.4.2 The life of the linguistic sign in society: Context, sign and sign users

Saussure often refers to 'community', locating therein the origin of language. He appeals to it in connection with conventionality; further a recognition of the community's linguistic behaviour is treated as relevant to the genesis of diachronic change. It should be obvious that a particular configurations of features define the boundaries of *états de langue*, a concept essential to the SYNCHRONIC LINGUISTICS of langue, whose origin is said to lie in parole. Despite the centrality of 'community' to such important issues 'culture' remains untheorized in Saussure, and this has infected other concepts including the relation of 'parole' to *langue* and of linguistic variation to synchronic linguistics, which is in effect the linguistics of langue. As pointed out, Saussure (2006) rejects the ability of common sense to scientifically analyse the sign; I suggest the same applies to the analysis of social context seen in relation to language as system and process: it needs to be theorized to provide a valid account of the relations of language and culture.

To SFL, oriented to discourse analysis (Halliday *et al.*, 1964) for decades, context and language variation have been familiar concepts; SFL has used context as a device for placing grids on language use, thereby introducing system into parole. Language use always occurs with reference to some social practice: the environments for social practices are culturally specific, which is what SFL refers to as context of SITUATION. It follows that situation must be 'aware' of CULTURE: just as behind parole lies the language system, so also culture is instantiated as situation. As linguists, our interest in culture and situation is from the perspective of language SYSTEM (*langue*) and language USE (*parole*), with the implication that the theorization of their relations should offer a valid account of the relations of these four categories. Figure 6.3 is Halliday's graphic representation (1999) of just such an account where the principal concepts and their relations are specified.

Figure 6.3 below should be seen as an extension of Halliday's theoretical concepts relating to register variation. According to it, the linguistic system is REALIZATIONALLY related to the context of culture, just as the use of language as text is to the context of situation[7]. Contexts of situation hosting social activities INSTANTIATE the system of culture, just as the process of language i.e., parole, in the shape of text(s), instantiates the system of language.[8] Figure 6.3 helps locate precisely the relations of categories such as language system, language use, culture, situation, linguistic varieties, and change: it is here that conventionality and innovation find their measure.

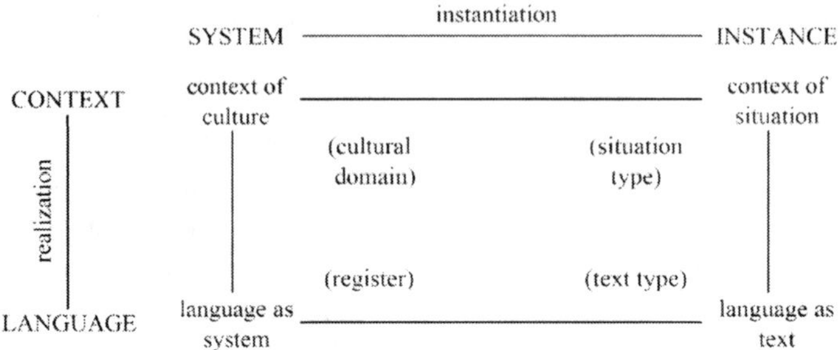

Note: Culture instantiated in situation, as system instantiated in text.

Culture realized in/construed by language; same relation as that holding between linguistic strata (semantics: lexicogrammar: phonology: phonetics).

Cultural domain and register are 'sub-systems': likeness viewed from 'system' end.

Situation type and text type are 'instance types': likeness viewed from 'instance' end.

Figure 6.3: Instantiation and realization relating language and context

6.4.2.1   Linguistic sign, context and social practice

The sign's signing function relies for its efficacy on the contexts of social activity: its status as a functional sign is confirmed only if it is active in some recognizable context. Thus, attention is paid to a road sign only if it is encountered in the proper context of driving; the same board showing the 'same sign' is not treated as 'a sign proper' *if found lying by the road-side*. A toddler, playing by his parents, ignores all linguistic signs passing between them; but as soon as the talk turns to, say, a visit to the zoo or the toyshop, the child will prick up his ears and attend to the linguistic signs more closely. So activities are central to sign use. Not all kinds of social activity are equally relevant to every member of the community: a selective sense of relevance develops in members of the community as they continue engaging in the range of social activities relevant to their patterns of life; people develop the ability to recognize the identity of types of social activity and the meanings appropriate to them simply by participating in acts of semiosis with other members of their speech fellowship (Firth, 1957; Bernstein, 1990).

Reflection on the last comment points to an exotic property of systems whose origin lies in communal life: 'would be' system users learn the systems only by using them with other members of the community. Consider, for example, the learning of the mother tongue: infants learn to speak by 'speaking' and 'being spoken to' by caregivers who know their mother tongue; their language develops by languaging even as the community's system of language evolves by being used. The linguistic sign system whose origin Saussure always located in the community is an extreme case of this kind. Above we discussed the inherent systemicity of linguistic sign: (sections 6.2 and 6.3 above) if the meaning of a particular linguistic sign lies in its relation to other signs, the same is true for the meaning of these *other* signs, and so on *ad infinitum*. This, in ordinary logic, implies that to 'know' *a* particular sign's meaning one must already know the *other* signs' meanings. If 'learning the mother tongue is learning how to mean' (Halliday, 1975), it should pose serious problems to the infant because of the hermetically sealed circle created by the inherently systemic nature of the linguistic sign system (Hasan, 1985a). How does the child break into this circle?

6.4.2.2   Learning the social semiotic of mother tongue in context

It was Malinowski (1923, 1935) who pointed to an answer: the key for entering the closed circle of meaning lies in the context of early child-adult interactions. Notably infants interact far less frequently with other infants than with their caregivers who are, by definition, acculturated adults: they use the language of the speech fellowship; they know its ways of being, saying and doing, i.e., its culture (Halliday, 1975, 2004; Hasan, 2005, 2009). The interactions occur most frequently in the material situational settings of everyday life; so the exchanges relate to the here and now; the sens-ible is foregrounded. In such contexts, the sign's SIGNIFICATION helps the child by referring directly to the world outside, thus opening the door to how the community means: *the context of interaction becomes the primary calibrator of meanings.*

The meanings the child learns thus are not the same as the adult's: they lack the power of systemic sign values. But parole is overwhelmingly systemic with reference *to* context; in everyday contexts of living, the meanings and the elements of everyday social activities are calibrated (Halliday *et al.*, 1964; Hasan, 1999, in press; Butt and Wegener, 2007). In this way, the sign-meaning introduced initially to the child through signification begins to turn systemic (Halliday, 1975, 2004; Painter, 1984; Torr, 1997).

6.4.2.3   From context to meaning to consciousness

Fascinating as the topic of mother tongue learning is, my concern here is with the general significance of that process: in Halliday's words (1980) it includes 'learning language, learning through language, learning about language'. For the child, learning the mother tongue is the way into internalizing his social universe: ways of being, doing and saying become routinized: nurture becomes 'second nature'. Now, *nurturing is a semiotic activity; it can only be achieved by using signs*: in the material world of 'real things', signs are the only 'meaningful things' capable of interpreting the world; and due to its *semiotic power*, language signs enter most areas of the internalized universe.[9] In and by this process, the physical brain is transformed into 'a personalised brain' (Edelman and Tononi, 2000; Greenfield, 2000; Damasio, 2010): *acculturated individual minds* with personalized forms of consciousness are created by semiosis in the community's cultural contexts; so nine-tenths of what is called 'cognition' is, in fact, the gift of parole. This is SFL theory's response to the so-called *Saussurean paradox of locating a psychological sign system in a social community*: to reiterate, in a community, an acculturated brain is not isolated; it is united by the means of intellection, developed communally in 'acts of meaning' (Halliday, 1993).

6.4.2.4 'Saussurean paradoxes' seen in context

Babies are not the only ones to interact in context. The adult contexts of talk vary more widely, each situation type hosting social practices regulated by the speakers' SOCIAL POSITIONING (Bernstein, 1990). Generalizing, speaking with reference to context is done systemically (Hasan, 1999), so that the semiotically developing child's language turns into the adult's 'ways of saying'.

Language active in social context implies a conjunction of doers (TENOR), doing (FIELD), and means of calibrating doer and doing (MODE). The specific features of these contextual parameters *vary systemically*, so in field, the sphere of social action may be *'quotidian'* or *'specialized'*; the tenor may be *'friendly'* or *'reserved'*; the mode may be *'spoken'* or *'written'*. Varying syndromes of such systemically valid contextual features constitute CONTEXTUAL CONFIGURATIONS (CC) which underlie specific varieties of REGISTERS and TEXT TYPES: on the one hand CC is relevant to the Generalized Structure Potential (GSP) of a register, and on the other, variation in the CC forms the basis of LINGUISTIC VARIATION ACCORDING TO USE. The second kind of variety is LINGUISTIC VARIATION ACCORDING TO USER; its distinguishing patterns are realized largely by features of the sign's signifier: in these varieties, known as ACCENT and SOCIAL DIALECT, the same meanings are exchanged but with distinct varieties of expression devices.[10] The distinctive contextual features correlating with these LECTAL VARIETIES pertain only to the tenor underlying the texts: they relate to certain user characteristics e.g. sex, age, age relation, and social and/or geographical location. The parole of socially highly significant groupings of users, in particular that according to social class, displays the linguistic variation known as SEMANTIC VARIATION (Cloran, 1994; Williams, 1995; Hasan, 2009): it is characterized by variation in SEMANTIC ORIENTATION.

The types of linguistic variation described here are common to *all états de langue*, which implies they inhere in language; to the extent that these inherent variation types are systemic, they would be 'in the *langue*' as studied in Saussure's synchronic linguistics. Ignoring variation would be acceptable only if it contributes nothing to the morphology of the sign system; this however is not the case (6.4.3.2 below). Further diachronic linguistic change is logically impossible without the simultaneous presence of innovation and large scale stability in chronolects. Establishing the systemicity of variation is SFL's response to the *Saussurean paradox of recognizing états de langue while treating linguistic variation as external to the linguistics of* langue.

The SFL theoretical framework has introduced a systematic account of TEXTURE and STRUCTURE in individual texts and text types, identifying the contextually regulated semantic structuring of texts in the three kinds of linguistic varieties mentioned above (Halliday, 1974; Hasan, 1984, 1985b). Frames have been produced for analysis demonstrating the systemic regularities of parole in everyday discourse (e.g. Cloran, 1994; Williams, 1995; Eggins and Slade, 1997; Hasan, 2009) as well as in specialist interactions in official pedagogy (e.g. Halliday and Martin, 1993; Williams, 1995; Martin and Veel, 1998; Christie and Martin, 2007; Christie and Maton, 2011). This theorization of the social context supports the claim that *parole is systemic;* it helps also in identifying linguistic varieties as a site for the evolution of sign meanings: *social context is not only integral to the growth of the mind but also to the growth and circulation of 'the interplay of signs'* (6.4.3, below).

Halliday (1973, 1979) suggests that the three parameters of the contexts of social practice leave their traces on the FUNCTIONAL-FORMAL ORGANIZATION of sign morphology: language is adaptively related to the classification of meanings by social parameters of activities, and so to the lexicogrammar due to the 'natural' relations of meaning and wording: this makes language METAFUNCTIONAL. If these claims are true, then obviously context cannot be ignored in the analysis of sign morphology.

The non-randomness of *parole* is evident from this account. The systemicity of context and semantics may differ from that of syntax and phonology; but to say that in parole the speaker is 'the master' is not only to underplay the power of cultural contexts, it is in fact to undermine the possibility of establishing a *conventional* relation between the signified and the signifier. Conventionality, an important concept in Saussure, requires regularity, and the measure of regularity is in the signs' systemic relation to contexts of talk. Without such regularities 'phonic shapes' such as 'appropriate' and 'relevant' would go begging for their meaning. With such a theorized context, when we claim that engagement in the use of linguistic signs is voluntary, it is with the understanding that the speaker, in all the uniqueness of his individuality, still works with a brain personalized by cultural experience; so this brain is as 'au fait' with language as it is with the contexts of social activities: the speaker would know when not/speaking is a viable option (Hasan, 1989). *Speaking is not simply a semiotic act*; it is also *social*: Saussure saw language system as a *semiotic* object, but to work in the community's life, the system *has* to be a *social-semiotic*.

6.4.3 The interplay of signs: developing descriptive categories

Turning to the second major issue, according to my reading, for Saussure meaning is the essence of the linguistic sign: systemicity counteracts the arbitrary relation of the signified and signifier; it generates 'value' and identity, while templates in language clearly depend on systemicity. So the concern will be with identifying the internal resources in language for establishing the signs' values. But before exploring this, a warning about the meaning of terminology is needed: some of the linguistic terms in use today are signalled by the same 'vocal forms' as used in Saussure's time but with significantly different meanings. For example, Saussure's (1966, 2006) term 'psychological' does not mean 'innate' or 'hard-wired', but 'internalized' and/or 'intellig-ible'. Similarly, the word 'form' does not refer to syntactic form as today, but to a *bona-fide* 'signifier'; his 'morphology of sign meaning' is pretty much the same as 'the lexicogrammatical realization of meaning' in SFL. And some time his usage may be inconsistent (6.4.3.2, below). This may be due to translation problems or because one is reading notes Saussure made only for himself. Sometimes confusions occur because Saussure 'has no words' for referring to some category or relation: in other words, theorization of some category or relation may not have been completed.

6.4.3.1 Morphology: The interplay of signs that is *langue*
For Saussure 'morphology' was concerned with explaining the mechanisms for realizing the sign's meaning; thus 'The real name of morphology should be: the theory of signs and not forms' (2006: 123); 'form' here equals 'the sign's expression'. The aim of his projected linguistics was to explain both the sign's meaning and its systemicity by the concept of morphology):

> The study of language as a system, in other words of its morphology, comes down either to the study of *use of forms*, or the study of *representation of ideas*. It is wrong to believe that there may be *forms* (existing in themselves, independently of their *use*) or *ideas* (existing in themselves, independently of their *representation*).

> A form without a use is a *vocal figure*: a physiological, acous-
> tic notion. Moreover this gives rise to an immediate contradiction,
> since there are many *forms* that are identical in terms of sound,
> though no one would dream of associating them. That is the best
> proof of the complete absurdity of an entity *form* divorced from its
> use. (Saussure, 2006: 15, *emphasis original*, RH)

So if there is a vocal figure that is not associated with some meaning it is simply a 'phonic' event, not a 'form'; and since it is not a sign, it cannot be treated as internal to the linguistics of *langue*.

Saussure offers the syntagmatic and associative relations of signs as the means of establishing the identity and value of particular signs (6.2.2–6.2.3 for discussion). He suggested that (a) there are systematic aspects of the syntagm which always display regularity (i.e., those we know as 'syntactic structure' today); they owe much to the sign's inherent systemicity; yet he maintained also that (b) syntagms carry other regularities than just that of syntax: thus (1966: 123, footnote 5; *emphasis introduced*, RH) 'It is scarcely necessary to point out that the study of syntagms is not to be confused with syntax. *Syntax is only one part of the study of syntagms*'. In other words, there is more to syntagm than syntax; other forms of syntagmatic continuity exist. What Halliday and Hasan (1976) referred to as the texture and structure of text types are two attested examples of such regular patterns of continuity in the syntagm; other strong candidates are RST patterns (e.g. Mann *et al.*, 1992) and rhetorical units (e.g. Cloran, 1994), and phasal analysis (Gregory, 2002). Saussure had reservations against the popular definitions of such terms as syntax, morphology, lexicology as used among his contemporaries, which still continue to be used in formalistic linguistics. Discussing the various 'sub-disciplines' recognized in his contemporary linguistics, he commented:

> the distinctions were illusory. ... Form and function are interde-
> pendent, and it is difficult, if not impossible, to separate them.
> Linguistically, morphology has no real, autonomous object. It
> (i.e., 'morphology as the study of declensions' RH) cannot form
> a distinct discipline from syntax. ... it is not logical to exclude
> lexicology from grammar. ... we notice at once that innumerable
> relations may be expressed as efficiently by words (i.e., lexeme/
> lexical item. RH) as by grammar. (Saussure, 1966: 135)

These Saussurean views on the 'science of linguistics' would perhaps be just as unpopular today in linguistics as they were in his times except for SFL, which has rejected the separation of lexicon and syntax by reconceptualizing the two in the unity of lexicogrammar. SFL is in fact quite close to Saussure's ideas about the essentials of how meaning and lexicogrammar should be studied in his linguistics. So in discussing the second issue the concern is more with the elaboration of his ideas, not so much with departures or extensions, except in the introduction of concepts that assist the study of sign morphology.

6.4.3.2   On realization across linguistic strata

The arbitrary relation in the sign is crucial to its make up and so to the description of *langue* as a whole; thus, SFL views stratification in multiple steps (Figure 6.2; section 6.4.1 above), the primary being the line of arbitrariness stratifying the signified and the signifier. The secondary step applies to each of these primary strata: the signified is stratified as (i) 'idea/ meaning' and (ii) 'meaning morphology', the signifier as (i) sound image and (ii) sound unit. These four strata are viewed as the *language internal* strata, each stratum representing a distinct order of abstraction, each with a unique concern and function, compared to the others. Together these two pairs of strata on either side of the line of arbitrariness provide the necessary and sufficient resources for the description of language as a semiotic system: *in principle, the sign system is analysable in its entirety*, and this is clearly necessary for the model's appliability.

As argued above (sections 6.4.2.1–6.4.2.4), a viable explanatory theory of the sign system must recognize the context of culture and situation; on this ground, with a third step in stratification, context forms the fifth stratum in the SFL theory, which, unlike the other four, is language-external: it acts as the environment for the language-internal strata and brings the linguistic system into relation with the community of its users. Figure 6.4 represents these relations.

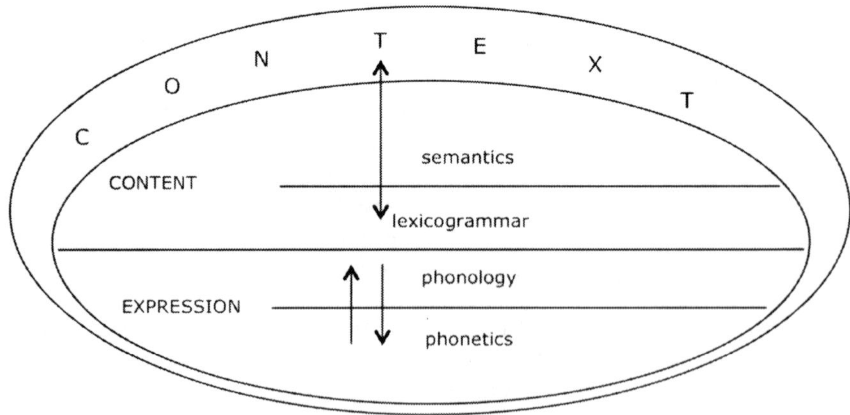

Figure 6.4: Language as a Social Semiotic System (Source: Hasan, 2012: 255)

SFL treats the five strata in Figure 6.4 as realizationally related: context of situation is realized as the largest semantic unit, text, which is realized as some lexicogrammatical unit(s), which is realized as some phonological unit(s), which is realized as some phonetic unit(s). In the normal course, a sign, no matter how big or small, is produced only with all strata working together; and, conversely, an analysis of the internal make up of the sign functioning in community should present the same five strata as necessary and sufficient to the description of language. This is a highly ambitious goal, in my knowledge, so far not achieved by any model.

6.4.3.3 The lexicogrammatical realization of meaning: Construing value
The nearest we come to a representation of the interplay of signs in Saussure is in the discussions of specific examples, i.e., instances of the category word/morpheme, as for example, in offering the associative bonds of 'enseignement' in Figure 6.5.

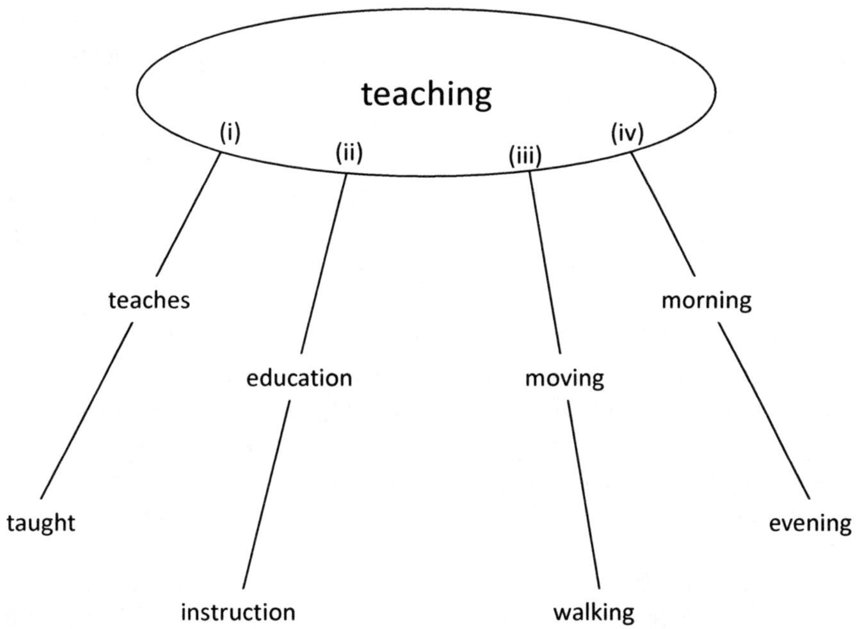

Figure 6.5: Associative bonds (adapted from Saussure, 1966: 126)

The English version retains the same four Saussurean distinctions. Saussure's comment (1966: 126) on his own diagram was: 'a particular word is like the centre of a constellation; it is the point of convergence of an indefinite number of co-ordinated terms.'

By contrast with Figure 6.5, SFL follows a more abstract route: it does not offer the description of single isolated signs, but begins its descriptive work from the concept of UNIT. Each unit at any language-internal stratum may function as the POINT OF ORIGIN for a SYSTEM NETWORK of FEATURES, the calibrated CHOICES of which provide a series of descriptions. The systemic description of every single sign of the language, in theory, demands a visit to every stratum in Figure 6.4. The system at issue pertains to some category not to an instance: thus there is no system network of 'eat' or 'love'; but there is a system network of the unit VERB which belongs to the VERBAL GROUP at the lexicogrammatical stratum. What these descriptions identify are templates for specific 'unit-types'. The working of the system networks and concepts associated with it have been discussed (in many places, e.g. Halliday and Matthiessen, 2004; Matthiessen, 2007; Halliday, 2009; Halliday and Webster, 2009; Hasan, 2009).

The description of the sign is thus dispersed into system networks across the entire linguistic system. Using this information each 'line of description' in Figure 6.5 can be located more precisely: thus, moving from left to right, for (i) in Figure 6.5, assume *teaching* is semantically a process, so time is relevant, the latter is lexicogrammatically realized as some tense, whose phonological realization is conditioned by (a) tense choice, and (b) the choice of number in the noun at Subject *if* primary tense is simple present; for (ii) assume semantically *teaching* is an activity; lexicogrammatically realized as nominalization functioning as Thing/Head in nominal group, whose phonological realization takes the form 'verb'+tion; for (iii) assume semantically *teaching* is again an activity, realized lexicogrammatically as nominalization functioning as Thing/Head in nominal group, the phonological realization taking the form 'verb'+ing; (implying —tion and —ing belong to the same class of lexicogrammatical unit, members of which occur under distinct conditions); and finally for (iv) by-pass semantic, grammatical description; assume all signs ending in the phonological form '—'+ing related by 'rhyming'.

Saussure sometimes highlights the 'difference' between signs as most important to their identity/value, and sometimes it is the similarities that are said to bring them together, as in Figure 6.5. SFL systemic description simultaneously tracks a sign's difference and similarities in relation to other signs in the language through the systemic features the relations of which count as a systemic description. Descriptions in SFL can vary in delicacy; the least delicate description is in terms of constituency; the most delicate grammatical system network is capable of describing units of lexis (Hasan, 1987; Tucker, 1998).

SFL descriptions of this kind for a substantial part of a language have not been produced, but (i) in theory the potential of such description is present in SFL: the sign in its entirety can be analysed; and (ii) the analyses of actual uses of language carried out up to certain degrees of delicacy have supported the belief that such descriptions are helpful in revealing the meanings of the texts (Halliday and Matthiessen, 1999; Hasan, 2009).

6.4.3.4 Morphology, templates and parole

Saussure made modern linguistics aware of the peculiar logic whereby the linguistic sign maintains itself in the communicative act by defying the logic of the logicians. So it is not clear why he insists on 'the morphology of meaning' as essential to the linguistics of *langue*, while at the same time treating parole as external to that discipline. In the absence of evidence from parole, the morphology of meaning could only make one simple statement: the meaning of a sign is produced by the sign's relation to other signs, because it could have no evidence of any relations except through parole. Clearly there can be no interplay of signs without parole: the linguistics of *langue* is impossible without treating parole as logically related to *langue* and therefore part of the science of linguistics.

Then, consider also the regularities in syntagm other than those attributable to syntax/structure: in SFL, the structure is 'built up' on the basis of realizational statements of systemic features; there is no descriptive value to a claim that at the stratum of semantics there is a type of question, whose underlying selection expression is (Hasan, 2009, 2013):

'demand;information:confirm:verify:reassure'

unless the claim can be backed up by stating: (i) what unit at the lexicogrammatical stratum is the point of origin for the system whose features realize these semantic features; (ii) what part of the lexicogrammar of that unit is relevant to realizational features; and (iii) how the selected features are realized as a structure. Without going into details (Hasan, 2009), the unit clause is the point of origin for the network whose features would realize the above selection expression; the relevant part in the lexicogrammar of the clause will be in MOOD; the realizing features of the clause:

declarative:tagged:reversed:negative

and the actual elements of the MOOD structure of the clause critical to its realization may be stated as follows:

Subject^Finite;positive polarity^Predicator ... Finite; negative polarity^Subject

An instance of this clause type would be: *you like dad, don't you?* where the elements critical to realization are highlighted in bold.

Selection expressions from a given system network specify a structure that Saussure would have called a templates: not the structure of just one instance, but rather the structure of every member of that class.

6.5   Conclusion: Appliable linguistic theory and the description of the sign

I began with the hypothesis that a valid conceptualization of the sign is 'the first principle' on which an appliable linguistics can be built by taking the sign's description to its logical end. SFL has adopted Saussure's widely accepted view of the sign, and in developing the sign's theorized description it has needed to widen the scope beyond Saussure's concept of the linguistics of *langue*. The most important moves in further theorizing some Saussurean concepts and relations are:

- Stratification as the relation between signified/signifier extended to language as a whole, entailing recognition of realizational relation across strata;
- Revealing the systemicity of parole by theorizing relations of community and *langue*, leading to identification of the basis of linguistic varieties;
- Relating systemic description to categories rather than to instances, leading to a systemic description potentially capable of identifying 'everything that is systemic in language'.

The strength of parole lies in its relation to the life of speakers doing ordinary things in ordinary ways. Much of sections 6.3 and 6.4 has insisted that the principles of its regularities argue for the recognition of parole. The mastery of syntax and lexicon is a necessary condition for speaking, but relevant speaking is impossible without the knowledge gained from using language in the day to day contexts of communal life.

Linguistic meanings intercede at every point in the living of life, but meanings in relation to each other are only encountered in parole, and best described by reference to the regularities of language use. Descriptions yielded by the use of scientific linguistics need to be validated: the reliability of the categories of the theory of linguistics needs to be established. In the absence of this, claims about the scientific status of linguistics is without basis. To accomplish this validation of the model the linguists' descriptions have to be matched with the patterns of the community's behaviour: there has to be a renewal of connection between the abstract principles and the real instances. The theorization of register and the description of the instances of the many registers, including the analysis of the text's texture and structure, can certainly be validated by reference to communal semiotic practices.

The development of linguistics to the point where it can produce linguistic descriptions of registerial categories, as SFL has done, would play an important role both in establishing the validity of the analysis and in increasing the resources of an appliable linguistic model. It is social practices of different kinds that act as the environment for the application of linguistics: this expertise will be in demand only if it can offer viable ways of describing 'how language works' (Halliday, 1964), for this is what opens the door to solving problems with their origin in linguistic semiosis. When a model is able to describe on a substantial scale the language used in many different classes of social activities, then it has become appliable: appliable linguistics is not dedicated to some particular problem; it should be capable of being used to help solve any problem that implicates language in any social activity.

I hope I have given some evidence of this ability arising from pursuing the study of a viable conception of the sign such as Saussure's to its logical end. I am suggesting this is the secret of the appliability of linguistic theories such as SFL.

Appendix A: domains of SFL applications

DOMAINS:	FOCI:
Education	Teaching mother tongue Teaching other tongues Language across the curriculum Classroom interaction: kindergarten; primary; secondary Classroom genres: primary, secondary Text books: primary; secondary Grammar pedagogy: primary; secondary Language assessment Academic discourse Multi-literacies
Knowledge production	Language of physical sciences Language of history Language of geography Language in mathematics Language in teaching language Language in verbal art Language in 'children's literature' Language based learning

Law	Language of legislature Language of court room interrogation Language of judgement
Politico-economic systems	Language and ideology Language and the market Language and politico-economic discourse Language of advertisement
Sociology	Code theory and semantic variation Social structure and language varieties Cultural knowledge and contextual construct Language and the sociology of pedagogy
Psychology	Linguistic interaction and formation of consciousness Semiotic mediation and socio-semantic variation
Language disorder	Aphasia: assessment, description, therapy Alzheimer's: description of language Schizophrenia: description of language Autism: assessment, description, therapy
Health and medicine	Doctor nurse interaction Doctor patient interaction Nurse patient interaction Patient's journey through the health care system
Language contact	Translation & interpretation
Alternative semiotic systems	Mathematics as a semiotic system Visual arts and images as a semiotic system Music (aural art) as a semiotic system Dance as a semiotic system Multi-semiotic analysis of discourse
Human animal interaction	Bonobo interaction with human users of 'English'
Pedagogic practices: private agents (based in cultural information circulation systems)	Language of tourism Language in the museum Language of recipes Language of religions
Pedagogic practices: private agents (based in circulation of information via Media Systems)	Reporting news: spoken (radio); written; televised Editorials Letter to editors Letter to 'Agony Aunts'
Pedagogic practices: private agents (based in everyday interactions)	Language in face to face commercial exchange Dinner time conversations Conversation analysis Mother-child interactions Mother-child book-reading at home
Computing	Multilingual analysis Text generation Software: representing analysis

Notes

1. This chapter is a distant relative of a plenary at the 10th Chinese National Conference of Functional Linguistics at Xiangxi Normal University, 2007. My thanks are due to Halliday for his comments on an earlier draft.
2. Two other declared varieties of SFL are (i) Martin's (e.g., 1992) genre based modelling of language; and (ii) Fawcett's (e.g., 2000) theory of systemic functional syntax. Both rely in many important aspects on Halliday's SFL, but diverge at some points, critical enough to the debate here. In this chapter read SFL as Halliday's SFL.
3. Prague School Linguistics has been applied, among other things, to the study of linguistic variation, translation, functionalism, and stylistics.
4. 'Semiology' has lost its currency today; it is now replaced by 'semiotics' following the philosopher, Peirce (e.g., 1955).
5. During the transition from proto-language to mother-tongue, Nigel invented as do other small children, some 'linguistic signs', such as 'quoise' for a particular shape, 'go-getti-go' for the shape of a Rugby ball; but hardly any such signs get transported into the mother tongue: they lack the communal support i.e., conventionality.
6. The term realization was used by Hjelmslev (1961: 40), who mentions other solidary relations, only some of which may be treated as realizational. The use of the term in SFL while at first in keeping with Hjelmslev's definition, has now been further elaborated (Hasan 2009; 2010) which distances it from Hjelmslev term.
7. Cultures are realized multi-semiotically; language is only one semiotic systems amongst the others. However, the semiotic power of language means it is the most pervasive.
8. For a discussion see Hasan (2009; 2012). For further discussion of language/ parole see Matthiessen (2007); Halliday (2008; 2009). For realization and instantiation as theoretical concepts; for context, register and text see Hasan (1999; in press); Butt (2009); Butt and Wegener (2007).
9. This is not to deny the efficacy of non-linguistic experience in the development of 'mind'; however the externalization of experience does imply the mediation of language (Hasan 2011).
10. Social dialects differ in accent as well as certain variant lexicogrammatical features e.g., the in/famous use of 'not' and concord (cf. copula deletion). Neither variety makes any difference to the meaning they 'give'; they however 'give off meaning' due to the association of the expression with a particular user groups. This latter is closest to Labov's sense of 'social meaning'.

References

Aarsleff, H. (1982) *From Locke to Saussure: Essays on the Study of Language and Intellectual History*. Minneapolis, MI: University of Minnesota Press.

Bernstein, B. (1990) Codes, modalities and the process of cultural reproduction: a model. In B. Bernstein (ed.) *The Structuring of Pedagogic Discourse, Volume IV: Class, Codes and Control*. London: Routledge.

Butt, D. G. (2009) The robustness of realizational systems. In J. J. Webster (ed.) *Meaning in Context: Implementing Intelligent Applications of Language Studies*. London: Continuum.

Butt, D. G. and Wegener, R. (2007) The work of concepts: Context and metafunction in the systemic functional model. In R. Hasan, C. M. I. M. Matthiessen and J. J. Webster (eds) *Continuing Discourse on Language: A Functional Perspective Volume 2*. London: Equinox.

Christie, F. and Martin, J. R. (2007) (eds) *Language, Knowledge and Pedagogy: Functional Linguistics and Sociological Perspectives*. London: Continuum.

Christie, F. and Maton, K. (2011) *Disciplinarity: Functional Linguistics and Sociological Perspectives*. London: Continuum.

Cloran, C. (1994) *Rhetorical Unit and Decontextualisation: An Enquiry into Some Relations of Context, Meaning and Grammar. Monographs on Systemic Linguistics 6*. Nottingham: Department of English, Nottingham University.

Damasio, A. (2010) *Self Comes to Mind: Constructing the Conscious Brain*. London: Heinemann.

Edelman, G. M. and Tononi, G. (2000) *Consciousness: How Matter Becomes Imagination*. London: Penguin.

Eggins, S. and Slade. D. (1997) *Analysing Casual Conversation*. London: Cassell.

Fawcett, R. P. (2000) *A Theory of Syntax for Systemic Functional Linguistics*. Amsterdam: Benjamins.

Firth, J. R. (1957) *Papers in Linguistics 1934–1951*. London: Oxford University Press.

Ghadessy, M. (1999) (ed.) *Text and Context in Functional Linguistics*. Amsterdam: Benjamins.

Goody, J. (1968) *Literacy in Traditional Society*. Cambridge. England: Cambridge University Press.

Goody, J. (1977) *The Domestication of the Savage Mind*. Cambridge: Cambridge University Press.

Greenfield, S. (2000) *The Private Life of the Brain*. London: Penguin.

Gregory, M. (2002) Phasal analysis within communication linguistics: Two contrastive discourses. In P. H. Fries, M. Cummings, D. Lockwood and W. Spruiell (eds) *Relations and Functions Within and Around Language*. London: Continuum.

Halliday, M. A. K. (1960) *General Linguistics and its Application to Language Teaching. Etudes de Linguistique Appliqué Vol. 1*. (reprinted in A. McIntosh and M. A. K. Halliday, *Patterns of Language*. London: Longman. 1966; reprinted in C. W. Halliday, Volume 9: 2007)

Halliday, M. A. K. (1961) Categories of the theory of grammar. *Word* 17 (3): 241–292. (Reprinted in C. W. Halliday, Volume 1: 2002.)

Halliday, M. A. K. (1963) Class in relation to the axes of chain and choice. *Linguistics* 2: 5–15. (Reprinted in C. W. Halliday, Volume 1: 2002)

Halliday, M. A. K. (1973) *Explorations in the Functions of Language*. London: Arnold.

Halliday, M. A. K. (1974) Language as social semiotic: Towards a general sociolinguistic theory'. In A. Makkai and V. B. Makkai (eds.), *The First LACUS Forum*. Columbia, S.C.: Hornbeam Press.

Halliday, M. A. K. (1975) *Learning How to Mean*. London: Arnold. (Reprinted in C. W. Halliday, Volume 4: 2004.)

Halliday, M. A. K. (1979) Modes of meaning and modes of expression: types of grammatical structures and their determination by different semantic function. In D. G. Allerton, E. Carney and D. Holdcroft (eds.), *Function and Context in Linguistic Analysis: Essays Offered to William Hass*. Cambridge: Cambridge University Press.

Halliday, M. A. K. (1980) Three aspects of children's language development: Learning language, learning through language, learning about language. In Y. M. Goodman, M. M. Haussler and D. Strickland (eds) *Oral and Written Language Development: Impact on Schools: Proceedings from the 1979 & 1980 IMPACT conferences*. Newark, DE: International Reading Association. (Reprinted in C. W. Halliday Volume 4. 2003.)

Halliday M. A. K. (1985) *Introduction to Functional Grammar*. 1st edition. London: Arnold .

Halliday, M. A. K. (1992) How do you mean? In M. Davis and L. Ravelli (eds) *Recent Developments in Systemic Functional Theory*. London: Pinter. (Reprinted in C. W. Halliday, Volume 1: 2002.)

Halliday, M. A. K. (1993) The act of meaning. In J. E. Alatis (ed.) *Language, Communication and Social Meaning*. Georgetown University Round Table on Language and Linguistics 1992. Washington, DC: Georgetown University Press. (Reprinted in C. W. Halliday, Volume 3: 2003.)

Halliday, M. A. K. (1999). The notion of 'context' in language education. In M. Ghadessy (ed.) *Text and Context in Functional Linguistics*. Amsterdam: Benjamins.

Halliday, M. A. K. (2002–2007) *The Collected Works of M. A. K. Halliday, Volumes 1–10*, J. J. Webster (ed.) London: Continuum. [entries as C. W. Halliday, Volumes 1–10, 2002–2007]

Halliday, M. A. K. (2004) *The Collected Works of M. A. K. Halliday, Volume 4: The Language of Early Childhood*, edited by J. J. Webster. London: Continuum.

Halliday, M. A. K. (2005) On matter and meaning: The two realms of human experience. *Linguistics and the Human Sciences* 1 (1): 59–82.

Halliday, M. A. K. (2008) *Complementarities in Language*. Beijing: The Commercial Press.

Halliday, M. A. K. (2009) Methods – techniques – problems. In M. A. K. Halliday and J. J. Webster (eds) *Continuum Companion to Systemic Functional Linguistics*. London: Continuum.

Halliday, M. A. K. and Hasan, R. (1976) *Cohesion in English*. London: Longman.

Halliday, M. A. K., A. McIntosh, and P. Strevens (1964) *Linguistic Sciences and Language Teaching*. London: Longmans.

Halliday, M. A. K. and Martin, J. R. (1993) *Writing Science: Literacy and Discursive Power*. London: Falmer Press.

Halliday, M. A. K. and Matthiessen, C. M. I. M. (1999) *Construing Experience Through Meaning: A Language-Based Approach to Cognition*. London: Continuum.

Halliday M. A. K. and Matthiessen, C. M. I. M. (2004) *An Introduction to Functional Grammar* (3rd edition). London: Arnold.

Halliday, M. A. K. and Webster J. J. (2009) (eds) *Continuum Companion to Systemic Functional Linguistics*. London: Continuum.

Hasan, R. (1984) Coherence and cohesive harmony. In J. Flood (ed.) *Understanding Reading Comprehension*. Newark, DE: International Reading Association.

Hasan, R. (1985a) Meaning, context and text – fifty years after Malinowski. In J. D. Benson and W. S. Greaves (eds) *Systemic Perspectives on Discourse Volume 1*. Norwood, NJ: Ablex.

Hasan, R. (1985b). Language, Context and Text: Aspects of Language in a Social-Semiotic Perspective, Part B. Geelong, Victoria: Deakin University Press.

Hasan, R. (1987). The grammarian's dream: Lexis as most delicate grammar. In M. A. K. Halliday and R. P. Fawcett (eds) *New Developments in Systemic Functional Linguistics, Volume 1: Theory and Description*. London: Pinter.

Hasan, R. (1989) The disempowerment game: Bourdieu on language in literacy. *Linguistics and Education*, 10 (1): 25–80. Reprinted in J. J. Webster (ed.) *The Collected Works of Ruqaiya Hasan, Vol 1: Language, Society and Consciousness*. London: Equinox.

Hasan, R. (1999) Speaking with reference to context. In M. Ghadessy (ed.) *Text and Context in Functional Linguistics*. Amsterdam: Benjamins.

Hasan, R. (2005) *The Collected Works of Ruqaiya Hasan, Vol 1: Language, Society and Consciousness* (ed.) J. J. Webster. London: Equinox.

Hasan, R. (2009) *The Collected Works of Ruqaiya Hasan, Vol 2: Semantic Variation: Meaning in Society and in Sociolinguistics* (ed.) J. J. Webster. London: Equinox.

Hasan, R. (2010) The meaning of 'not' is not in 'not'. In A. Mahboob and Na. Knight (eds.), *Appliable Linguistics*. London: Continuum.

Hasan, R. (2011) On the process of teaching: a perspective from functional grammar. In *Language and Education: Learning and Teaching in Society: The Collected Works of Ruqaiya Hasan, Volume 3*, edited by Jonathan J Webster. London: Equinox.

Hasan, R. (2012). A view of pragmatics in a social semiotic perspective. *Linguistics and the Human Sciences* 5 (3): 251–271.

Hasan, R. (in press) *The Collected Works of Ruqaiya Hasan, Vol 4: Context in the System and Process of Language* (ed,) J. J. Webster. London: Equinox.

Hasan, R. (2013). Choice, system, realization: describing language as meaning potential. To appear in L. Fontaine, T. Bartlett and G. O'Grady (eds) *Systemic Functional Linguistics: Exploring Choice*. Cambridge: Cambridge University Press.

Hasan, R., Matthiessen, C. M. I. M. and Webster, J. J. (eds) (2005) *Continuing Discourse with Language: A Functional Perspective Volume 1*. London: Equinox.

Hasan, R., Matthiessen, C. M. I. M. and Webster, J. J. (eds) (2007) *Continuing Discourse on Language: A Functional Perspective Volume 2*. London: Equinox.

Hjelmslev, L. (1961) *Prolegomena to a Theory of Language* (F. J. Whitfield trans.) Bloomington, IN: Indiana University Press.

Malinowski, B. (1923) The problem of meaning in primitive languages: Supplement 1. In C. K. Ogden and I. A. Richards (eds) *The Meaning of Meaning*. London: Kegan Paul.

Malinowski, B. (1935) An ethnographic theory of language. In B. Malinowski, *Coral Gardens and Their Magic, Volume 2 Part IV*. London: Allen & Unwin.

Mann, W. C., Matthiessen, C. M. I. M. and Thompson, S. A. (eds) (1992) Rhetorical structure theory and context analysis. In W. C. Mann and S. A. Thompson (eds) *Discourse Descriptions: Diverse Linguistic Analyses of a Fund-Raising Text*. Amsterdam: Benjamins.

Martin, J. R. (1992) *English Text: System and Structure*. Amsterdam: Benjamins.

Martin, J. R. and Veel, R. (1998) (eds) *Reading Science: Critical and Functional Perspectives on Discourse of Science*. London: Routledge.

Matthiessen, C. M. I. M. (2007) The architecture of language according to systemic functional theory: developments since the 1970s. In R. Hasan, C. M. I. M. Matthiessen and J. J. Webster (eds) *Continuing Discourse on Language: A Functional Perspective, Volume 2*. London: Equinox.

Painter, C. (1984) *Into the Mother Tongue: A Case Study in early Language Development*. London: Pinter.

Peirce, C. S. (1955) *Philosophical Writings of Peirce*, selected and edited by J. Buchler. New York: Dover Publications, Inc.

de Saussure, F. (1966) *Course in General Linguistics* (W. Baskin trans.). Glasgow: Fontana.

de Saussure, F. (2206) *Writings in General Linguistics* (eds) S. Bouquet and R. Engler (C. Sanders and M. Piers trans.). Oxford: Oxford University Press.

Torr, J. (1997) From Child Tongue to Mother Tongue. *Monographs in Systemic Functional Linguistics*, No. 9. Department of English Studies: Nottingham University.

Tucker, G. H. (1998) *The Lexicogrammar of Adjectives: A Systemic Functional Approach to Lexis*. London: Cassell.

Webster, J. J. (2009) (ed.) *Meaning in Context: Implementing Intelligent Applications of Language Studies*. London: Continuum.

Williams, G. (1995). Joint Book-Reading and Literacy Pedagogy: a Socio-Semantic Interpretation. Doctoral dissertation. Sydney: Department of Linguistics, Macquarie University.

Wittgenstein, L. (1953) *Philosophical Investigations*. Oxford: Blackwell.

7 Appliable Discourse Analysis

Christian M. I. M. Matthiessen[*]

7.1 Appliable linguistics, appliable discourse analysis

There is general agreement that linguistics is the scientific study of language; in Wikipedia, it is characterized as 'the scientific study of human language'.[1] However, there is as yet no consensus about what actually constitutes the – or even a – scientific study of language and there is also as yet no agreement about the nature of language (see e.g. Halliday, 1977, and Seuren, 1998, on two currents running through the history of scholarly thinking about language – language as resource/ecologists vs. language as rule/formalists): linguists differ in their views about the nature of data, of methodology, and of theory; and they also differ in their views regarding the relationship between data and theory, between description and theory, and between theory and application.

In the second half of the twentieth century, **theoretical linguistics** and **applied linguistics** tended to be pushed quite far apart; they have often been pursued by fairly distinct communities of scholars and students, and, in universities, they have often been institutionalized as different disciplines within different departments. My own experience after my undergraduate studies at Lund University was of the situation at UCLA: by the mid-1980s, linguistics and applied linguistics had drifted quite far apart, operating as separate departments. After a long rich foundational period of broad-based linguistics, the Department of Linguistics increasingly became a kind of 'MIT West'; by the mid- to late 1980s, linguists who had pioneered other theoretical approaches to language had left for UC Santa Barbara or the University or Oregon, and, by the turn of the century, founding and pioneering members representing the broad foundation had retired or passed away. Thus linguistics at UCLA came to mean the study of the 'sentence' and units below in formal terms; the study of text in context and areas of

* Christian Matthiessen is affiliated to ENGL, PolySystemic Research Group, FH, PolyU.

activity crucially dependent on this kind of conception of language were the concern of the department of applied linguistics. Variations of this theme of the opposition between linguistics and applied linguistics have been played out around the world in the last few decades. The channels of publications of linguistics and applied linguistics, including journals and book series, and their conferences also tend to be distinct. In this way, they have come to be treated as a thesis and antithesis pair in the scholarly engagement with language. However, there is a possible synthesis position of the kind proposed by Halliday (e.g. 2007; cf. also 1964): see Figure 7.1. The synthesis is **appliable linguistics** – a conception of linguistics where theory and application remain in constant dialogue as related phases of the ongoing scientific engagement with language. Theory is developed to support application; and application is a way of testing theory (as has long been the case in different branches of engineering in relation to theories produced by sciences of the material world).

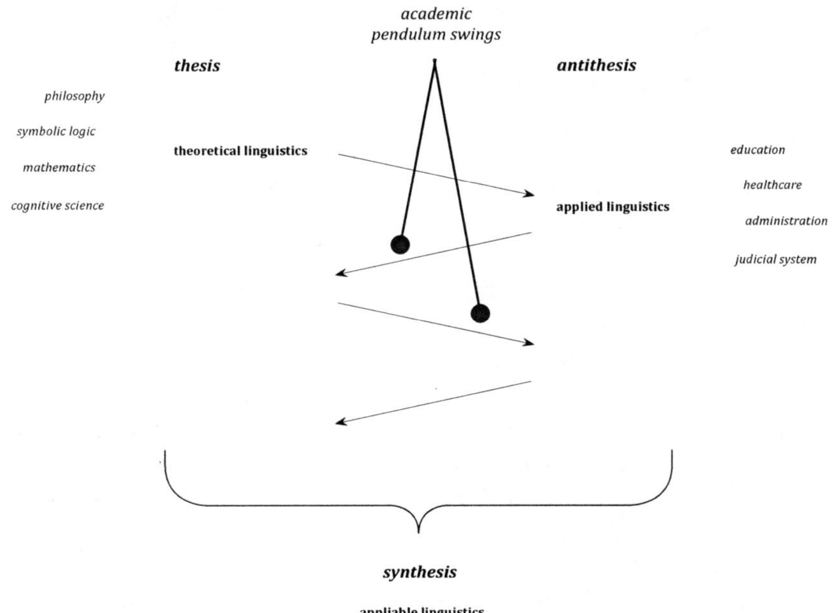

Figure 7.1: Appliable linguistics as a synthesis of theoretical linguistics and applied linguistics – a kind of linguistics whose theories can be applied (i.e. have the potential to be applied).

One type of appliable linguistics is Halliday's own **Systemic Functional Linguistics** (SFL; for recent overviews, see e.g. Hasan *et al.*, 2005, 2007;

Halliday and Webster, 2009; Matthiessen *et al.*, 2010). His approach to the scientific study of language is grounded in data and empowered by theory, and theory is in constant dialogue with application. Like any other type of appliable linguistics, SFL has the ***potential to be applied***; this potential may or may not be taken up in a given context, but it has been built into the 'architecture' of SFL. As a special case of appliable linguistics, we can speak of **appliable discourse analysis** (ADA) – the potential to apply discourse analysis to problems addressed in different contexts of research and development.

Analysis is one of the key scientific activities in linguistics, together with the activities of **description, comparison** and **theorizing**. These activities can be placed in a hierarchy of activities involving increasingly more demanding tasks, ranging from analysis to theory: see Figure 7.2.

Analysis is always the analysis of *instances* of language – of **texts (discourses)** in their contexts of situation; but it involves a move up **the cline of instantiation** (see e.g. Halliday, 1991; Matthiessen, 1993), from instances to descriptions of systems located at some point higher up the cline: in analysis, we match patterns that we can detect in instances to specifications of recurrent patterns in the description of the system, as illustrated in Figure 7.3. Naturally, analysis can be very demanding and involve considerable challenges; but the analytic challenges we face are in principle restricted to be the particular instances that we are concerned with in our analysis.

In contrast, **description** is focused not on instances but rather on regions higher up the cline of instantiation; the goal of the process of description is to produce descriptions (accounts) of *systems* – either of the overall system of a language in context, or of subsystems located midrange along the cline of instantiation. While analysis deals with instances, description thus deals with potential – with the potential instantiated by instances. Description therefore has to cover much more semiotic ground than analysis: since systemic functional description is always based on text, it presupposes the analysis of a considerable volume of texts.

Just as analysis presupposes the existence of the description of a language, **comparison** of two or more languages presupposes the existence of descriptions of these languages. We can posit a metatheoretical cline from comparison applied to a few languages to generalized comparison, or typology, applied to many languages (cf. Halliday, 1957; Matthiessen *et al.*, 2008). Thus when we engage with comparison or typology, we have to range over comprehensive descriptions of at least a handful of languages: we must manage the combined complexity of these languages, coping for example with the quite different models for construing time embodied in systems of tense and of aspect (cf. Halliday and Ellis, 1951; Matthiessen, 2004).

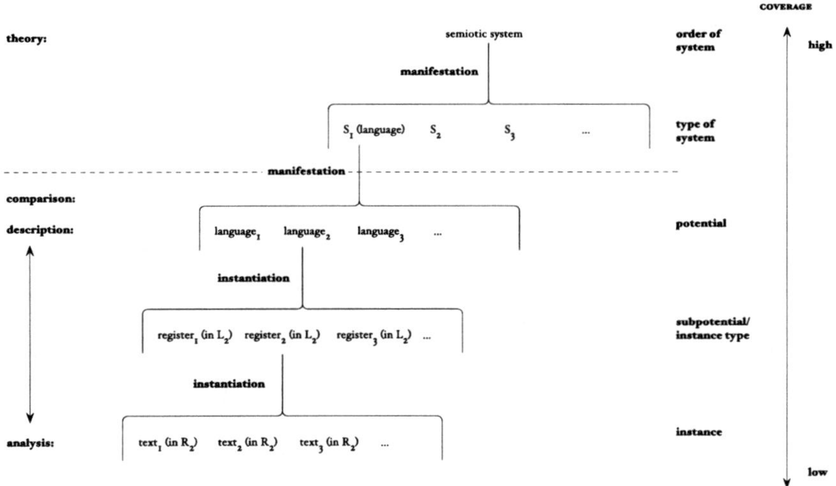

Figure 7.2: Analysis, description, comparison and theory in relation to one another

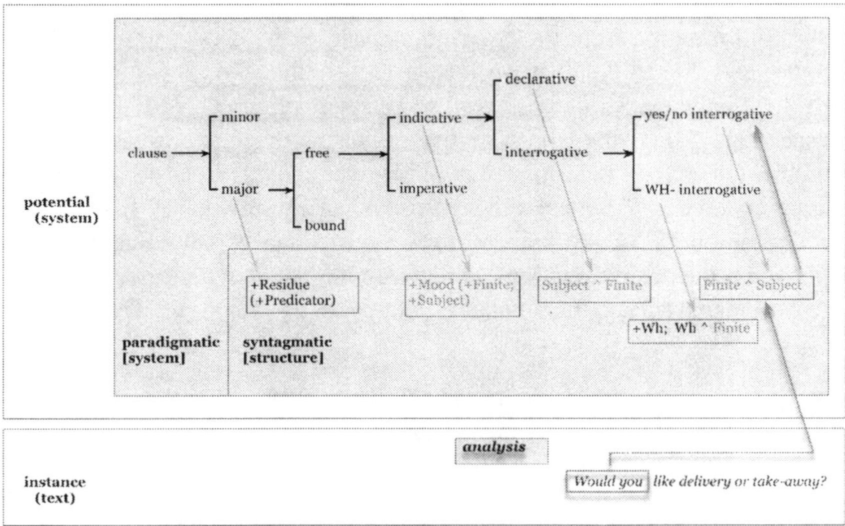

Figure 7.3: Analysis as move up the cline of instantiation from instance to potential (or subpotential) – from text to system (or subsystem), matching patterns in the text (e.g. *would you*) to specifications in the description of the system (e.g. Finite ^ Subject)

Finally, **theory** is concerned with human language in general – with the defining properties of the human system of language (cf. Matthiessen and Nesbitt, 1996), so it presupposes the existence of descriptions and comparisons of many languages – as many languages as possible: these descriptions and comparisons of descriptions constitute the ***empirical*** base of linguistic theory, but the distance between the general theory of language and 'data' in the sense of texts from particular languages that can be observed, sampled and analysed is of course much greater than the distance between the description of a particular language and such data.

It is difficult to determine how many languages in 'as many languages as possible' would actually be. However, it is clear that there are far fewer comprehensive descriptions of languages to work with in the development of theory than what would ideally be the case. Out of the 6,900 or so languages that are still spoken around the world according to the Ethnologue[2] – which is probably a considerably lower number of languages than the number of languages spoken around 10K years ago at the time when agriculture and settlement began to emerge in a few places around the world (cf. Nichols, 1992), only around 30-40 (perhaps up to 100) are described in reasonably comprehensive terms – one measure of descriptive comprehensiveness being whether a 'reference grammar' has been produced for a given language based on extensive evidence from naturally occurring texts; perhaps up to 400 to 600 languages have been described in such a way that we can extract a great deal of information from the descriptions; and perhaps we can increase the number to 1,200 to 2,000 if we include descriptive sketches. In the World Atlas of Language Structures (WALS; Haspelmath *et al.*, 2005; Dryer and Haspelmath, 2011).[3] the largest sample of languages for any of the linguistic variables ('features') investigated is a little over 2,500; but the number of languages covered by a large number of variables is just over 100 (e.g. Comrie and Cysouw, n.d.). These numbers are very difficult to estimate, but the important point is the inverse relationship between the extent of the descriptive coverage of languages and the number of languages described: see Figure 7.4.

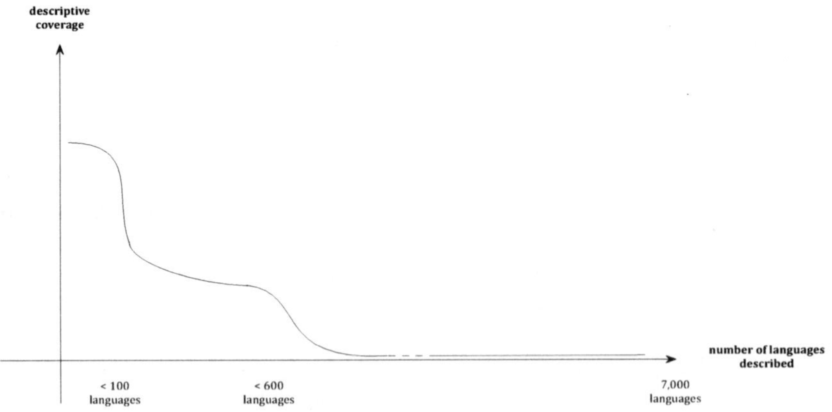

Figure 7.4: The relationship between descriptive coverage and the number of the world's languages that have been described

The notion of 'theory' should therefore be treated with a great deal of care and caution: linguistic theory cannot be derived from a single language or even from a small handful of languages. And now that systemic functional theory has been extended to include semiotic systems other than language and proto-language, it is important to make sure that any claims about *semiotic* theory are empirically grounded in the descriptions of a wide range of semiotic systems.

In summary, any kind of approach to discourse analysis (DA) must be seen against the background of the hierarchy of linguistic activities shown in Figure 7.5: analysis depends on (and feeds) description and comparison, and these depend, in turn, on (and feed) theory.

7.2 Types of Discourse Analysis

7.2.1 Immanent and transcendent problems in DA

Like SFL in general, ADA informed by SFL is a ***resource for solving problems that arise in the community*** – in the case of ADA, specifically through the analysis of discourse. Problems that can be addressed through discourse analysis may be either internal to the linguistic community, **immanent** problems, or external to it, **transcendent** problems (cf. Hjelmslev, 1943; Halliday, 1978). Both types are valued in SFL, and there is of course no sharp divide between the two: see Table 7.1. As scholars have produced more and more extensive descriptions of languages, the problem-solving potential of discourse analysis has increased with respect to both types in the last couple of decades; but our challenge is to expand this potential considerably further, to define 'discourse analyst' as a profession, and to create career opportunities for discourse analysts.

Table 7.1: Examples of internal and external problems that can be addressed through discourse analysis

Orientation	Area	Examples of problems
Internal	Theoretical linguistics	What are similarities and differences between the processes of analysis and of synthesis (generation)?
	Descriptive linguistics	How can we produce discourse-based generalizations about linguistic system?
		What are the meanings at risk in a certain register?
Internal/external	Translation studies	What are the translation equivalents of certain linguistic features?

	Multisemiotic studies	What is the division of labour between language and other semiotic systems in different documents and presentations?
	Computational linguistics	How can the analysis of text be automated so that it can serve as part of a natural language processing system?
External	Healthcare linguistics	How can people interacting with a person suffering from a certain kind of aphasia like Broca's aphasia learn strategies to facilitate exchanges?
	Educational linguistics	What challenges will learners face in engaging with texts in a particular subject, and how is 'knowledge transmitted' by these texts?
	Institutional linguistics	What is the function of code switching and of code mixing in different institutional settings in multilingual groups and in multilingual societies?

7.2.2 Specialized forms of DA

Certain transcendent problems have been given special attention in the naming and development of particular currents within discourse analysis because they relate centrally to human relationships in the community, and to the political 'ecosystem' in which these relationships operate. One prominent example is **Critical Discourse Analysis** (CDA, see e.g. Fairclough, 1989, 1992, 1995, 2003, 2005, 2006; Caldas-Coulthard and Coulthard, 1996; Fairclough and Wodak, 1997; Chouliaraki and Fairclough, 1999; van Dijk, 2001; Meurer, 2004; Young and Harrison, 2004; Veloso, 2006). The scholars who developed it drew on both SFL and on the SFL-inspired development of Critical Linguistics (cf. Fowler *et al.*, 1979), and focused on the tenor parameter of power (status): it has been applied to reveal inequities relating to this parameter in a range of institutions – to reveal the abuse of power (cf. Matthiessen, forthcoming).

Complementing this focus on inequality, J. R. Martin (e.g. 2004, 2007) has shifted the focus from power to solidarity, still within the tenor parameter of context, and developed **Positive Discourse Analysis** (PDA) as an approach designed to give us insight into socio-political approaches that have served to address problems in communities, e.g. discourses of reconciliation (e.g. Martin, 2002), of restorative justice (e.g. Martin *et al.*, 2009) – or more generally of 'discourses of hope' (e.g. Gouveia, 2006/7), 'discourse which attempts to make the world a better place' (Martin, 2008). PDA is of course a way of deploying the general descriptive and theoretical resources that Martin and his colleagues have developed over the last three decades or so (see Martin, 1992; Martin and Rose, 2003, 2008), and in this respect it is quite different from CDA: while CDA is an approach designed specifically to deal with a particular set of issues such as those that are related to inequality, PDA is a 'registerial setting' of parameters within a general approach to discourse analysis.

In addition to CDA and PDA, there are of course a number of other specialized forms of discourse analysis that have been 'tailored' to deal with some particular type of discourse rather than with any and all types of discourse. The focus of each specialized form of discourse analysis can be characterized in terms of the well-known contextual variables of **field**, **tenor** and **mode** (see e.g. Halliday, 1978): see Table 7.2. The examples given in the table vary in degree of specialization. For instance, approaches to the analysis of dialogue, in particular to conversation (see Matthiessen and Slade, 2010), include both frameworks that have been designed specifically to analyse conversation, like 'Conversation Analysis', and frameworks that are 'registerial settings' of a general approach to the analysis of discourse, as in the case of systemic functional work on conversation (e.g. Halliday, 1984; Eggins and Slade, 1997; Halliday and Greaves, 2008).

Table 7.2: Specialized forms of discourse analysis (DA) dealing with discourses corresponding to a certain setting of values within a field, tenor or mode system

Contextual parameter	Contextual system in focus	Example of approaches to DA
Tenor	Power (status): control, dominance, inequality	Critical Linguistics (CL); Critical Discourse Analysis (CDA)
	Familiarity: inclusion, solidarity	Positive Discourse Analysis (PDA)
	Institutional role: professional roles	Professional DA
Mode	Turn: dialogic	CA (Conversation Analysis)
	'Modality': multimodal	MDA (multimodal Discourse Analysis)
Field	Socio-semiotic process: recreating	Stylistics, literary analysis, narrative analysis
	Socio-semiotic process: (various)	Media discourse analysis, medical discourse analysis, academic discourse analysis

In Table 7.2, a number of approaches to DA are characterized in terms of the contextual parameters of field, tenor and mode. All approaches to DA are concerned with the analysis of text, or discourse; thus they are concerned with the instance pole of the cline of instantiation, regardless of whether they are general or specialized approaches: see Figure 7.5.

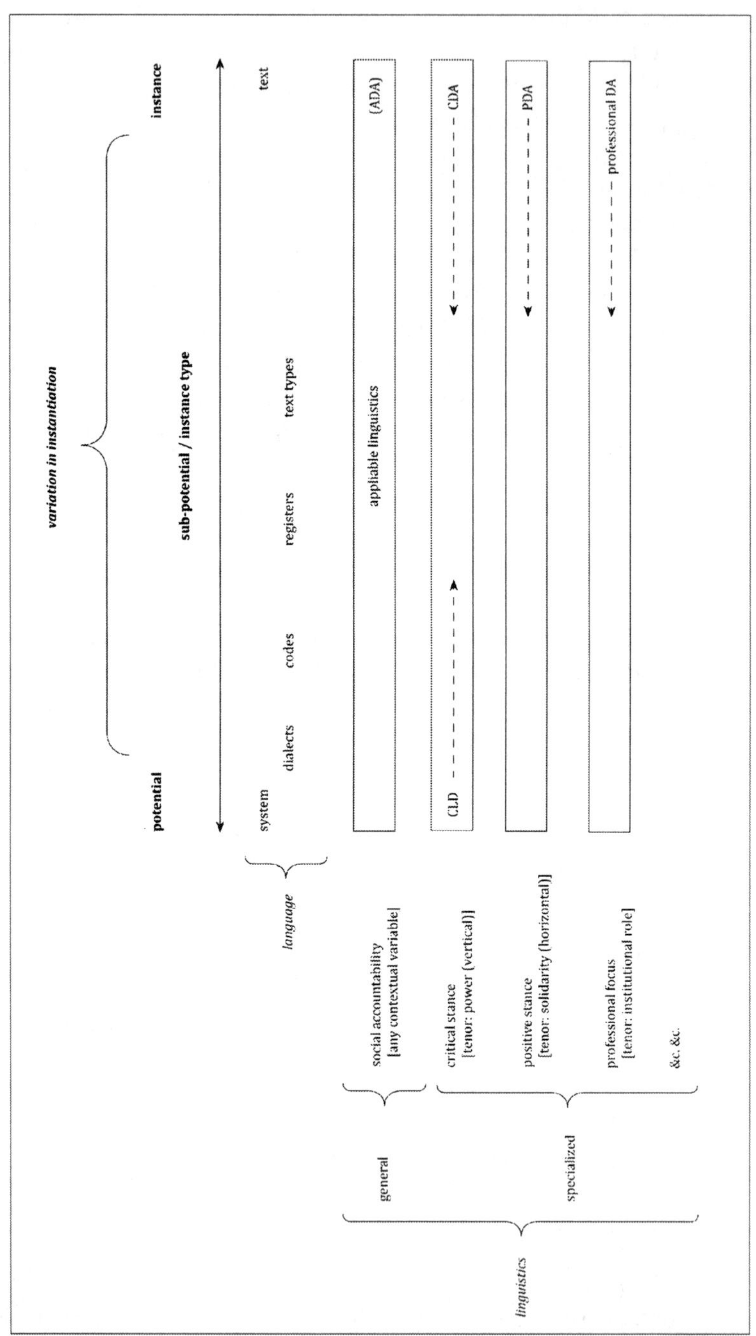

Figure 7.5: Coverage of regions of the cline of instantiation by socially accountable discourse analysis, socially accountable linguistics, and critical approaches

By locating the concerns of approaches to DA at the instance pole of the cline of instantiation, we raise the possibility that they may be complemented by comparable forms of description. For example, it makes sense to explore the possibility of Critical Language Description (CLD) as a complement to Critical Discourse Analysis. In CLD, we would develop descriptions of languages from a critical vantage point, showing the implications of the characteristics of different linguistic systems. This is, in fact, precisely what Halliday (1992) does: he shows how certain key modes of meaning that evolved in purely agrarian societies can get in the way of ecological insights and modes of action that are now central to the continued survival us and our fellow creatures – of the whole biosphere of our planet.

In short, it is important to explore correspondences between approaches to DA and approaches to language description. Thus ADA corresponds to Appliable Language Description, the two being complementary aspects of appliable linguistics.

After having contextualized ADA, let me now focus on the properties that are characteristic of this approach to DA.

7.2.3 Generalized DA: Properties of ADA

In order to be maximally appliable, ADA needs to empower its practitioners to engage with a very wide variety of tasks; it must have a number of properties:

- It must be grounded in a **holistic theory** of language in context – one in which language is approached in ecological terms as a system operating in an environment of other systems (cf. Capra, 1996), both other semiotic systems and non-semiotic systems (cf. Halliday and Matthiessen, 1999: Chapter 13).
- It must reference a **comprehensive description** of the particular language-in-culture that is in focus. This means that as many 'regions' as possible of language-in-culture must have been described (cf. Matthiessen, 2007) so that the analyses of texts-in-situations can be done systematically – either in terms of all systems described or in terms of an informed selection of a subset of systems.
- It must be reasonably **explicit** so that analysts can easily relate manual analysis to automated analysis (cf. Teich, 2009; Wu, 2009), treating these as two complementary forms of analysis. This means among other things that relations between strata, axes and ranks should be spelt out by means of realization statements (cf. Fawcett, 1988).

- It must be both **multilingually and multisemiotically oriented**. It must be able to deal with different languages, either one by one or in combination (as in translation and comparative studies), and it must be able to deal with different semiotic systems, again either one by one or in combination (cf. Kress and van Leeuwen, 2001; Bateman, 2008; Kress, 2010).
- It must provide an account of the **context** in which we undertake discourse analysis so that it is possible to relate features of this context to the nature of the analysis undertaken and to reason about analytical choices (cf. Ghadessy, 1999).

In addition, it must support communities of analysts who are likely to be working in different places around the world over extended periods of time:

- It must be geared towards data **sharing and reuse** of (analysed) texts.

This last property is of crucial importance, since it will allow a breakthrough to long-term collective discourse analysis designed to address problems that are beyond the scope of individual research projects. Sharing and reuse of analysed texts will depend on agreed standards for representing analyses, and on computational tools that do not encode the analyses in some proprietary format but instead use an open format, a generally available form of representation that is independent of particular tools: see Teich (2009: 114).

ADA has the power to empower thanks to a number of properties that are key to the success of SFL as a form of appliable linguistics. The most central of all properties is probably its potential for comprehensive analysis.

7.3   Comprehensiveness: Systemic orders of analysis

The holistic theory of SFL has paved the way for comprehensive descriptions of particular languages (see e.g. Caffarel *et al.*, 2004, for a sample of descriptions of languages other than English), and comprehensive description can and should now also be a goal for the description of semiotic systems other than language. Comprehensive descriptions of a wide range of semiotic systems in turn make it possible to undertake comprehensive analyses of texts in ADA – or alternatively, informed selective analyses (see further below, Section 7.5). Such comprehensive descriptions are needed, among other things, to support comprehensive analyses of texts.

7.3.1 Systemic orders of analysis: Semiotic, sociological, biological and physical

A comprehensive analysis of a text, or of a set of texts, is one where the analysis is carried out in terms of all the systems that have been covered in the descriptions relevant to the text(s). In other words, a comprehensive analysis of a text *exhausts* the description of the system that lies behind the text.

A comprehensive analysis of a text ranges across all its manifestations within different orders of system, as shown Table 7.3. It involves the **semiotic analysis** of the text not only at its own systemic order as a semiotic process (or product), but also at lower orders of manifestation[4] – **sociological analysis** of the text as (interactive) behaviour, **biological analysis** of the text as physiological (embodied) activity (e.g. neural processes, articulatory processes), and **physical analysis** of the text as physical events (e.g. acoustic analysis of text as sound waves). For instance, Halliday and Greaves (2008) show how intonational analysis of spoken text involves physical (acoustic), biological (auditory) and semiotic (phonological, and lexicogrammatical) analyses, and how they complement one another in the engagement with, and understanding of, text.

Table 7.3: Orders of analysis

Order of analysis		Type within order	Form of analysis
Immaterial analysis:	Semiotic analysis (meaning) [4th order]	Contextual analysis [connotative semiotic analysis]	Field – tenor – mode analysis of context of situation of text, with contextual stages
		Linguistic and other denotative semiotic analysis	Semantic analysis of text as meaning, lexicogrammatical analysis of text as wording; phonological and phonetic analysis of text as sounding
	Sociological analysis (value) [3rd order]		Sociological (ethnographic) analysis of text as interactive behaviour
Material analysis:	Biological analysis (life) [2nd order]		[Spoken language] physiological-neurological analysis, e.g. auditory analysis of text as perception of sound waves
	Physical analysis [1st order]		[Spoken language] acoustic analysis of text as sound waves

A comprehensive analysis of a text could – or should – in principle involve all four systemic orders shown in Table 7.3 (and this kind of comprehensiveness is likely to be needed for example in the contexts of neuroscience and medicine); but let me focus on the two **immaterial orders of system**, social and semiotic systems:

- **Social systems** – sociological, anthropological, ethnographic analysis: analysis of discourse as social process (behaviour), and of social processes and systems in their own right – using descriptions of social phenomena, e.g. Steiner's (1985, 1991) systemic functional account of social activity (influenced by the activity theory developed by Russian scholars), Martinec's (2000) analysis of action, van Leeuwen's (1996, 2008) work on the representation of social actors and events (e.g. Caldas-Coulthard and van Leeuwen, 2002), Butt's (1991) approach to persons in social role networks; or using ethnographic observation methods (e.g. shadowing people operating in their institutional roles) and interview techniques (e.g. Slade *et al.*, 2008).

- **Semiotic systems** – linguistic analysis (in its broadest sense), multimodal analysis, contextual analysis: prosodic analysis of spoken text (Halliday and Greaves, 2008), lexicogrammatical analysis, including systems from all metafunctions across the rank scale (e.g. Halliday and Matthiessen, 2004), semantic analysis, including all metafunctions (e.g. Eggins and Slade, 1997; Halliday and Matthiessen, 1999; Martin and Rose, 2003), contextual analysis, including field, tenor and mode and contextual (generic, schematic) structure (e.g. Ghadessy, 1999); analysis of semiotic systems other than language and multisemiotic analysis (e.g. Kress and van Leeuwen, 1996, 2001; Baldry and Thibault, 2006; Bateman, 2008a; Kress, 2010; Bateman and Schmidt, 2012).

Both semiotic systems and social systems are 'materialized', i.e. manifested materially, through biological and physical systems (cf. Thibault, 2004). For example, in the case of face-to-face interaction, selections in semiotic and social systems are realized through biological (neurological and physiological) activities, which in turn are realized physically. This means that there may be semiotic, social and biological competition for the same bodily resources. For example, at a dinner table, talking and gesturing (semiotic) and eating (social) must in principle alternate (cf. injunctions against talking with food in one's mouth in certain cultures), although people will of course gesture even in the course of eating. Similarly, a team of removalists carrying a heavy piece of furniture must in principle alternate between gesturing to coordinate the direction of movement and carrying. Thus, the material channel will place constraints on what range of semiotic and social systems can operate simultaneous in the exchange of meanings and in the performance of interactive behaviour. (People may gesture and use facial expressions when they speak on the phone, but these expressions are inaccessible to their listeners unless the telephonic channel is complemented by a video channel.)

In this connection it is important to note that the relation between the immaterial and the material is many-to-one. Looking at some activity 'from below', we can identify some particular **material situational setting** – using the term introduced by Hasan (e.g. in Halliday and Hasan, 1985: 99); but, as Hasan points out, this is distinct from the **context of situation**. The context of situation – or situation for short – is immaterial; as suggested below, it can be interpreted twice, as social (behaviour) but also as semiotic (meaning). A given material situational setting that we identify 'from below' may accommodate a single immaterial situation; but very often more than one such situation will be unfolding within one and the same material situational setting, as illustrated schematically in Figure 7.1. Such immaterial situations may be unfolding in parallel, or they may interrupt one another, perhaps with some overlap. The degree to which and the way in which they relate to one another will vary considerably across different immaterial situations and material settings.

For example, if human beings are seated around a table engaged in feeding, there may be several semiotic and social situations unfolding simultaneously or in partial succession: the persons around the dinner table may be sharing personal experiences and values, they may be engaged in the social ritual of having a meal together, serving one another, passing dishes around the table and of course ingesting food and drink (potentially facilitated by semiotic processes), and if there is a hierarchic relationship, e.g. between the head of the family and the rest, the ones in more powerful positions may be regulating the behaviour of the others (as happens when parents control their children's behaviour, seizing the opportunity of a 'teachable moment').

These different strands of activity should be teased out in the analysis, hopefully with the aid of computational analysis tools that enable analysts to distinguish the different strands while at the same time indicating how they relate to one another temporally.

immaterial situations (semiotic [text] and social)

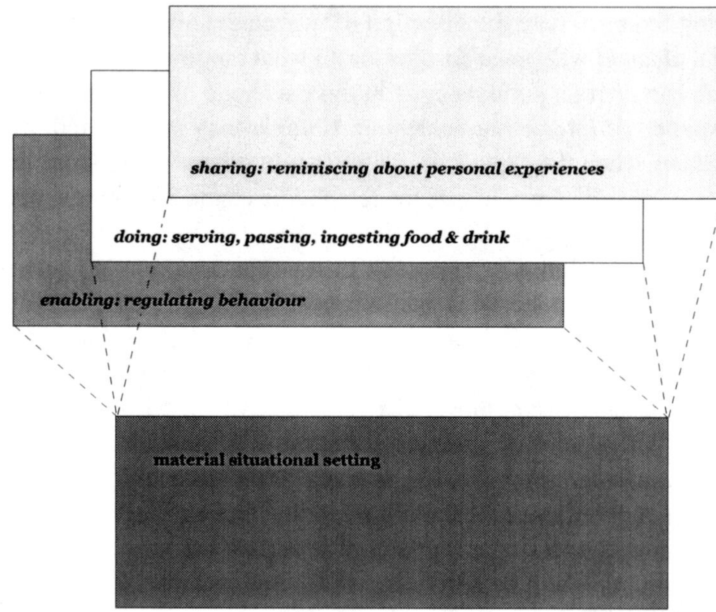

Figure 7.6: Multiple immaterial situations (semiotic and social orders) mapped onto one and the same material situational setting (biological and physical orders)

A comprehensive 'immaterial' analysis of a text in its context of situation would involve both semiotic and social analysis, as shown diagrammatically in Figure 7.7. I will discuss semiotic analysis first (Section 7.3.2), and then turn to sociological analysis (Section 7.3.3).

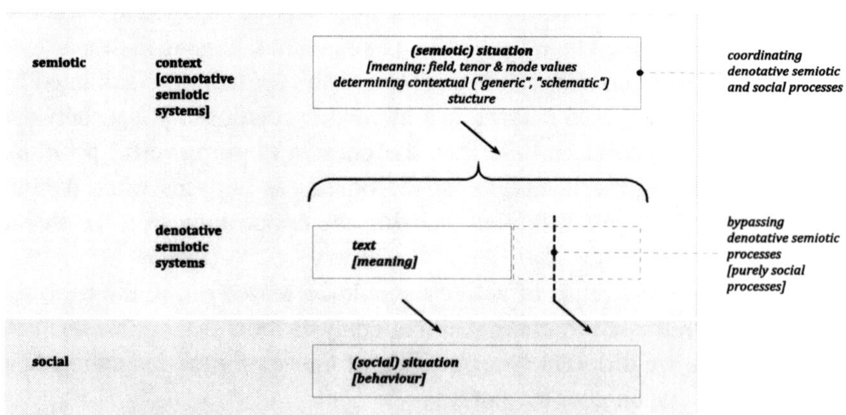

Figure 7.7: Semiotic and social systems – semiotic situation, text and social situation

7.3.2 Semiotic analysis: Contextual (connotative) and denotative

Semiotic analysis is in a sense the overarching form of analysis since semiotic systems are 4th-order systems, i.e. systems of the highest order in the ordered typology of systems, and are therefore also manifested through the lower orders of system. The world of human affairs is choreographed semiotically. Within semiotic analysis, **contextual analysis**, or connotative semiotic analysis, will serve to bring out the way in which denotative semiotic processes, investigated through **denotative semiotic analysis**, and social processes, investigated through **sociological analysis**, complement one another and are coordinated within a situation (interpreted as a process of meaning).

7.3.2.1   Contextual (connotative semiotic) analysis

Contextual (connotative semiotic) analysis includes both systemic and structural analysis of situations:

- the analysis of a situation in terms of the contextual parameters of field, tenor and mode, identifying the terms in the **systems** within these parameters;
- the analysis of the **structure** of the situation realizing the combinations of field, tenor and mode terms;[5]
- and specifications of how the elements of this structure are realized by denotative semiotic patterns (processes of meaning) or by purely social patterns (processes of doing/behaving), bypassing denotative semiotic systems, as shown in Figure 7.7 above.

Here context is interpreted theoretically as a connotative semiotic system along the lines of Martin (1992), referring to Hjelmslev (1943) and drawing on Halliday's (1978) interpretation of context as a system of meanings. Contextual patterns of meaning (systemic and structural) may be realized by denotative semiotic patterns, e.g. in face-to-face interaction, language, gesture, facial expression, gaze, posture and other semiotic systems with the body as their expression plane (i.e. somatic semiotic systems [Matthiessen, 2009] based on the signifying body [Thibault, 2004]) but they may also be realized by purely social patterns, bypassing denotative semiotic systems (cf. Figure 7.7 above), as in social-interactive team work during phases of behaviour unfolding between directive or collaborative talk. In the former case, denotative semiotic systems are constitutive of the semiotic context; in the latter, social systems are constitutive of it, with denotative semiotic systems coming in merely to facilitate the performance of social behaviour (the traditional notion of language in action).

7.3.2.2   Denotative semiotic analysis

Denotative semiotic analysis ranges over all the denotative semiotic systems operating in a given semiotic situation; thus comprehensive analysis is inherently **multisemiotic analysis,** covering all the systems in operation. There is clearly an abundance of such systems; examples are given in Figure 7.8 classified 'from below' according to the (primary) sensory system used by the addressee to process them (cf. again Thibault, 2004): **visual semiotics, auditory semiotics, somatic sensory semiotics** (including tactile semiotics), **gustatory semiotics** and **olfactory semiotics.**

The nature of the analysis – and of the description that it is based on – will clearly depend on what kind of semiotic system we are concerned with. For example, there are now widely available computational tools for conducting automated analysis of some aspects of expression plane patterns within visual and auditory semiotic systems – video analysis and acoustic analysis, but the same is not the case for the other types of semiotic system identified in Figure 7.8: they would involve more specialized equipment (and the same is of course true of non-acoustic analysis of speech; see e.g. Hardcastle and Laver, 1999: Part I). The nature of the analysis will also depend on whether the semiotic system or systems being analysed are more like speech or more like writing (cf. Halliday, 1985) – that is, whether they are produced and analysed by 'speaker' and 'listener' as *process* in real time, as with spoken language and paralanguage (e.g. voice quality) and 'body language' (e.g. gesture, gaze, facial expression and posture), or whether they are processed as *product* in (potentially) extended time, as with written language and accompanying images such as drawings, graphs, maps and photographs. The implications for temporal alignment in the analysis are obviously somewhat different. For example, a product such as a printed page or a computer screen can be viewed in different ways, as can be shown by the tracking of a viewer's eye movements (see Bateman, 2008a: 63–65, for discussion of research on reading or viewing paths).

Multisemiotic, or multimodal, analysis has of course been an area of intense research for quite a while now, and scholars are still developing descriptions of different semiotic systems. For language, see below. Among non-linguistic denotative semiotic systems, the first to be described in systemic functional terms were those whose expression planes are accessible to addresses through their visual systems in the first instance – although the focus was not on face-to-face interaction of the kind found in casual conversation but rather on texts transmitted through print; see e.g. Kress and van Leeuwen (1996) on images of different kinds (drawings, paintings, photographs), and O'Toole (1994) on 'displayed art' (painting, sculpture, architecture). Auditory semiotic systems followed with van Leeuwen's (1999), although there had been precursors, including Winograd (1968). These systems shade into language with paralinguistic features such as voice quality, investigated in systemic functional terms by Wan (2011).

Semiotic systems based on the other sensory systems also need exploring – somatic sensory, gustatory and olfactory semiotic systems, although they are likely to be less elaborated, in view of the human orientation towards visual and auditory sensory systems (reflected in how sensory systems are construed lexicogrammatically in languages; cf. Viberg, 1984). Surely a systemic functional description of olfactory semiotics, applied to e.g. perfume and aromatherapy, is just around the corner, if one hasn't been produced already! Systemic functional accounts of 'body language' (cf. Thibault, 2004, on the 'signifying body') include work on gesture (see more generally e.g. McNeill, 2000, 2005), e.g. Muntigl (2004), Martinec (2004); and Hood (2011), with a focus on textual and interpersonal meaning and discussion of 'metafunctional fusion'. (For non-systemic functional work, see e.g. McNeill, 2000, 2005; Hübler, 2001; Kendon, 2004.)

In addition to describing separate semiotic systems, systemic functional researchers have turned their attention to the way in which such systems work together (e.g. Kress and van Leeuwen, 2001; O'Halloran, 2005; Baldry and Thibault, 2006; Bateman, 2008a; Kress, 2010; Bateman and Schmidt, 2012).

Let me just give one brief example, from a context where the field of activity is that of 'recreating' (see Section 7.4, Figure 7.9, below). In John Huston's film *Beat the Devil*,[6] about 23 minutes into the film, there is a scene where Julius O'Hara, played by Peter Lorre, visits Billy Dannreuther, played by Humphrey Bogart, and his wife, played by Gina Lollobrigida, in their hotel room. As Julius arrives, Billy is about to leave; but Julius is in his way, so Billy lets him in. This brief extract from the film lasts only a short while, but it's full of semiotic and social activity. Some of the complexity is illustrated in the sequences of screenshots shown in Figure 7.9 together with my transcription of the dialogue. I took each screenshot at the end of the (partial) utterance transcribed under it, so changes between screenshots are, of course, not shown. Here I have tried to illustrate some of the correlations between the spoken dialogue and gestures. There would be many other ways of segmenting the sequence with screenshots, e.g. to track changes in facial expression and gaze. What we really need are analysis tool such as the video and audio analysis tool ELAN (from the Max Plank Institute for Psycholinguistics, Nijmegen),[7] Michael Kipp's ANVIL,[8] Baldry and Thibault's (2006) tool, or the new powerful analysis tool being developed by Kay O'Halloran and her team at her Multimodal Analysis Lab of the National University of Singapore – or Praat[9] for phonetic analysis (used extensively by Halliday and Greaves, 2008).

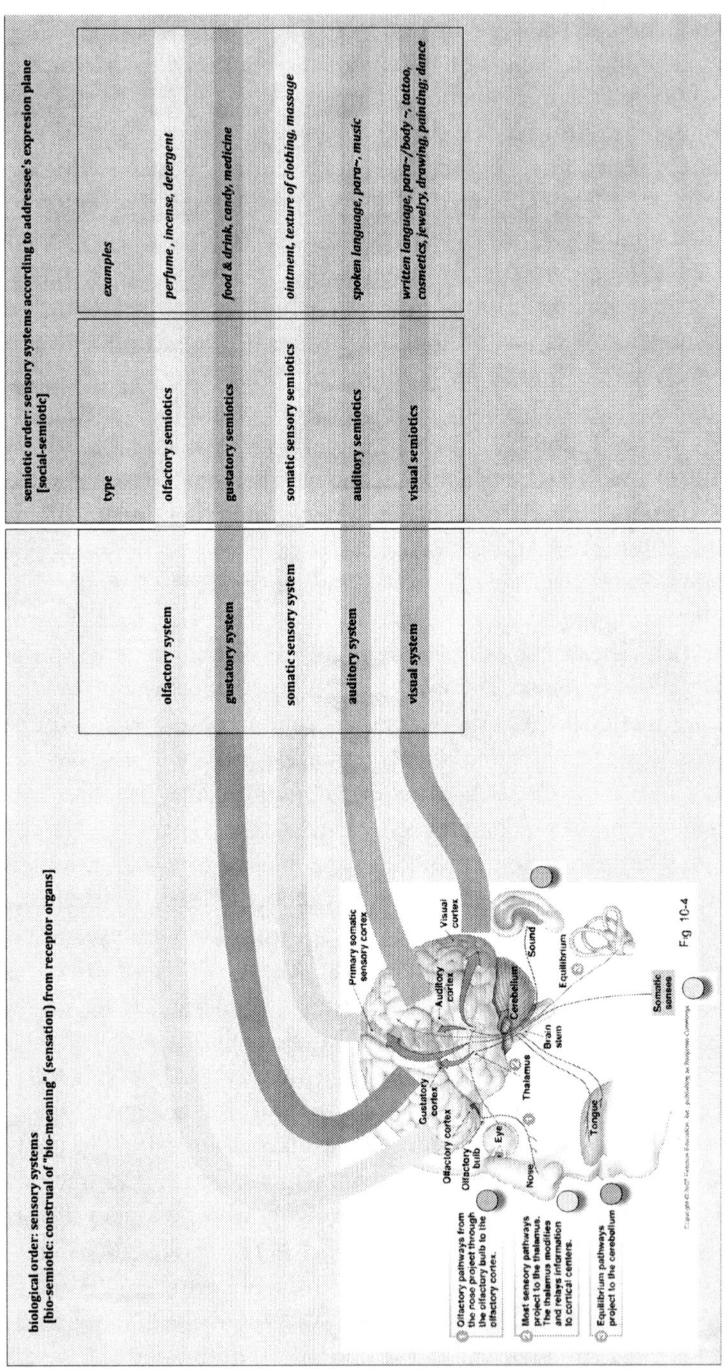

Figure 7.8: Examples of semiotic systems differentiated according to addressee's sensory systems.

Figure 7.9: Extract from John Huston's *Beat the Devil*.[10]

Such video annotation tools make it possible to keep the different semiotic analyses separate as different 'tiers' while at the same time showing how they are synchronized. For example, when Peter Lorre (Julius O'Hara) says *Oh it's not so much a difference of age*, we could analyse selections in accompanying semiotic systems as shown in Figure 7.10 (drawing on some of the proposals in Arndt and Janney, 1987, InterGrammar framework; see also Hübler, 2001: 228–255). Obviously even a short example such as this one changes semiotically (and socially) as it unfolds; approaching it 'from below', we can see and hear this variation over time by tracking prosody (intonation and rhythm), facial expression (including gaze), gesture and posture, as illustrated in Figure 7.11. However, from the point of view of ADA, the approach 'from below', focused on the expression plane, is not enough; we have to reveal how these different systems work alongside each other by viewing them 'from round-about' and how they are coordinated and integrated when viewed 'from above'. Viewed 'from above', Lorre's performance is a holistic one – what we might call a *Gesamtkunstwerk*, using Richard Wagner's term for the kind of opera he advocated (cf. Matthiessen, 2009).

Figure 7.10: Semiotic systems in face-to-face interaction – somatic semiotic systems (Peter Lorre in a scene from *Beat the Devil*: Oh it's not so much a difference of age).

Figure 7.11: Phases within *Oh it's not so much a difference of age*.

As the sequence from *Beat the Devil* shown in Figure 7.9 illustrates, semiotic processes and purely social processes (like opening doors, moving around, sitting down, providing drinks, drinking, and smoking) proceed in parallel, sometimes overlapping, sometimes alternating and sometimes occurring at the same time. And, as noted above, they are all 'materialized' by physiological activities, and thus have to compete for material resources; for example, when Peter Lorre says *we are in with the money*, he has to shift his glass from his right hand to his left one to free up his right hand so that he can use it to make the sign for money.

7.3.3 Sociological analysis

Sociological analysis is concerned with (interactive) behaviour within social systems, one step down from semiotic systems in the ordered typology of systems, as shown in Figure 7.7 above. It will, of course, involve contributions from various disciplines concerned with social systems – sociology, anthropology, ethnography, social psychology, and also disciplines concerned with organization, management and administration. From the point of view of ADA, it is important that the sociological analysis should be able to be related to the semiotic analysis and that it should complement it. Systemic functional linguists and semioticians have made connection with a number of important contributions coming from the sociological perspective (though much bridging work of course still remains to be done). A key contribution is Steiner's (1985, 1991) account of social activity mentioned immediately above. He shows how processes can be described in terms of a rank scale – a social analogue of the notion of rank scale proposed by Halliday (1961) in the study of language; **social activities** consist of **social actions**, which in turn consist of **social operations**, as illustrated by Figure 7.12. Steiner describes this rank model as follows:

> Within the structure of activity on the individual level, we shall distinguish three ranks: activity, action, operation. [...] Activity is a type of human behaviour which is aroused by a cultural and/ or physiological need, expressed as a state of the individual in relation to his/her environment. We shall call the activity successful only if the execution of the activity is a sufficient condition for the reaching of another state of the individual in relation to his/her environment, a state which we shall call 'objective'. The objective is a projected, i.e. subjective state as long as it is not reached. [...] An action is a unit of human activity to which we attribute a goal, formulated as a state of affairs. If an activ-

ity is filled by one action, which is a marginal case, then the goal of the action must be a sufficient condition for the reaching of the objective. If an activity is filled by more than one action, the goals taken together must provide a sufficient condition for the reaching of the objective in a given situation. [...] The unit of action is compounded of the following elements: Motivation, Planning, Execution, Evaluation. These will typically be filled by operations, units from again one rank below [...] Operations are units of activity filling elements of structure of actions. An operation is interpreted as having a task formulated as a state of affairs (Steiner, 1991: 24–27).

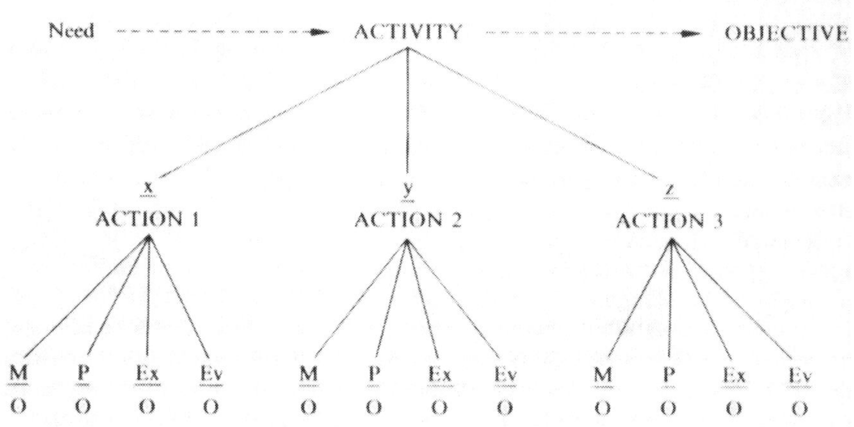

Figure 7.12: Steiner's (1991: Figure 4) schematic representation of the ranked composition of social activities.

Looked at semiotically, in terms of context, Steiner's account of what we might call social process (or behaviour, as a cover term for activity, action and operation) corresponds to the **field** parameter of context – the semiotic nature of processes (activities) within context. From a sociological point of view, we are concerned with processes of **behaviour**; from a semiotic point of view, we are concerned with processes of **meaning** (cf. Halliday, 1984).

Complementing the sociological account of social process, we can also add considerations of **tenor** – of the **roles** the persons taking part in the social processes enter into and the **relationships** that they enact serving in these roles. This was a perspective Firth (1951) pioneered as part of the account of language in context; and Butt (1991) has developed it further, relating it to social network theory in sociology. Together these two facets of social systems – social processes and the persons ('social subjects' or 'actors') taking part in them in different roles – constitute a powerful contribution to sociological analysis (cf. again Steiner, 1991: e.g. 36).

Social processes and the persons taking part in them within a context of situation can be integrated in terms of the social domain of **institution** – a unit of analysis that Malinowski argued was central in the study of 'culture'.

> An ethnographer taking a rapid survey of various types of human culture, from the most primitive to highly developed ones, would make an interesting discovery. He would find that the work of culture is not done by any community as a whole, nor yet by individuals, but by smaller organized groups, that is, institutions, which are organized and integrated to form the community. The significance of this discovery is due to two facts, first, that an institution always presents the same structure, and second, that institutions are of universal occurrence; thus the institution is the real isolate of culture. [...] The study of any culture must therefore be carried out in terms of institutions. This means in other words that an object or artifact, a custom, an idea or an artistic product, is significant only when placed within the institution to which it belongs. Certain institutions are to be found in all human societies; other types of institutions, though less universal, can be found in many cultures although some of them are more characteristic of highly developed societies. As culture advances we find that various organized activities, which on the primitive level were carried out as a by-product of other institutions, become organized in their own right. (Malinowski, 1944: 154–155)

Institutions are, among other things, characterized by systematic correlations between field (the field of activity: social processes) and tenor (social roles, and persons interpreted as aggregates of social roles);[11] these correlations represent the division of labour within a given institution.

In my brief remarks on sociological analysis, I have not, of course, been able to present a comprehensive framework for such forms of analysis; but I hope that my references to past contributions have shown that there is already a considerable potential within ADA for sociological analysis.

7.4 Semiotic analysis: Dimensions

While sociological analysis interprets text as **behaviour** – together with other kinds of behaviour that are 'purely' social in character without an

162   *Developing Systemic Functional Linguistics*

added layer of semiosis, **semiotic analysis** interprets text as **meaning**. Semiotic analysis can be considered comprehensive when it covers all strata identified in the hierarchy of **stratification** (context – language [content: [semantics – lexicogrammar]] – [expression: [phonology – phonetics]]) and all functions identified in the spectrum of **metafunctions** (ideational [logical ~ experiential] ~ interpersonal ~ textual).

7.4.1 Mapping dimensions of analysis: Matrices

By intersecting these two semiotic dimensions, we can produce a comprehensive map in the form of a **function-stratification matrix**, as illustrated for language-in-context in Table 7.4.

Table 7.4: Function-stratification matrix (for language in context, exemplified by English)

plane	stratum	ideational		interpersonal	textual
context		FIELD		TENOR	MODE
language: content	semantics	IDEATION		NEGOTIATION	PRESENTATION
		RHETORICAL RELATION	FIGURATION		
	lexicogrammar	COMPLEXING: TAXIS & LOGICO-SEMANTIC TYPE	TRANSITIVITY	MOOD & MODAL ASSESSMENT	THEME, INFORMATION
language: expression	phonology	COMPLEXING: TONE GROUP COMPLEXES	—	TONE	TONICITY

Using the matrix in Table 7.4, we specify what would be included in a comprehensive contextual-linguistic analysis, in terms of both systems, the names of which are given in small capitals in the table, and the structures that realize combinations of features from these systems. For example, Matthiessen *et al.* (2005) present a multistratal analysis of telephonic service encounters focused on interpersonal systems. In the matrix, whole regions are of course compressed into single cells; for example, the 'lexicogrammar' row can be expanded according to the grammatical rank scale (clause – group/phrase – word – morpheme), giving us a more detailed map in the form of a **function-rank** matrix, as illustrated for the lexicogrammar of English in Table 7.5 (see e.g. Halliday and Matthiessen, 2004: 63; Halliday and McDonald, 2004, for Chinese; and Teruya, 2007, for Japanese).

Table 7.5: Function-rank matrix, lexicogrammatical stratum (for language in context, exemplified by English)

metafunction		ideational			interpersonal	textual	
rank	*class*	*logical*		*experiential*			
clause		TAXIS, LOGICO-SEMANTIC TYPE		TRANSITIVITY	MOOD; MODAL ASSESSMENT (incl. MODALITY, POLARITY); VOCATIVE	THEME; VOICE [CULMINATION]	CONJUNCTION; ELLIPSIS/ SUBSTITUTION
		1 2 3...; α β γ		Process + Medium (+Agent) (+Range) (+Beneficiary) (+ circumstances)	Mood (Subject • Finite • Adjunct) + Residue (Predicator, Complement, Adjunct) (+Moodtag) + Adjunct [comment] + Vocative	Theme ^ Rheme [... ^ Culminative]	Adjunct [conjunctive]
group/ phrase	phrase	TAXIS, LOGICO-SEMANTIC TYPE		MINOR TRANSITIVITY	MINOR MOOD	MINOR THEME	
		1 2 3...; α β γ		Process ^ Range	Predicator ^ Complement	↑Theme/ Complement	
	nominal	TAXIS, LOGICO-SEMANTIC TYPE	MODIFICATION	THING TYPE, EPITHESIS, CLASSIFICATION, QUALIFICATION	PERSON, NOMINAL MOOD, ATTITUDINAL EPITHESIS	DETERMINATION	ELLIPSIS/ SUBSTITUTION, REFERENCE
		1 2 3...; α β γ	γ β α	Deictic ^ post-Deictic ^ Numerative ^ Epithet ^ Classifier ^ Thing ^ Qualifier			
	verbal	TAXIS, LOGICO-SEMANTIC TYPE	TENSE	EVENT TYPE, ASPECT	POLARITY, MODALITY	CONTRAST, VOICE	ELLIPSIS/ SUBSTITUTION
		1 2 3...; α β γ	α β γ	Finite ^ Auxiliary 1...n ^ Event			
	adverbial	TAXIS, LOGICO-SEMANTIC TYPE	MODIFICATION	CIRCUMSTANCE TYPE	COMMENT TYPE	CONJUNCTION TYPE	
		1 2 3...; α β γ	α β γ				
word		TAXIS, LOGICO-SEMANTIC TYPE	DERIVATION	DENOTATION	CONNOTATION		LEXICAL COHESION
		1 2 3...; α β γ	α β γ				
info unit					KEY	INFORMATION	
						Given + New	
		complexes		simplexes			

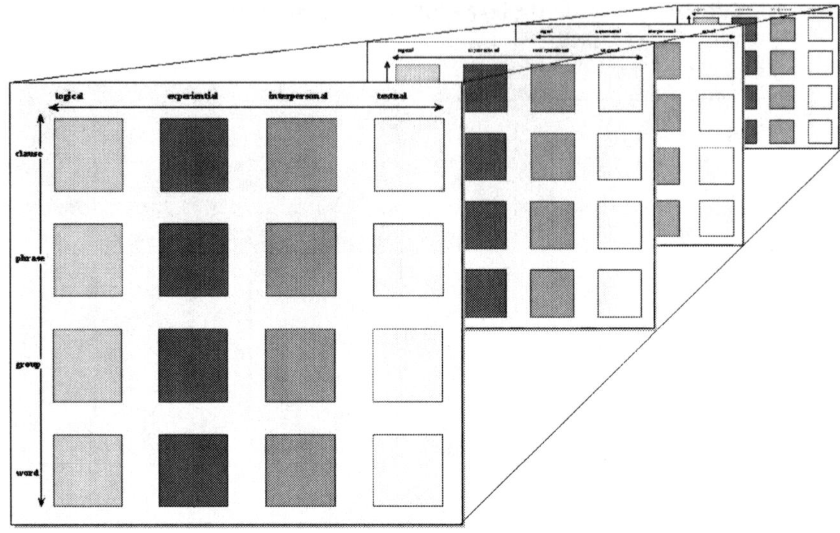

Figure 7.13: Schematic function-rank matrix indicating different degrees in delicacy along the grammar to lexis continuum

Since lexicogrammar is a continuum from grammar to lexis extended along the cline of delicacy, it will also be helpful, in future, to add the **cline of delicacy** as a third dimension to the matrix, as envisaged in Figure 7.13. This will enable analysts to locate sub-systems that may be accessible through automated lexical analysis (see below) of large corpora such as delicate systems of PROCESS TYPE (see e.g. Neal, 2006) or delicate systems of ATTITUDINAL EPITHESIS (involving adjectives listed in accounts of 'appraisal'; cf. Tucker, 1997).

At the same time, the stratification-function matrix in Table 7.4 needs to be supplemented with matrices for (denotative) semiotic systems other than language (here exemplified by English) – both for systems that may operate alongside language like gesture, facial expression and (other) forms of paralanguage operating alongside spoken language and drawings, paintings, photographs, graphs, diagrams and other forms of 'visual' semiotics operating alongside written language and for systems that are more likely to be 'stand-alone' like ballet, mime and architecture (though obviously with lots of little texts attached) and sculpture. O'Toole (1994) presents function-rank matrices for painting, sculpture and architecture, and O'Halloran (2005: 135–137) presents function rank matrices for 'mathematical visual images'; and these can provide models for exploring similar maps of other semiotic systems to support what is now sometimes called MDA, Multimodal Discourse Analysis or (better) Multi-semiotic Discourse Analysis. In the case of semiotic systems that are likely to operate alongside language, analysts also need the support of matrices that show how and where they related to language in the overall account.

In this section, I have presented overviews of systems that can be referenced in discourse analysis:

- systems of different systemic orders: semiotic, social, biological and physical systems (Table 7.3);
- systems of the semiotic (4th) order: language, viz. the function-stratification matrix (Table 7.4);
- language: the function-rank matrix of the lexicogrammar of English (Table 7.5) and the function-rank matrix with the added dimension of delicacy (Figure 7.13).

These overviews start with the most global view of systems of different orders and zoom in on semiotic subsystems, with lexicogrammar as the representative example. They all represent overviews of the resources at the potential pole of the cline of instantiation.

7.4.2 The cline of instantiation and register variation

As already noted, as we conduct analyses of instances of meaning (semiotic) and behaviour (social), we reference descriptions of meaning potentials and behaviour potentials that lie behind these instances, moving up the cline of instantiation from instances to – or at least towards – the potential (as illustrated for mood analysis in Figure 7.3 above): see Figure 7.14. Analysts may move all the way up to the potential pole of the cline of instantiation, analysing instances in terms of the overall potential of semiotic systems in context. However, there are important insights to be gained by relating instances to patterns midway along the cline of instantiation.

Intermediate between the two poles of the cline of instantiation – between instance and potential, we can discern patterns of variation in the instantiation of the overall meaning potential according to context of use. This functional variation is what has been called **register variation** (or **diatypic variation**; see e.g. Halliday *et al.*, 1964; Gregory, 1967; Hasan, 1973; Halliday, 1978: 35; Matthiessen, 1993; Lukin *et al.*, 2008). As we analyse a text in its context of situation, moving up along the cline of instantiation towards the potential pole (as shown in Figure 7.14), we locate the text within a text type and the situation within a situation type; in other words, in analysing instances, we refer them to the instance types that they instantiate. Or, looked at from the potential pole of the cline of instantiation, we identify the subpotential within which the instance operates – the institution or cultural domain within which the situation operates and the register within which the text operates.

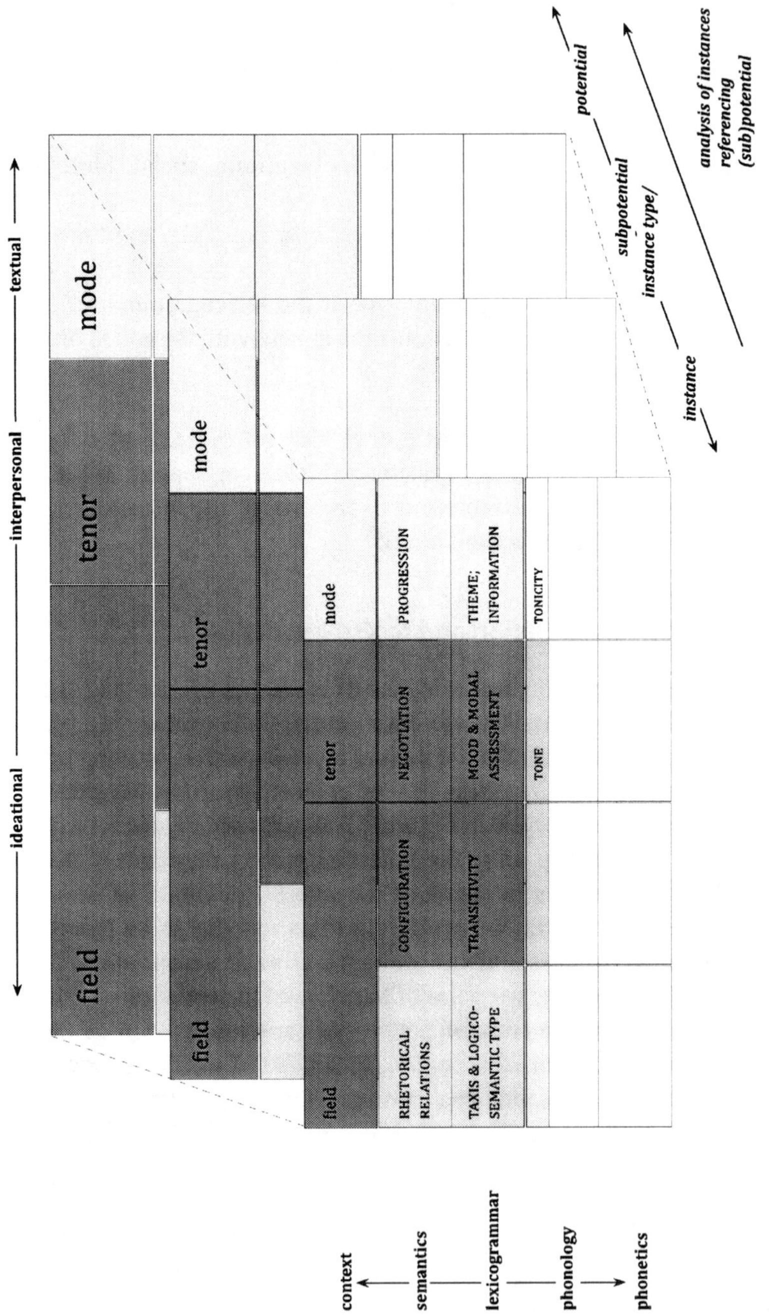

Figure 7.14: Analysis of instances as move up the cline of instantiation referencing a subpotential or the overall potential.

To be able to analyse texts in their contexts of situation in terms of these patterns intermediate between instance and potential, we need a comprehensive description of them – a **map of the functional varieties of language in context**. There have been quite a few proposals developed within different disciplines, e.g. linguistics (e.g. Longacre's classic account, 1974, updated and elaborated in Longacre, 1996, and Longacre and Hwang, 2012; and within a different tradition, Werlich, 1975) – including schemes used in the compilation of traditional corpora in corpus linguistics (e.g. Greenbaum and Svartvik, 1990), rhetoric (e.g. Kinneavy, 1971), translation studies (e.g. Snell-Hornby, 1995). Such proposals have been given different names such as 'text typology', 'register typology', 'genre typology' and 'genre agnation'. They have been based on different criteria; using Halliday's (e.g. 1996: 26–27) notion of trinocularity, we can say that text typologies have been based on criteria 'from above' (contextual considerations), 'from roundabout' (semantic considerations) and 'from below' (lexicogrammatical considerations);[12] these approaches to text typology are represented diagrammatically in Figure 7.15. If the classification of texts is manual, all three angles are possible; but if it is automated, criteria 'from below' need to be used since only fairly 'low-level' features can be identified through automated analysis (e.g. Biber, 1988).

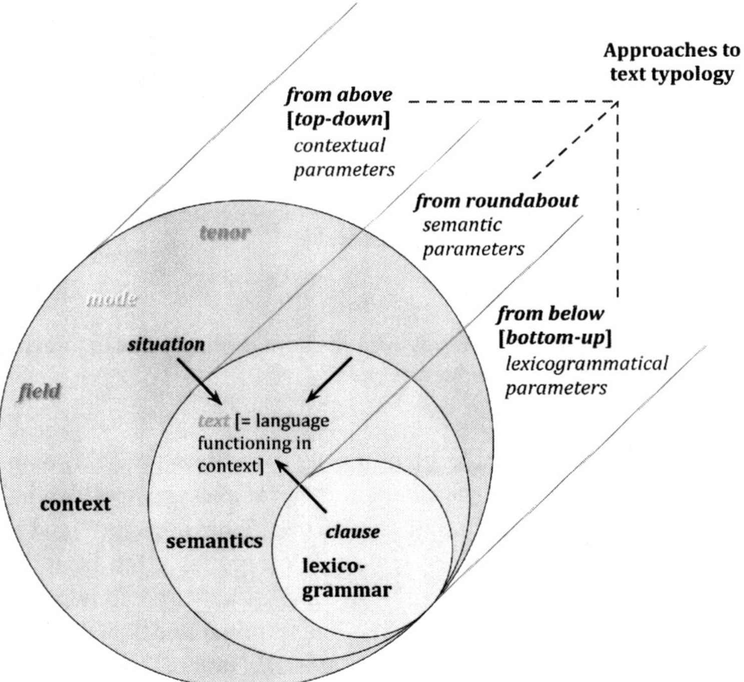

Figure 7.15: Approaches to text typology interpreted in terms of trinocularity

From a systemic functional point of view, it makes sense to start with criteria 'from above' – i.e. with contextual considerations since text is a semantic unit characterized as 'language functioning in context' (cf. Halliday and Hasan, 1976: 1–2). As we identity different types of context, we shunt (cf. Halliday, 1961), and look for semantic correlates, and also, by a further stratal step, for lexicogrammatical ones. A typology based on context will involve the three major contextual parameters – field, tenor and mode (see Lavid, 1995: 31ff). It will thus be multi-dimensional embodying intersections from parallel field, tenor and mode systems, as shown schematically in Figure 7.16.

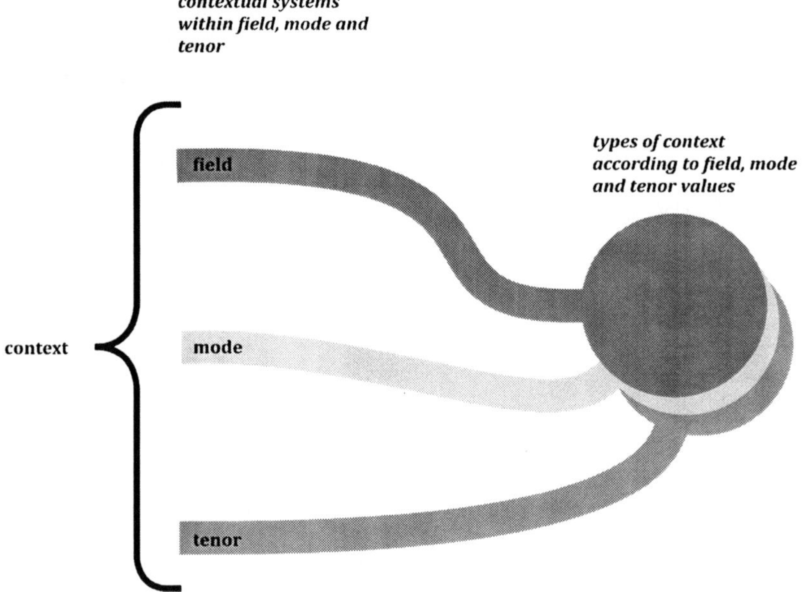

Figure 7.16: Context-based typology – multi-dimensionality due to intersections of values within field, mode and tenor systems.

Typologies proposed in the literature tend to draw on field, tenor and mode categories in different measures; some examples are provided in Table 7.6. Typologies used in the compilation of traditional corpora[13] tend to mix field, tenor and mode categories; but mode categories often figure prominently, partly because they obviously play a significant role in how texts are sampled in the compilation of a corpus. The terminal nodes of such classifications are often folk categories such as 'stories', 'letters', 'speeches', 'circulars' and 'plays'. Such folk categories may of course embody field, tenor and mode features, but Martin (1992) notes that they tend to be mode-oriented.

Table 7.6: Examples of field, tenor and mode categories in genre / text typologies

	field ~ ideational		tenor ~ interpersonal	mode ~ textual
	[activity]	[domain]	[formality, "style", interactant provenance]	[medium, channel, turn]
General	types of activity: narration, instruction, persuasion, and so on	subject area: popular, administrative, business, legal, academic, and so on	formality: formal, informal; "style": expert, non-expert (lay)	medium: spoken, written; channel: face-to-face, telephone, printed, non-printed etc.; turn: dialogue, monologue
Longacre (1974)	narrative, drama, procedural, expository, hortatory			
Werlich (1975)	description, narration, exposition, argumentation, instruction		subjective, objective	
Kinneavy (1971)	expressive, referential, literary, persuasive			[orientation: encoder, decoder, reality, signal]
Greenbaum & Svartvik (1990) [Survey of English Usage]	<written: printed> informative, instructional, persuasive, imaginative	<informative> academic, popular, administrative & legal <persuasive> religious, political, commercial	(<dialogue> public discussion, conversation	spoken, written; dialogue, monologue

To provide a comprehensive map of registers/text types that can be used in ADA, let me present ***part*** of one context-based typology that we have been developing over a number of years and testing in various contexts of use, including those of language description, translation studies and educational linguistics (e.g. Matthiessen, 2006; Teruya, 2007; and see also entries in Matthiessen *et al.*, 2010). Drawing on work by Jean Ure, we have been ranging across field, tenor and mode; but for present purposes, let me focus on field — more specifically, on field in the sense of what's going on in a given context, i.e. on the **field of activity**. We call this the SOCIO-SEMIOTIC PROCESS parameter of field (the other major field parameter being the semiotic domain — the domain of experience, 'topic' or 'subject matter'; cf. Hasan, 1994) because the activity is either a purely social process or a semiotic one. Purely social processes are processes of (interactive) behaviour

– processes of 'doing'. They include team work such as constructing buildings, moving furniture, performing surgery and engaging in recreational team activities such as team games. Semiotic processes may be present as the social processes unfold, but they are activated to facilitate the social processes – they do not constitute the field of activity.[14] This is the traditional category of language in action. Other processes are semiotic as well as social – not purely social; being semiotic, they are also social since semiotic processes are manifested through social processes.

We can summarize the socio-semiotic processes of field, grouping them into three superordinate categories – semiotic processes, semiotic processes potentially leading to social processes and social processes:

- **semiotic processes** (i.e. 'meaning' processes – semiotic processes constitutive of context, manifested through social processes):
    - **expounding** knowledge about general classes of phenomena (rather than particular phenomena), theorizing our experience of the world in terms of a commonsense (folk) or uncommonsense (scientific) model by explaining why general classes of events take place or by categorizing general classes of entities (in terms of taxonomies, hyponymic and/or meronymic, and/or characterization);
    - **reporting** on particular phenomena (rather than general classes of phenomena), by recording or chronicling (the flow of) particular events, inventorying particular entities, or surveying particular places;
    - **recreating** various aspects of life – any of the eight different types of context according to field of activity, typically imagined (fictional) rather than experienced (personally or vicariously), as verbal art with a 'theme' (in the sense of Hasan, 1985), through narration and/or dramatization;
    - **sharing** personal experiences and values (opinions) as part of establishing, maintaining and calibrating, negotiating interpersonal relationships – in terms of tenor, ranging from (and potentially transforming) strangerhood to intimacy, but in sustained form involving fairly intimate relationships; in terms of mode, traditionally and prototypically in private face-to-face interaction, but increasingly enabled by new technologies opening up new channels of sharing (epistolary, telegraphic, telephonic – and now with an explosion of mobile and Internet based possibilities, with a tendency to blur the distinction between private and public spheres);

- o **exploring** public values (opinions) and positions (ideas, hypotheses) by reviewing commodities (assigning them values on a scale from very positive to very negative) or by arguing about positions, debating or discussing them – in terms of tenor, typically between one person (a professional or a member of the general public) and some segment of the general public, so between strangers; in terms of mode, typically using media channels, either 'old' media channels (print, radio, TV) or 'new' media channels (mobile and/ or Internet-based);[15]
- **semiotic processes** potentially leading to **social processes** (i.e. 'meaning' leading to 'doing'):
  - o **recommending** some course of action (typically some kind of social process – in the strong form, exhortation), either for the sake of the addressees by advising them to undertake it for their own good or for the sake of the speaker by promoting some type of goods-&-services;
  - o **enabling** some course of action (typically some kind of social process), either literally enabling (empowering) them by instructing them in some type of procedure or constraining them by regulating their behaviour;
- **social processes** (i.e. 'doing' processes – social processes constitutive of context, semiotic processes facilitating [i.e. 'meaning' facilitating 'doing']):
  - o **doing** – performing some form of social behaviour, on one's own or as part of a team, with semiotic processes ('meaning') coming in to facilitate this social behaviour through direction or collaboration.

There are thus eight primary types – types that can be grouped into three categories (semiotic, semiotic leading to social, and social processes); and the eight types all have subtypes; we can extend the account in delicacy, as shown schematically in Figure 7.17. This display is designed to suggest a **topological** perspective on the **typology** of fields of activity – of socio-semiotic processes (cf. Martin and Matthiessen, 1991; Matthiessen, 1995). Extending the account of the eight primary types in delicacy is, of course, an ongoing long-term project; but let me take just one step further in delicacy: see Figure 7.18. This differentiation of socio-semiotic process types within field can be located midway along the cline of instantiation between the two outer poles of potential and instance: see Figure 7.19.

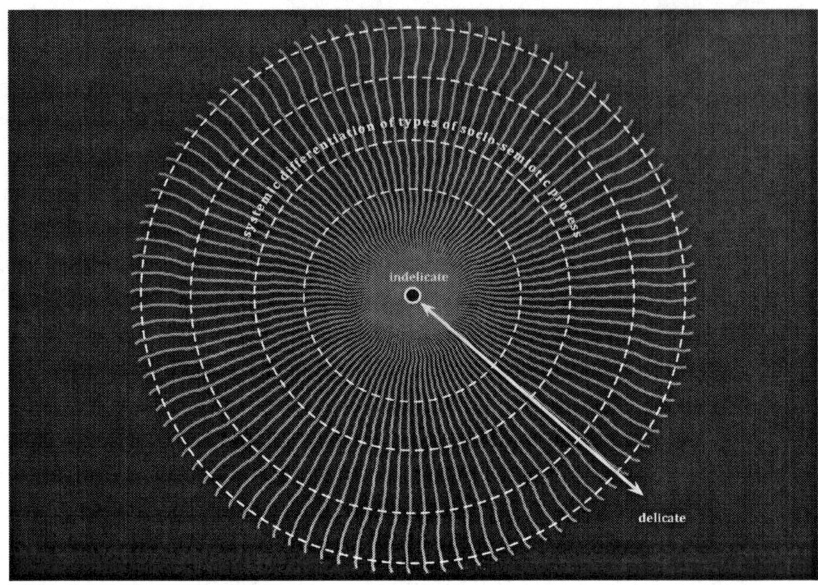

Figure 7.17: Field within context – increasing delicacy in the differentiation of types of socio-semiotic process

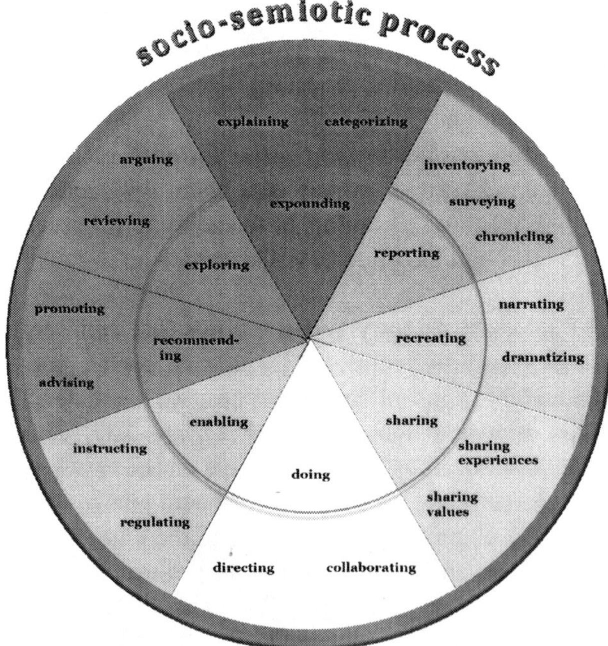

Figure 7.18: Field – types of socio-semiotic process (what's going on in context – activity)

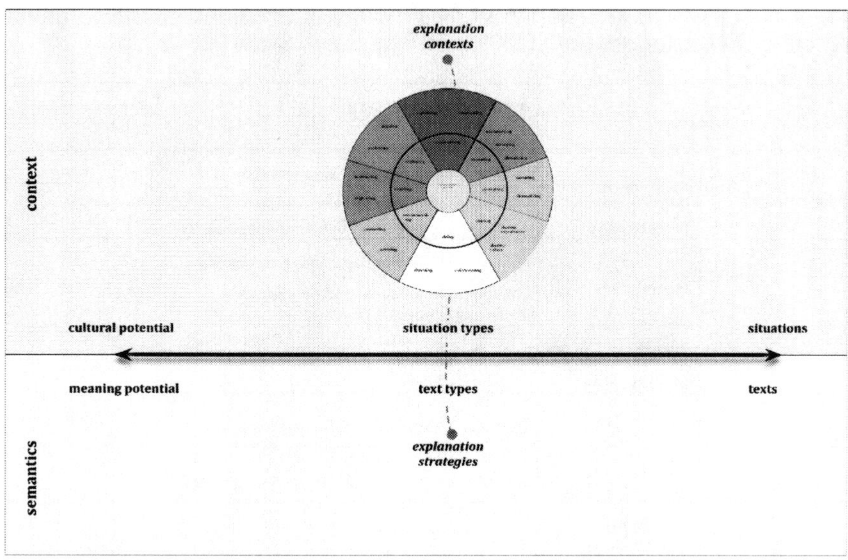

Figure 7.19: The location of types of socio-semiotic process within field (Figure 7.18) along the cline of instantiation

Once we have taken this step in delicacy to secondary types (Figure 7.18), we can begin to see many connections with the very rich and detailed work on 'genre agnation', typically 'genres' of writing, from J. R. Martin and his colleagues and students within the 'genre model' (e.g. Martin, 1985, 1992; Martin and Rose, 2008), and also the 'genres' of casual spoken discourse described by Eggins and Slade (1997). For example, within 'expounding', we can recognize two modes of expounding – expounding phenomena by explaining events and by categorizing entities; and here we can make contact with the work on explanations within the 'genre model' (e.g. Veel, 1997; Martin and Rose, 2008: 150–165). To locate 'genres' in terms of the account of the system of SOCIO-SEMIOTIC PROCESS in Figure 7.18 above, I have sorted the 'genres' of writing that are described in Martin and Rose (2008) and those of spoken conversation described by Eggins and Slade (1997) in terms of the different socio-semiotic process types in Table 7.7. As the table shows, certain socio-semiotic process types are presented in these accounts of the 'genres' of writing and speaking – with a particular focus on educational contexts in the case of writing.

Table 7.7: Terms in the system of socio-semiotic process (field) and 'genres' described in Martin and Rose (2008) and Eggins and Slade (1997)

SOCIO-SEMIOTIC PROCESS		Martin & Rose (2008): "Genre model"	Eggins & Slade (1997)
expounding	explaining	(Chapter 4 Reports and Explanations) explanations	
	categorizing	(Chapter 4 Reports and Explanations) reports	
reporting	chronicling	(Chapter 3 Histories) recounts, biographies (Chapter 5 Procedures and procedural recounts) procedural recounts	
	surveying		
	inventorying		
recreating	[narrating, dramatizing]	(Chapter 2 Stories) stories: narratives	
sharing	[experiences, values]	(Chapter 2 Stories) stories: anecdotes, exempla	chat; opinion, teasing, gossip
doing	[directing, coordinating]		
recommending	promoting		
	advising		
enabling	instructing	(Chapter 5 Procedures and procedural recounts) procedures	
	regulating	(Chapter 5 Procedures and procedural recounts) protocols <or: embedded in procedures>	
exploring	arguing	(Chapter 3 Histories) expositions, discussions	
	evaluating		

Let me use the 'expounding' type of semiotic process within field as an example of how the account of socio-semiotic processes given here can be related to descriptions of particular genres within the genre model and how, by a second step, the elements in the structure of a genre – or situation type in the terms I use here, can be related to semantic strategies through realization. There are two types of expounding processes, as shown in Figure 7.18 above: we can expound knowledge about general classes of phenomena by 'explaining' them or by 'categorizing' them. Within the 'explaining' type, we can differentiate different explanatory strategies, following Veel (1997), as indicated schematically in Figure 7.19 above; these are set out in the system network in the top half of Figure 7.20. Each situation type of explanation ('explanation genre') is characterized by a characteristic contextual structure; for example, factorial explanations are structured as a sequence of two contextual elements, Phenomenon identification $\wedge$ Factor$^{1\text{-}n}$ (see again Veel, 1997). These contextual elements are realized semantically (as shown by Hasan, 1984, for the element of Placement in traditional nursery tales).

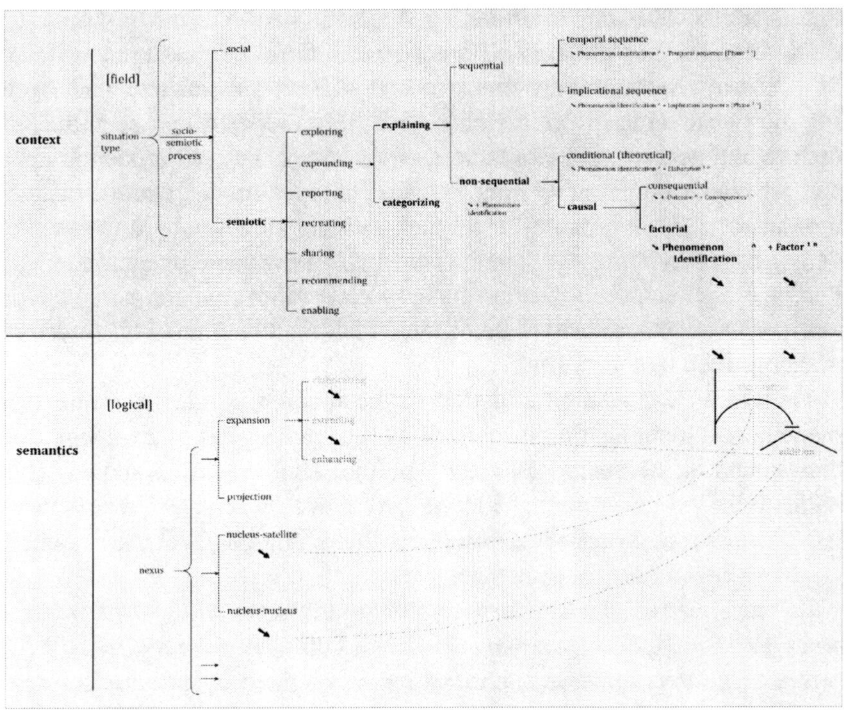

Figure 7.20: Context (field) and semantics (logico-semantic relations) – the realization of the elements of a context of factorial explanation by text segments linked by logico-semantic relations

The semantic realization of the elements of a situation involves all the metafunctional modes of meaning; but for present purposes I will focus on the logico-semantic realization of an element of contextual structure, stating it in terms of RST (Rhetorical Structure Theory; see e.g. Mann *et al.*, 1992; Matthiessen, 2002; and Cloran *et al.*, 2007, for a comparison with other accounts used in SFL of the organization of text). In terms of RST, a text is developed relationally, semantic segments being linked to existing ones through some type of logico-semantic relation. Such logico-semantic relations, or rhetorical relations, can be classified according to Halliday's TYPOLOGY OF LOGICO-SEMANTIC RELATIONS as involving either 'expansion' or 'projection' (see e.g. Halliday and Matthiessen, 1999: Chapter 3; Halliday and Matthiessen, 2004: Chapter 7). Relations of 'expansion' are further differentiated into 'elaborating', 'extending' and 'enhancing' relations, each of which leads to more delicate subtypes. Relations of 'projection' are further differentiated into the projection of 'ideas' and of 'locutions', again with further differentiations in delicacy. At the same time as logico-semantic relations are differentiated in terms of the nature of the relation, they are also differentiated in terms of the NUCLEARITY of the relation; a relation may link two text segments as nucleus and satellite, the two having unequal status, or it may link two text segments as nucleus and nucleus, the two having equal status. The two systemic variables of type and nuclearity intersect; for example, there are multi-nuclear relations of the 'elaborating' type such as restatement, where two nuclei are construed as being equivalent construals of the same phenomena, and there are nucleus-satellite ones such as elaboration, where a nucleus is construed as a generalization being specified in more detail, characterized or exemplified by a satellite.

Thus in an explanation situation of the factorial kind, the element of Phenomenon Identification is realized by the nuclear part of an elaboration relation and the elements of Factor^{1-n} by the satellite part, as shown schematically in the lower part of Figure 7.20 above. Whenever there is more than one factor as part of the explanation, these multiple factors are realized in the text by an additive sequence.

Let me illustrate the logico-semantic organization of a text realizing a situation of the factorial explanation kind, taken from Veel (1997):[16] see Figure 7.21. Phenomenon Identification is realized by the nuclear segment of the whole text, which in turn is realized by clauses [1], *This process is the cause of the breaking up of large rocks into smaller pieces*, and [2], *Physical processes can cause changes in rocks*. The next element of the structure of the explanation situation, Factor^{1-n}, is realized by a satellite segment that stands in a relation of elaboration to the nucleus. This segment, which constitutes the main bulk of the text, is in turn realized by clauses [3] through [18]. There are altogether six factors identified in the text. These are not in fact presented simply as a list of six factors; but they are instead grouped semantically into two sets, the two most important factors and the remainder. As shown in Figure 7.21, these two sets are represented by an additive sequence of two text segments, both of which start with a nuclear generalizations about factors, [3] and [4] respectively. Elaborations of these nuclear generalizations then introduce the different factors, organized into additive sequences. Thus while the contextual structure of factorial explanations is 'flat', the semantic structure involves considerable further organization in the form of the internal nesting of logico-semantic complexes.

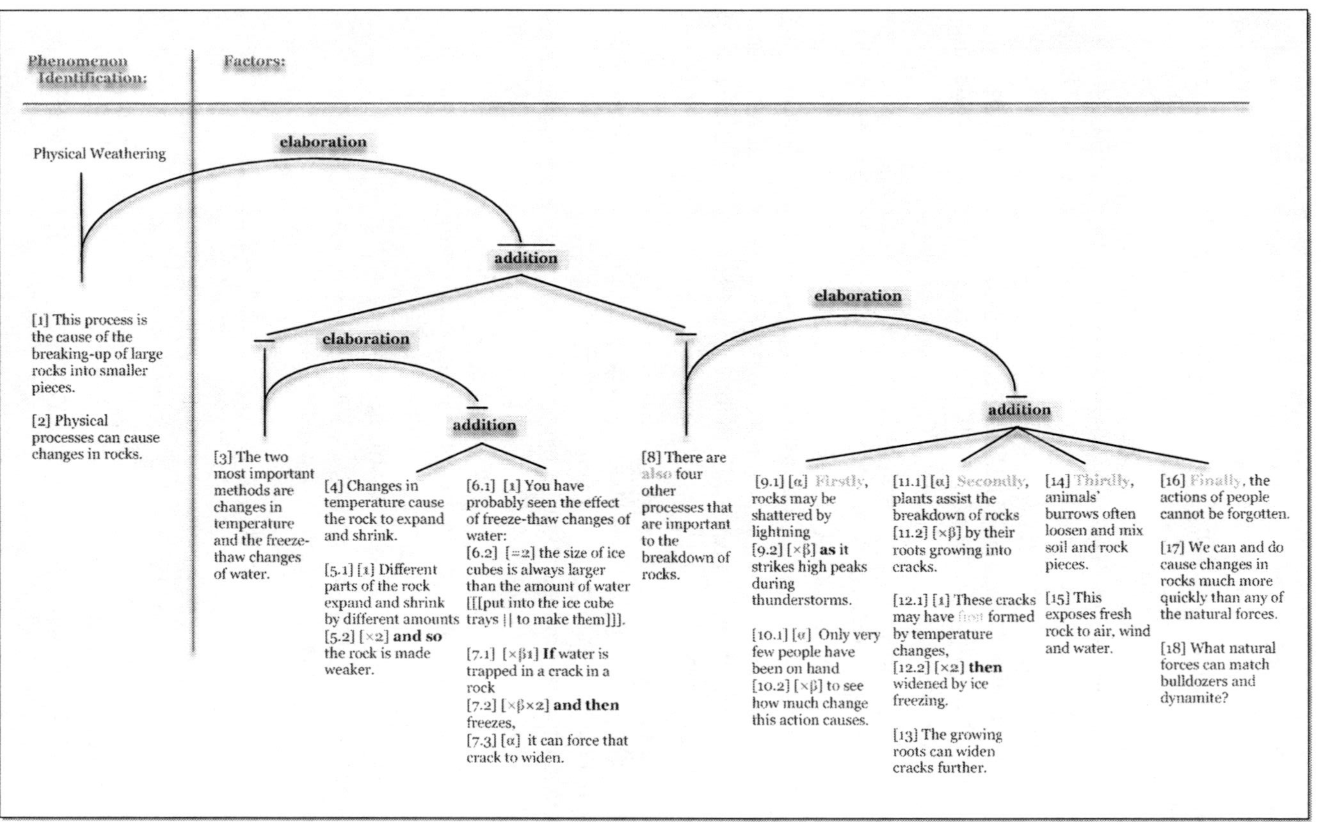

Figure 7.21: Semantic analysis of a factorial explanation in terms of logico-semantic relations (as represented in RST)

The logical analysis of text in terms rhetorical relations is, as noted, only one strand of analysis; the other strands are experiential, interpersonal and textual. The logical organization of text works together with contributions from the other metafunctional modes of meaning (see Table 7.4 above); for example:

- As part of the ideational semantic system of IDEATION, RHETORICAL RELATIONS contribute to the development of experiential patterns of FIGURATION into larger ideational text segments such as episodes in narratives (recreating contexts), procedures in instructions (enabling contexts) and taxonomies in reports (expounding contexts).
- Supporting the interpersonal semantic system of NEGOTIATION, RHETORICAL RELATIONS contribute to the formation of move complexes in the development of dialogic exchanges.
- Working alongside the textual semantic system of PRESENTATION, RHETORICAL RELATIONS contribute to the development of waves of information in a text (cf. Matthiessen, 1992, on textual transitions and textual statuses).

Ideationally, texts construe human experience of the world as meaning. As just noted, the logical and experiential modes of construing experience – as sequence and as configuration, respectively – work together to construe episodes, procedures, taxonomies and other 'chunks' of experience. The nature of the 'chunk' depends to a large extent on the field of activity. For example, in recreating contexts where the primary method of recreating is that of narrating, the logical and experiential modes of construing experience work together to construe episodes that together form a plot or event line. This can be illustrated in a very schematic way for an episode in a traditional folk tale, *The Hummingbird King*: see Figure 7.22.

One day, Kukul was hunting in the forest. He heard the rustling of leaves and raised his bow and arrow. With a flurry, a magnificent hummingbird, larger than any hummingbird Kukul had ever seen, fluttered next to him. The hummingbird spoke these words, 'I am your guardian, Kukul. My job is to warn you. Beware. Death is circling you. Beware of a man.'

'Magnificent hummingbird, my guardian, what man should I beware of?' asked Kukul.

'Someone very close to you. Be careful, Kukul,' said the bird. Then it flew away.

Kukul walked on through the forest. As he came to a thicket, he heard the faint rustling of leaves. He pointed his arrow, but saw nothing. Kukul crouched low to the ground and moved slowly. He had not gone far when … sss … it came. An arrow pierced his chest.

In pain, Kukul pulled out the arrow and headed for the river to wash his wound. 'Surely, it is not deep,' he tried to convince himself, but his strength began to fade as his chest turned scarlet with blood.

A few more steps and Kukul had to lean against a tree. 'It is so dark,' he moaned. He fell onto a sea of emerald grass and there he died. Alone. Betrayed. Then, something extraordinary happened. Slowly, Kukul's body changed to the color of grass, but his chest remained scarlet. His skin became feathers and his hair, a gorgeous crest.

By the time Chirumá came out of the thicket, Kukul's arms had turned into wings. All Chirumá could see was a glowing green bird with a scarlet chest and a long, long tail, flying off into the sunlight.

This episode realizes one element in the contextual structure of traditional folk tales (or nursery tales), Sequent Event, according to Hasan's (1984) description. The episode is organized globally by means of enhancing relations of time – temporal circumstance and temporal sequence; and the local organization is also dominated by temporal sequence – by relations of temporal succession linking one figure to another.

Textually, texts create waves of information (cf. Halliday, 1979, 1981, 1985b; Matthiessen, 1992; Martin, 1993); these ripple through the whole text globally, but also unfold on smaller scales – rhetorical paragraphs; and (within the domain of the grammar) clause complexes and clauses (Halliday's 'hierarchy of periodicity'). For instance, the episode mentioned above and represented schematically in Figure 7.22, is presented textually as a move from Theme, *one day he was hunting in the forest*, where the spatio-temporal setting is given as an orientation, to New, starting with *then, something extraordinary happened* and continuing through the last couple of (orthographic) paragraphs. The main point is thus Kukul's transformation into a beautiful bird, a quetzal. The Theme is a satellite that relates to the whole remainder of the text segment, serving (as noted) as an orientation to what follows. The New is the last segment in the temporal sequence in Figure 7.22.

The relationship between peaks of textual prominence as Theme and as New and the logico-semantic organization of texts varies according to the registerial nature of texts: some examples of global text patterns are provided in Table 7.8. For instance, while the expounding text analysed in Figure 7.22 has a global nucleus that is given the status of macro-Theme

– which is characteristic of factorial explanations, persuasive texts, which operate in recommending and exploring contexts, tend to end with a global nucleus with the status of macro-New: the body of the text provides evidence for a nuclear proposition or motivation for a nuclear proposal, and this proposition or proposal is presented has the main point of the text, the new information to be taken away from it.

Table 7.8: Nuclearity in rhetorical-relational organization of text in relation to textual statuses

Field of activity		'Genre'	Macro-Theme	(Body of text)	Macro-New
Expounding	Classifying	Report	Nuclear segment	Elaboration of nuclear segment	–
Recreating	Narrating	Story	Satellite segment, circumstantially related to multi-nuclear segment	Multi-nuclear segment organized by temporal sequence	(Evaluative elaborating satellite)
Recommending	Promoting	Advert		Satellite segment, motivating nucleus	Nuclear segment [command/ offer]

Interpersonally, text relation between speaker (writer) and addressee through successions of moves selecting in the system of SPEECH FUNCTION and thereby forming exchanges between speaker and addressee (see Halliday, 1984; Martin, 1992: Chapter 2; Eggins and Slade, 1997; Halliday and Matthiessen, 2004: Chapter 4). Monologic texts tend, of course, to unfold as sequences of moves that are predominantly statements; but stories may have passages of dramatic dialogue spliced into them, as in the folk tale above:

> The hummingbird spoke these words, 'I am your guardian, Kukul. My job is to warn you. Beware. Death is circling you. Beware of a man.'

> 'Magnificent hummingbird, my guardian, what man should I beware of?' asked Kukul.

> 'Someone very close to you. Be careful, Kukul,' said the bird.

Here the hummingbird's first contribution is a move complex – a complex of moves related to one another logico-semantically by rhetorical relations. This complex involves nuclear warnings (*beware*; *beware of a man*) and motivating satellites (*my job is to warn you*; *death is circling you*) – supported by a satellite related through a relationship of justification (*I am your guardian, Kukul*).

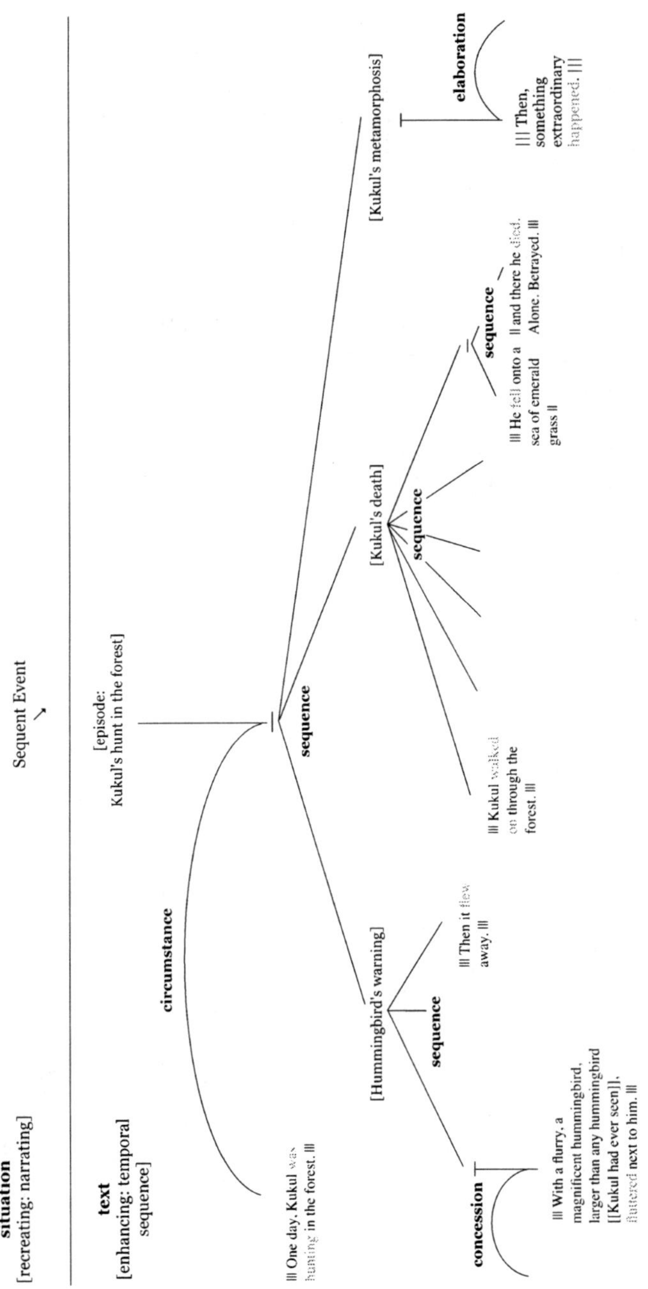

Figure 7.22: Construal of an episode realizing Sequent Event in a traditional narrative

Such move complexes are very common in dialogue: a speaker's turn in an exchange very often involves a nuclear move (or set of moves) with the key speech function supported by other moves, typically statements (cf. Ventola, 1988). Let me just give one illustration – a contribution by a call centre agent in a telephonic service encounter: see Figure 7.23. Here the nuclear move is an offer, an offer by the agent to provide further assistance to the caller; the other segments are related to this nuclear segment as supporting satellites linked to the nucleus directly or indirectly through different rhetorical relations. If the addressee chooses the 'expected' type of response – rather than a 'discretionary' one, this response will be focused on the nucleus of the move complex. In this particular case, the exchange does not quite work, so the agent decides to move things along:

> Agent: As I mention earlier, I'll be connecting your phone to a specialist regarding your request, is there anything I can assist you before I connect the call?

> Caller: Um …

> Agent: May I put you on hold now, and I'll connect the call, Mr. Green?

> Caller: Yeah.

> Agent: You're welcome.

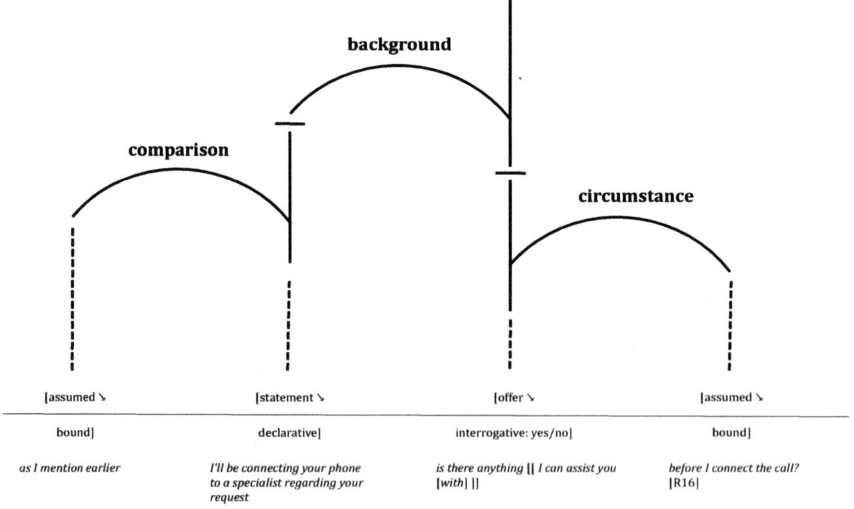

Figure 7.23: Semantic analysis – logical (rhetorical relations) and interpersonal (speech function) of a turn in a telephonic service encounter

Part of the negotiation between speaker and listener is the ongoing assessment of the commodities that they're exchanging and also of the acts of exchanging these commodities. Like interpersonal features in general, such assessments tend to be realized prosodically (cf. Halliday, 1979; Martin 1996), so they are not confined to any particular nuclear or satellite text segment but tend to extend across segments. However, the deployment of the resources of assessment varies from one field of activity to another (see Figure 7.18 above), and this variation is also reflected in the logico-semantic organization of texts. For instance, narrative texts may end with a text segment that serves as a Moral (cf. Hasan, 1984); and this means that the moral assessment is given the status of macro-New.

7.4.3 Compositional scale: From macro via meso to micro

Up to now, I have focused on generalizations about units of a certain size – viz. texts in their contexts of situation. At the stratum of context, these generalizations are stated syntagmatically in terms of the kind of generic or schematic structures illustrated above. Staying within context, we can move down and up from situations and situation types along a **compositional scale**.

> (1) Moving down, we can examine **sub-situational** patterns – contextual phases characterizing the development of an element of structure such as Factors in a factorial situation type (cf. Figure 7.20 above).
>
> (2) Moving up, we can examine **supra-situational** patterns – situations combining to form supra-situational units of context. For example, a patient's journey through the emergency department of a hospital can be interpreted and described as a sequence of situation types extending from admission to discharge or transfer to a ward (cf. Slade *et al.*, 2008).

There thus at least three ranks of contextual units on this compositional scale: (i) macro – supra-situations, (ii) meso – situations, and (iii) micro – sub-situations. Thus, as just noted, a patient's journey through the emergency department of a hospital can be analysed as a supra-situation – i.e. as a structured multivariate sequence of situation types, as illustrated in Figure 7.24.[17] The supra-situation is, naturally, quite complex, involving many semiotic and social activities (cf. Steiner's, 1991, analysis of social activities in Figure 7.12 above). The situation types that make up the supra-situation will, of course, occur in other supra-situations as well; or rather, variants of them will. For instance, it is quite illuminating to compare and contrast situation types of consultation across different healthcare supra-situations – say that of a visit to an emergency department with that of a visit to a GP (cf. Halliday, 1998), where the time is much less foregrounded as a source of pressure than in an emergency department.

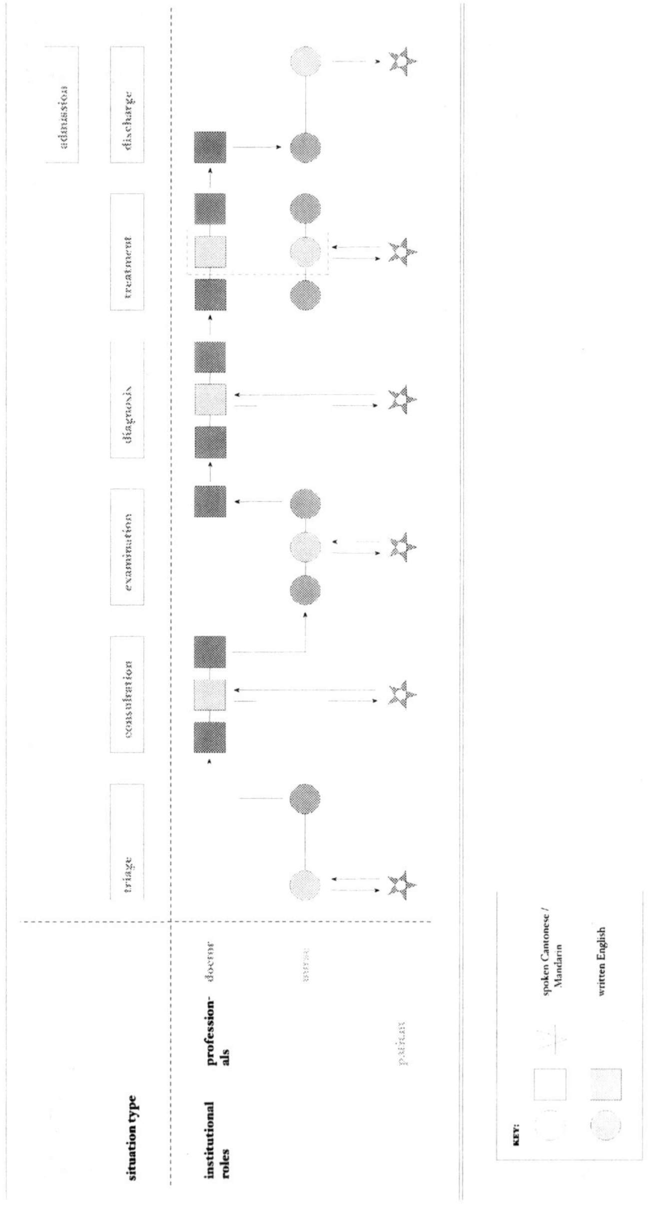

Figure 7.24: A patient's journey through an accident and emergency department as a supra-situational construct

The situation types that make up a supra-situation such as a patient journey through an emergency department are likely to be quite diverse, e.g. involving different kinds of socio-semiotic process within field (see Figure 7.18) but also involving variation within both tenor and mode as well as within the 'subject matter' variable of field.

Texts of different sizes operate within sub-situations, situations and supra-situations. 'Text' has usually been defined by reference to situation (cf. Halliday and Hasan, 1976, 1985), so as we move up and down the compositional scale, we can identify sub-texts (cf. Halliday, 1994) operating in sub-situations and supra-texts – or macro-texts (see Martin, 1994, on 'macro-genres') – operating in supra-situations.

The variation along the compositional scale in terms of both text and context can be illustrated by reference to a patient's journey, but let me instead give a highly schematic illustration of this variation by reference to the context of print media (cf. e.g. Iedema *et al.*, 1994), from the consumer's point of view: see Figure 7.25. Here the supra-situation is that of engagement with a quantum of mass media in the form of a newspaper (or its web equivalent). This supra-situation covers certain ranges of field, tenor and mode values; in terms of field (in the sense of socio-semiotic activity), it includes not only situations characterized by the key activity of 'reporting' but also situations characterized by 'expounding', 'exploring', 'enabling' and 'recommending' activities. The supra-situation is the semiotic environment of the whole newspaper, which we can interpret as a complex of texts related in different ways through logico-semantic relations (cf. again Martin, 1994; and see e.g. Mann *et al.*, 1992, on logico-semantic, or 'rhetorical', relations). The texts that make up the macro-text – the newspaper – have long been recognized under various headings in accounts of the media and may be indicated in newspapers, e.g. news reports, news features, editorials, opinion pieces, reviews, advertisements (see again Iedema *et al.*, 1994). The situations that they operate in can be characterized in terms of generic or schematic structures such as Headline ^ Lead ^ Lead development (^ Wrap-up).

The kind of compositional scale discussed here was explored a long time ago in Sinclair and Coulthard's (1975) pioneering study of classroom discourse, where they drew on Halliday's (e.g. 1961) notion of rank: see Figure 7.26 for an interpretation of their Figure 1 (p. 24) in the terms used here. The categories they posit, in particular course, period, topic, lesson and transaction, are of course specific to the contexts and texts of classroom-based education. They developed the framework further, and by the late 1970s they were working on a more generalized model (reported by Sinclair in a talk at the Department of English, Lund University, around 1978). At the same time, their context-specific account embodies the important insight that contexts vary considerably in complexity and therefore also in the nature of their compositional scales. The nature of the 'macro' in institutions of education has been further illuminated by Christie (e.g. 1997), in her work on 'curriculum macrogenres', and also by other educational linguists.

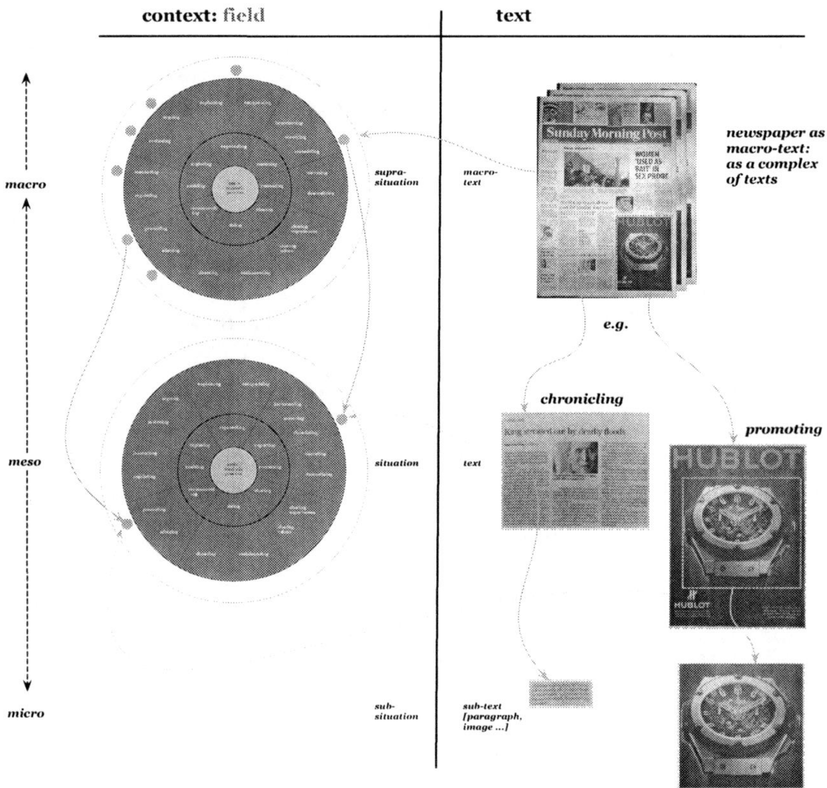

Figure 7.25: Scale in context and text – from macro via meso to macro

The compositional scale can, in principle, be extended upwards so that we can analyse and interpret contextual phenomena that extend beyond supra-situations such as a patient's journey through an emergency department or a student's journey through a course during a semester. However, at this point, we face the interesting question of whether such extensions are best interpreted and modelled in terms of compositional scales or in terms of the cline of instantiation (cf. Section 7.4.2 above) – or both, in a kind of knight's move (cf. Matthiessen, 2009: Section 7.3.6, on the interpretation of institutions in terms of the cline of instantiation and the hierarchy of stratification).

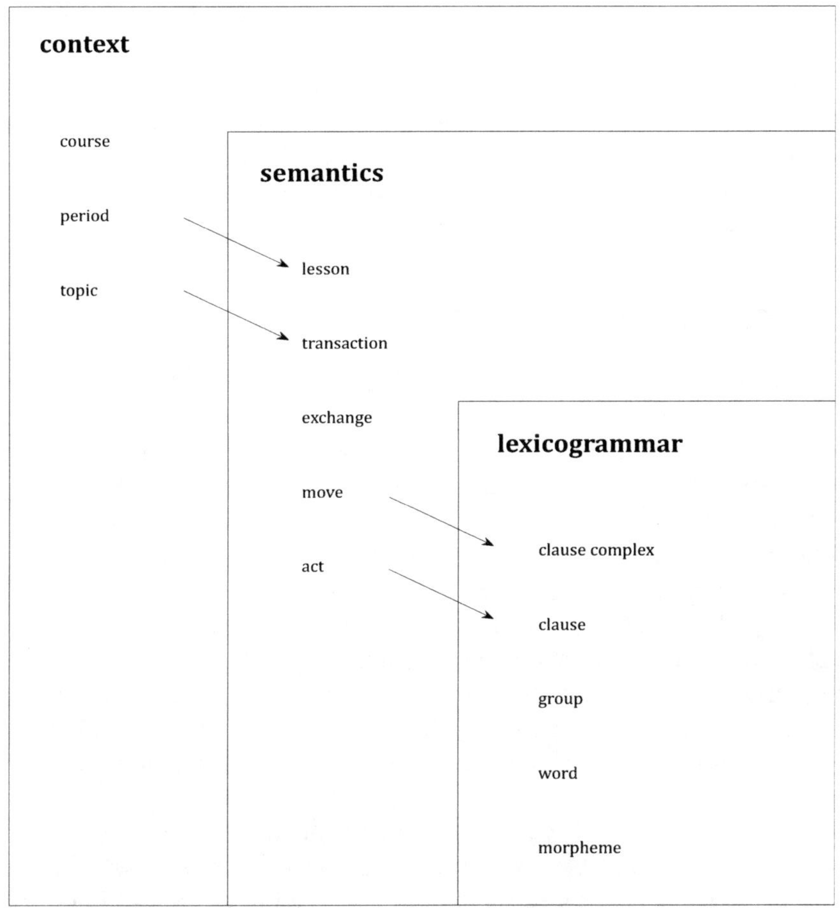

Figure 7.26: Adaptation of Sinclair and Coulthard's (1975) 'levels and ranks' for the analysis of classroom discourse

7.5   Trade-offs in analysis

Analysis always involves **choices** on the part of analysts; and in making such analytic choices, analysts must weigh different objectives against one another: analysts are always faced with **trade-offs**, e.g. between the coverage of the analysis of text and the volume of text analysed. Such trade-offs are particularly important to consider in relation to ADA, Appliable Discourse Analysis, because the choices analysts make obviously affect the appliability of the results of the analysis.

Assuming for the moment that all the combinations of metafunction and stratification have been described in some detail.[18] we can define a **comprehensive analysis** of a given text in its context of situation, or of a given set of texts in their context of situation, as one where all the systems identified in the description have exhaustively been taken into account, in both qualitative and quantitative terms. However, it is not always possible – or even desirable – to undertake a comprehensive analysis of a text.

7.5.1 Comprehensive vs. selective analysis

Comprehensiveness is costly – if we assume that the analysis is manual, then the more comprehensive the analysis is, the smaller the volume of text that can be analysed within a given quantum of research labour; but by reducing the comprehensiveness of the analysis – by being more selective, we can increase the volume of text analysed. This inverse relationship between comprehensiveness of analysis and volume of text analysed is shown schematically in Figure 7.27.

Comprehensive analysis and selective analysis are thus the outer poles on a cline of the comprehensiveness of the analysis of text in context. A **selective analysis** of text in context is one where only certain systems have been included in the analysis – e.g. only textual systems of THEME or only interpersonal systems of APPRAISAL (these systems being two popular choices in selective analysis).

As noted, comprehensiveness is a matter of degree; there are any number of intermediate points between fully comprehensive, or exhaustive, analysis and highly selective analysis. Relating this scale to the question of the volume of text being analysed, we can differentiate between **minimally reliable analysis** and **maximally reliable analysis**, as shown in Figure 7.27. Reliability must, of course, be interpreted in terms of the claims that the analysis is made to support.

- Minimally reliable analysis simply means that very few systems have been considered in the analysis, and the analysis has been applied to a very small volume of text, such as an extract from a single text.
- Maximally reliable analysis means that the analysis involves as wide a range of systems as possible, and that it has been applied to a very large volume of text.

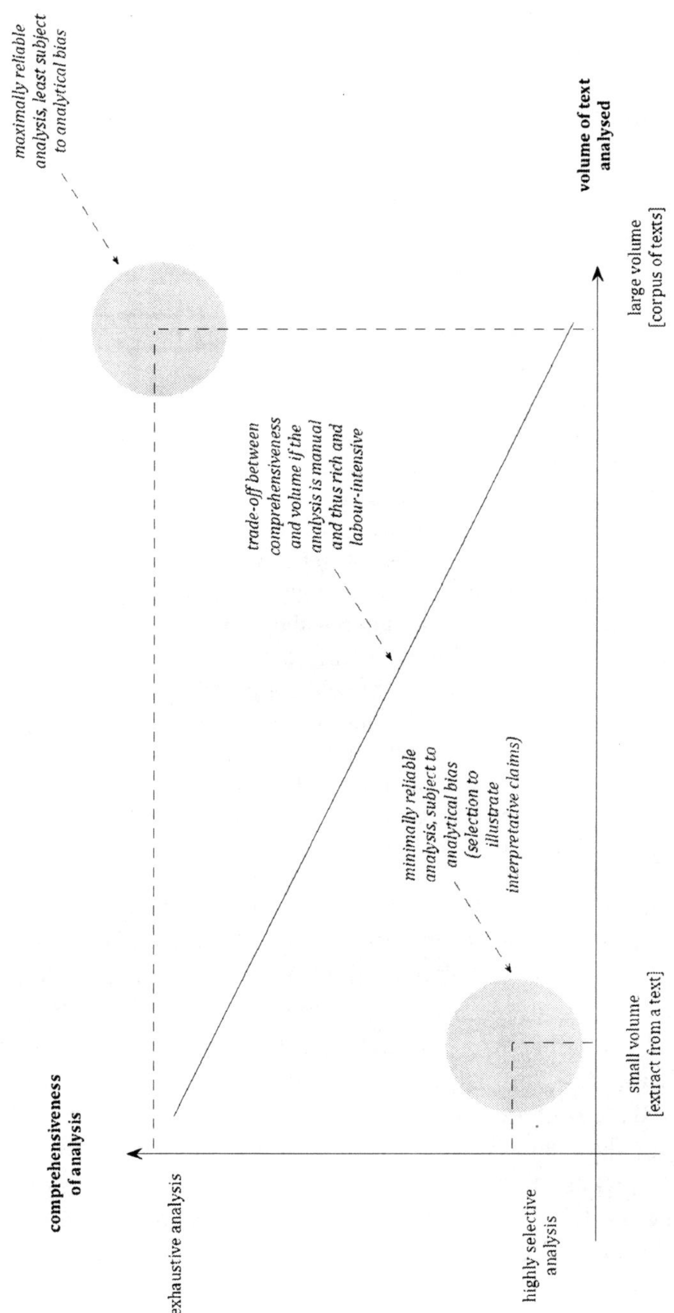

Figure 7.27: The inverse relationship between the comprehensiveness of (manual) analysis of volume of text analysed

In the case of minimally reliable analysis, the danger is that the analyst makes the choice of the sample of text and the systems to analyse in order to illustrate (or, more worryingly, to 'prove') a claim. Halliday's (2010) comments on the angle and attitude adopted in the analysis are directly relevant:

> An interesting feature of discourse analysis (and one that might serve to distinguish 'discourse analysis' from 'text analysis', or 'text linguistics') is that many of those who undertake discourse analysis approach the task from a particular angle, with a particular attitude towards the text and a view of their own responsibility as analysts. In modern parlance, they have their own agenda.
>
> This may be seen in the choice of the text to be analysed, which is often a text displaying, or seen as displaying, some socio-political stance of which the analyst disapproves: racism, perhaps, or colonialism, or a one-sided attitude to some contemporary or earlier conflict. This has the danger that the analyst might have picked out certain portions of the text which display the features in question without noting how far they are typical of the text as a whole – though it might be argued that this does not matter; the fact that they are there at all reveals a possibly unadmitted bias on the part of the writer. What is more problematic is whether the analyst might unwittingly have selected just those features of the lexicogrammar which support them in their argument. This arises if the argument is based on the choice of vocabulary without regard for colligation with the grammar.

If the analysis is selective rather than comprehensive, it is important to be able to articulate the criteria according to which the selection has been made. These criteria may be derived from the dimensions of the theory – e.g. a metafunctional slice across strata in the analysis of a particular corpus of texts, as in Matthiessen *et al.* (2005); or they may be derived from practical concerns, as in the analysis of communication in institutions of health-care, e.g. Slade *et al.* (2008).

Whether the analysis is comprehensive or selective, it is usually followed by a process of **interpretation** of the results of the analysis. By interpreting the results of the analysis, we try to bring out the significant patterns revealed by the analysis, determining how they relate to one another (e.g. interpersonal patterns to textual ones, or interpersonal patterns to experiential ones). Here we may again refer to the description of the system to determine whether the text(s) we have analysed are typical or atypical in one respect or another.

7.5.2 Complementarity of manual and automated analysis

If we want to achieve great reliability in our text analysis, we can increase the volume of texts analysed, as indicated in Figure 7.27 above. We can of course do this by involving more analysts and devoting more hours of manual analysis to the task, but this quickly becomes very costly and even with a large team of analysts there is a limit to the volume of text that can be analysed – and also to the consistency and reliability of the multi-person analysis (inter-analyst reliability). Alternatively, we can automate the analysis; we can deploy existing computational tools or design new ones. However, currently, the potential to automate analysis is still severely restricted. The higher the 'level' of analysis – in terms of strata and ranks within a given stratum, the harder it is to automate it (see e.g. Teich, 2009; Wu, 2009). For example, while it is easy to base computational analysis on graphological patterns (as in concordancing programmes), it is much harder to base it on semantic patterns, or even on grammatical patterns at grammatical ranks higher than that of the morpheme or word. Therefore we face another analytic trade-off, one between the 'level' of analysis and the volume of text analysed: see Figure 7.28.

For many uses of ADA, the best solution is to develop a two-pronged approach based both on manual 'high-level' analysis of small samples of texts and on automated analysis of large samples of text. In a sense, this means combining the techniques of text or discourse analysis and the techniques of corpus linguistics.

As corpora – samples of texts based on systematic criteria – have grown in size from around one million words in the 1960s (e.g. the BROWN and LOB corpora) to tens of millions of words or even hundreds of million of words (e.g. the British National Corpus [BNC] and the Corpus of Contemporary American English [COCA]), it is becoming possible to detect patterns that were not previously visible – just as natural scientists began to do several hundred years ago with the aid of telescopes and microscopes; we are moving further into technologically empowered discourse analysis. This trend is reinforced by tools enabling us to search texts available on the World Wide Web such as WebCorp and the Google book Ngram Viewer; but while texts on the WWW constitute vast text samples, they are not, of course, corpora in a strict sense since they have not been compiled according to systematic criteria – they are simply opportunistic samples whose composition we know very little about.

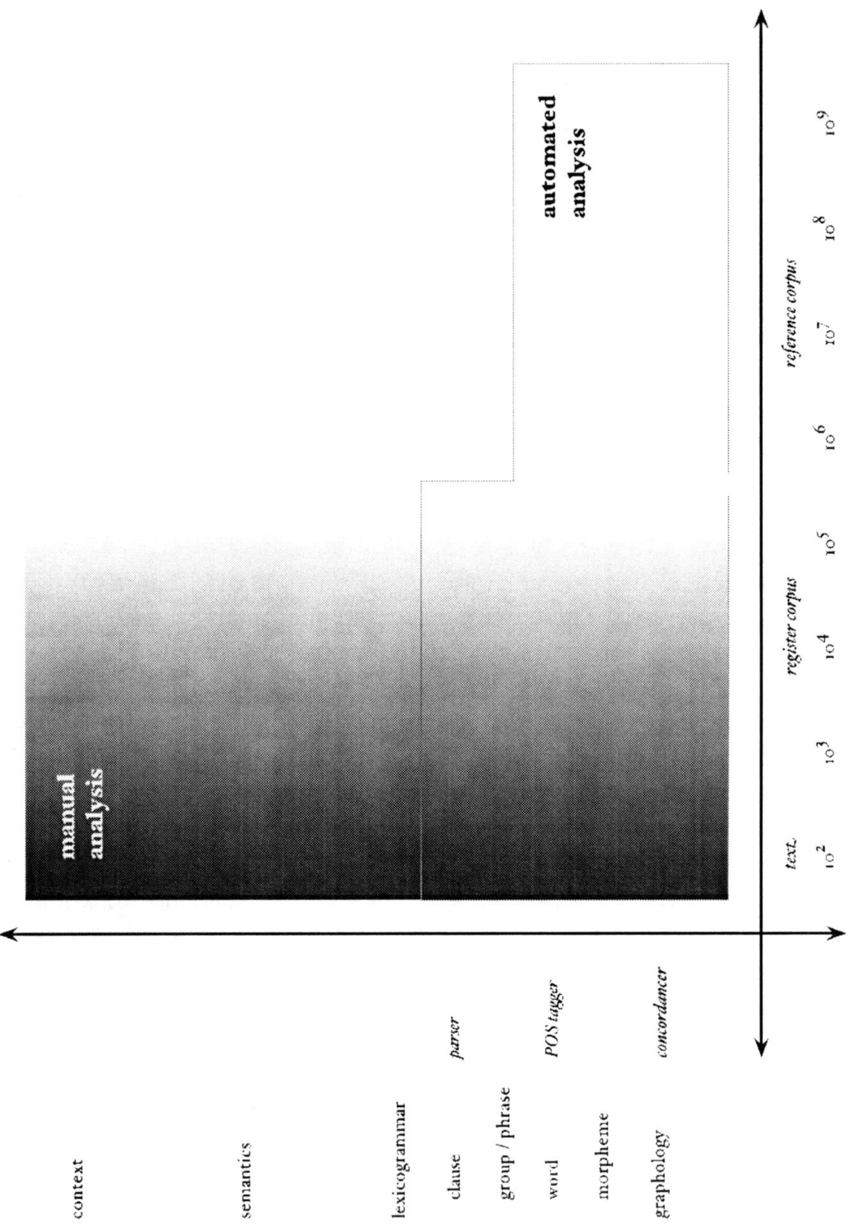

Figure 7.28: Complementarity of manual and automated analysis in terms of (1) 'level' of analysis and (2) volume of text analysed

These large corpora and text collections open up new possibilities for ADA. For example, it is now possible to attempt to track cultural or subcultural trends and fashions discursively. Thus Google's Ngram Viewer reveals that there has been a fairly sharp and steady increase in the frequency of instances of *emotional intelligence* since 1992;[19] and in the Brigham Young historical corpus of *Time Magazine* from the 1920s to the 2000s, there are six instances in the 1990s and eight in the 2000s but none at all before the 1990s. According to the Wikipedia,[20] the term *emotional intelligence* was first introduced by Wayne Payne in his 1985 PhD thesis *A Study of Emotion: Developing Emotional Intelligence*, though earlier uses are also mentioned. It seems plausible that this is part of a **cultural syndrome** – such as an increasing orientation towards emotions and feelings, at least in the academic world: this is roughly the period when scholars have begun to explore notions like 'emotion', 'evaluation', 'attitude', 'stance' and 'appraisal' (although as always with precursors, such as Charles Osgood's psycholinguistic research). It would of course be interesting if it turns out that that is possible to show that the syndrome extends beyond the world of scholarly fashions. For instance, the expression *I feel good about* has increased rather dramatically in frequency since the late 1960s, and it is matched by *I feel bad about*, although with a somewhat earlier start and a less dramatic increase during the same period (see Figure 7.29). In the *Time Magazine* historical corpus, there is 1 instance of *feel good about* in the 1920s, then nothing until the 1960s: 1960s – 1, 1970s – 5, 1980s – 18, 1990s – 17, and 200s – 15. However, this is just an exploratory fishing expedition. It is not possible to draw any conclusions based on *feel good about* on its own. We have to ensure that we are exploring trends in meaning rather than just trends in wording; that is, we have to explore changes in terms of semantic fields realized through a variety of wordings.

7.5.3 Large-scale automated analysis

There are now a number of initiatives involving automated analysis of very large samples of texts. These initiatives come largely from outside linguistics, and have been applied to a range of research questions relevant to ADA. One prominent example is a longitudinal study of language learning based on very extensive video recording of one child and his caregivers in a home equipped with recorders for total coverage: Roy *et al.* (2006) characterize their research as the 'human speechome project'. To cope with the huge volume of recordings (230,000 hours; Roy, 2009), the team had to design and use computational tools for analysis, e.g. BlitzScribe (Roy and Roy, 2009). One of the concerns has been to related 'word learning' to the contexts in which words are learned, as shown by Roy *et al.* (2012). This research can be interpreted as providing significant support of Halliday's (e.g. 1975) account of how young children learn how to mean.

Figure 7.29: Increase in the occurrences of *I feel good about* and *I feel bad about* according to Google's Ngram viewer

Research efforts involving very large samples of texts are often concerned with some kind of 'content analysis' using 'data mining' techniques. The 'content' may of course be conceived of in ideational terms, as when researchers track themes or motifs in large volumes of text (e.g. Havre *et al.*, 2000); but it may also be interpersonal in nature, concerned with connotations or 'appraisal', as in forms of 'sentiment mining' (e.g. Hu and Liu, 2004).

One promising development in 'content analysis' based on massive volumes of text is what has been called 'Culturomics'. Michel *et al.* (2011: 186) define it as 'the application of high-throughput data collection and analysis to the study of human culture'. They investigate cultural trends based on 'a corpus of digitized texts containing about 4% of all books ever printed', e.g. showing evidence of censorship and suppression in Nazi Germany. In another recent contribution, Leetaru (2011) uses the techniques of Culturomics to investigate motifs in a 30-year large sample of news, retroactively predicting major events based on analysis of 'global news tone'. One tool of Culturomics has been made freely available, the Ngram viewer of Google Labs,[21] already mentioned above.

To bring out patterns identified in large-scale samples of texts through various sophisticated forms of analysis, researchers have also turned their attention to the development of tools for visualizing such patterns to make it easier to identify trends and to interpret them. One type of helpful visualization is the kind of 'streamgraph' (Byron and Wattenberg, 2008) used in ThemeRiver visualizations (e.g. Havre *et al.*, 2000): themes are represented as currents in a virtual river, with the size of the currents representing the frequency of occurrence of lexical items associated with the theme. Similarly, the patterns identified by Culturomics researchers are brought out by sophisticated visualization tools.

7.6 Conclusion

In this chapter, I have discussed the nature of ADA – Appliable Discourse Analysis – as one of the aspects of appliable linguistics: discourse analysis explicitly conceived and designed as a resource in a wide variety of contexts of research and application. In addition, I have outlined some of the key features that I believe are needed in order to ensure the continued development of comprehensive discourse analysis within SFL and to enhance its appliability.

To be a powerful resource capable of being applied to a wide range of problems, ADA needs to be part of a comprehensive account of language in context, or more generally, of a comprehensive account of denotative semiotic systems in context – i.e. of denotative semiotic systems embedded in the connotative semiotic system of context. The power of ADA depends critically on the continued development of comprehensive descriptions of languages and of other semiotic systems. Even for a well-described language such as English, Chinese or Japanese, there are still many descriptive gaps to be filled – including centrally large areas of the semantic systems of these languages and of the contexts in which they operate. These descriptions need to be comprehensive, but they also need to be explicit enough so that it will one day become possible to automate extensive analysis drawing on the descriptions (cf. O'Donnell and Bateman, 2005; Bateman, 2008a; Teich, 2009; Wu, 2009), bridging the gap between low-volume high-level manual analysis and high-volume low-level automated analysis.

When we explore the nature of discourse analysis, it is helpful to theorize it in semiotic terms as a form of meta-semiosis taking place in a meta-context, as shown in Figure 7.30.

The increasing need for appliable discourse analysis can also be viewed institutionally in terms of professional roles. While many commercial and public institutions recognize the need to employ people in various general professional roles such as the company psychologist, the company accountant, the company marketing person, we can certainly make a good case that many such institutions also need the company appliable discourse analyst – a professional equipped to address a wide range of tasks through discourse analysis. There is a growing awareness of the value of discourse analysis in the fields of education, health care, translation and the law.

If various sectors of the community come to realize that they need professional discourse analysts, how do we meet the demand in educational terms? It would make sense to develop MA programmes specifically geared towards ADA – programmes where students with various undergraduate backgrounds can study to become professional discourse analysts, drawing on the areas of expertise of their undergraduate degrees. The curricula of such programmes would include the areas of theoretical expertise and of practical skills needed by professional discourse analysts to make effective contributions in a wide range of institutions: a theoretical framework for understanding and engaging with language and other semiotic systems in context; comprehensive descriptions of one or more particular languages, of other particular semiotic systems, and of the system of context; methods for carrying out both manual and automated analyses, together with computational tools for recording, transcribing and analysing semiotic (and social) data; methods complementing discourse analysis such field notes, ethnographic interviews, questionnaires; familiarity with representative case studies of projects centrally involving discourse analysis; practical, legal and ethical issues involved in sampling discourse needed for analysis; project planning and management; strategies for working with professionals from other areas of expertise.

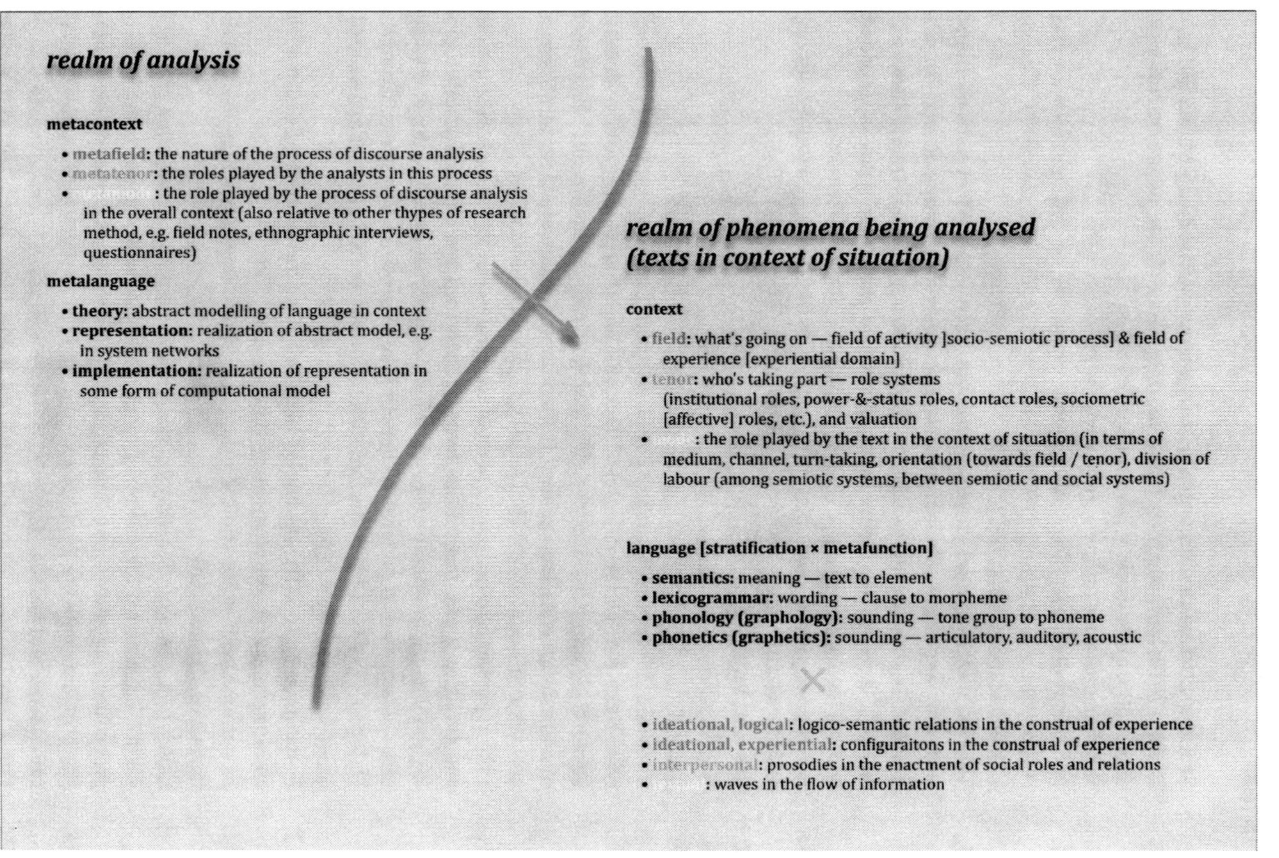

Figure 7.30: Discourse analysis as meta-semiotic process in meta-context

Notes

1. See: http://en.wikipedia.org/wiki/Linguistics (accessed 26 March 2011).
2. Dixon (2010: xiii) suggests that a more accurate figure would be 'no more than 4,000, quite likely a fair number fewer'.
3. For the up-to-date online version, see: http://wals.info/
4. For the ordered typology of systems operating in different phenomenal realms, see e.g. Halliday (1996), Halliday and Matthiessen (1999: Chapter 13) and Matthiessen (2007).
5. That is, the contextual structure that has been explored in various frameworks in linguistics (including discourse analysis), computational linguistics and AI under headings such as 'generic structure', 'schematic structure', 'script', 'schema' (or terms more specific to particular types of situation, such as 'narrative structure', 'story structure', 'lesson structure').
6. See e.g. http://www.imdb.com/title/tt0046414/ ; http://en.wikipedia.org/wiki/Beat_the_devil
7. See e.g.: http://www.lat-mpi.eu/tools/elan/
8. See: http://www.anvil-software.de/
9. See: http://www.fon.hum.uva.nl/praat/
10. This film is supposedly in the public domain: see http://en.wikipedia.org/wiki/Beat_the_Devil_(film) – '*Beat the Devil* is in the public domain because of unrenewed copyright, and is freely available and distributed over the internet as seen below.' It's available for download at: http://www.archive.org/details/BeatTheDevil1953. [Accessed i/2012.]
11. Like a number of other phenomena of the immaterial world such as situations and situation types, institutions must be theorized and described both sociologically and semiotically: they exist both as patterns of behaviour and social role systems and as patterns of meaning and speech role systems. Compare Halliday's (1978: 144) important distinction between first-order and second-order field and tenor.
12. Sometimes these different angles have taken as the sources of distinct but simultaneous and complementary typologies.
13. In contrast with more context-oriented corpus samples such as Gu's (n.d.) corpus of situated spoken Chinese.
14. Other types of situation may of course be operating at the same time (cf. Figure 7.6 above); for example, team members carrying out some type of procedure may at the same time engage in a situation of casual conversation.
15. For problems with the term 'new media' and for an account of 'social media', see Macnamara (2010).
16. For a general account of explanations along these lines, see Matthiessen and Pun (forthcoming). The systemic distinctions among different kinds of explanation have been adapted from Martin and Rose (2008).
17. This schematic diagram is based on observations and analyses by Andy Fung and Jack Pun.

18. A description can be comprehensive in coverage even if it's fairly indelicate; but increasing the delicacy of the description naturally also increases the comprehensiveness of the description in terms of detail.
19. Interestingly, the variant spelling with initial capitals, *Emotional Intelligence*, levelled off in frequency around 2003.
20. Entry on 'emotional intelligence': http://en.wikipedia.org/wiki/Emotional_intelligence
21. http://books.google.com/ngrams/ ; http://books.google.com/ngrams/info

References

Arndt, H. and Janney, R. W. (1987) *InterGrammar: Toward an Integrative Model of Verbal, Prosodic and Kinesic Choices in Speech.* Berlin: Mouton de Gruyter.

Baldry, A. and Thibault, P. J. (2006) *Multimodal Transcription and Text Analysis: A Multimedia Toolkit and Coursebook.* London: Equinox.

Bateman, J. A. (2008a) *Multimodality and Genre: A Foundation for the Systematic Analysis of Multimodal Documents.* London and New York: Palgrave Macmillan.

Bateman, J. A. (2008b) Systemic functional linguistics and the notion of linguistic structure: Unanswered questions, new possibilities. In J. J. Webster (ed.), *Meaning in Context: Implementing Intelligent Applications of Language Studies*, 24-58. London and New York: Continuum.

Bateman, J. A. and Schmidt, K. H. (2012) *Multimodal Film Analysis: How Films Mean.* London and New York: Routledge.

Biber, D. (1988) *Variation Across Speech and Writing.* Cambridge: Cambridge University Press.

Butt, D. G. (1991) Some basic tools in a linguistic approach to personality: A Firthian concept of social process. In F. Christie (ed.), *Literacy in Social Processes: Papers from the Inaugural Australian Systemic Functional Linguistics Conference, Deakin University, January 1990*, 23–44. Darwin: Centre for Studies of Language in Education, Northern Territory University.

Byron, L. and Wattenberg, M. (2008) Stacked graphs – geometry & aesthetics. IEEE InfoVis 2008 Available online at: http://www.leebyron.com/else/streamgraph/download.php?file=stackedgraphs_byron_wattenberg.pdf

Caffarel, A., Martin, J. R. and Matthiessen, C. M. I. M. (eds) (2004) *Language Typology: A Functional Perspective.* (Current Issues in Linguistic Theory 253.) Amsterdam: Benjamins.

Caldas-Coulthard, C. R. and van Leeuwen, T. (2002) 4. Stunning, shimmering, iridescent: Toys as the representation of gendered social actors. In L. Litosseliti and J. Sunderland (eds), *Gender Identity and Discourse Analysis*, 91–108. Amsterdam: John Benjamins.

Capra, F. (1996) *The Web of Life.* New York: Doubleday.

Chouliaraki, L. and Fairclough, N. (1999) *Discourse in Late Modernity: Rethinking Critical Discourse Analysis.* Edinburgh: Edinburgh University Press.

Christie, F. (1997) Curriculum macrogenres as forms of initiation into a culture. In

F. Christie and J. R. Martin (eds), *Genres and Institutions: Social Processes in the Workplace and School*, 134–160. London: Cassell.

Cloran, C., Stuart-Smith, V. and Young, L. (2007) Models of discourse. In R. Hasan, C. M. I. M. Matthiessen and J. Webster (eds) *Continuing Discourse on Language: A Functional Perspective,* Volume 2, 645–668. London: Equinox Publishing.

Comrie, B. and Cysouw. M. (n.d.) New Guinea through the eyes of WALS. Available online at: http://web.mac.com/cysouw/publications/index_files/cysouwNEWGUINEAtext.pdf

Dixon, R. M. W. (2010) *Basic Linguistic Theory. Volume 1: Methodology.* Oxford: Oxford University Press.

Dryer, M. S. and Haspelmath, (eds) (2011) *The World Atlas of Language Structures Online.* Munich: Max Planck Digital Library. Available online at http://wals.info/

Eggins, S. and Slade, D. (1997) *Analysing Casual Conversation.* London: Cassell.

Fairclough, N. (1989) *Language and Power.* London: Longman.

Fairclough, N. (1992) *Discourse and Social Change.* Cambridge: Polity.

Fairclough, N. (1995) *Critical Discourse Analysis: The Critical Study of Language.* London: Longman.

Fairclough, N. (2003) *Analysing Discourse: Textual Analysis for Social Research.* London: Routledge.

Fairclough, N. L. and Wodak, R. (1997) Critical discourse analysis. In T. A. van Dijk (ed.) *Discourse Studies: A Multidisciplinary Introduction, Vol. 2. Discourse as Social Interaction,* 258–284. London: Sage.

Fawcett, R. P. (1988) What makes a 'good' system network good? In J. D. Benson and W. S. Greaves (eds) *Systemic Functional Approaches to Discourse,* 1–28. Norwood, NJ: Ablex.

Firth, J. R. (1950) Personality and language in society. *Sociological Review* 42(1): 37–52. Reprinted in J. R. Firth (1957) *Papers in Linguistics 1934–1951,* 177–189. London: Oxford University Press.

Fowler, R., Hodge, B., Kress, G. and Trew, T. (1979) *Language and Control.* London: Routledge & Kegan Paul.

Ghadessy, M. (ed.) (1999) *Text and Context in Functional Linguistics.* Amsterdam: Benjamins.

Gouveia, C. A. M. (2006/7) The role of a Common European Framework in the elaboration of national language curricula and syllabuses. *Cadernos de Linguagem e Sociedade (Papers on Language and Society)* 8: 8–25.

Greenbaum, S. and Svartvik, J. (1990) The survey of English usage. In J. Svartvik (ed.) *The London Corpus of Spoken English: Description and Research.* Lund Studies in English 82. Lund: Lund University Press.

Gregory, M. J. (1967) Aspects of varieties differentiation. *Journal of Linguistics* 3: 177–198.

Gu, Y. (n.d.) Sampling situated discourse for spoken Chinese corpus. The Institute of Linguistics, The Chinese Academy of Social Sciences.

Halliday, M. A. K. (1957) Some aspects of systematic description and comparison in grammatical analysis. *Studies in Linguistic Analysis,* 54–67. Oxford: Basil Blackwell.

Halliday, M. A. K. (1961) Categories of the theory of grammar. *Word* 17 (3): 242–292.

Halliday, M. A. K. (1964) Syntax and the consumer. In C. I. J. M. Stuart (ed.) *Report of the Fifteenth Annual (First International) Round Table Meeting on Linguistics and Language*, 11–24. Washington, DC: Georgetown University Press. Reprinted in M. A. K. Halliday (2003) *On Language and Linguistics.* Volume 3 of *Collected Works of M. A. K. Halliday* (ed. Jonathan Webster), Chapter 1: 36–49. London and New York: Continuum.

Halliday, M. A. K. (1975) *Learning How to Mean: Explorations in the Development of Language.* London: Edward Arnold.

Halliday, M. A. K. (1977) Ideas about language. In M. A. K. Halliday, *Aims and Perspectives in Linguistics.* Applied Linguistics Association of Australia (Occasional Papers 1), 32–49. Reprinted in M. A. K. Halliday (2003) *On Language and Linguistics.* Volume 3 of Collected Works of M. A. K. Halliday. (ed. Jonathan Webster), Chapter 4: 92–115. London and New York: Continuum.

Halliday, M. A. K. (1978) *Language as Social Semiotic: The Social Interpretation of Language and Meaning.* London and Baltimore, MD: Edward Arnold and University Park Press.

Halliday, M. A. K. (1979) Modes of meaning and modes of expression: Types of grammatical structure and their determination by different semantic functions. In D. J. Allerton, E. Carney and D. Holdcroft (eds) *Function and Context in Linguistic Analysis: A Festschrift for William Haas*, 57–79. Cambridge: Cambridge University Press.

Halliday, M. A. K. (1981) Text semantics and clause grammar: Some patterns of realization. *Seventh LACUS Forum*, 31–59. Columbia, SC: Hornbeam Press. Reprinted as Text semantics and clause grammar: How is a text like a clause? in M. A. K. Halliday (2002) *On Grammar.* Volume 1 of Collected Works of M. A. K. Halliday (ed. Jonathan Webster), Chapter 9: 219–260. London and New York: Continuum.

Halliday, M. A. K. (1984) Language as code and language as behaviour: A systemic-functional interpretation of the nature and ontogenesis of dialogue. In M. A. K. Halliday, R. P. Fawcett, S. Lamb and A. Makkai (eds.), *The Semiotics of Language and Culture*, Volume 1: 3–35. London: Frances Pinter. Reprinted in M. A. K. Halliday (2003) *On Language and Linguistics.* Volume 3 of Collected Works of M. A. K. Halliday (ed. Jonathan Webster), Chapter 10: 226–250. London and New York: Continuum.

Halliday, M. A. K. (1985a) *Spoken and Written Language.* Geelong, Vic.: Deakin University Press.

Halliday, M. A. K. (1985b) It's a fixed word order language is English. *ITL Review of Applied Linguistics* 67–68: 91–116.

Halliday, M. A. K. (1991) The notion of 'context' in language education. In T. Le and M. McCausland (eds) *Interaction and Development: Proceedings of the International Conference, Vietnam, 30 March–1 April 1991*, 1–26. University of Tasmania: Language Education. Reprinted in M. A. K. Halliday (2007), *Language and Education.* Volume 9 in the Collected Works of M. A. K. Halliday (ed. Jonathan Webster), 269–290. London and New York: Continuum.

Halliday, M. A. K. (1992) New ways of meaning: A challenge to applied linguistics. *Greek Applied Linguistics Association, Journal of Applied Linguistics* 6: 7–36.

Halliday, M. A. K. (1994) So you say 'pass' ... thank you three muchly. In A. D. Grimshaw (ed.), *What's Going On Here: Complementary Studies of Professional Talk,* 175–229. Norwood, NJ: Ablex.

Halliday, M. A. K. (1996) On grammar and grammatics. In R. Hasan, C. Cloran and D. Butt (eds) *Functional Descriptions: Theory into Practice,* 1–38. Amsterdam: Benjamins. Reprinted in M. A. K. Halliday (2002) *On Grammar.* Volume 1 of Collected Works of M. A. K. Halliday (ed. Jonathan Webster), Chapter 15: 384–417. London and New York: Continuum.

Halliday, M. A. K. (1998) On the grammar of pain. *Functions of Language* 5 (1): 1–32. Reprinted in M. A. K. Halliday (2005). *Studies in English Language.* Volume 7 in the Collected Works of M. A. K. Halliday (ed. Jonathan J. Webster), Chapter 12: 306–337. London and New York: Continuum.

Halliday, M. A. K. (2007) Applied linguistics as an evolving theme. In *Language and Education,* Volume 9 of Collected Works of M.A.K. Halliday (ed. Jonathan J. Webster), 1–19. London: Continuum.

Halliday, M. A. K. (2010) 'Text, discourse and information: A systemic-functional overview.' Written version of plenary paper presented the biannual conference on Discourse Analysis, Tongji University, Shanghai, November 2010.

Halliday, M. A. K. and J. O. Ellis (1951) Temporal categories in the Modern Chinese verb. In M. A. K. Halliday (2006) *Studies in Chinese Language* (ed. Jonathan J. Webster) 177–208. London and New York: Continuum.

Halliday, M. A. K. and W. S. Greaves (2008) *Intonation in the Grammar of English.* London: Equinox.

Halliday, M. A. K. and R. Hasan (1976) *Cohesion in English.* London: Longman.

Halliday, M. A. K. and C. M. I. M. Matthiessen (1999) *Construing Experience Through Meaning: A Language-based Approach to Cognition.* London: Cassell. Study edition in 2006. London: Continuum.

Halliday, M. A. K. and C. M. I. M Matthiessen (2004) *An Introduction to Functional Grammar.* Third Edition. London: Arnold.

Halliday, M. A. K. and E. McDonald (2004) Metafunctional profile of the grammar of Chinese. In A. Caffarel, J. R. Martin and C. M. I. M. Matthiessen (eds), *Language Typology: A Functional Perspective,* 305–396. Amsterdam: Benjamins.

Halliday, M. A. K. and J. J. Webster (eds) (2009) *Continuum Companion to Systemic Functional Linguistics.* London and New York: Continuum.

Halliday, M. A. K., A. McIntosh and P. Strevens (1964) *The Linguistic Sciences and Language Teaching.* London: Longman.

Hardcastle, W. J. and J. Laver (eds) (1999) *The Handbook of Phonetic Sciences.* Oxford: Blackwell.

Hasan, R. (1973) Code, register and social dialect. In B. Bernstein (ed.) *Class, Codes and Control: Applied Studies Towards a Sociology of Language,* Volume 2, 253–292. London: Routledge & Kegan Paul.

Hasan, R. (1984) The nursery tale as a genre. *Nottingham Linguistic Circular* 13. Reprinted in R. Hasan (1996) *Ways of Saying: Ways of Meaning: Selected Papers of Ruqaiya Hasan* (ed. C. Cloran, D. Butt and G. Williams), 51–72. London: Cassell.

Hasan, R. (1985) *Linguistics, Language and Verbal Art*. Geelong, Vic.: Deakin University Press.

Hasan, R. (1994) Situation and the definition of genre. In A. D. Grimshaw (ed.), *What's Going On Here: Complementary Studies of Professional Talk*, 127–172. Norwood, NJ: Ablex.

Hasan, R., C. M. I. M. Matthiessen and J. J. Webster (eds) (2005, 2007) *Continuing Discourse on Language: A Functional Perspective*, Volume 1 (2005) and Volume 2 (2007). London: Equinox Publishing.

Haspelmath, M., M. S. Dryer, D. Gil and B. Comrie (eds) (2005) *The World Atlas of Language Structures*. Oxford: Oxford University Press.

Havre, S., B. Hetzler and L. Nowell (2000) ThemeRiver: Visualizing theme changes over time. *Proceedings of the IEEE Symposium on Information Visualization*.

Hjelmslev, L. (1943) *Omkring sprogteoriens grundlæggelse*. København: Akademisk Forlag. (English version. 1961 *Prolegomena to a Theory of Language*. Madison, WI: University of Wisconsin Press.)

Hood, S. (2011) Body language in face-to-face teaching: A focus on textual and interpersonal meaning. In S. Dreyfus, S. Hood and M. Stenglin (eds), *Semiotic Margins: Meaning in Multimodalities*, 31–52. London and New York: Continuum.

Hu, M. and Bin L. (2004) Mining and summarizing customer reviews. *KDD '04: Proceedings of the Tenth ACM SIGKDD International Conference on Knowledge Discovery and Data Mining*, 168–177.

Hübler, A. (2001) *Das Konzept 'Körper' in den Sprach- und Kommunikationswissenschaften*. Tübingen und Basel: A. Francke Verlag.

Iedema, R., S. Feez and P. White (1994) *Media Literacy* (Write it right industry research report no. 2) Sydney: NSW, Department of Education, Disadvantaged Schools Program Metropolitan East.

Kendon, A. (2004) *Gesture: Visible Action as Utterance*. Cambridge: Cambridge University Press.

Kinneavy, J. L. (1971) *A Theory of Discourse*. New York: W.W. Norton & Company.

Kress, G. (2010) *Multimodality: A Social Semiotic Approach to Contemporary Communication*. Milton Park and New York: Routledge.

Kress, G. and T. van Leeuwen (1996) *Reading Images: The Grammar of Visual Design*. London: Routledge.

Kress, G. and T. van Leeuwen (2001) *Multimodal Discourse: The Modes and Media of Contemporary Communication*. London: Arnold.

Lavid, J. (1995) Towards a text type taxonomy: A functional framework for text analysis and generation. *Procesamiento del Lenguaje Natural, Revista 16, Abril de 1995:* 29–43.

Leetaru, K. H. (2011) Culturomics 2.0: Forecasting large-scale human behavior using global news media tone in time and space. *First Monday* [Online], Volume 16 Number 9 (17 August 2011).

Longacre, R. E. (1974) Narrative vs other discourse genres. In R. Brend (ed.) *Advances in Tagmemics*, 357–376. Amsterdam: North-Holland.

Longacre, R. E. (1996) *The Grammar of Discourse*, 2nd edition. New York: Plenum.

Longacre, R. E. and Shin Ja J. Hwang (2012) *Holistic Discourse Analysis*. Dallas, TX: SIL International Publications.

Lukin, A., A. Moore, M. Herke, R. Wegener and C. Wu (2008) Halliday's model of register revisited and explored. *Linguistics and the Human Sciences* 4 (2): 187–243.

Macnamara, J. (2010) *The 21st Century Media: (R)evolution – Emergent Communication Practices.* New York: Peter Lang.

Malinowski, B. (1944) *A Scientific Theory of Culture and Other Essays.* Chapel Hill, NC: University of North Carolina Press.

Mann, W. C., C. M. I. M. Matthiessen and S. A. Thompson (1992) *Rhetorical Structure Theory and Text Analysis.* USC/ISI Report. Also in W. C. Mann and S. A. Thompson (eds), *Discourse Description: Diverse Linguistic Analyses of a Fund Raising Text,* 39–78. Amsterdam: Benjamins.

Martin, J. R. (1985) *Factual Writing: Exploring and Challenging Social Reality.* Geelong, Vic.: Deakin University Press.

Martin, J. R. (1992) *English Text: System and Structure.* Amsterdam: Benjamins.

Martin, J. R. (1993) Life as a Noun. In M. A. K. Halliday and J. R. Martin, *Writing Science: Literacy and Discursive Power,* 221-267. London: Falmer.

Martin, J. R. (1994) Macro-genres: The ecology of the page. *Network* 21: 29–52.

Martin, J. R. (1996) Types of structure: Deconstructing notions of constituency in clause and text. In E. Hovy and D. Scott (eds) *Burning Issues in Discourse: A Multidisciplinary Perspective,* 39–66. Heidelberg: Springer.

Martin, J. R. (2002) Blessed are the peacemakers: Reconciliation and evaluation. In C. Candlin (ed.) *Research and Practice in Professional Discourse,* 187–227. Hong Kong: City University of Hong Kong Press.

Martin, J. R. (2004) Positive discourse analysis: Power, solidarity and change. *Revista Canaria de Estudios Ingleses* 49: 179–200.

Martin, J. R. (2007) English for peace: Towards a framework of Peace Sociolinguistics: Response. *World Englishes* 26 (1): 83–85.

Martin, J. R. (2008) Intermodal reconciliation: Mates in arms. In L. Unsworth (ed.), *New Literacies and the English Curriculum: Multimodal Perspectives,* 112–148. London: Continuum.

Martin, J. R. and C. M. I. M. Matthiessen (1991) Systemic typology and topology. In F. Christie (ed.) *Literacy in social processes: Papers from the Inaugural Australian Systemic Functional Linguistics Conference,* 345–383. Deakin University, January 1990. Darwin: Centre for Studies of Language in Education, Northern Territory University. Reprinted in J. R. Martin (2010) *SFL theory,* Volume 1 in the collected works of J. R. Martin (ed. Wang Zhenhua), 167–215. Shanghai: Shanghai Jiao Tong University Press.

Martin, J. R. and D. Rose (2003) *Working with Discourse: Meaning Beyond the Clause.* London and New York: Continuum.

Martin, J. R. and D. Rose (2008) *Genre Relations: Mapping Culture.* London and Oakville: Equinox.

Martin, J. R., M. Zappavigna, P. G. Dwyer (2009) Negotiating narrative: Story structure and identity in youth justice conferencing. *Linguistics and the Human Sciences* 3 (2): 221–253.

Martinec, R. (2000) Types of process in action. *Semiotica* 130 (3-4): 243–268.

Martinec, R. (2004) Gestures that co-occur with speech as a systematic resource:

The realization of experiential meanings in indexes. *Social Semiotics* 14 (2): 193–213.

Matthiessen, C. M. I. M. (1992) Interpreting the textual metafunction. In M. Davies and L. Ravelli (eds) *Advances in Systemic Linguistics: Recent Theory and Practice*, 37–82. London: Pinter.

Matthiessen, C. M. I. M. (1993) Register in the round: Diversity in a unified theory of register analysis. In M. Ghadessy (ed.) *Register Analysis: Theory and Practice*, 221–292. London: Pinter.

Matthiessen, C. M. I. M. (1995) Fuzziness construed in language: A linguistic perspective. *Proceedings of FUZZ/IEEE*, 1871–1878.Yokohama, March 1995.

Matthiessen, C. M. I. M. (2002) Combining clauses into clause complexes: A multi-faceted view. In J. Bybee and M. Noonan (eds) *Complex Sentences in Grammar and Discourse: Essays in Honor of Sandra A. Thompson*, 237–322. Amsterdam: Benjamins.

Matthiessen, C. M. I. M. (2004) Descriptive motifs and generalizations. In A. Caffarel, J. R. Martin and C. M. I. M. Matthiessen (eds) *Language Typology: A Functional Perspective*, 537–673. Amsterdam: Benjamins.

Matthiessen, C. M. I. M. (2006) Educating for advanced foreign language capacities: Exploring the meaning-making resources of languages systemic-functionally. In H. Byrnes (ed.) *Advanced Instructed Language Learning: The Complementary Contribution of Halliday and Vygotsky.* 31–57. London and New York: Continuum.

Matthiessen, C. M. I. M. (2007) The 'architecture' of language according to systemic functional theory: Developments since the 1970s. In R. Hasan, C. M. I. M. Matthiessen and J. Webster (eds) *Continuing Discourse on Language*, Volume 2, 505–561. London: Equinox.

Matthiessen, C. M. I. M. (2009) Multisemiotic and context-based register typology: Registerial variation in the complementarity of semiotic systems. In E. Ventola and A. J. M. Guijarro (eds) *The World Shown and the World Told,* 11-38. Basingstoke: Palgrave Macmillan.

Matthiessen, C. M. I. M. (2009b) Ideas and new directions. In M. A. K. Halliday and J. Webster (eds) *A Companion to Systemic Functional Linguistics,* 12–58. London and New York: Continuum.

Matthiessen, C. M. I. M. (2012) "Systemic Functional Linguistics as appliable linguistics: social accountability and critical approaches." D.E.L.T.A. (Revista de Documentacao de Estudos em Linguistica Teorica e Aplicada) 28: 437–471.

Matthiessen, C. M. I. M. (in press) Applying Systemic Functional Linguistics in healthcare contexts. Submitted to guest editor of special issue of *Text and Talk.*

Matthiessen, C. M. I. M., A. Lukin, D. G. Butt, C. Cléirigh and C. Nesbitt (2005) Welcome to Pizza Hut: A case study of multistratal analysis. *Australian Review of Applied Linguistics* 19: 123–150.

Matthiessen, C. M. I. M. and C. Nesbitt (1996) On the idea of theory-neutral descriptions. In R. Hasan, C. Cloran and D. Butt (eds) *Functional Descriptions: Theory in Practice,* 39–85. Amsterdam: Benjamins.

Matthiessen, C. M. I. M. and J. Pun (forthcoming) Expounding knowledge through explanations: generic types and rhetorical-relational patterns.

Matthiessen, C. M. I. M. and D. Slade (2010) Analysing conversation. In R. Wodak, B. Johnstone and P. Kerswill (eds), *The SAGE Handbook of Sociolinguistics*, 375–395. Los Angeles, London, New Delhi, Singapore and Washington DC: SAGE.

Matthiessen, C. M. I. M., K. Teruya and C. Wu (2008) Multilingual studies as a multi-dimensional space of interconnected language studies. In J. Webster (ed.), *Meaning in Context*, 146–221. London and New York: Continuum.

Matthiessen, C. M. I. M., K. Teruya and M. Lam (2010) *Key Terms in Systemic Functional Linguistics*. London and New York: Continuum.

McNeill, D. (ed.) (2000) *Language and Gesture*. Cambridge: Cambridge University Press.

McNeill, D. (2005) *Gesture and Thought*. Chicago, IL: Chicago University Press.

Meurer, J. L. (2004) Role prescriptions, social practices, and social structures: A sociological basis for the contextualization of analysis in SFL and CDA. In L. Young & C. Harrison (eds) *Systemic Functional Linguistics and Critical Discourse Analysis: Studies in Social Change*, 85–99. London and New York: Continuum.

Michel, J-B., Y. K. Shen, A. P. Aiden, A. Veres, M. K. Gray, The Google Books Team, J. P. Pickett, D. Hoiberg, D. Clancy, P. Norvig, J. Orwant, S. Pinker, M. A. Nowak, E. L. Aiden (2011) Quantitative analysis of culture using millions of digitized books. *Science* 331: 176–182.

Muntigl, P. (2004) Modelling multiple semiotic systems: The case of gesture and speech. In E. Ventola, C. Charles and M. Kaltenbacher (eds), *Perspectives on Multimodality*, 31–50. Amsterdam: Benjamins.

Neale, A. (2006) Matching corpus data and system networks: Using corpora to modify and extend the system networks for TRANSITIVITY in English. In S. Hunston and G. Thompson (eds), *System and Corpus: Exploring Connections*, 143–163. London and Oakville: Equinox.

Nichols, J. (1992) *Linguistic Diversity in Space and Time*. Chicago, IL: Chicago University Press.

O'Donnell, M. and J. A. Bateman (2005) SFL in computational contexts. In J. Webster, R. Hasan, C. Matthiessen (eds) *Continuing Discourse on Language: A Functional Perspective*, 343–382. Equinox: London.

O'Halloran, K. L. (2005) *Mathematical Discourse: Language, Symbolism and Visual Images*. London and New York: Continuum.

O'Toole, M. (1994) *The Language of Displayed Art*. London: Leicester University Press (Pinter).

Roy, D. (2009) New horizons in the study of child language acquisition. *Proceedings of Interspeech 2009*. Brighton, England.

Roy, B. C. and D. Roy (2009) Fast transcription of unstructured audio recordings. *Proceedings of Interspeech*. Brighton, England.

Roy, B. C., M. C. Frank and D. Roy (2012) Relating activity contexts to early word learning in dense longitudinal data. *Proceedings of the 34th Annual Meeting of the Cognitive Science Society*. Sapporo, Japan.

Roy, D., R. Patel, P. DeCamp, R. Kubat, M. Fleischman, B, Roy, N. Mavridis, S. Tellex, A. Salata, J. Guinness, M. Levit and P. Gorniak (2006) The Human

Speechome Project. *Proceedings of the 28th Annual Cognitive Science Conference.*

Seuren, P. A. M. (1998) *Western Linguistics: An Historical Introduction.* Oxford: Blackwell.

Sinclair, J. McH. and M. Coulthard (1975) *Towards and Analysis of Discourse: The English Used by Teachers and Pupils.* London: Oxford University Press.

Slade, D., H. Scheeres, M. Manidis, C. M. I. M. Matthiessen, R. Iedema, M. Herke, J. McGregor, R. Dunston and J. Stein-Parbury (2008) Emergency Communication: The discursive challenges facing emergency clinicians and patients in hospital emergency departments. *Discourse & Communication* 2 (3): 289–316.

Snell-Hornby, M. (1995) *Translation Studies: An Integrated Approach,* 2nd edition. Amsterdam: Benjamins.

Steiner, E. (1985) The concept of context and the theory of action. In P. Chilton (ed.) *Language and the Nuclear Arms Debate: Nukespeak Today,* 215–230. London: Pinter.

Steiner, E. (1991) *A Functional Perspective on Language, Action and Interpretation.* Berlin and New York: Mouton de Gruyter.

Teich, E. (2009) Computational linguistics. In M. A. K. Halliday and J. J. Webster (eds) *Continuum Companion to Systemic Functional Linguistics,* 113–127. London and New York: Continuum.

Teruya, K. (2007) *A Systemic Functional Grammar of Japanese,* 2 volumes. London and New York: Continuum.

Thibault, P. J. (2004) *Brain, Mind and the Signifying Body: An Ecosocial Semiotic Theory.* London and New York: Continuum.

Tucker, G. H. (1997) *The Lexicogrammar of Adjectives: A Systemic Functional Approach to Lexis.* London: Cassell.

van Dijk, T. (2001) Critical Discourse Analysis. In D. Tannen, D. Schiffrin and H. Hamilton (eds), *Handbook of Discourse Analysis,* 352–371. Oxford: Blackwell.

van Leeuwen, T. (1996) The representation of social actors. In C. R. Caldas-Coulthard and M. Coulthard (eds). *Text and Practices: Readings in Critical Discourse Analysis,* 32–70. London: Routledge.

van Leeuwen, T. (1999) *Speech, Music, Sound.* London and New York: Palgrave Macmillan.

van Leeuwen, T. (2008) *Discourse and Practice: New Tools for Critical Discourse Analysis* (Oxford studies in sociolinguistics). Oxford: Oxford University Press.

Veel, R. (1997) Learning how to mean – scientifically speaking: Apprenticeship into scientific discourse in the secondary school. In F. Christie and J. R. Martin (eds) *Genre and Institutions: Social Processes in the Workplace and School,* 161–195. London: Cassell.

Veloso, Francisco O. D. (2006) '*Never awake a sleeping giant…*': *A multimodal analysis of post 9-11 comic books.* Universidade Federal de Santa Catarina: Ph.D. thesis.

Ventola, E. (1988) The logical relations in exchange. In J. D. Benson and W. S. Greaves (eds), *Systemic Functional Approaches to Discourse,* 51–72. Norwood, NJ: Ablex.

Viberg, Å. (1984) The verbs of perception: A typological study. In B. Butterworth, B. Comrie and Ö. Dahl (eds), *Explanations for Language Universals,* 123–162. The Hague: Mouton.

Wan, Y. N. (2011) *Call centre communication: An analysis of interpersonal meaning.* Hong Kong Polytechnic University: Ph.D. thesis.

Werlich, E. (1975) *Typologie der Texte. Entwurf eines textlinguistischen Modells zur Grundlegung einer Textgrammatik.* Heidelberg: Quelle & Meyer.

Winograd, T. (1968) Linguistics and the computer analysis of tonal harmony. *Journal of Music Theory,* 21: 2–49. Reprinted in M. A. K. Halliday and J. R. Martin (eds) (1981) *Readings in Systemic Linguistics,* 257–270. London: Batsford.

Wu, C. (2009) Corpus-based research. In M. A. K. Halliday and J. J. Webster (eds) *Continuum Companion to Systemic Functional Linguistics,* 128–142. London and New York: Continuum.

Young, L. and C. Harrison (eds) (2004) *Systemic Functional Linguistics and Critical Discourse Analysis: Studies in Social Change.* London and New York: Continuum.

8 Labelling discourse acts: Interpersonal projection across registers

Geoff Thompson*

8.1 Introduction

It is generally accepted within Systemic Functional Linguistics (SFL) that projection is a key resource by means of which interpersonal meaning potential can be expanded through grammatical metaphor. The focus of studies in this area until recently has been on metaphorical expressions of modality (Halliday and Matthiessen, 2004: 613). For example, Hewings and Hewings (2004) compare the different ways in which expert and novice academic writers use anticipatory 'it' modal clauses such as *it is possible* to achieve the appropriate degree of impersonality; and Iedema (1997) explores the use of indirect, metaphorical expressions of obligation in directives issued by administrators. However, there is a parallel category of metaphor which also exploits the grammar of projection for interpersonal ends, and which has been less fully investigated. Speakers/writers can make explicit the speech function that they are carrying out by representing it as a proposition in its own right. They do this by realizing the interpersonal meaning of mood as a separate clause such as *I suggest (that ...)*, which is often structurally dominant, but is not the proposition/proposal that is to be negotiated with the addressee. Halliday and Matthiessen (2004: 626–631) provide the first systematic treatment of this phenomenon. It is presented there in terms of metaphors of mood, and the account focuses on the major speech functions particularly at the level of the interpersonal projection of propositions (statements and questions) vs. proposals (commands and offers). The aim of the present chapter is to extend the analysis in delicacy, looking at the ways in which sub-categories of speech functions (such

---

* Geoff Thompson is an Honorary Senior Fellow in the School of English at the University of Liverpool.

as 'concession' or 'assertion') may be signalled in projecting clauses, and the uses which are made of the resource. Since these clauses can be seen as a type of metadiscourse, I draw on the terminology used by Hyland (2005: 49) in referring to these more delicate categories as 'discourse acts'; and apply the term 'discourse act label' to the projecting clause.

Two corpora of two contrasting registers – academic writing and personal blogs – are compared in terms of the frequency of use of such labels and of the range of discourse acts that are labelled, and especially in terms of the functions for which they are used in each register.

8.2   Defining discourse act labels

8.2.1   Locating the phenomenon

The present study is part of a wider project which aims at mapping the types of relations that can be established between clauses onto the three metafunctions identified in Systemic Functional Linguistics, thus viewing conjunction as operating in the experiential, interpersonal and textual domains (Thompson, 2005, forthcoming). The term 'domain' here is taken from Sweetser (1990): the experiential domain corresponds to her 'content' domain, while the interpersonal domain covers her 'epistemic' and 'speech act' domains (see further details below). Sweetser does not include any relations corresponding to the textual domain, possibly because her primary focus is on casual conversation where certain kinds of textual relations are extremely rare (Thompson, forthcoming). However, the phenomenon that I see as textual conjunction is well recognized in SFL, although not given that label. It is part of what is instead called 'internal' conjunction (Halliday and Hasan, 1976; Martin, 1992; Halliday, 1994). As Martin (1992) notes, internal relations serve two main functions: one is to establish links between moves in an exchange, and the other is 'to organise the argument ... to scaffold the schematic structure of a text' (1992: 181). In my view, the first of these functions, which has been less fully explored in SFL terms (even Martin, who provides an illuminating overview of internal conjunction in his 1992 chapter, touches on it only briefly), is better seen as operating in the interpersonal domain. The latter function is the one that has typically been highlighted in SFL studies: for instance, Halliday (1994: 338) cites '*first* [I say this], *next* [I say that], *finally* [I say the other]' as typical examples of internal conjunction. This involves the relations between stretches of text from the perspective of their role in the unfolding discourse: time in the world of the text rather than time in the external world.

Like Martin (1992), in the main project I make no essential distinction in types of relations between inter- and intra-complex connectivity. However, for my present purposes, the focus is on clause complexing; and the relevant logico-semantic type is projection: 'the logical-semantic relationship whereby a clause comes to function not as a direct representation of (non-linguistic) experience but as a representation of a (linguistic) representation' (Halliday and Matthiessen, 2004: 441). The relevant domain is the interpersonal. As noted above, the distinction between projection in the experiential and interpersonal domains is a familiar one.[1] It can be illustrated in Examples (1) and (2) (collected via Google™):

(1)   he said // it was fun at least, // didn't he?
(2)   I believe // it's the longest running parade, // isn't it?

Example (1) is a representation of a speech event in the external world, whereas (2) is an instance of interpersonal grammatical metaphor, in which the resource of projection is deployed to realize a modal meaning. The difference in the tag questions reflects the difference in the semantic status of the two projecting clauses: in (1) the tag picks up on the clause which is structurally dominant, as normally happens (*he said ... didn't he*), whereas in (2) the tag picks up on the clause which is technically subordinate (*it's ... isn't it*). In (2), *I believe* is primarily functioning not as an experiential representation of a mental act by the speaker (though it does, of course, retain traces of its congruent origins), but as an expression of the speaker's stance towards the main proposition in the projected clause. Such clauses have traditionally been termed 'epistemic parentheticals' (e.g. Urmson, 1952; Dehé and Wichmann, 2010).

Having identified the general category of projection in the interpersonal domain, it is then possible to see three main sub-domains, corresponding to the three main areas of interpersonal meanings in general: modality, appraisal (Martin and White, 2005) and mood. The first is to do with the expression of modal stance, as in example (2) above (this essentially corresponds to Sweeter's epistemic domain). The second involves the exploitation of projection (in the form of embedded projections – cf. footnote 1 on textual projection) to realize evaluation of propositions, as in (3):

(3)   The odd thing is, is [[that I can access from other computers]]

The third, and the one which is the focus of the present study, is oriented to mood and speech roles (Sweetser's speech act domain). This is illustrated in Example (4):

(4)   I'd like to point out // that Canadian McDonalds are a very nice
       workplace.

Although there are variations, the prototypical features of such speech act projecting clauses, or discourse act labels, are as follows (see also Thompson, 2009):

- the Subject is *I* or *we* (or *you*, typically in interrogatives or in the expression *you could say* – see Example (8) below)
- the verb is non-past (present or modalized)
- the verb realizes a verbal process
- the clause labels a projected clause in which the act specified in the projecting clause is performed
- if there is a tag, it normally picks up on the projected clause
- the projecting clause can be omitted without affecting the ideational content
- polarity transfer is possible in at least some cases.

All of these features can be seen in Example (5) and variants:

(5)   I'd say it's a fair deal, isn't it?

Here the Subject of the projecting clause is *I*; the clause is modalized; the process is a verbal one; by uttering the projected clause the speaker is performing the speech act of 'saying' something announced in the projecting clause; and the tag picks up *it's* rather than *I'd*. Version (5a) shows that the speaker would express the same propositional content if the discourse act label were omitted:

(5a)   It's a fair deal, isn't it?

Finally, the two versions in (5b) can be seen as near-equivalents, demonstrating that negative polarity may be expressed either in the projecting clause or in the projected clause:

(5b)   I wouldn't say it's a fair deal – I'd say it's not a fair deal

The features listed above are, of course, exactly those which are characteristic of modal projecting clauses such as in Example (2), with the crucial exception that the process is verbal rather than, as in (2), mental.

8.2.2   Delimiting the phenomenon

The summary of the features of discourse act labels above may appear to make it a simple task to decide what counts as a label and what does not; but the precise boundaries of the category are in fact somewhat blurred. There are some cases which look similar in certain respects but serve different, albeit related, functions. In (6), for example, *say* pre-signals the speaker's utterance of *thursdays* as a suggestion; but this involves the framing of a single clause constituent rather than of a whole proposition. In my data, this use of *say* is strongly associated with single constituents or individual words – in this it can be compared with Examples (8) and especially (9) below.

> (6)   we could do it on *say*, thursdays

In (7), *I mean*, which is anyway not unambiguously a verbal process, is better treated as a discourse marker, particularly since, unlike core discourse act labels, this use does not normally allow the addition of the *that*-complementizer:

> (7)   The older I get, the less I care. *I mean*, the less I care about important things.

The exclusion of *I mean* (which is extremely common in one of the two corpora that I explore in this study) is parallel to the way in which *you know* is not usually included in counts of metaphors of modality.

On the other hand, instances of the kind illustrated in Examples (8) and (9) were counted as labels:

> (8)   I suppose *you could say* that it was a lot nicer when we were a more homogeneous community.
> (9)   *Let's say*, like Steve Wynn, you've punched a hole in your Picasso.

The label *(I suppose/guess) you could say* illustrated in (8) serves to offer a formulation of a proposition to be accepted by the addressee. Like *say*, it can be used to frame single constituents (in fact most discourse act labels can be used in this way, so it is a matter of degree rather than of fundamental difference). However, it does not exhibit the same marked preference for single constituents as *say*; and, as (8) shows, unlike *say* it may be followed by the *that*-complementizer. Although the reference is to what 'you' *could say*, it is the speaker who utters the labelled proposition: this is the so-called impersonal *you*, replaceable by *one* (Kitagawa and Lehrer, 1990), which actually includes the speaker in its reference. The inclusion of both speaker and addressee is more salient in *let's say* in (9), and this label is much more frequently used with propositions. Its function is to signal that a proposition is being put forward as hypothetical as part of developing a line of reasoning.[2]

The problematic cases above all came from the blog data. The journal article data threw up a different kind of problem of identification, illustrated in (10) and (11).

> (10)   In what follows, we propose an alternative explanation for the data. We suggest that the acquisition of relative clauses is determined by multiple factors affecting different types of relative clauses.
>
> (11)   *We suggest* that the inconsistency of the conversion errors can be explained by the fact that certain types of relative clauses are more easily ACTIVATED than other types.

In (10), *we suggest* fits most of the recognition criteria outlined in section 7.2.1, but the context (most obviously *in what follows*) makes it clear that this functions as an advance label, indicating what will come later in the text. The act of suggestion is not actually performed in the projected proposition: instead, the reader is given the promise of a future discourse act. In (11), on the other hand, the same wording is used later in the same article to label the discourse act as it is performed – this is in fact the fulfilment of part of the 'suggestion' promised in (10). Of the two, only instances of the type shown in (11) were included in the counts.

Topologically, comparing discourse act labels with related areas of meaning around them, labels seem to make contact with two kinds of meaning in particular. On one side, there are some in the data which are very close to metaphors of modalization: e.g. *I would say* is often used in a way which is very similar to *in my opinion*. On the other side, other labels, such as *I swear, I declare,* and *I guarantee,* look very much like performatives, in that, at least in some of the instances, it would be possible to add *hereby* without greatly affecting the meaning (although the formality would be markedly increased). Some, however, do not overlap easily with either of those areas (e.g. *I will say, I'm saying, I would argue*). Those which could be classified as performative verbs are in fact usually closely related to modalization (at least in my data), in that they are to do with vouching for the truth of what the person is saying. This connection has long been recognized in pragmatic/philosophical approaches to performatives (e.g. Urmson, 1952; Recanati, 1987). It is worth noting, however, that work on performatives excludes modalized cases, although these occur about as frequently as Simple Present cases in my data. There is no space in this chapter to explore the precise interrelations between these three areas of meaning; but it is an issue that will be worth returning to in future work.

8.3   Discourse act labels in registers

8.3.1   The data

In order to explore the ways in which discourse act labels are used, I constructed corpora from two contrasting registers. Personal blogs and academic journal articles in Linguistics were selected as representing relative extremes on the clines of formal/informal and planned/spontaneous discourse. Journal articles are clearly at one extreme on both clines: formal and carefully planned. Personal blogs, while in the written mode and quite possibly redrafted and crafted to a greater or lesser extent, are typically designed to appear spontaneous and to mimic casual speech in a number of respects: most bloggers of this kind aim to sound as though they are talking face to face with the addressees. Extract (12) is a representative example of the spoken tone of the blogs, with dialogic discourse markers, direct appeals to the reader, sentence fragments, informal lexis, interpolations, etc.:

> (12)   I will explain the game in a minute. Oh no, wait, I can now: It's basically like rounders, but with extra made-up rules. And strategy. And things.
>
> And then the people start walking up and down the aisles shouting 'PEANUTS!' and 'CRACKERJACK!' ('ooh, I could crush a grape....') and selling ice cream, corn dogs (a hot dog dipped in corn bread batter and deep fried on a stick, as far as I can tell? Is that right?), and bags of candy floss, and something we couldn't identify called 'dabs', I think.

The contrast with academic journal articles is therefore very marked, which makes this type of text appropriate for the comparison.

The two corpora are of very different sizes, for practical reasons. It is relatively easy to compile a corpus of academic journal articles, since they are available online. The blogs, on the other hand, presented more of a problem. A great many were ruled out because of inappropriate subject matter – often of a sexual nature – or because they were not 'personal' blogs in the sense that I wished to focus on: they were (semi)commercial or (semi)professional, the latter often dealing with political issues or with some aspect of computer programming. The final word count was just over 500,000 for the academic articles and 50,000 for the blogs. In order to compare the frequencies of occurrence of discourse act labels, the results below are normalized per 10,000 words. However, the unavoidable difference in size does mean that results for the blogs, in particular, need to be treated with some degree of caution.

An initial automatic search of the corpora was carried out by creating concordances of all instances of *I*, *we*, *you* and *let's/let us*. These were then manually checked to identify all relevant cases. In the academic corpus, this was a simple matter: as could be predicted given the general characteristics of the register, the frequency of occurrence of the search items was much lower (despite the far greater size of the corpus), and a higher proportion of these occurred in labels. In the blog corpus, where interactant pronouns occur far more frequently, the process was more time-consuming, despite various short-cuts such as checking within each set of concordances for all the verbs found in labels in the academic corpus; but the more limited size of the corpus made the task manageable.

8.3.2   Findings

The basic frequency results are shown in Table 8.1.

Table 8.1: Frequency of discourse act labels in the two corpora

	Blogs			Linguistics articles		
	no.	norm.*	%	no.	norm.*	%
Present Simple	12	2.4	29%	57	1.1	52%
Modal	15	3.0	37%	27	0.5	24%
Desiderative	2	0.4	5%	14	0.3	13%
Present Continuous	5	1.0	12%	8	0.2	7%
To-INF	5	1.0	12%	1	0.02	1%
Other	2	0.4	5%	3	0.1	3%
TOTAL	41	8.2	100%	110	2.2	100%

* normalized per 10,000 words

In addition to the frequency, the spread should also be taken into account: 9 out of 10 blogs (90%) contain at least one instance of a discourse act label, compared with 22 out of 38 Linguistics articles (58%).[3]

The occurrences in Table 8.1 are divided according to the form of the verb, mainly to highlight the fairly wide range of forms which are used in labels. The two most frequent structures overall are the Present Simple and modalized forms (each 3.5 occurrences per 10,000 words). Present Simple is by far the most frequent choice in the Linguistics articles, but it still accounts for over one-quarter of the instances in the blogs:

(13)   It's not that my accent has changed (it hasn't, it honestly hasn't, *I promise you*) [BLOGS]

(14)   that is, *we maintain* that the conversion errors are due to the activation of the wrong grammatical pattern. [LINGUISTICS]

Modalized forms, most often with *would*, make up the single largest group in the blogs, but are also fairly frequent in the Linguistics articles:

(15)   *I'd say* all this time we've spent teaching them how to do things is rubbing off on them. [BLOGS]

(16)   Here, too, *I would argue* that there is no distinction of meaning according to subject-verb word order. [LINGUISTICS]

The less frequently occurring forms include desiderative labels. These most often have *would like to*, but other forms are also found:

(17) I could go into the details, but *I would rather say* simply that they are far more prosaic than profound. [BLOGS]

(18) *We would like to emphasize* that this picture of what constitutes grammatical status is function-based. [LINGUISTICS]

When the Present Continuous is used, the label is negative in five of the total of 13 cases (it is one of the two forms which appear to be more strongly associated with negatives):

(19) I mean, *I'm not saying* you can walk down the road with your genitals hanging out. Not every day, anyway. [BLOGS]

(20) With Schegloff (1996a, 2001b (see note 1)), then, *we are claiming* that the favorite unit of linguists, the *clause*, is a unit of interaction. [LINGUISTICS]

The *to*-infinitive occurs only with *say*, and is mostly found in the fixed phrases *suffice/needless to say*, but can appear in other structures such as *this is not to say*. This is the other form which seems to be associated with negatives (three out of the total of six instances):

(21) She used to buy these really tough cuts of beef, the sort that you'd use for pot roast or beef stew, and cut them into 'steaks' and cook them that way. *needless to say*, they were impossible to chew. [BLOGS]

(22) *I think it is reasonable to say* that examples such as (71), (72) … are not as strongly conducive as the positive 'accept' truncated interrogatives. [LINGUISTICS]

It is worth noting that, while initial position is the default one for labels in the data, they may occur in final position (as in (13) above) or in medial position, as in (23):

(23) Such a corpus-informed, systematic, contextualised method, *we would propose*, moves beyond the type of analysis (appraisal or otherwise) that falls into the trap of saying more about the analyst than about the way in which a text is likely to position its target readership. [LINGUISTICS]

As Table 8.1 shows, even allowing for the relatively small size of the blogs corpus, discourse act labels occur with markedly greater frequency and with greater spread in the blogs than in the linguistics articles; and while all the main structures are found in both corpora, they are all more frequent in blogs. Bloggers thus appear more concerned with framing their discourse acts in some way than academic writers. On the other hand, the academic corpus shows great variety than the blogs in the verbs that are used (although the much larger size of the academic corpus, which may be a factor in the wider range of verb types, means that this finding must be regarded as provisional). Tables 8.2 and 8.3 show the individual verbs that appear more than once in the blogs and more than four times in the academic articles.

Table 8.2: Verbs in labels in blogs

	no.	**norm.**	**%**
say	23	4.6	56%
admit	2	0.4	5%
promise	2	0.4	5%
swear	2	0.4	5%
other (12 types)	12	2.4	29%
TOTAL (16 types)	41	8.2	100%

Table 8.3: Verbs in labels in academic text

	no.	**norm.**	**%**
suggest	32	0.6	29%
argue	21	0.4	19%
note	8	0.2	7%
claim	8	0.2	7%
propose	7	0.2	6%
say	5	0.1	5%
other (18 types)	29	0.6	27%
TOTAL (24 types)	110	2.2	100%

There are five verbs which appear in labels in both corpora: *argue, claim, maintain, point out* and *say*. Of these, only *say* appears in both lists of more frequent verbs above, and the difference here in relative, and even absolute, frequency is very marked: in blogs it is by far the most frequently used verb, whereas in the linguistics articles it only just reaches the threshold level. The verbs which appear once in the blogs corpus include *bet, dare, (not) deny, guarantee* and *tell (you)*; those which appear fewer than five times in the academic corpus include *add, advocate, assert, emphasize, reiterate* and *stress*. It is worth noting that the most frequent verb in the blogs, *say*, is the most neutral verbal process, especially when compared with the relative semantic complexity of verbs like *suggest* and *argue*, which make up nearly half of the instances in the Linguistics articles.[4] This suggests that in the blogs the precise specification of the discourse act itself is less important than other considerations (see discussion of functions in section 8.3.3).

The differences in these two sets reinforce the impression that will no doubt have been gained from the paired examples in (13)–(22) above: that the two registers make very different use of this resource.

8.3.3   Functions of labels

These differences emerge even more clearly when the functions of the discourse act labels are considered.

The main function in the academic articles is to grade the degree of epistemic investment in the proposition. This is most obvious when the labels include the verbs *suggest, argue, claim* or *propose* (which together account for over half the labels found in the data), since these verbs are inherently more or less strongly associated with tentativeness and reasoning. Roughly 90% of the instances of these labels can be grouped in this category: most indicate awareness that a claim is being made which needs to be advanced with caution, allowing for the possibility that some readers may not automatically accept it as valid, as in (24):

> (24)   We observe that Mary's response (line 16) to Alice's complaint in lines 9–15 is positioned at the end of the clause 'Ron, ... usually doesn't get home till nine or ten'. It is not positioned after 'Ron' (line 14), although Alice's pause in line 15 might have provided Mary with an opportunity to come in. This, *we suggest*, can be related to the fact that on the occurrence of 'Ron' the clausal unit is not yet complete. [LINGUISTICS]

The negative in the second sentence (*it is <u>not</u> positioned after 'Ron'*) reflects the authors' acknowledgement that the reasons for the position of Mary's response are not self-evident and need to be explained. By opting to attribute the explanation given in the third sentence explicitly to themselves (note that *we suggest* could be omitted with some degree of hedging still being realized by *can*), the authors signal simultaneously that the explanation is offered tentatively but that it is a key step in the argument that they are constructing (cf. Myers, 1989, on self-attribution in academic articles). The negotiation with the reader in (25) is rather similar:

> (25)   In this extract there is no direct judgement of officials' incompetence in the sense of explicitly labelling them as inept or disorganised. However, *we would argue* that the phrase 'completely unprepared' functions as an indirect judgement since it is likely to prompt many readers to judge government officials' and, in turn, the government's lack of preparedness as ineptitude. [LINGUISTICS]

Again, there is a negative in the first sentence; and in this case it sets up a potential context of concession which is made explicit by *However*. The label *we would argue* then enacts a dialogue with the reader-in-the-text (Thompson, 2001) who is constructed as viewing the fact that there is *no direct judgement of officials' incompetence* as critical for the interpretation. The label flags up the authors' acknowledgement of the need to allow for this absence of direct judgement, but also signals that what follows is their counter-proposal.

In some cases, the dialogue with the reader-in-the-text is more overt. Rather than framing a claim as they make it, the authors may use a discourse act label to frame a denial of possible objections to claims that they have made earlier. In (26), the authors have indicated immediately before that they intend to demonstrate certain limitations of existing definitions of evidentiality. They then hasten to forestall possible reactions from readers who may accept (or even have formulated) those definitions:

> (26)   *We would like to emphasize* that it is not our intention to criticize the cited accounts of evidentiality as such; in fact we have selected them because we regard them as centrepieces of the linguistic literature on evidentiality. [LINGUISTICS]

In (27), the reader-in-the-text is constructed as drawing certain conclusions about the authors' focus on the imperative which the authors feel must be contradicted:

> (27)   Although we have here concentrated on the imperative as a discrete grammatical structure, *we in no way want to imply* that the choice of imperatives versus some more staid or more formal circumlocutions is either a unique or an isolated choice. [LINGUISTICS]

It is, of course, not an accident that both (26) and (27) involve negation in the label or in the framed proposition (*not our intention, in no way*): in such cases, the function is to correct a possible mistaken response from the reader by explicitly denying the validity of the response.

The main uses of discourse act labels outlined above are to frame propositions; but in a small number of cases (7, or 6%) in the data they frame proposals (i.e. commands or offers). The label in these cases not only signals the speech function (*propose* and *suggest* are the most frequent verbs) but is often used to mitigate the possible face-threatening act (Brown and Levinson, 1987) by incorporating modalization, as in (28):

> (28)   *I would want to suggest* that the term 'utterer' might be usefully reserved for this definition. [LINGUISTICS]

Discourse act labels in the Linguistics data can thus be seen as serving a restricted number of broad functions: the variations in verb choice mentioned above mainly serve to realize different points along the same cline of commitment, with different aspects of negotiation with the reader becoming more or less salient in different contexts, most obviously through the choice of different verb forms in the projecting clause. When we turn to labels in the blogs, on the other hand, the picture is much more diverse. This is partly because many of the individual labels have become more or less formulaic and have developed specialized pragmatic functions. This specialization of function has already been seen with *(I suppose/guess) you could say* and *let's say* (Examples (8) and (9) above). Other instances include *I will (simply/just) say*, which typically follows a reference to a topic that the writer is not going to talk about and introduces an exception to this avoidance:

> (29)   My mother's adversities aren't ones that I'm going to write about. …
> I would happily serve as her biographer, but somehow I don't think
> that's very likely to happen. *I will say* simply that the years in which
> I was in junior high and high school were hard for her. [BLOGS]

On the other hand, *I can honestly/truthfully/truly say* tends to be used in a context where the writer feels that the reader may not necessarily accept the proposition as valid – the focus is as much on the writer's assertion of veracity as on the signal of the speech act to come:

> (30)   He also likes to say my Ty hurts me too much and that I'm too
> good for him and that he doesn't treat me right. *I can honestly say* I
> disagree with that. [BLOGS]

This is even more strongly the case with *I swear*, which serves to emphasize the accuracy of a fact or claim that the writer has just expressed in contexts where the reader-in-the-text is constructed as disbelieving it:

> (31)   And if she served corn with the beef, she called it 'corned beef'. *I
> swear* I am NOT making this up. [BLOGS]

When used as a true performative, *I promise* realizes an undertaking (i.e. a proposal); but in the blogs data it is used to reassure the addressee:

> (32)   And yes I do know there is a 'recession' on at the moment and now
> really isn't the time (supposedly!) to be starting a business but there
> is a method to my madness *i promise*. [BLOGS]

As Examples (31) and (32) suggest, *I swear* and *I promise* are close in use and could sometimes be seen as interchangeable. From the evidence in the data, the main difference appears to be that *I swear* typically projects an addressee who feels at risk of being deceived, whereas *I promise* is more likely to be used in contexts where it is the writer who is in some way at risk (e.g. of starting a business at an unpropitious time). However, more examples would be needed to confirm this. A final example of the special-ised pragmatic uses, *I must admit*, has already been investigated by Hunston (2002). She notes (p. 59) that it reflects the 'need for speaker to protect their own face or that of their hearer'. In Example (33), it is the blogger's own face that needs protecting, as he admits to what could be seen as a lack of stamina:

> (33)   My whole state of mind and body feels better for several hours after a workout, though *I must admit* I get tired early when I work out heavy and have been known to go to bed at 9pm at night after working out heavily during the day. [BLOGS]

The single most frequent label in the blogs data (five instances) is *I'd/ would say*, which generally performs a function that is similar in some ways to the functions of labels in the Linguistics articles. It typically intro-duces an evaluation or a claim, and construes the writer as cautious, but also as thoughtful, considering all the possible factors before arriving at the conclusion:

> (34)   Some people keep blogs with the honest intent that no one will read them (though they are, *I would say*, the vast minority). [BLOGS]
>
> (35)   In most cases *I would say* the parents have the absolute decision to choose what medical care their child receives, especially when the child is less than 16 years of age. [BLOGS]

In (34) the writer projects himself as having weighed up the options care-fully,[5] while in (35) the writer is advancing a view that he knows is con-tentious (he has started the blog entry by referring to the debate as 'a really hot button'). In both cases, the label signals the claim as the writer's own, thus acting simultaneously to hedge it and to set down a marker of the writer's ownership of the claim. In (36), on the other hand, the func-tion appears to be to elicit agreement with an evaluation that rounds off the preceding anecdote:

> (36)   Remember how I talked about how they told us that if we removed Mike from that cesspool *against medical advice*, that our insurance would refuse to pay? So I called Blue Cross/Blue Shield, and was told that they would never refuse to pay due to people changing hospitals due to being unhappy with the quality of care. Well, now it's official. Today we got a letter from the insurance company, saying that they approved the stays at both the hellhole and the Lahey Clinic for payment. ...
>
> *I'd say* we had an EPIC WIN this time! [BLOGS]

There is some evidence that *I would say* is used for the 'writer as thoughtful' function, and *I'd say* for the 'invitation to agree' function; but again more examples would be needed before this could be stated with certainty.

8.4   Conclusion

As a broad generalization, the data suggests that Linguistics research articles exploit the resource of discourse act labelling primarily for the single purpose of hedging, grading the degree of epistemic investment in the proposition, whereas in blogs their use is generally more varied and pragmatically specialized. This latter point is in fact to be expected in that the function of labels is interpersonal, and interpersonal resources tend to be used more extensively and in more complex ways in informal, spoken (or spoken-like) contexts. Whereas formal written language typically achieves complexity through ideational grammatical metaphor (nominalization and the associated 'remapping' of clause functions – see Halliday and Matthiessen, 2004: 639), informal spoken language makes more extensive use of interpersonal metaphor, since this resource is associated with central aspects of interaction such as politeness and negotiation. The greater variety in verbs used in the linguistics articles is not, as it might at first sight appear, counter-evidence to this claim, since it is primarily related to field and ideational meaning: the primary function of the labels remains the same, with the different verbs allowing writers to position their claims at different points along the scale of commitment. However, the function of labels is inherently interpersonal even in the academic register; and it should be borne in mind that there are areas where the functions in the two registers overlap. In particular, the use of modalized labels (*I would say,* or *we would argue/claim/propose*) to construe the speaker as carefully working through options before arriving at a conclusion is relevant in the academic articles as well as in blogs.

As I have stressed above, the analysis presented here is an exploratory one, especially in relation to the blogs, and a number of the claims made above would need to be checked in a larger corpus. It is also exploratory in that the focus has been on investigating the functions of the labels in terms of their pragmatic force. It would certainly be illuminating to view them from other perspectives, such as their role in the system of ENGAGEMENT in the APPRAISAL model (Martin and White, 2005).[6] What the study has aimed to do is to work towards a fuller understanding of discourse act labelling as a type of interpersonal grammatical metaphor, in particular by defining the phenomenon and throwing some light on how labels are used in two contrasting registers.

Notes

1. Textual projection is a minor motif in the lexico-grammar, and is not directly relevant to the discussion here. However, for the sake of completeness, the following example (found via Google™) illustrates this phenomenon:

    > Mirroring, which is one of several NLP techniques, is the art of copying another person's behavior to create a relaxed communication situation. *The reason being is* [[that we like people who are like us]].

    The projection in the second sentence involves embedding rather than two ranking clauses. The key justification for labelling it as textual projection is that the matrix clause 'frames' the embedded clause in very much the same way as does the matrix clause in instances of explicit objective modality (e.g. *it is possible [[that ...]]*); but it functions to express not the speaker's stance towards the proposition but the conjunctive relation between the proposition and the preceding sentence (which might more congruently be expressed by *because*). The relatively frequent occurrence of the 'ungrammatical' form *being is* (or *is is*) in such clauses can be argued to be a reflection of the speaker's unconscious awareness that the clause has a textual, discourse organising, function rather than a purely experiential one. (The same applies to Example (3), where embedded projection is used to realize evaluation.)

2. Part of my initial hesitation over including *let's say* is that it has the specific function of marking the labelled proposition as hypothetical. However, discourse labels are often hypothetical to some degree (as in (8) or, for example, *I would argue*), and it appears that *let's say* is simply at the extreme end of the scale in this respect.

3. It should be stressed that the findings for academic text in this chapter refer specifically to Linguistics research articles. As part of another study (Thompson, 2009), I also investigated labels in Biochemistry research articles, and found markedly different patterns of use. Labels do occur in Biochemistry, but they are much less frequent and less widely distributed than in Linguistics, they use less tentative verbs (60% of labels use *note* or *conclude*), and with very few exceptions they only take up the one structural option of Simple Present. This reinforces the general point that we need to bear in mind issues of registerial specificity of corpora and tailor our claims to the corpus.

4. 'Semantically more complex' in that *suggest* can be somewhat crudely decomposed as 'say' + 'tentatively' + 'for the addressee to think about', and argue as 'say' + 'writer's opinion' + 'on the basis of reasoning'.

5. It is quite possible that the writer of (34) is being ironic. He may assume that his readers will think it self-evidently implausible that any blogger 'honestly' does not want other people to read their blog. If so, the impression of the writer weighing up the options introduced by *I would say* would then be the source of the irony, since this is a claim that does not in fact need careful deliberation. This would reinforce my argument that the label is used with

this particular function: conscious exploitation of the pragmatic force of an expression for ironic purposes indicates that the pragmatic force is salient for the writer and, by implication, the addressee.

6.   I am grateful to Jim Martin for pointing this line of enquiry out to me.

References

Brown, P. and Levinson, S. C. (1987) *Politeness: Some Universals in Language Usage*. Cambridge: Cambridge University Press.

Dehé, N. and Wichmann, A. (2010) The multifunctionality of epistemic parentheticals in discourse: Prosodic cues to the semantic-pragmatic boundary. *Functions of Language* 17 (1): 1–28.

Halliday, M. A. K. (1994) *An Introduction to Functional Grammar* (2nd edition). London: Edward Arnold.

Halliday, M. A. K. and Hasan, R. (1976) *Cohesion in English*. London: Longman.

Halliday, M. A. K. and Matthiessen, C. M. I. M. (2004) *An Introduction to Functional Grammar* (3rd edition). London: Arnold.

Hewings, A. and Hewings, M. (2004) Impersonalizing stance: A study of anticipatory 'it' in student and published academic writing. In C. Coffin, A. Hewings and K. O'Halloran (eds), *Applying English Grammar*, 101–117. London: Arnold/The Open University.

Hunston, S. (2002) *Corpora in Applied Linguistics*. Cambridge: Cambridge University Press.

Hyland, K. (2005) *Metadiscourse: Exploring Interaction in Writing*. London: Continuum.

Iedema, R. (1997) The language of administration: Organizing human activity in formal institutions. In F. Christie and J. R. Martin (eds), *Genre and Institutions: Social Processes in the Workplace and School*, 73–100. London and Washington: Cassell.

Kitagawa, C. and Lehrer, A. (1990) Impersonal uses of personal pronouns. *Journal of Pragmatics* 14 (5): 739–759.

Martin, J. R. (1992) *English Text: System and Structure*. Amsterdam: John Benjamins.

Martin, J. R. and White, P. R. R. (2005) *The Language of Evaluation: Appraisal in English*. Basingstoke: Palgrave Macmillan.

Myers, G. (1989) The pragmatics of politeness in scientific articles. *Applied Linguistics* 10 (1): 1–35.

Recanati, F. (1987) *Meaning and Force: The Pragmatics of Performative Utterances*. Cambridge: Cambridge University Press.

Sweetser, E. (1990) *From Etymology to Pragmatics: Metaphorical and Cultural Aspects of Semantic Structure*. Cambridge: Cambridge University Press.

Thompson, G. (2001) Interaction in academic writing: Learning to argue with the reader. *Applied Linguistics*, 22 (1): 58–78.

Thompson, G. (2005) But me some buts: A multi-dimensional view of conjunction. *Text* 25 (6): 763–791.

Thompson, G. (2009) Linguists *would argue* – biochemists *conclude*: A cross-disciplinary comparison of discourse act labeling in research articles. In S. Slembrouck, M. Taverniers and M. Van Herreweghe (eds), *From* will *to* well*: Studies in Linguistics Offered to Anne-Marie Simon-Vandenbergen*, 405–414. Ghent: Academia Press.

Thompson, G. (forthcoming) *Conjunctive Relations in Discourse: A Tri-functional Study of Six English Registers*. London: Equinox.

Urmson, J. O. (1952) Parenthetical verbs. *Mind* 61 (4): 480–496.

9 Modelling ellipsis in EFL classroom discourse

YANG Xueyan*

9.1 Introduction

Ever since Halliday established Systemic Functional Grammar (SFG), a grammar that is oriented towards semantics, one of the challenges facing systemicists has been to give an account of the semantic system of a language that is realized by its grammatical system. Martin (1992; Martin and Rose, 2003) made a step forward by setting up a series of systems of discourse semantics based on Halliday's SFG – as the semantic system network of the English language focusing on 'text-size rather than clause-size meanings' (Martin, 1992: 1). While Martin's efforts are aimed at the 'potential', i.e. a general semantics that applies to any individual texts; it is believed that efforts are also needed to aim at the 'subpotential', i.e. a specific semantics that applies to a register or text type. For one thing, discourse meanings are context-specific: when associated with a given situation type, not only do clause-size meanings adjust their probabilities (Halliday, 1991, 2004), but text-size meanings also adjust their sequences (Yang, 2010). It is thus significant to view semantics as the **semantics of text types** or, as Halliday (1978: 114) calls it, 'the semantics of situation types'. For another, a description of the subpotential is a way into that of the potential, since a description of the general semantic system of a language is no other than the generalization of a set of context-specific semantic descriptions.

Ellipsis has been given an extensive account in SFG, as a cohesive device performing textual function (see Halliday and Hasan, 1976; Halliday, 1994, 2004). In particular, it is described as a cohesive tie in 'question-answer and other rejoinder sequences' (Halliday and Hasan, 1976: 206). Martin (1992) further proposes that an ellipsis system should be subsumed into the Mood system, as a resource for tying a responding move to an initiating move. However, ellipsis has so far hardly been modelled as text-size meanings of a

* Yang Xueyan is Professor at the School of English and International Studies, Beijing Foreign Studies University, China.

particular text type, where meanings shift their probabilities and sequences. As an attempt at the semantics of ellipsis in a specific text type, which in turn is considered a step towards the semantics of text types as well as a way into general semantics, this chapter presents an analysis of ellipsis choices occurring in EFL classroom discourse, offering a description of the different types of elliptical clauses as identified in the analysis, followed by a proposed semantic system of ellipsis specific to EFL classroom discourse, referred to as DALOGIC SEQUENCE. EFL classroom discourse is chosen as the object of analysis both because it is a text type featuring ellipsis, and because classroom discourse has been much studied in the SFL tradition (e.g. Sinclair and Coulthard, 1975; Berry, 1987; Christie, 2002) but not equally so within an EFL context. It is held that a systemic-functional account of ellipsis in EFL classroom discourse has practical implications for the ways EFL teachers 'manage' classroom interaction (Allwright and Bailey, 1991; Walsh, 2006).

The rest of this chapter is divided into three parts: (a) a description of the analysis, (b) the ellipsis types as identified in the analysis, and (c) a semantic system of ellipsis thus set up.

9.2   Description of the analysis

The data used in the analysis were 10 texts transcribed from 10 audio-recorded EFL classes taught by 10 different teachers from eight well-known universities in Beijing, each class lasting 45 or 50 minutes (i.e., 1 class hour). Given the actual level of average EFL teachers in China (see Yang, 2003; Zhou, 2005), only 'good' teachers were chosen – 'good' in the sense of having both an outstanding record in Teaching Evaluations and a reputation among students and colleagues alike as a highly competent teacher. Nevertheless, differences among the 10 teachers came out quite strongly in terms of their academic title, age, gender, the type of university they were affiliated to, and the type of course being taught. See Table 9.1 for details.

Table 9.1: Teacher differences involved in the data

academic title	lecturers: 3	professors: 2	associate professors: 5	
age	20-30: 2	30-40: 3	40-50: 3	over 50: 2
gender	male: 3	female: 7		
affiliation	comprehensive universities: 2		normal universities: 2	
	foreign language universities: 2		specialized colleges: 4	
course type	Intensive Reading: 5		Integrated English Skills: 2	
	Extensive Reading: 2		Oral Interpretation: 1	

The ellipsis system in SFG (Halliday and Hasan, 1976; Halliday, 1994, 2004) was applied in the analysis of all ellipsis choices identified in the 10 texts. According to Halliday's ellipsis theory, ellipsis is a form of anaphoric cohesion realizing textual meaning. It applies where two clauses in the same grammatical structure occur successively: while the first clause is complete in structure, the second has certain element(s) missing but retrievable from – and hence presupposes – the first. To supply the missing elements in the elliptical clause and to insert them in place, the addressee must go back to the complete clause, thus the cohesive function of ellipsis. Actually, the ellipsis system in SFG consists of three options: nominal, verbal and clausal. But in the analysis of the data, the system was found to shift its probabilities: only clausal ellipsis was frequently found, while nominal ellipsis was rarely found, and verbal ellipsis was mostly found overlapping with clausal ellipsis – a phenomenon also noted by Halliday (1994: 321) and Halliday and Hasan (1976: 194). After an initial analysis, therefore, it was decided that the ellipsis choices in the data should be analysed entirely by reference to the system of clausal ellipsis, with occasional instances of nominal ellipsis being ignored.

According to Halliday and Hasan (1976), clausal ellipsis occurs in responses in question-answer or other rejoinder sequences, functioning to join a responding move to an initiating move. Martin (1992: Chapter 2) explicitly states that ellipsis is a device tying up an adjacency pair. As both moves in an adjacency pair are described in SFG in terms of speech functions realized by different mood structures of the clause, ellipsis is also considered to be related to the Mood system, in its textual function of organizing interpersonal meanings. See Table 9.2 for a brief description of Halliday's clausal ellipsis system (where brackets enclose an optional element while a slash indicates an alternative), as summarized from Halliday and Hasan (1976) and Halliday (1994, 2004).

As shown in Table 9.2, clausal ellipsis appears in two types of mood: declarative and interrogative. While the declarative occurs in a response to a question, or a rejoinder to a statement/command; the interrogative occurs, not in a question, but in a disclaimer to a question, or a request for clarification or confirmation in response to a statement/command. In other words, clausal ellipsis occurs only in responding moves – either as a response to a question, or as a rejoinder to a statement/command – although there are a variety of response types realized by a variety of grammatical forms; and it serves to link no more than two adjacent moves.

Table 9.2: A summary of Halliday's clausal ellipsis system

mood	speech function		absent	present
decl	direct	answer	clause	reporting clause + *so/not*
	response	to yes/no Q		modal adjunct + *so/not*
	to Q			polarity/modal Adjunct
				(*not* +) qualifier
			Residue	polarity/modal Adjunct + Mood
		answer	clause	WH- responsive element
		to WH-Q	Residue	Mood
			Mood	Residue
	indirect	commentary	clause	reporting clause (+WH- element)
	response to Q	supplementary	clause	coordinated /conditional clause
int	indirect	disclaimer	clause	WH- element
	response to Q		Residue	Mood
decl	rejoinder	assent/	Residue	*so/nor* + Mood
	to statement	contradiction		(polarity Adjunct+) Mood
	/command	consent/refusal	Residue	(polarity Adjunct+) Mood
int	rejoinder	clarification	clause	WH- element + *so/not*
	to statement	request		
	/command	confirmation	Residue	Mood
		request	remainder	existing element
			clause	new element /corresponding
				existing element WH- element
				expanded by coordination

This clausal system, however, when applied to the actual analysis of
ellipsis choices in the data, was found to shift its systemic probabilities. Many
of the options in the system rarely showed up, including the various types of
indirect response to a question or rejoinder to a statement/command; while
quite a number of ellipsis choices found prominent in the data were simply
unaccountable by reference to the system. Therefore it was decided that the
analysis should be made based on Halliday's ellipsis theory in general, with
reference to the clausal ellipsis system only where it is applicable. At the
same time, following Halliday in examining clausal ellipsis in relation to its
adjacent move, it was decided that the unit of analysis should be the entire
dialogic sequence involved rather than the elliptical clause alone.

9.3   Ellipsis types as identified in the analysis

As a result of the analysis, it is found that clausal ellipsis appears in three
types of mood: declarative, interrogative and imperative; and that it occurs
in both responding and initiating moves, serving to tie up both an adjacency pair and a much longer dialogic sequence. The following is a detailed

description of the different types of elliptical clauses as identified in the analysis, which are classified according to their speech function as well as their specific cohesive function in the on-going EFL classroom dialogue.

9.3.1 As answer

One type of elliptical clause as identified in the analysis is declarative in mood, functioning as a response to a question. Actually this is the only type found in the data which has been described in Halliday's system of clausal ellipsis. But here, the elliptical clause functions merely as a direct answer, with fairly limited realizational forms in comparison with the range of forms described in Table 9.2.

In this type of elliptical clause, there is only one element present, with the whole clause being omitted. If the clause functions as an answer to a yes/no question, the element left in the clause is a mood Adjunct of polarity (*yes* or *no*), which serves to either affirm or negate the proposition set out in the preceding question (see Example[1] 1). If the clause functions as an answer to a WH-question, the element present is one given in response to the WH-element in the preceding question (see Example 2).

Example 1 [from Text 7]

4-T	OK, so 'furious' – this is the word I'd like you to pay attention to – <u>can we say 'I feel furious'</u>, 'I feel furious'?
5-S(n)	No.

Example 2 [from Text 4]

9-T/4	So, then, "it is devoid of all theme and principle except appetite and racial domination", "it is devoid of ..." and here, 'devoid', what <u>does it mean, 'devoid'</u>?
10-S/a	'Without'.
11-S/b	'Absent'.

In both cases, the elliptical clause functioning as an answer enables a student to give the particular information being demanded in the teacher's question. The specific cohesive function performed by ellipsis is to join the question and its answer into a coherent dialogic sequence, which is here referred to as an **information exchange**. But it should be pointed out that the term 'exchange' used here does not refer to a clause in its speech function (i.e. an interact, see Halliday, 1994/2004: Ch 4), but a sequence of moves centred on the same proposition or proposal – following the conventional use of the term initiated by Sinclair and Coulthard (1975) as well as the redefinition of the term by Yang (2010: Section 6.2.3).

9.3.2 As question

In Halliday's system of clausal ellipsis, the interrogative mood does not occur in a question demanding information and initiating an exchange. But it does here in the data, for example:

Example 3 [from Text 1]

105-T/2	All right, now, I'd like you to tell me, what people did in this disaster, er, what <u>did they do</u> – they actually did many things?
105-T/3	Yes, xxx.
106-S	er, she cried to her husband.
107-T/1	She cried to her husband, (laugh) yes.
107-T/2	And what else?
107-T/3	Xxx.
108-S	Then they go to the job.
109-T/1	Uh-huh, right, the husband went to see his job, yes.

In this example, the interrogative mood first occurs in a complete clause in 105-T/2 and then in an elliptical clause in 107-T/2. The latter may appear like a rejoinder to a statement, especially a request for confirmation of an existing element in the preceding statement by expanding that element through coordination, e.g. – *John is coming to dinner. – And who else?* (for more see Halliday and Hasan, 1976: 215). But the elliptical clause in 107-T/2 does not belong to this category. For one thing, a confirmation request comes immediately after a statement produced by a different speaker, but the statement in 107-T/1 is produced by the same speaker, i.e. the teacher, as a feedback to the student's answer in 106-S. For another, a confirmation request – if elliptical – presupposes the immediately preceding statement; but the elliptical clause in 107-T/2 presupposes, instead, the non-elliptical question that is several moves apart and produced again by the same speaker. In other words, it does not mean *what else did **she** do* but *what else did **they** do*. What is more, both the student's answer in 108-S and the teacher's feedback in 109-T/1 prove that the student is not confirming *what else **she** did* but answering the question *what else did **they** do.*

Therefore, this kind of elliptical clause is regarded, not as a confirmation request, but as a question, or more precisely, a rotational question, since it can be raised several times addressing different students but focusing on the same proposition. Here the specific cohesive function performed by ellipsis is to link two or more questions, thus joining several successive information exchanges into a much longer dialogic sequence than an adjacency pair. In fact, the sequence may even extend over a considerable span of text as shown in Example 4, where the two elliptical questions are respectively 33 and 44 turns apart from the presupposed non-elliptical one. In this way, ellipsis serves well for the teacher to make sure that a question should get fully answered from various respects and that more students could have a chance to speak.

Example 4 [from Text 1]
19-T/2   All right, <u>have you ever experienced</u> any disaster <u>in your life</u>?

....

52-T   OK, any other disasters?

....

64-T/2   OK, flood, earthquake, anything else?

In terms of clause structure, all elements in the elliptical clause can be omitted except one, which is typically the Complement (*disaster* in Example 4), including a WH- Complement (*what* in Example 3), combined with a comparative reference item (*else, other, different, etc.*) that marks a different member of the Thing and hence highlight the element remaining in the clause. Alternative elements present in the clause include a circumstantial Adjunct (*by the time 1650* and *by 1930* in Example 5) or the Subject (*'video'* in Examples 6). A conjunctive item expressing extension (*and* or *but*) is found to co-occur sometimes with the Complement, and always with the Adjunct or Subject; and when being placed in the thematic position of the elliptical clause, the extension item well enhances the cohesive relationship set up by ellipsis between the successive information exchanges.

Example 5 [from Text 6]
15-T/2   OK, can anyone tell me, say, at the time A.D. 1, how many people there
            were in the world – say, <u>what's the population</u> in A.D. 1, remember?

....

17-T/2   But by the time 1650?

....

21-T/2   And by 1930, by 1930?

Example 6 [from Text 9]
25-T/4   Ok, 'text', <u>what's</u> a 'text'?

....

27-T/2   And 'video'?

9.3.3 As command

Another type of elliptical clause identified in the teachers' utterances initiating an exchange performs the speech function of a command, i.e. a proposal (vs. proposition). However, it should be pointed out that, while a 'proposal' is defined by Halliday (2004: 111) as 'the semantic function of a clause in the exchange of goods-&-services [vs. information]', it is here redefined, following (Yang, 2010: 82), as 'a move in the semantic function of demanding or producing an action', since EFL classroom discourse is concerned with action – verbal action in particular – rather than goods-&-services in general. So, it can be said that this type of elliptical clause is used to initiate an **action exchange**, and it tends to occur repeatedly during an in-class-exercise session. See Examples 7 and 8.

Example 7 [from Text 1]
167-T/3   Now, let's <u>do</u> the exercises.
167-T/4   Now, the first one, xxx, please.

....

169-T/3   All right, Number 2.

Example 8 [from Text 10]
16-T/2   Now, let's <u>read</u> the statements <u>and then decide it's true or false</u>.
16-T/3   First you <u>read</u> the statement <u>and then</u> you <u>tell they are true or false</u>.
16-T/4   xxx, Number 1, please.
17-S   I think it's true

....

53-T/4   Now, the 8th statement, xxx, please.

....

61-T/6   And the last one, Effie, would you please?

As can be seen in the examples, an in-class-exercise session usually begins with one or two moves realized by a complete imperative clause, which orientates the class (*let's*...) towards the coming exercise and/or gives the students directions (*you*...[2]). Then there is a series of commands, each initiating an action exchange that is realized by an elliptical clause.

The mood of this type of elliptical clause can be congruently imperative, where the element present is the Complement (*the first one, number 1, the eighth statement, the last one*), which specifies the target of the action. Or else, the mood is metaphorically interrogative, where the element left in the clause is the Complement plus the Mood element (*would you* in 61-T/6 in Example 8). In either case, the element missing is the Predicator, which specifies the action to be carried out, and which has to be retrieved from the initial non-elliptical imperative clause. Other elements that optionally turn up in the elliptical clause include (a) a vocative,[3] which addresses the person responsible for carrying out the action; (b) the interjection *please*, which mitigates the command.

This type of elliptical clause performs the cohesive function of linking a command with a command. No matter how many times an elliptical command recurs, each time it is equally linked – through ellipsis – with the initial, non-elliptical command. In this way, ellipsis serves to link recursive action exchanges into a coherent dialogic sequence, a resource that enables the teacher to organize the students' actions within a lengthy in-class-exercise session efficiently and without losing track.

9.3.4 As elicitation

In the data, there is another type of elliptical clause in the interrogative mood, but it does not function the same way as a question. It is here referred to as an 'elicitation' – in the sense of drawing out a response. See an example:

> **Example 9 [from Text 5]**
> 47-T/2   Now, was it so important – <u>why was it the biggest problem</u>, have you got
>   any idea?
> 47-T/3   Anyone?
> [more than 6 seconds, no response]
> 47-T/4   xxx, have you got any idea?
> 48-S   No.

In this example, 47-T/4 is actually an elliptical clause in which the question *why was it the biggest problem* is presupposed. The clause *have you got any idea* is not a proposition in its own right, but part of the metaphorical realization of a proposition. In the form of a projecting clause, it congruently expresses a logical relationship between two clauses within a clause complex. But in the particular form of [*I/you* + present tense], this logical resource is made to do an interpersonal service, i.e. to make explicit the subjective orientation of a proposition, thus being referred to as 'interpersonal projection' (Halliday, 2004: 626). So, in the elliptical clause in 47-T/4, the only element present is the interpersonally projecting clause while the entire projected question is absent; consequently, the subjective orientation of the question is given an unusual prominence. Clearly, this type of elliptical clause – which comes as a separate move after a question (with enough wait-time in between) – is not used to raise a question, but to orientate a question raised earlier explicitly towards an addressee in an effort to elicit an answer from the addressee. It is, therefore, viewed as an elicitation rather than a question.

As found in the data, elliptical clauses functioning as an elicitation have two other variant forms. First, everything else in the projecting clause is also omitted except the Participant, i.e. the Sensor or Sayer, such as *Anyone?* in 47-T/3 in Example 9, which means *has any one of you got any idea* [*why it was the biggest problem*], with the indefinite pronoun *anyone* added so as to address all students in class. Second, the only element present in the projecting clause is the mental or verbal process (*think, suggest, say*) which, however, is nominalized (*idea, suggestion, version*) to function as the 'Range' of the process (see Halliday, 1994: 146), such as in 3-T/3 in Example 10 (where 3-T/2 is an elliptical clause functioning as a command, that is, demanding a translation of a Chinese sentence into English).

Example 10 [from Text 3]
3-T/2   The first sentence: 全国每分钟生产1,267吨煤 [quanguo mei fenzhong shengchan 1,267 dun mei].
[confusion for more than 12 seconds]
3-T/3   Come on, any idea?
4-S   It produces one thousand, two hundred and sixty-seven tons coal per minute in the country.

In fact, the speech function of this kind of elliptical clause varies according to the type of move in which the missing projected clause is retrievable. If it can be retrieved from a preceding question, such as in Example 9, the elliptical clause functions to elicit an answer to a previously raised question. If it has to be retrieved from a preceding command, such as in Example 10, where 3-T/3 presupposes the elliptical command 3-T/2 ([*translate*] *the first sentence…*), then the elliptical clause functions to elicit a verbal action that complies with a previously given command (*do you have any idea [how to translate the first sentence]?*). In other words, an elliptical clause functioning as an elicitation may occur in either an information exchange or an action exchange.

The cohesive function of ellipsis as applied here is either to link a question with an answer elicitation, or to join a command with a compliance elicitation. Thus it turns a simple exchange, which is composed of adjacent moves only, into a complex one with inserted moves. In EFL classroom discourse, it often occurs when an exchange is about to fail (thought it may still fail after all, as in Example 9), a resource the teacher resorts to in an effort to put the exchange back on track.

9.4   A semantic system of ellipsis in EFL classroom discourse

Based on the above classification of the elliptical clauses as found in EFL classroom discourse, a semantic system of ellipsis has been set up. It is called a 'semantic system' in the sense of a system of text-size meanings as created by ellipsis. Also, it is part of the semantics of a specific text type, i.e. EFL classroom discourse.

As text-size meanings in EFL classroom discourse as created by ellipsis constitute dialogic sequences of different types, the system is given the name DIALOGIC SEQUENCE. For an illustration of the system see Figure

9.1, where both the elliptical clause and the presupposed complete clause are presented in terms of speech function (question, command). Capitalization is used to represent a speech function realized by a complete clause (Q, C), and lower-case is used to represent a speech function realized by an elliptical clause (q, c). The caret sign indicates order, while the three dots indicate other bound moves in the exchange. The right downward arrow introduces the grammatical form of the elliptical clause, including (a) its mood, and (b) its clause structure (optional elements excluded) placed inside a square, in which the element absent but retrievable from the preceding complete clause is given a grey background.

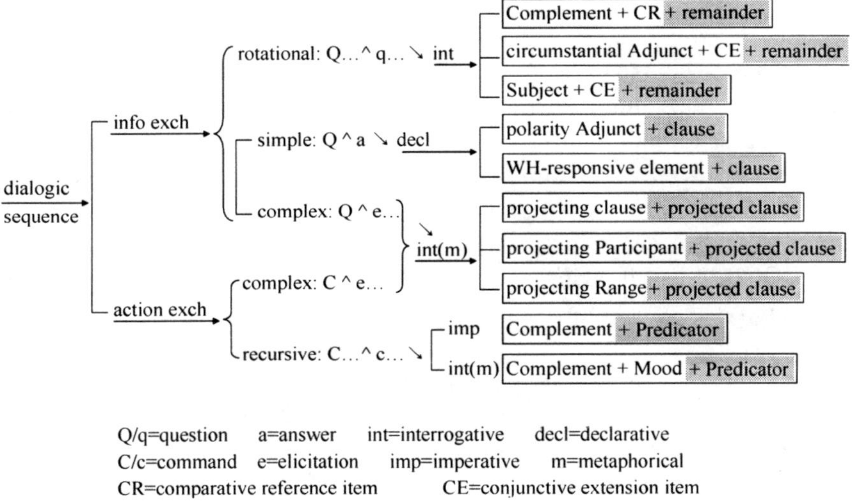

Figure 9.1: The DIALOGIC SEQUENCE System of EFL Classroom Discourse

As shown in Figure 9.1, all dialogic sequences tied up by ellipsis in EFL classroom discourse can be classified into two major types, according to whether the elliptical clause performs a speech function in an information exchange or an action exchange.

In an information exchange, ellipsis is found in (1) an answer to a question, (2) an elicitation of an answer to a question, and (3) a rotational question; serving to tie up respectively (1) a simple information exchange, (2) a complex information exchange, and (3) a series of rotational information exchanges, simple or complex. Although the element present in the three types of elliptical clauses varies, the element absent invariably presupposes, and is retrievable from, the preceding question that is complete in structure.

In an action exchange, ellipsis is found in (1) an elicitation of a compliance to a command and (2) a command that can be repeated as many times as required by the number of items in an in-class-exercise. Thus it serves to tie up (1) a complex action exchange and (2) a series of recursive action exchanges, including complex ones. In both cases, the element absent from the elliptical clause can be retrieved from the initial command that is complete in clause structure; and it is the case with every elliptical command occurring in every recursive action exchange.

9.5   Concluding remarks

In sum, presented above is an analysis of ellipsis choices occurring in EFL classroom discourse, intended as an effort to model text-size meanings as created by ellipsis in a specific text type. While ellipsis used to be described as a resource for joining a response to an initiation and applied in a question-response or statement/command-rejoinder sequence; in this analysis ellipsis is found to occur in both a responding and an initiating move, thus tying up both an adjacency pair and other types of dialogic sequences. The DIALOGIC SEQUENCE system presented above is a description of the different types of dialogic sequences created by ellipsis in EFL classroom discourse.

As a semantic system of a specific text type, DIALOGIC SEQUENCE is a model of text-size meanings in a specific situation type. In the EFL classroom situation, the field of discourse, i.e. foreign language teaching and learning, requires sufficient verbal actions; the tenor of discourse, i.e. one teacher faced with multiple students, requires that the teacher give as many practice opportunities to as many students as possible; and the mode of discourse, i.e. face-to-face dialogue, makes available both aural and visual channels that more or less help to reduce misunderstandings. So, when ellipsis occurs in teachers' initiations – as question, command or elicitation – it serves well to push the dialogue forward in an efficient as well as organized manner, apart from doing such specific jobs as engaging more students in class discussions, assigning different exercise items to different students, and encouraging students to answer a question or to produce a verbal action. As such, ellipsis constitutes an important resource for textualizing dialogue in EFL classrooms.

Meanwhile, the system has been shown as informing about both the sequence types realized through ellipsis, and the grammatical forms of the elliptical clauses functioning in such sequences. Regarding the former, much longer sequences than an adjacency pair have been identified, such as a complex exchange, an information exchange rotation, or even an entire action phase. Regarding the latter, metaphors of mood have been identified in elliptical clauses realizing some of the speech functions, such as interrogative mood realizing a command, or interpersonal projection realizing an elicitation. In addition, it has been noticed that other cohesive devices such as comparative reference and conjunctive extension tend to co-occur with ellipsis to enhance the cohesive relation between moves that are apart from each other, although further studies are needed in this regard. Also, in order to step further towards the general semantics of ellipsis, more text types need to be studied.

Notes

1.   In all examples in this chapter, Arabic numbers before a hyphen are used to number turns, and those after a hyphen to number moves in the same turn. T stands for teacher, S for student, and S/a or S/b for different students. Double quotation marks enclose a sentence (or part of it) taken from the text that is being taught in class, while single quotation marks enclose a linguistic item of any size or part of speech that is being explained in class and hence used as a nominal group in the sentence being produced. Underlining indicates an element that is absent from an elliptical clause but retrievable from the current complete clause.
2.   The use of *you* in an imperative clause may be a feature of the Chinese variety of English and deserves further study.
3.   A vocative may occur either within an elliptical clause, or more than 6 seconds after a question, a command or an elicitation. In the latter case, it is taken as a distinct move selecting the next speaker (see 105-T/3 in Example 3).

References

Allwright, D. and Bailey, K. (1991) *Focus on the Language Classroom: An Introduction to Classroom Research for Language Teachers*. Cambridge: Cambridge University Press.

Berry, M. (1987) Is teacher an unanalyzed concept? In M. A. K. Halliday and R. P. Fawcett (eds) *New Developments in Systemic Linguistics Volume 1: Theory and Description*, 41–63. London: Pinter.

Christie, F. (2002) *Classroom Discourse Analysis: A Functional Perspective*. London: Continuum.

Halliday, M. A. K. (1978) *Language as Social Semiotic: The Social Interpretation of Language and Meaning*. London: Edward Arnold.

Halliday, M. A. K. (1991) Towards probabilistic interpretations. In E. Ventola (ed.) *Functional and Systemic Linguistics: Approaches and Use*, 39–61. New York: Mouton de Gruyter.

Halliday, M. A. K. (1994) *An Introduction to Functional Grammar* (2nd edition). London: Edward Arnold.

Halliday, M. A. K. (revised by Matthiessen, C. M. I. M.) (2004) *An Introduction to Functional Grammar* (3rd edition). New York: Edward Arnold.

Halliday, M. A. K. and Hasan, R. (1976) *Cohesion in English*. London: Longman.

Martin, J. R. (1992) *English Text: System and Structure*. Philadelphia, PA: Benjamins.

Martin, J. R. and Rose, D. (2003) *Working with Discourse: Meaning beyond the Clause*. London: Continuum.

Sinclair, J. M. and Coulthard, M. (1975) *Towards an Analysis of Discourse*. Oxford: Oxford University Press.

Walsh, S. (2006) *Investigating Classroom Discourse*. London: Routledge.

Yang, X. (2003) On the study, of foreign language teachers' classroom strategies. *Foreign Language Teaching and Research* 1: 40–46 (杨雪燕, 外语教师课堂策略研究：状况与意义,《外语教学与研究》(1): 40–46).

Yang, X. (2010) *Modelling Text as Process: A Dynamic Approach to EFL Classroom Discourse*. London: Continuum.

Zhou, Y. (2005) Needs analysis of EFL teacher development in Chinese universities. *Foreign Language Teaching and Research* 3: 48–52 (周燕, 高校英语教师发展需求调查与研究,《外语教学与研究》(3): 48–52).

10 Genre and appraisal theories in Functional Discourse Analysis – with reference to accounts in *Dragon Carving and the Literary Mind*

LI Zhanzi[*]

10.1 Introduction

This chapter examines the genre and evaluation thoughts in a Chinese classic *Dragon Carving and the Literary Mind* (hereafter, for short, *Dragon Carving*), with the aim of drawing insights from this single longest treatise in Chinese literary criticism.

On the one hand, the holistic approach in *Dragon Carving* which incorporated stylistics, author-subjectivity, writing process and rhetoric studies constitutes a rich heritage in accounting for the relationship between genres and appraisals. On the other hand, the chapter argues that the socio-cultural concern carved out by functional discourse analysis can answer the need of the present time better if the holistic approach and the more sophisticated categorization of genre and appraisal in ancient Chinese classics can be given due attention.

10.1.1 A Brief Introduction to Dragon Carving and the Literary Mind

A possible paraphrase of the title of this great work would be the 'expression of feeling and thought in embellished language' (Yang, 2003: 61).[1] (As the book by Yang is the major source; hereafter, the date is deleted.) The book has attracted unprecedented interest in the recent decades. It is not an exaggeration to say that the book establishes a philosophy of literature that revitalizes the Chinese culture (Yang: 68).

[*] Prof. Li Zhanzi teaches at the Foreign Language School, Nanjing International Studies University, Jiangsu Province, China.

It is the single longest treatise in Chinese literary criticism with 37,000 characters in 50 chapters that holds an everlasting charm for later scholars. The studies of this literary text have achieved a quasi-disciplinary status with the name of 'Dragonology' (Yang: 44; Hu and Li, 2006; Liu, 2009).

The author of the book, Liu Xie, was well versed in Buddhist sutras; his work, written about 501 CE, was deeply influenced by Buddhism. Unlike a typical text of Chinese literary criticism, the work is structured more like a Buddhist sutra (Yang: 45).

'Liu Xie's sense of humility and human frailty makes him a warm and sympathetic critic, no less sharp or insightful for that, yet utterly sensitive and humane' (Yang: 70). In Chapter 50, *my intensions or postscript,* the author states that:

> To evaluate one piece of work is easy; to give an overview of so many is hard. Although I have mentioned briefly some minor issues and treated in detail the essentials of writing, there must have been subtleties and nuances that have eluded my vision or gone beyond my power of language. If some of the ideas here coincide with past opinion, it does not mean that I have copied them but that they are irrefutable. If they differ, it does not mean that I deliberately set out to contradict past opinion but that I have no reason to accept them as true. ... My foremost concern is to combine close analysis with unbiased judgments. (Yang: 70–71)

From this statement of intentions or postscript, we can clearly see that Liu's mission in the book is to make judgements about the styles of his own classification and aspire to objectivity in this formidable task. Across the linguistic and cultural space and time, this concern corresponds well to the genre and appraisal theories in functional discourse analysis (Cao, 2008). So in what follows I am going to survey this long discourse and compare Liu's accounts and the related theories with contemporary Hallidayan functional linguistics.

10.2 Theorization of genre in *Dragon Carving*

Dragon Carving has broached many important issues of literature and literary criticism. Its discussions of various literary genres extend from Chapter 6 to Chapter 25, while its discussions of relationship between genres/styles and appraisals/evaluations are scattered throughout the book.

According to the book's translator Yang Guobin, 'Liu Xie's genre theory is the consummation of his time. Before him, Cao Pi, Lu Ji, Zhi Yu and Xiao Tong, the Crown Prince, had all touched on the question of genres in their literary discourse. ... In many ways, therefore, the way for the exploration of this conception had been paved for Liu Xie, and yet he was able to break new ground.' And Yang gives Liu Xie the highest appraisal in terms of his creative work – 'If Liu's predecessors had touched on the stylistic implications of individual genres and treated generic development in a haphazard manner, Liu was more of a system builder' (Yang: 53, 54).

First, Liu makes a clear distinction between *wen* (rhymed writing/genre), which covers Chapters 6 to 15, and *bi* (unrhymed writing/genre), which extends from Chapter 16 to Chapter 25.

Second, Liu puts forward the critical method in genre study: he describes this method in his postscript and considers it to be the guideline for the first part of his book, in terms of the following four steps:

> trace their origins to demonstrate their developments;
> define terms to clarify their meanings;
> list exemplary pieces to illustrate the points;
> and discuss the general characteristics of each genre. (Chapter 50,
> My Intentions, or Postscript) (Yang: 717)[2]

Now I am going to summarize the main aspects of Liu's theorization of genre in *Dragon Carving*.

10.2.1 Centrality of the sages' writings

Liu establishes the classics as the source of all later genres in Chapter 3, 'Modeling on the classics':

> *The Book of Changes* is the fountainhead of treatise, discourse, preface and verse; *the Book of Documents* is the source of edict, decree, laudatory address, and reports to the throne; *the Book of Poetry* is the origin of rhyme-prose, hymn, song, and eulogy; *the Book of Rites* is the beginning of inscription, mourning-song, admonition, and prayer; and *the Spring and Autumn Annuals* is the root of chronicle, biography, oath, and dispatch. They all reach great heights and establish the ultimate criteria, opening up boundless territories of writing. No matter how much various writers aspire to, they cannot reach beyond this range. (Chapter 3, 'Modeling on the Classics') (Yang: 31)

From this quote we can see the classics listed include *The Book of Changes, the Book of Documents, the Book of Poetry, the Book of Rites,* and *the Spring and Autumn Annuals*[3]. These sages' writings are given the status of canon and considered the source of all later genres. In this way, the study of genre by Liu Xie has something to refer back to and the status of these classics is also strengthened in the process.

10.2.2 Theory of generic continuity and change

When it comes to the laws of genre change and genre continuity, Liu is highly ingenious. For instance, he dismisses the bias in earlier criticisms (represented by Sima Qian's work *Records of the Grand Historian*) of *The Songs of the South* by Qu Yuan[4] and other poets, and sums up four positive qualities that Qu Yuan's works share with those of the classics. First, in terms of theme continuity, they adopt the themes of *The Book of Documents*. Second, the illocutionary function of Qu Yuan's writing is aimed at giving warnings and admonitions. Third, Qu's work follows the classical model of comparison and metaphor, and fourth, in terms of the main content, Qu's writings express the plaint of loyal ministers.

Liu also suggests that Qu Yuan deviates from the classics in four respects, namely, absurd descriptions, chimerical phantasies, narrow-minded pride, and licentiousness. The qualities that Liu Xie rejects are those that are to lead later literature, especially the works of rhyme-prose produced in the Han Dynasty, namely, qualities of extravagance and shallow novelty. That is why Liu Xie puts *The Songs of the South* below *The Book of Poetry* but above rhyme-prose (Yang: 56).

10.2.3 Genre comparisons based on functions

Liu has also distinguished different genres according to their functions. For instance, in the following description, he distinguishes an admonition and an inscription in terms of their different functions and their related language features. He also touches on the development and the change of these two similar genres:

> An admonition is chanted by an official, an inscription is carved on an object. Though their names and functions differ, their purpose is to give warning. An admonition is used solely to warn against mistakes, so its language should be accurate and precise. An inscription gives praises in addition to warnings, so its style should be grand and gracious. Both should express exact, clear, concise, and profound ideas. These are the essentials. However, as the tradition of making honest admonitions lapsed and the practice of inscribing merits on vessels declined, these two types of writing have become more and more rare. Only men of letters need to know their far-reaching significance. (Chapter 11, 'Inscription and Admonition') (Yang: 143)

10.2.4 Genre delicacy – miscellaneous writings subdivided into 16 types

One of the most impressive of Liu's scholarly deeds is that he subdivides miscellaneous writings into different groups and types. In the following paragraph from his work, altogether 16 types are named and they are listed in four groups according to their similarities:

> Since the Han Dynasty, all sorts of names have been given to miscellaneous writings. One group includes *dian* (code), *gao* (announcement), *shi* (oath), *wen* (question); another *lan* (synopsis), *lue* (summary), *pian* (discourse), *zhang* (chapter); a third *qu* (ditty), *cao* (strain), *nong* (lay), and *yin* (prelude); a fourth *yin* (chant), *feng* (satire), *yao* (ballad), and *yong* (song). Miscellaneous writings can be separately discussed by distinguishing them according to their respective genres. This will be done in separate chapters, so there is no need to dwell upon them here. (Chapter 14, 'Miscellaneous Writing') (Yang: 185)

10.2.5 Genre delicacy – epistolary writing and miscellaneous records (not in terms of literary value)

In his book, Liu also introduces various types of practical writings as follows:

> The scope of epistolary writings and miscellaneous records is vast, covering a variety of subjects. In the course of time, they have been given various names. *Pu* (genealogy), *ji* (register), *bu* (account book), and *lu* (chronicle) are used for the general administration of the population. *Fang* (formula), *shu* (arithmetic), *zhan* (divination), and *shi* (pattern) are used in medicine, establishing the calendar, astrology, and prophecy. *Lu* (regulation), *ling* (decree), *fa* (stratagem), and *zhi* (military command) are used in proclaiming laws and military orders. *Fu* (tally), *qi* (contract), *quan* (bond), and *shu* (sales slip) are used as market credentials, government officials use *guan* (pass), *ci* (inquiry), *jie* (solution), and *die* (memorandum) to obtain information. The common people use *zhuang* (account), *lie* (list), *ci* (speech), and *yan* (proverb) to express their sentiments. They are all honest expressions. Insignificant as literary forms, they are essential for handling government affairs. (Chapter 25, 'Epistolary Writing and Miscellaneous Records') (Yang: 357)

Here we see 24 types mentioned and considered essential for handling government affairs. Again they are grouped according to different functions, namely, the general administration of the population, medicinal practice, astrology and prophecy matters, legal and military matters, and expression of sentiments by common people. A vista of the social life at that time is captured by Liu's listing and classification of these practical genres. His vision lies in dealing with genre delicacy not in terms of their literary value but in terms of their social value. This vision comes very close to the genre studies in contemporary functional discourse analysis which will be explored in more detail in Section 4 of the chapter.

10.2.6 Special genres for political purposes – Jesting Rhymes and Puzzles

Worth noticing in Liu's work are the special genres for political purposes. Liu advocates the Jesting Rhymes and Puzzles and explains them as follows:

> In the past, comic rhymes and puzzles
> Helped to check crises and ease sufferings.
> Although not as useful as silk and hemp,
> They served their purposes like straw and rushes.
> Used justly, on proper occasions,
> They provide advice or reproof.
> Mere jesting and meaningless farce
> Are damaging to virtue and morality. (Chapter 15, 'Jesting Rhymes and Puzzles') (Yang: 197)

10.3 Appraisal of genres in *Dragon Carving*

From what we have discussed in the previous sections, it is clear that genres are studied in detail and are appraised alongside the description. When Liu emphasizes the appreciation of language, he comes to terms with the idea of style. Genres and styles are interrelated but different in Liu Xie's accounts. In this section we focus on how he evaluates the genres and how he dwells on the classification of styles and relates styles to personality.

As far as I can see, Liu Xie demonstrates three different senses of style in his work: (1) the style of a person, i.e. the sum-total of an individual; (2) the style in the sense of the combination of the genres and the stylistic features of such genres; and (3) the style of a genre, namely, the appraisal of the language of the genre.

10.3.1 On the style of a person

Style is seen by Liu Xie as the sum-total of an individual – his talent, vitality, learning and cultivation. Differences in these respects yield different styles. The styles of previous writers are evaluated as follows by Liu Xie in his book as:

> Thus bright and sharp, Jia Yi (literary scholar and writer of political treaties in the Western Han Dynasty.) had a pure and fresh style. Proud and unrestrained, Sima Xiangru (alias Chang Qing, rhyme-prose writer of the Western Han period.) used inflated language to make inflated arguments. Quiet and pensive, Yang Xiong (alias Zi Yun, writer and philosopher in the Western Han Dynasty) reached depth beyond his surface meanings. Simple and plain, Liu Xiang (alias Zi Zheng, scholar of Confucian classics and bibliographer in Western Han) wrote with clarity and breadth. Graceful and genial, Ban Gu (alias Meng Jian, historian and writer in the Eastern Han period) was good at organization and thorough in thought. Learned and erudite ... restless and pugnacious ... Narrow-minded by temperament, ... Free and unfettered, ... Frivolous yet keen, ... Reserved and sedate ... They show how a writer's style corresponds to the man, and how his talent and natural endowments affect the style. (Chapter 27, 'Style and Natural Endowments') (Yang: 393)

In Chapter 27, Liu describes the relationship between Style and Natural Endowments as:

> Mediocrity or brilliance of language and thought depends on talent, masculinity or effeminacy of style is determined by personality, depth or shallowness of meaning is related to learning, elegance or baseness of style is contingent on cultivation. Each writer follows his own heart and the differences between one and another are as clear as different faces. (Chapter 27, 'Style and Natural Endowments') (Yang: 389)

Later on in the book, he supplements the above observation by noting 'As natural endowments are different, so styles are diverse and uncertain. ... Given persistent application, nurture can compensate for nature' (Chapter 27, 'Style and Natural Endowments') (Yang: 397).

10.3.2 Eight styles

Having shown the close relationship between style and the person, Liu Xie goes on to distinguish eight styles, namely, the elegant, the recondite, the concise, the plain, the ornate, the sublime, the eccentric, and the frivolous. According to him, the eight styles fall into four pairs: the elegant vs. the exotic eccentric, the recondite vs. the plain, the ornate vs. the concise, and the sublime vs. the frivolous. They represent the whole tree of writing, roots, branches, leaves and all (Chapter 27, 'Style and Natural Endowments') (Yang: 395).

As for *fenggu*, a special quality of the style, it is perhaps more appropriate to say that it is of itself not a style, but an important quality of a good style. This is the quality of strength and vigour as represented by the signification of the term *feng* (wind) and *gu* (bone or structure) (Yang: 63).

Works with 'wind' and 'bone' are good, according to Liu Xie, but not good enough. The ideal composition should be both forceful and graceful. Liu Xie himself frequently mentions 'elegantly beautiful' as a highly desirable style. At the end of Chapter 27, he writes, 'The elegant and beautiful resemble perfect silk embroideries; the excessive and frivolous are like the mixture of red and purple.' In Chapter 6, Liu regards elegance as the proper style of four-character verse, which had developed from *the Book of Poetry*. He considers 'beauty' as the ideal style of five-character verse, which originated in *the Book of Poetry* and in early folk songs (Yang: 64).

10.3.3 Genre and appraisal

A central sense of style in *Dragon Carving* is style as the overall appraisal of a specific genre. The following are three examples of appraisals of three genres, namely: (1) Classics; (2) *Sao – Songs of the South;* and (3) *Zhuzi*, Philosophical Writings.

First let us briefly look at appraisal of classic pieces of literary works (I have put the evaluative elements in italics):

Cao Zhi wrote a poem called 'The Yellow Bird'; Liu Zhen has one entitled 'The Green Pine'. *Forceful and vigorous*, both make good use of indirections to offer moral messages. Ji Kang's poem 'The Scholar-Soldier' and Ruan Ji's 'Song of My Heart' describe mystic realms and other-worldly thoughts: these are marked by *repose and unconstraint.* Lu Ji's 'Unrestrained Courage' and Tao Yuanming's 'Free Spirit' are *precise in ideas and lucid in language*: they may be characterized as *splendidly colourful* (Chapter 40, 'Concealed and Evident Excellence') (Yang: 559).

Liu evaluates the classics with a revealing simile: they are like trees, with deep roots, tall branches, and lush foliage. Their language is concise, meaning rich, exemplified in *Sao*, or *the Songs of the South*. The passage below is so full of evaluation that I just present it here in its original instead of marking many places with italics:

> The structures and linguistic textures show that although many themes are borrowed from the classics, these songs have their own lofty style. 'Encountering Sorrow' and 'Nine Declarations' are lucid, beautiful, and sorrowful. 'Nine Songs' and 'Nine Arguments' are elaborate and melancholy. 'Journey Afar' and 'Questioning Heaven' are gorgeous, exotic, and resourceful. 'Summoning of the Soul' and 'Great Summons' are dazzling and full of inner beauty. 'Divination' expresses the ideal of unrestrained freedom and 'The Fisherman' embodies the proud spirit of a self-exiled genius. That is why *the Songs of the South* surpasses past and contemporary works in spirit or excellence of language. Its brilliance and exquisite beauty are insurmountable. (Chapter 5, 'Evaluating *Sao*, or the Songs of the South') (Yang: 55)

The third example is Liu's appraisal of philosophical writings. For these writings, Liu makes extensive, accurate and varied evaluation. I have jotted down the evaluative lexis as below, when he mentions Mencius, Xunzi, Guan Zhong, Yan Ying[6] and a large group of great thinkers: '*fine thoughts in elegant language; accurate and concise, colorful and rigorous, extravagant yet powerful, plainly, using no ornament, sound theories in crude language, clarity and emotional depth, brevity and precision, meticulous analysis, combines broad visions with a careful style, weaves rich material into splendid fabrics*' (Chapter 17, 'Philosophical Writings') (Yang: 233).

Finally it is necessary to call attention to Liu's overall appraisal concept in the work. Liu argues that evaluation should be focused on the desirability of the literary pieces and styles. Liu establishes *Dao* as the origin of literature and asks the big question about what writings are the most desirable. The answer is scattered in many places in the book – namely the sages' writings, sages being the wisest interpreters of *Dao* (Yang: 51).

Having gone this far about the profound conceptions of genre and appraisal in Liu's work, we now turn to the functional linguistic study of genre and appraisal (Martin and Rose, 2003, 2008), in the hope that the two approaches may shed light on each other.

10.4 Functional genre theory and the appraisal cline

In this part a summary on the cline of evaluation in Chapter 4 of *The Language of Evaluation: Appraisal in English* (Martin and White, 2008: 164) will be presented. Below is the table of the cline of instantiation. The left column 'appraisal' is one of the many systems of language, and the right column 'system' stands for the overall language system.

10.4.1 Cline of instantiation – from system to reading

Appraisal	System
Key	Register
Stance	Text type (sub-selections of evaluative options within text)
Evaluation	Instance
Reaction	Reading

The idea of a cline is crucial in understanding the realization of evaluative reading. Martin and White stress the notion that instantiation is a cline, and there is no way of drawing a categorical distinction between key and stance along this cline (Martin and White, 2008: 203).

Stances are reconfigurations which we predict will be recurrent across a range of texts and a range of authors in a given discourse domain, and perhaps across different discourse domains. In their work, Martin and White study three stances – damning, excusing and sceptical as illustration of the focusing on the sub-selections of evaluative options within a text. And they express uncertainty about whether these stances will stand the test of time. 'This depends of course on the extent to which the configurations of appraisal recourse we have noted concur, and how they compare with related judgmental configurations we have not taken time to explore' (Martin and White, 2008: 208).

Indeed, it seems a bit difficult to draw a clear-cut line between 'key' and 'stance'. It seems that key is more related to voice, and stance is the finer judgemental types that are the broad types of keys; they are related to the journalistic field in Martin and White; stance transgresses to the macro speech acts realized by such genres as an essay, a letter, or even a short story. In Liu Xie's *Dragon Carving* as we have explored in previous sections (see 10.2.6), special genres for political purposes and even jesting rhymes and puzzles can be the realizations of some stances like checking crises and easing sufferings.

10.4.2 Evaluation and reaction

Evaluations can never be the final word – as part of the interpersonal meaning; evaluation is open to negotiations (Bakhtin, 1986). We might argue that a range of readings is being facilitated by evaluation, if not encouraged.

Reaction in the table refers to the reading one makes of the evaluative meaning in a text. In terms of solidarity, this amounts to the way in which readers commune with feeling and align themselves in and around the community under negotiation (Martin and White, 2008: 206).

10.4.3 Syndromes of evaluation

Evaluation and reaction do not occur in isolation from one another. In Martin and White's work, they discuss syndromes of evaluation, to try to understand 'how appraisal values operated in texts, not as individual, isolated moments of meaning, but as elements integrated into broader syndromes of co-occurring meanings' (Martin and White, 2008: 207–208). As we can perceive from the table, this analysis of syndromes of evaluation can be conducted at greater or lesser degree of delicacy, such as at the level of key, or stance or signature.

10.4.4 Evaluation style

As a text is constructed by heteroglossic voices and viewpoints, 'evaluation style' is the term used by Martin and White to describe the relationships which the author constructs with the text's heteroglossis. They hope an approach like this will lay the foundations for a grammar of solidarity which integrates the lexicogrammar with the discourse semantics (Martin and White, 2008). It looks like the most ambitious effort on their part to connect the lexicogrammar with the discourse semantics through the filter of interpersonal, especially evaluative meaning.

10.4.5 Genre theory

Genre theory in the functional vein looks at a text as composed of functionally distinct stages or steps. To put it in more dynamic ways, the genre analysts examine how a text unfolds through the sequence of specific stages or steps. Genre theory suggests that texts which are doing different jobs in the culture will unfold in different ways, working through different stages or steps. When it comes to relationship between context and text, these analysts perceive it as probabilistic, not deterministic (Batia, 2000). In other words, in order to achieve a particular cultural goal, a text of a particular genre is likely to be produced, and that text is most likely to unfold in a particular way; but no static one to one relationship is implied, as alternatives for different genres are inherent in the dialogic relationship between language and context (Eggins and Martin, 1997: 236).

The systemic approach has been developing detailed specifications of the staging structures and realization features of different genres, as well as accounts of how genres can relate to and evolve into other genres, thus providing replicable and functionally motivated accounts of different genres in our culture (Eggins and Martin, 1997: 236–237).

10.5 Comparison and further discussion

In this part we are going to further explore a few aspects of the above surveyed two approaches of genre and appraisal. It is hoped that this brief discussion will provoke more thoughts on these cross-cultural ancient and contemporary linguistic concerns (Cao, 2008: 123).

10.5.1 Signature (MARTIN AND WHITE) VS. Account on personality (LIU)

First of all we look at the definition of signature in *The Language of Evaluation*. Signatures refer to 'the ideolectal reconfigurations of meaning-making potentials by which individual authors achieve a recognizable personal style' (Martin and White, 2008). Here the idea of a discourse community is implied, in order for signature to come into being. When we talk about signature, it is important to bear in mind that the syndrome of appraisal resources, which distinguishes individuals, one from another, is within a specific community, as relevant values always rest with communities.

On the other hand, in *Dragon Carving*, we find an enlightening account on personality. First, Liu Xie holds that one personality decides one configuration of styles, and in Chapter 27 on 'style and natural endowments' (Yang: 389), he lists talent, personality, learning and cultivation as four paradigms that distinguish each individual writer's characteristics. (See section 10.3.1 for his original words.)

Liu Xie goes on by rationalizing the relationship between great writers and various styles. He holds that only truly great writers can master all styles. 'He can manipulate styles as different as the fanciful and the orthodox, and easily handle such divergent styles as the masculine and effeminate' (Chapter 30, 'Choosing the style, or natural tendency') (Yang: 425).

From the above comparison, we can conclude that the former emphasizes addressivity and attitudinal community, while the latter dwells on style and natural endowments. The difference lies in that the concept of 'community' is not emphasized in *Dragon Carving*, while it is of critical importance to the recognition of signature according to Martin and White. Other related concepts such as 'addressivity', 'attitudinal communities', 'a text's heteroglossic backdrop', etc. in Martin and White are not discussed in *Dragon Carving*. However, the miracle of *Dragon Carving* lies in that it explores the potential of great writers who are capable of creating divergent styles, even though they are defined by a particular personal style or signature for that matter. This is indeed an area worth further exploring when we have the teaching of creative writing in mind.

10.5.2 Stance discussed with different ranges

In Martin and White (2008), three stances are exemplified in journalistic commentator voice, namely, Damning, Excusing, and Sceptical. In *Dragon Carving*, genre names already take on the meaning of 'stances'. For instance, Report and Memorandum – they are two stances in themselves and also used as the names for the two genres. Another example: Jesting is the stance, while rhymes and puzzles are the range of texts that we can find jesting. Hence jesting rhymes and puzzles.

Stance is arrived at through careful analysis of evaluative configurations in Martin and White (2008) while in *Dragon Carving*, stance is a starting point to mark the functions of different genres. While the former can expand to the analysis of more types of stances, the latter can go deep into each genre to examine the relationship between evaluative configurations and the function of the genre.

10.5.3 The chain, with different emphasis

In narratology studies, the sequence of 'writer – implied author – text – heteroglossia in the text – reader reaction – reader' is generally observed in analysis. Taking this well established chain as a point of departure, we notice that Liu Xie, adopting the sequence of 'writer – implied author – text – literary critics as an ideal reader/analyzer' in *Dragon Carving*, further explores the relationship between the 'writer' and the style. We also note that Martin and White employ the sequence of 'Text – heteroglossia in the text – reader reaction – attitudinal communities' in the appraisal theory they propose.

Functional genre theory tries to reach the level of reader interpretation as represented by the stratum of appraisal analysis, but it has not incorporated the writer-personality and the writing process into the theory. A comprehensive approach to discourse analysis may eventually include all of the above (Zhang, 2008: 19). At the moment, it is practical to take the middle of the road.

10.5.4 Unlimited genres

With the advent of digital age, it is impossible to classify all the genres as neatly as Liu Xie did with the ancient writings. The functional approach to genre can enable us to deal with everyday life types of discourse with a cutting edge on their socio-cultural meanings. The difference between classic writings (including the pragmatic types such as mentioned above) and mass media genres lies in their different focuses of concern in terms of genres. In this aspect, functional approach to genre gives us an efficient way to come to terms with the emerging new genres.

The systematic approach to genres advocated by genre theory answers well to the concern of revealing a genre's socio-cultural significance as argued by Eggins and Martin (1997: 243): 'Analysis at the level of genre has concentrated on making explicit just which combinations of field, tenor and mode variables a culture enables, and how these are mapped out as staged, goal-oriented social processes.'

By way of concluding, this chapter implies a holistic approach to the interrelated studies of genre and appraisal. The sophisticated categorization and insightful depiction in the representative ancient Chinese classic *Dragon Carving* may shed new lights on the current studies, and the functional linguistic endeavours capture well the socio-cultural concerns in the new age genres.

Notes

1. Liu, Xie (2003) *Dragon Carving and the Literary Mind* (Yang Guobin, Trans.). Beijing: Foreign Language Teaching and Research Press. (Hereafter, I will cite the translator Yang as the note.)
2. It is quoted from Chapter 50 in Liu Xie's original work and appears on page 717 of Yang's translation edition. The other notes in the rest of the chapter follow this format.
3. All of these are ancient Chinese classics.
4. An ancient Chinese poet who lived during the Warring States Period (475–221 BC) in ancient China.
5. All these are famous Chinese literary scholars. Cao Zhi, Ruan Ji and Ji Kang lived in the Three Kingdoms' period of 200–280 AD; Liu Zhen at the end of Han Dynasty; Lu Ji in Western Jin and Tao Yuanming in Eastern Jin.
6. All were philosophical thinkers in the Spring and Autumn period or the Warring States period around 770–221 BC.

References

Bakhtin, M. (1986) *Speech Genre and Other Genres*. Austin, TX: University of Texas Press.

Batia, V. K. (2000) *Analysing Genre – Language Use in Professional Settings*. London and New York: Longman

Eggins, S. and Martin, J. R. (1997) *Discourse as Structure and Process*. Thousand Oaks, CA: Sage.

Liu, Xie (2003) *Dragon Carving and the Literary Mind* (Yang Guobin trans.). Beijing: Foreign Language Teaching and Research Press. (Original work completed 501.)

Martin, J. R. and Rose, D. (2003) *Working with Discourse*. London & New York: Continuum.

Martin, J. R. and Rose, D. (2008) *Genre Relations—Mapping Culture*. London & New York: Continuum.

Martin, J. R. and White, R. R. (2008) *The Language of Evaluation: Appraisal in English*. Beijing: Foreign Language Teaching and Research Press and Palgrave Macmillan.

Yang, Guobin (2003) *Dragon Carving and the Literary Mind*. Trans. Beijing: Foreign Language Teaching and Research Press.

Cao, Shunqing (2008) 'Discourse of Chinese literary criticism and dialogue between the east and the west / 中国文化话语及中西文论对话'. *Journal of Zhejiang University*, 38: 123–129.

Hu, Jingzhi and Li, Jian (2006) *Classic Chinese Literary Studies / 中国古典文艺学*. Beijing: Guangming Daily Press.

Li, Zhanzi (2006) 'Style and evaluation / 文体与评价'. *Foreign Languages and Their Teaching*, 211: 25–28.

Liu, Yin (2009) 'On the studies and English translation of Dragon Carving / 关于《文心雕龙》的英译和研究'. *Foreign Language Teaching and Research*, 41.

Zhang, Yan (2008) 'Dynamic approach to genre in the topological perspective / '拓扑'视角下的动态体裁研究'. *Rhetorical Studies*, 2008 (1): 19-24.

11 Analyzing the reporting clause in translating Confucius's *Lun Yu* (*The Analects*)

HUANG Guowen*

11.1 Introduction

The aim of this chapter is to discuss the analysis of the reporting clause in translating Confucius's *Lun Yu* (or 'Lunyu'; Lún Yǔ; 論語) into English, with special focus on translating the reporting clause in a section of Chapter 14 in *Lun Yu*. The discussion shows that even the analysis of a single example from *Lun Yu* can provide implications for translation studies within a systemic functional linguistics framework.

Lun Yu or the Confucian 'Lun Yu', also known in the English world as 'The Analects of Confucius', or simply, *The Analects*, is considered a record of the words and behaviours of the central Chinese thinker and philosopher Confucius (551–479 BC) and his disciples, as well as the conversations they had. It is regarded as the representative work of Confucianism and as one of the most influential canons in human history, which continues to have a tremendous influence on Chinese and East Asian thought and values even today. As Yang (1999: 36) argues, 'every Chinese, every act and every move of his or hers may be originated in one book – *The Confucian Analects*, a canon formed 2,400 years ago.'

According to existing studies, *Lun Yu* was written on bamboo strips over a period of 30 to 50 years. It is assumed that the writing was begun some time during the Spring and Autumn Period (770–476 BC) and was finished during the Warring States Period (479–221 BC). There are 20 chapters (also called 'books') in it, each of which consists of different numbers of sections (also called 'chapters'). The sections of *Lun Yu* were mainly recorded by Confucius's students, his students' students, and quite a few by others. Most of the sections are sayings and conversations but there are a few sec-

* Professor Huang Guowen is Dean of the School of International Studies, Sun Yat-sen University, Guangzhou.

tions which are concerned with the description of events and ideas, and in some sections there are detailed descriptions of Confucius's acts and behaviour in various daily activities. According to the literature, there are three main versions of *Lun Yu* available but the one that is most popular today is the *Lun Yu of Marquis Zhang*.

The Confucian *Lun Yu* has been translated into many foreign languages, and as far as the English translation is concerned, there are over 50 different translations of the same text by translators of different cultural, social, ideological and professional backgrounds. The first translation, which is not a complete one, was rendered from Chinese to Latin, and published in Paris in 1687 and the first English translation was published in 1691, redacted from Latin to English. The very first complete translation of *Lun Yu* from Chinese to English was undertaken by James Legge (1815–1897), who was a noted Scottish sinologist, a Scottish missionary, representative of the London Missionary Society in Malacca and Hong Kong (1840–1873), and the first professor of Chinese at Oxford University (1876–1897). During his residence in Hong Kong, he translated *The Confucian Analects* (1861).

In this chapter, the source text (ST) is described in terms of its lexicogrammatical structure. Then the translated versions are analysed, and through the explanation it is argued that any English (or other foreign language) translation of classic works such as *Lun Yu* may be based on the result of an 'intralingual translation' (Jakobson, 1959/2000) of some kind (STa), which may be the result of another intralingual translation (STb), which may be the result of yet another intralingual translation (STc), and so on and so forth. Throughout the chapter, a number of issues concerning the analysis and translation of *Lun Yu* are further discussed.

There are several systemic functional linguistic studies of *Lun Yu* and its translations as text in the literature to date. For example, Fang (2006) investigates 'the socio-historical and ideological environment' for the 'engendering' of *Lun Yu*, with a focus on contextual features, the hierarchical structure and the ways of realizing Confucius' ideas in terms of the lexicogrammatical choices. Wei and Zhang (2006) offer a register analysis and study translated texts by interpreting them within their context of situation. By contrast, Zou's (2007) study focuses on the context of culture. And Chen (2009) looks at translated texts from a functional discourse analysis perspective with a focus on the lexicogrammatical stratum.

11.2 Observation

For more than 100 years, missionaries, sinologists, philosophers have been translating Confucius's *Lun Yu* into different languages. Here we will take one section from the Chinese *Lun Yu*, which is a dialogue, as an example. It is from Chapter 14 (for the sake of analysis, the clauses/clause complexes are numbered):

1. zǐ（子）lù（路）wèn（問）jūn（君）zǐ（子）
2. zǐ（子）yuē（曰）xiū（修）jǐ（己）yǐ（以）jìng（敬）
3. yuē（曰）rú（如）sī（斯）ér（而）yǐ（已）hū（乎）
4. yuē（曰）xiū（修）jǐ（己）yǐ（以）ān（安）rén（人）
5. yuē（曰）rú（如）sī（斯）ér（而）yǐ（已）hū（乎）
6. yuē（曰）xiū（修）jǐ（己）yǐ（以）ān（安）bǎi（百）xìng（姓）
7. xiū（修）jǐ（己）yǐ（以）ān（安）bǎi（百）xìng（姓）
8. Yáo（堯）Shùn（舜）qí（其）yóu（猶）bìng（病）zhū（諸）

And below are two English translations. The first one was taken from Ku's (1898) translation and the second from Waley's (1938). Basically this section in the source text is made up of three questions (i.e., 1, 3, 5) and three answers (i.e., 2, 4, 6–7–8), the first question being an indirect one. In order to make it easy for us to discuss in detail, labels and numbers are added (Ku = Ku's translation, Q = Question, A = Answer, Waley = Waley's translation):

1. (Ku-Q1) A disciple of Confucius enquired what constituted a wise and good man. (Ku-A1) Confucius answered, "A wise and good man is one who sets himself seriously to order his conversation aright?" (Ku-Q2) "Is that all?" asked the disciple. (Ku-A2) "Yes," replied Confucius, "He wants to order his conversation aright for the happiness of others." (Ku-Q3) "Is that all?" asked the disciple again. (Ku-A3) "Yes," replied Confucius, "He wants to order his conversation aright for the happiness of the world; and, judged by that, even the great ancient Emperors felt their shortcomings."
2. (Waley-Q1) Tzu-lu asked about the qualities of a true gentleman. (Waley-A1) The Master said, He cultivates in himself the capacity to be diligent in his tasks. (Waley-Q2) Tzu-lu said, Can he not go further than that? (Waley-A2) The Master said, He cultivates in himself the capacity to ease the lot of other people. (Waley-Q3) Tzu-lu said, Can he not go further than that? (Waley-A3) The Master said, He cultivates in himself the capacity to ease the lot of the whole populace. If he can do that, could even Yao or Shun find cause to criticize him?

In terms of the discourse structure, we have three pairs of turn-taking: Q1 → A1, Q2 → A2, Q3 → A3. Since this section is made of questions and answers, some translators prefer to show the relationship by having different paragraphs. The following is taken from Watson (2007):

3.   (Watson-Q1) Zilu asked about the gentleman. (Watson-A1) The Master said, He trains himself to be respectful.

(Watson-Q2) Is that all?

(Watson-A2) The Master said, He trains himself in order to give ease to others.

(Watson-Q3) Is that all?

(Watson-A3) The Master said, He trains himself in order to give ease to all men and women. But training himself in order to give ease to all men and women – even the sages Yao and Shun found that hard to do.

In terms of the discourse structure, these three different translations are basically the same, and the roles taken by the two participants in the dialogue are clear: Zilu/Tzu-lu, a disciple of Confucius, is the questioner and Confucius the Answerer.

11.3 Description

Before we describe the translations in terms of their lexicogrammatical structures, we must say something about the source text. As the text *Lun Yu* was written more than 2,000 years ago, the Chinese then was different from what it is today: at that time there was no punctuation between the characters and the text was segmented and punctuated by scholars of Chinese studies many years later, thus giving rise to different interpretations due to the different segmentations by different punctuations.

Differences in translation may also arise from differences in lexicogrammatical structures between classical and modern Chinese. Present day Putonghua (modern Chinese) may be traced back to the May 4th Movement of 1919, together with other changes brought about by the New Culture Movement in China. There are a number of obvious linguistic differences between old Chinese (in which *Lun Yu* was written) and modern Chinese, which is beyond the scope of the present study. Relevant to the present study is the fact that the grammatical Subject in the classical Chinese clause is often missing while the logical Subject can be identified according to the co-text, as Clauses (3), (4), (5) and (6) in the source text show.

Therefore, most (if not all) English translators of classical Chinese texts have had to rely on one's interpretation of the source text, which means that the source text of the English translation is not the real source text in the normal sense. In other words, an 'intralingual translation' serves as the basis for the Chinese-English translation, which helps explain why there are various interpretations in different translations. This point will be taken up later.

Let us first look at the first clause in the source text in Chinese: (1) Zǐlù [name of one of Confucius's disciples] wèn [ask] jūnzǐ [gentleman]. When this was translated into English, the first nominal group 'Zǐlù' [a proper noun] was respectively translated into 'a disciple of Confucius' (Ku-Q1), 'Tzu-lu' (Waley-Q1) or 'Zilu' (Watson-Q1), the verb [process] 'wèn' into 'enquired' (Ku-Q1) and 'asked about' (Waley-Q1 and Watson-Q1), and the last nominal group 'jūnzǐ' into a nominalized clause 'what constituted a wise and good man' (Ku-Q1), and a nominal group 'the qualities of a true gentleman' (Waley-Q1) or 'the gentleman' (Watson-Q1). Both in terms of the lexicogrammatical structure and the meanings expressed, the three translations are different.

In the second Chinese clause (clause complex): (2) zǐ [Confucius] yuē [say] xiū [cultivate] jǐ [oneself] yǐ [so that] jìng [respectfulness], the first two characters ('Confucius', 'say') are the reporting clause and the other four characters form the reported clause. In Ku's translation, the reported clause is treated as a direct quote, while in both Waley's and Watson's translations, it was treated as a direct quote without quotation marks, which is sometimes called 'free direct speech'.

In the third Chinese clause complex: (3) yuē [say] rú [like, prep.] sī [this] ér yǐ [mood marker] hū [mood marker], the first character is a verb (a verbal process), and the other five characters form the verbiage. Here the Sayer does not appear but can be inferred from the context: It was Zilu who asked the question.

The fourth clause complex in Chinese is: (4) yuē [say] xiū [cultivate] jǐ [oneself] yǐ [so that] ān [bring peace to] rén [people], and like the third clause complex it is made up of a reporting clause (yuē [say]) without the Sayer and the reported clause (xiū [cultivate] jǐ [oneself] yǐ [so that] ān [bring peace to] rén [people]).

The fifth clause is the same as the third clause in terms of its structure and its basic meaning: yuē [say] rú [like, prep.] sī [this] ér yǐ [mood marker] hū [mood marker].

The sixth clause complex is the same as the fourth clause complex in Chinese except the last nominal group [bǎi xìng] (instead of [rén]): (6) yuē [say] xiū [cultivate] jǐ [oneself] yǐ [so that] ān [comfort, verb] bǎi xìng [populace], and like the third, fourth and fifth clause complexes the first character in the sixth clause complex forms a reporting clause (yuē [say]) without the Sayer and the rest forms the reported clause (i.e., Clause (6) without the first character 'yuē' [say]).

The seventh Chinese clause complex is the same as the reported clause in the sixth clause complex: (7) xiū [cultivate] jǐ [oneself] yǐ [so that] ān [comfort, verb] bǎi xìng [populace]. And the final Chinese clause ((8)Yáo [the first great emperor] Shùn [the second great emperor] qí [probably] yóu [still] bìng [worry] zhū [mood marker]), the seventh clause complex (i.e., xiū [cultivate] jǐ [oneself] yǐ [so that] ān [comfort, verb] bǎi xìng [all the people]) and the reported clause in the sixth clause complex (i.e., xiū [cultivate] jǐ [oneself] yǐ [so that] ān [comfort, verb] bǎi xìng [all the people]) together form the verbiage of the verbal process of yuē [say] in the six clause complexes.

To summarize, in the Chinese text the Questioner (Zǐlù) and the Answerer (Confucius) each are mentioned once only and the remaining two questions and answers were introduced by the verb 'yuē [say]' (which is the reporting clause without Subject). In both Ku's and Waley's translations, the Questioner and the Answerer were given in the three pairs of turn-taking. In Watson's translation, the reporting clauses to introduce the two direct questions were not realized 'explicitly' (see Watson-Q2 and Watson-Q3), while the reporting clauses introducing the last two answers (Watson-A2: 'The Master said', Watson-A3: 'The Master said') were provided.

11.4 Analysis

Comparing different translations of the same section from *Lun Yu* will show that there are interesting examples which are related to the interpretation and expression of the assumed ideas in the original text. From a linguistic perspective, we can examine the language at different strata, and even a single concept (e.g. 'jūnzǐ' in our example) requires numerous explanations.

Here our focus will be on the translation of the reporting clause in our Chinese source text example. In Ku's (1898) translation, the role of the Questioner and that of the Answerer are clearly identified by the use of two different verbs: enquire → answer, ask → reply, ask (again) → reply. By contrast, in Waley (1938), the verbs are not so explicit: ask → said, said → said, said → said. A comparison of Ku's and Waley's choices of the verbs realizing the verbal processes shows that Waley's use of 'said' accords better with the Chinese source text than Ku's choice, because the same verb (yuē [say]) is repeated five times in Chinese. By contrast, in Watson's (2007) translation, there is only one verbal process (Watson-Q1: '... asked about...') associated with the Questioner (in terms of introducing the question; i.e., Watson-Q1: 'Zilu asked about the gentleman.') and there are three reporting clauses introducing the three answers (Watson-A1, Watson-A2, Watson-A3: 'the Master said').

In Xu's (2005) translation (i.e., (4) below), the three questions were treated as indirect questions, and the questions and the answers in the three pairs of turn-taking were treated as forming three groups of clause nexus (Halliday, 1994), thus producing three clause complexes of the hypotactic type:

> 4.   When Zi Lu asked about an intelligentleman, the Master said, 'He should cultivate himself and do his duty with respect.' When asked whether it was all, the Master said, 'He should cultivate himself so as to make others live in comfort.' When asked again whether it was all, the Master said, 'He should cultivate himself so as to make people live in comfort. Such is the end the sagacious emperors would have attained.'

Note that in (4) above the temporal meaning is reinforced by the three clause complexes which all begin with a '*when*-clause', expanding by enhancing (Halliday, 1994). One of the features of classical Chinese is that the relationship between clauses is usually not expressed by conjunctions (either by Linkers or Binders), and the interpretation of the meaning is left to the reader. In Xu's translation of the dialogue, the temporal relationship is made explicit and strengthened, which is in contrast with translations such as Ku's (1898), Waley's (1938) or Watson's (2007). Because Xu chooses to introduce the questions indirectly, the original questions 'rú [like, prep.] sī [this] ér yǐ [mood marker] hū [mood marker]' have become indirect questions in the *when*-clause. Note that in Xu's (2005) translation, each of the clause complexes involves both Expansion and Projection; in terms of Expansion, the *when*-clauses function as clauses expressing the meaning of Enhancement, whereas in terms of projection, the verbiage of Confucius's three answers is quoted.

With Ku's translation, on the one hand, specific meanings are made general; thus, 'Zilu' (definite and specific in meaning) became 'a disciple of Confucius' (indefinite and non-specific) and 'Yáo Shùn' (the first great emperors) became 'the great ancient Emperors' (also from definite to indefinite, specific to non-specific). On the other hand, in the reporting clause introducing the third question, 'again' was added to indicate that the same question (in the second pair of turn-taking) was asked for the second time, apart from translating the same general 'yuē [say]' into specific verbs: 'answer' (in Ku-A1), 'ask' (in Ku-Q2), 'reply' (in Ku-A2), 'ask (again)' (in Ku-Q3) and 'reply' (in Ku-A3).

In Lau's (1979) and Slingerland's (2003) translations, only the first implicit question and the first answer was introduced by verbal processes, with the remaining two questions and two answers un-introduced by reporting clauses. If other translations are used as examples for comparison, it is likely that there are other differences as well.

It should be noted that in Ku's translation, the feature of question-answer is made more explicit because the yes-no questions (Ku-Q2: 'Is that all?', Ku-Q3: 'Is that all?') are answered with 'yes' (Ku-A2: 'Yes,'…, Ku-A3: 'Yes,'…). By contrast, in Waley's translation, the second and third questions were introduced by 'Tzu-lu said' (Waley-Q2, Waley-Q3) and the answers were also introduced by 'The Master said' (Waley-A1, Waley-A2, Waley-A3). The obvious difference between Ku's translation and Waley's is that Ku uses 'enquire → answer, ask → reply, ask (again) → reply' whereas Waley uses 'ask → said, said → said, said → said', which means that Ku makes the question-answer relationship more explicit than Waley. A comparison of these two versions of translation with the Chinese source text shows that Waley's translation is closer (and more equivalent in terms of word choice) to the source text than Ku's, which reflects a freer style of translation. Looking at Watson's translation, we observe that only the first pair of question-answer has verbal processes (i.e. 'asking' and 'saying') with Sayers (i.e. 'Zilu' and 'the Master'). This reflects a simplification strategy which is in clear contrast with Ku's strategy, because the latter is more explicit in choosing verbs representing the verbal process: the same Chinese yuē [say] is translated differently.

11.5 Explanation

There are a number of different interpretations of the section from *Lun Yu* which we use as an example above. It seems that with most of the sections in *Lun Yu*, different people offer different interpretations and that is why the meanings expressed are quite different in many cases. In Huang's (1997: 150) translation, 'jūnzǐ' in the first clause is translated as 'the gentleman' (cf. 'a wise and good man' in Ku, 'a true gentleman' in Waley, 'the gentleman' in Watson, and 'an intelligentleman' in Xu) which he said that it refers to 'the sovereign'. Huang (1997: 150) interprets Confucius's three answers by saying that there are three steps in the answers: 'The first step of the gentleman's cultivation is to cultivate himself in acquiring the rituals and revering himself. The second step is to cultivate himself in bringing peace to the nobility … The third step is to cultivate himself in bringing peace and good order to all the people in the empire.' There are of course many other interpretations and the different explanations reflect different ideological beliefs and philosophical assumptions.

Being an ancient Chinese text, the Confucius's *Lun Yu* is, like other Chinese classics, made up of rich meaning-making Chinese characters without having any punctuation or spaces between them. Therefore, we would say that before any interlingual translation was conducted, there already existed many versions of intralingually translated texts. From the history of the interlingual translation of *Lun Yu*, one can see that all the interlingual translations (target text) are based on the kind of source text that was in fact the result of intralingual Chinese translations of some kind. Therefore, the simple translation process of 'source text being translated into target text' does not apply here. I would argue that any interlingual translation of classic works may have been based on the product (result) of an intralingual translation, which is the product of another intralingual translation, and so on and so forth. And this is true of the English translation of classic works such as *Lun Yu*.

The situation becomes more complicated with the fact that an English translator of *Lun Yu* may not only rely on many source texts (which are the results of various intralingual translations) but also consult existing English translations (which are the result of interlingual translations). This can be seen from the acknowledgements in many publications of translated works, such as the following:

> After a decade of researching, writing, and revising, I offer this new English version of *Lun Yu* as finally ready for print. I dare not claim it solely as my own work, for many are the scholars ancient and modern, Eastern and Western, who have contributed to its completion. First of all, I am immensely indebted to the major *Lun Yu* commentators, from the time of the Han Dynasty down to the present day, whose writings have greatly enhanced my comprehension of the text and the truthfulness of my translation. Thanks are also due to some of my predecessors in the translation of this monumental work, namely, Messrs. James Legge, Arthur Waley, D. C. Lau, James R. Ware, and Raymond Dawson, both the merits and the demerits of whose works have benefited my new rendition considerably. (Huang, 1997: vii).

Another translator, Xu Yuanchong (a professor at Peking University), who is said to be the king of Chinese-English and Chinese-French translations of ancient Chinese works, admits that when he was translating Confucius's *Lun Yu* (i.e., Xu, 2005), he consulted both intralingual translations such as Yang (1980) and Li (2004) and interlingual translations such as Legge (1861) and Waley (1938) (as reported in Wu, 2012: 106).

Owing to the characteristics of the process of translating ancient classics such as *Lun Yu*, it is not difficult to see why the Chinese text (the 'same' source text) has been translated quite differently. A comparison of the different versions of translation provided above from a linguistic perspective reveals considerable differences between them in terms of the choice of words, word groups, and clauses. In a text like *Lun Yu*, the key concepts (e.g. 'jūnzǐ' in our example) are vitally important and behind the translations there are philosophical, religious, cultural, political, historical, societal considerations and motivations. This will highlight the importance of the study of the translators in relation with their cultural backgrounds and motivations.

From a systemic functional perspective (e.g. Halliday, 1994), as linguists, in examining translated texts, what we must pay attention to is the motivation behind each choice of meaning and expression. A speaker (or translator) may use certain words and structures unconsciously, but 'what we aim to uncover through a functional analysis are the reasons why the speaker produces a particular wording rather than any other in a particular context' (Thompson, 1996: 8).

11.6 Discussion

From a systemic functional viewpoint, any clause in a text can be analysed from a metafunctional (i.e. experiential, logical, interpersonal, textual) perspective, and in terms of the analysis of translated text, we can see whether the translated text is experientially equivalent, logically equivalent, interpersonally equivalent, and/or textually equivalent.

If we compare clauses (1) (i.e. 'zīlù [name of one of Confucius's disciples] wèn [ask] jūnzǐ [gentleman]') and (2) (i.e. 'zǐ [Confucius] yuē [say] xiū [cultivate] jǐ [oneself] yǐ [so that] jìng [respectfulness]') in the source text with Clauses (1) (i.e. 'Watson-Q1: Zilu asked about the gentleman') and (2) (i.e. 'Watson-A1: The Master said, He trains himself to be respectful') in Watson's (2007) translation, we can argue that the clauses in the translated text are experientially equivalent, logically equivalent, interpersonally equivalent, and textually equivalent. However, a comparison of clauses (1) and (2) in the source text with clauses (1) and (2) in Xu's (2005) translation (i.e. 'When Zi Lu asked about an intelligentleman, the Master said, "He should cultivate himself and do his duty with respect"') reveals that the translated version is nearly experientially equivalent and nearly interpersonally equivalent, but logically and textually non-equivalent. Another example is Clause (3) in the source text and its translated versions by Waley (1938), Watson (2007) and Xu (2005):

> Source clause: (3) yuē [say] rú [like, prep.] sī [this] ér yǐ [mood marker] hū [mood marker].

> Target text (Waley-Q2): Tzu-lu said, Can he not go further than that?

Target text (Watson-Q2): Is that all?

Target text (Xu): When asked whether it was all,

From the viewpoint of the logical mentafunction, the six Chinese characters are the realization of a clause complex with the first character (yuē [say]) realizing the reporting clause (without Subject/Sayer) and the remaining characters as the reported clause (the Verbiage). Comparing this clause with Waley's translation, one can see that the Sayer ('Tzu-lu') is added. By contrast, in Watson's version, instead of adding the Subject as Waley did, the whole reporting clause is deleted. And in Xu's (2005) translation, this clause is treated as a dependent clause and as a result Clauses (3) and (4) (Xu: 'When asked whether it was all, the Master said, "He should cultivate himself so as to make others live in comfort"') are regarded as forming a clause nexus (hypotaxis) with Clause (3) as a dependent clause of enhancement. Clearly, a comparison with other existing translated versions will indicate more experiential, logical, interpersonal, and textual differences between the source text and the target text.

It can be assumed that there are translated texts that are metafunctionally equivalent to their corresponding source texts and that there are also translated texts that are not metafunctionally equivalent to the source texts. And this fact is concerned with the quality of translation and the quality assessment of translation. In the model of systemic functional linguistics, the three (or four) metafunctions are equally important in the analysis and description of a clause in a language because they are the different strands of meaning in a clause. However, if we apply the 'metafunctional equivalence' concept to our study of translated texts, the 'metafunctional equivalences' are not the same on the cline of importance. Strictly speaking, in terms of the meaning expressed (experientially), if the translated text is not equivalent with its corresponding source text it is not a translation at all. This is in line with Halliday's (2001: 16) argument that 'if a text does not match its source text ideationally, it does not qualify as a translation'.

Compared with experiential equivalence, logical, interpersonal and textual equivalences are not as crucial in evaluating the quality and effectiveness of translated text. For example, if a translated text is not logically, interpersonally or textually equivalent to the corresponding source text, it does not mean that it does not qualify as a translation. Therefore, the questions to be asked should be: Why is the translated text logically, interpersonally or textually non-equivalent to the corresponding source text? How do the differences (non-equivalences) affect the meaning being expressed? Why did the translator choose the non-equivalence option when there was an equivalence option available?

Halliday (1994: xv), in his discussion on discourse analysis, says that 'there are always two possible levels of achievement to aim at', one of which is 'a contribution to the understanding of the text: the linguistic analysis enables one to show how, and why, the text means what it does' and the other, which is the higher level of achievement, is 'a contribution to the evaluation of the text: the linguistic analysis may enable one to say why the text is, or is not, an effective text for its own purposes – in what respects it succeeds and in what respects it fails, or is less successful', and this higher level is more difficult to reach, because 'it requires an interpretation not only of the text itself but also of its context (context of situation, context of culture), and of the systematic relationship between context and text' (Halliday, 1994: xv). We would assume that these systemic functional ideas can be applied to the study of translated texts such as the translations of *Lun Yu* and other Chinese classic works.

Considering the fact that the Chinese text was written and compiled by many people from before 55 BC and that there are over 2,000 intralingual translations of *Lun Yu* and over 50 English versions of interlingual translation, there is no way to achieve a generally-accepted version in Chinese, let alone in English or other foreign languages. This explains why it is impossible to produce a universally-accepted version of translation.

Although there are preliminary attempts to study *Lun Yu* and its English translations from situational and cultural perspectives (e.g. Wei and Zhang, 2006; Zou, 2007), the context of situation and the context of culture are not easily identified, no matter how hard one tries to re-contextualize the text. Many of the utterances and questions have no clear or identifiable addressees.

Some people even challenge the coherence of the text, claiming that *Lun Yu* is a collection of unrelated questions and descriptions. By contrast there are others who argue that the text is both coherent and cohesive, because it has been treated as a text (as opposed to 'non-text) with its own texture for more than 2,000 years, and therefore it has been considered as a coherent text. Following Halliday (1994: 339) in saying that 'for a text to be coherent, it must be cohesive', Huang (2011) illustrates the cohesive chains of *Lun Yu* by emphasizing the importance of the chapter numbering and section numbering.

Like other classic works, *Lun Yu* is a text that allows different interpretations and explanations. For example, the last clause complex in the Chinese source text is translated both as a statement (e.g. Watson-A3: 'But training himself in order to give ease to all men and women – even the sages Yao and Shun found that hard to do') and a question (e.g. Waley-A3: 'If he can do that, could even Yao or Shun find cause to criticize him?'). This highlights the importance of the translator's roles: as a reader, as an interpreter, as a text analyst, as a re-writer and as a translator. In doing such jobs, the translator's perception and understanding play a vital role, and the purpose and motivation in doing the translation are related to his manipulation of both the interpretation and expression.

A functional linguistic analysis of the translated texts indicates that the application of systemic functional linguistics 'to understand[ing] the quality of texts: why a text means what it does, and why it is valued as it is' (Halliday, 1994: xxix). As a general linguistic theory and as appliable linguistics, systemic functional linguistics has much to offer to the study of translated texts (e.g. Halliday, 2001, 2009a; Steiner and Yallop, 2001), but the question we should ask is: To what extent can systemic functional linguistics help us in our studies of the translation of classic works?

The discussion so far indicates that there is still much to be done before we will have a fully-developed systemic functional approach to the study of translated texts of classic works such as Confucius's *Lun Yu*.

11.7 Conclusion

This chapter offers a preliminary investigation of the language of translated texts of Confucius's *Lun Yu* from a lexicogrammatical perspective. Although we only take one simple example and analyse it partially, focusing on the level of clause complex, this may be enough to illustrate complicated issues relating to the study of translations of ancient Chinese writings.

As the literature to date shows, many of the studies of Confucius's *Lun Yu* are from a literary perspective, and the approach taken here is linguistics-oriented, which is an alternative approach to the study of text, both literary and non-literary.

Following Halliday (2009b: 61), we characterize systemic functional linguistics as a problem-oriented theory, which means that 'it is designed to assist towards identifying and tackling problems that arise from outside itself – that is, not problems that the theory identifies for itself'. The literature to date (e.g. Halliday, 2001, 2009a; Steiner and Yallop, 2001) shows that systemic functional linguistics can help us solve problems in translation studies. As Halliday (2001:13) observes, both translators and linguists are interested in theorizing about translation in its entirety and they are 'concerned with a general theory of translation'. For linguists, 'translation theory is the study of how things are: what is the nature of the translation process and the relation between texts in translation'. What we need is a theory of language both as a general linguistics theory (focusing on the system) and an appliable linguistics theory (focusing on the instances). This is systemic functional linguistics (e.g. Halliday, 1994).

References

Chen, Y. (2009) A functional analysis of quotations from *Lun Yu. Foreign Languages and Their Teaching* (*Waiyu yu Waiyu Jiaoxue*) 2: 49–52.

Fang, Y. (2006) Constructing a harmonious world: Linguistic studies on The Analects of Confucius. In G. Huang *et al.* (eds) *Functional Linguistics as Appliable Linguistics* 95–112. Guangzhou: Sun Yat-sen University Press.

Halliday, M. A. K. (1994) *An Introduction to Functional Grammar* (2nd edition). London: Arnold.

Halliday, M. A. K. (2001) Towards a theory of good translation. In E. Steiner and C. Yallop (eds) *Exploring Translation and Multilingual Text Production: Beyond Context,* 13–18. Berlin: Mouton de Gruyter.

Halliday, M. A. K. (2009) The Gloosy Ganoderm: Systemic functional linguistics and translation. *Chinese Translators Journal* (*Zhongguo Fanyi*) 1: 17–26.

Halliday, M. A. K. (2009b) Method – techniques – problems. In M. A. K. Halliday and J. J. Webster (eds) *Continuum Companion to Systemic Functional Linguistics,* 59–86. London: Continuum.

Huang, C. (1997) *The Analects of Confucius (Lun Yu)*. Oxford: Oxford University Press.

Huang, G. (2011) The textual structure of Confucius *Lun Yu* in relation to the English translation of the book title and chapter headings. *Foreign Languages in China (Zhongguo Waiyu)* 6: 88–95.

Jakobson, R. (1959/2000) The linguistic aspects of translation. In L. Venuti (ed.) *The Translation Studies Reader,* 113–118. London: Routledge.

Ku, H. M. (1898) *The Discourses and Sayings of Confucius*. Shanghai: Kelly and Walsh, Ltd.

Lau, D. C. (1979) *Confucius: The Analects*. New York: Penguin Books.

Legge, J. (1861) *Confucius: Confucian Analects, The Great Learning and The Doctrine of the Mean*. Oxford: Clarendon Press.

Li, Z. (2004) *Lun Yu Jin Du (A New Reading of Lun Yu)*. Beijing: Sanlian Book Store.

Slingerland, E. (2003) *Confucius Analects: With Selections from Traditional Commentaries*. Indianapolis, IN: Hackett Publishing Company, Inc.

Steiner, E. and Yallop, C. (2001) (eds) *Exploring Translation and Multilingual Text Production: Beyond Context*. Berlin: Mouton de Gruyter.

Thompson, G. (1996) *Introducing Functional Grammar*. London: Arnold.

Waley, A. (1938) *The Analects of Confucius*. London: George Allen & Unwin Ltd.

Watson, B. (2007) *The Analects of Confucius*. New York: Columbia University Press.

Wei, H. and Zhang, X. (2006) On the translation of Lun Yu: A perspective of Systemic-Functional Grammar. *Journal of Lianyungang Teachers College (Lianyungang Shifan Gaodeng Zhuanke Xuexiao Xuebao)* 2: 51–54.

Wu, G. (2012) Classic translation and cultural transmission: A review of the 1st conference on translating Confucius's Lun Yu. *Foreign Languages in China (Zhongguo Waiyu)* 1: 104–107.

Xu, Y. C. (2005) *Confucius Modernized: Thus Spoke the Master*. Beijing: Higher Education Press.

Yang, B. (1980) *Lun Yu Yi Zhu (Translation of and Notes on Lun Yu)*. Beijing: Zhonghua Book Store.
Yang, F. (1999) Introduction. In *The Analects of Confucius* (A. Waley trans.), 36–63. Changsha: Hunan People's Publishing House.
Zou, C. (2007) *The Genre Analysis of the Analects of Confucius from the Systemic Functional Perspective*. Unpublished MA dissertation, South China Normal University.

12 Challenges and solutions for multimodal analysis: Technology, theory and practice

Kay O'Halloran, Alexey Podlasov, Alvin Chua, Christel-Loic Tisse, Victor Lim Fei and Bradley Smith[*]

12.1. Introduction

Multimodal analysis, also called multimodal discourse analysis (MDA) and more generally 'multimodality', is a rapidly expanding interdisciplinary field in linguistics and language-related fields of study, including education (see Jewitt, 2009). Multimodal analysis is concerned with theorizing and analysing the multiple resources (e.g. language, image, audio resources, embodied action and three-dimensional objects) which combine to create meaning in different contexts (e.g. print media, film, digital media and day-to-day events). Inspired by Kress and van Leeuwen's (2006 [1996]) and O'Toole's (2011 [1994]) foundational works of the mid-1990s, multimodal research has largely derived from Michael Halliday's (1978; Halliday and Matthiessen, 2004) social semiotic theory which provides a comprehensive theoretical platform for the study of semiotic resources and their integration in media and events. Other major approaches include multimodal interac-

[*]   Kay L. O'Halloran is Associate Professor in the School of Education at Curtin University, Western Australia. She was founding Director of the Multimodal Analysis Lab and Deputy Director of the Interactive & Digital Media Institute at the National University of Singapore. Alexey Podlasov is a Principal Investigator at Sheer Industries Group, Singapore. He was formerly Research Fellow at the Multimodal Analysis Lab in the Interactive & Digital Media Institute at the National University of Singapore. Victor Lim Fei is Senior Specialist (Educational Technology) and Senior Head for Technologies for Learning, Educational Technology Division, Ministry of Education in Singapore. Bradley Smith is currently a Tutor in Higher Education at the University of Melbourne. He was formerly Research Fellow at the Multimodal Analysis Lab in the Interactive & Digital Media Institute at the National University of Singapore.

tional analysis (e.g. Norris, 2004; Scollon, 2001) and cognitive approaches to multimodality (e.g. Forceville and Urios-Aparisi, 2009).

Much progress has been made in multimodal research, particularly in systemic functional (social semiotic) approaches to MDA (SF-MDA) (e.g. Baldry and Thibault, 2006b; Royce and Bowcher, 2006; Bateman, 2008; Unsworth, 2008; Bednarek and Martin, 2010; Dreyfus *et al.*, 2011; O'Halloran and Smith, 2011; Ventola and Moya, 2009), which have moved beyond the study of individual semiotic resources – for example, speech, music and sound (van Leeuwen, 1999, 2009; Caldwell, 2010; McDonald, 2005), gesture and action (Martinec, 2000, 2001) and three dimensional space (Ravelli, 2000; Stenglin, 2009, 2011) – to the study of the inter-semiotic (or 'inter-modal') relations which give rise to semantic expansions in multimodal phenomena – for example, text and image (Royce, 1998; Martinec, 2005; Liu and O'Halloran, 2009; Unsworth and Cleirigh, 2009), language, image and symbolism in mathematics and science (Lemke, 1998; O'Halloran, 1999b, 2005) and gesture and phonology (Zappavigna *et al.*, 2010) (see Zhao (2011) for a comprehensive overview of SF-MDA research).

However, as Bateman (2008) and others (e.g. Baldry and Thibault, 2006a; Smith *et al.*, 2011) have pointed out, the complexity of multimodal analysis has limited the type of analytical, and as a result, theoretical developments which have been made, particularly for dynamic media such as video, film and interactive digital media. Many analysts have resorted to tabular descriptions of unfolding semiotic choices (e.g. Tan, 2009; Bednarek, 2010; Zappavigna *et al.*, 2010) which is a laborious and time-consuming task and furthermore, the resemioticization of dynamic phenomena in static tables necessarily has limitations with regard to capturing the underlying multimodal semantic patterns. As a result, multimodal research has tended towards generalizations which lack a empirical basis, or at best are based on the study of a limited number of texts (Bateman, 2008). Multimodal researchers have developed different approaches to address this issue, most notably the Genre and Multimodality (GeM) model (Bateman, 2008; Bateman *et al.*, 2007) and the Multimodal Corpus Authoring (MCA) system (Baldry and Thibault, 2006a, 2006b) which are designed to support empirical corpus-based research. As part of this research initiative, this chapter describes *Semiomix*, a software application developed in the Multimodal Analysis Lab in the Interactive and Digital Media Institute (IDMI) at the National University of Singapore, which provides digital tools specifically developed for multimodal analysis of static and dynamic media.

Semiomix is designed to link low-level features in different media (text, image and video) to higher-order semantic information using social semiotic theory and computer-based techniques of analysis. The software provides a range of graphical user interfaces (GUIs) so the analyst can import and view different media, enter systems networks, create time-stamped tier-based annotations and overlays, and use automated tools (e.g. image processing tools, shot detection and so forth) and audio functionalities for multimodal analysis. The analysis is stored in a database format for later retrieval and visualization of the results. *Semiomix* is the first known application to model the integration of language, image and audio resources on a common computational platform, thus providing analysts with digital tools specifically designed for multimodal analysis.

The analyst remains central to the analytical process, however, and thus *Semiomix* provides a theoretical and conceptual space for advancing multimodal study via modelling, testing and application of theory (O'Halloran *et al.*, 2011; Smith *et al.*, 2011). In fact, the operationalization of systemic functional theory in an interactive digital media environment means that key theoretical issues, such as the usefulness, consequences and limits of modelling systemic grammars as sets of inter-related hierarchical classification systems organized according to metafunction, rank, stratum and system/structure cycles (see Bateman, 2011; Martin, 2011) and other issues such as search and the visualization techniques for dynamic multimodal analysis (O'Halloran *et al.*, 2011; Smith *et al.*, 2011; Zappavigna, 2010; Zhao, 2010) are foregrounded. These issues could not be ignored during development of *Semiomix*, which functions as a 'metasemiotic tool' (Smith *et al.*, 2011) for semioticizing both multimodal social semiotic theory and analysis. The major theoretical issues and problems were not solved during the software development process, but they were understood with greater clarity, as hopefully the ensuing discussion reveals.

In what follows, the principal functionalities of *Semiomix* are first described (see also O'Halloran *et al.*, 2012) and then illustrated via screenshots from Professor W. Gilbert Strang's first lecture in Linear Algebra from Massachusetts Institute of Technology (MIT) Open Courseware (OCW).[1] Following this, Professor Strang's use of language and gesture are interpreted in relation to the different stages of the mathematics lecture. Finally, the achievements and limitations of the existing version of *Semiomix* are described with view to future research.

12.2   Principal Functionalities of *Semiomix*

In what follows, we outline our vision of the principal functions expected from multimodal annotation and analysis software.

1.   The software must provide the means to organize analysts' work so that the analyses and media files are structured to facilitate efficient utilization and reuse of available and user-created data.

2. The software must provide functions and efficient GUIs to access multimedia under analysis. Due to multimodal nature of analysed phenomena, the GUIs have to be customized to provide efficient interaction with media, whether it is an image, video or text file.
3. The software must provide tools to localize regions of interest in the media and facilitate annotation of such regions. Again, means of localization depend on the nature of media under analysis and may be implemented in terms of recorded timestamps for sound and video, 2D coordinates for static images or both for dynamic overlays in video. Created annotations must be stored in a database, which must provide efficient retrieval and search functions.
4. The software must contain facilities for inter-relating the created annotations, annotating such inter-relations and storing these structures in the database. This aspect is important to enable multimodal analysis of inter-semiotic, cohesive and inter-textual relations, where annotations localized within and across different types of recorded media are analysed in relation to each other, and furthermore, these inter-relations themselves are annotated and analysed.
5. The software must provide tools for analysis of annotation data created by the analyst, since intuitive understanding of such complexity is not possible. These tools must include, but not be limited to, efficient search and visualization functions.
6. Finally, the software must provide instruments to enhance productivity of the analyst. Annotation work may often involve low-level tasks, which can be semi- or fully automated with help of modern computer technology – for example, shot, motion and face detection and tracking for video, optical character recognition for images, speech and silence detection for audio, and similar techniques. In the hands of multimodal analysis experts, these tools will save time and effort, and they may also provide insights into phenomena otherwise missed due to the tedious and mechanical nature of such annotation tasks. These automated tools are referred to as 'media analytics' tools in our software.

In the following sections we describe how the above-mentioned aspects have been incorporated in *Semiomix*, our multimodal analysis software.

12.2.1 Organization of *Semiomix*

Semiomix is used to produce multimodal analysis of media recorded in digital form. The analysis consists of three components: a set of media files, a set of annotation units (co-ordinates) and a set of categorical descriptions (systems) used in the annotation. These three components are critical for the consistency of any particular multimodal analysis, and the loss of any component would make the analysis invalid. We also consider that in real-life analytical tasks, the analyst is likely to create multiple analyses of the same or related media using the same or similar annotation systems. There-fore, implementing the multimodal analysis as a standalone entity consist-ing of all its components (media files, annotation units and systems) would result in an inefficient utilization of storage space, since media files are usu-ally large in size. Proper organization of the analysis components saves space by re-using the same media files, annotation systems and annotation units in different analyses, so that the various components are organized into a coherent and transparent data structure.

Semiomix imposes a workflow for the user organized in terms of *Solution – Library – Project – Analysis*. The *Analysis* is an actual multimodal analysis doc-ument consisting of media objects (i.e. files), annotation units (coordinates) and annotation systems. The *Project* organizes the different Analyses sharing the same or related media objects, facilitating reuse of media files. The *Library* is a set of annotation systems used in different Analyses. Since the Library may be quite large, Analysis is associated with a subset of the Library called the *Catalogue* (i.e. Systems Catalogue). The Library facilitates reuse of annota-tion systems throughout the Analyses. The *Solution* is a global placeholder for Library and Projects, where data is not shared between the different Solutions. The organization of user's workflow is illustrated in Figure 12.1.

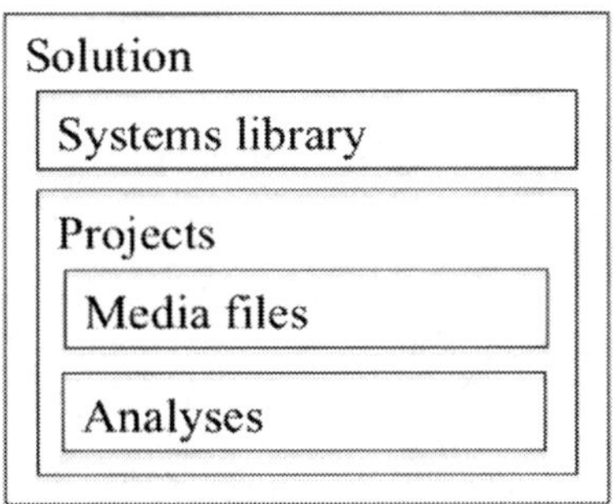

Figure 12.1: Organization of user workflow

12.2.2   Access to media

Semiomix provides access to the following media types: plain text, images, sounds and videos. These types cover to a major extent the ways multimodal phenomena can be digitally recorded (hypertext is excluded at this stage because of time constraints). Due to a great variety of modern compression formats, the software relies on open source FFMPEG[2] library to provide file format access and decompression functions. Among different text file formats, the software supports only unformatted plain text files, since text formatting is considered to be out of the scope of the current version of the software.

12.2.3 Annotation

The implementation of efficient annotation GUIs is critical for successful multimodal annotation software. The palette of annotation GUIs is fully motivated by the supported media types and the way the localization (i.e. coordinates) of annotation units can be stored. In particular, there are interfaces for annotating:

- Text via word and clause indexes
- Images via 2D coordinates
- Sound via timestamps
- Video via 2D coordinates and timestamps.

In what follows, the screenshots of *Semiomix* have been modified in the interests of space and the annotations illustrate the functionalities of the different GUIs. In cases where the GUIs are still under development, mock-up images are provided (and labelled as such).

12.2.3.1 Text annotation GUI

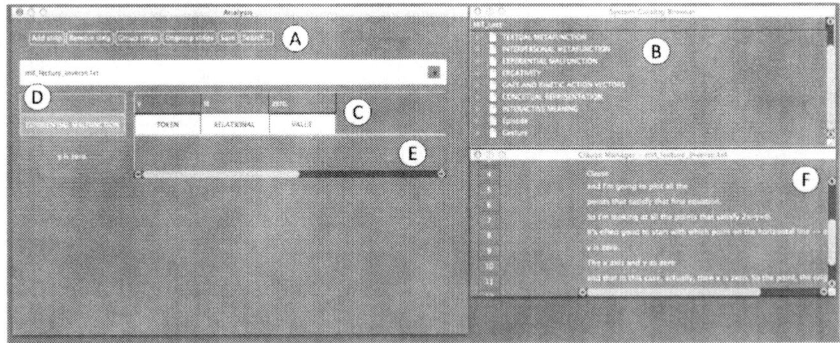

Figure 12.2: Text annotation interface: (A) General controls; (B) Systems catalogue browser; (C) Word-level annotation; (D) Strip organization view; (E) Clause-level annotation; and (F) Clause editor

Text annotation is the process of associating descriptions with words and/ or clauses of text using word/clause index as a reference point. An example of the text annotation GUI is presented in Figure 12.2. Area (A) contains general controls; (B) provides a view of the available annotation systems, which are "Episode" and "Gesture" for Professor Strang's mathematics lecture (these systems are described in Sections 12.3.1 and 12.3.2); (C) provides word-level annotation interface (in this case, for "x is zero"); (D) visualizes the organization of annotation strips; (E) provides clause-level annotation interface; and (F) provides the clause browsing and editing interface.

12.2.3.2 Image annotation GUI

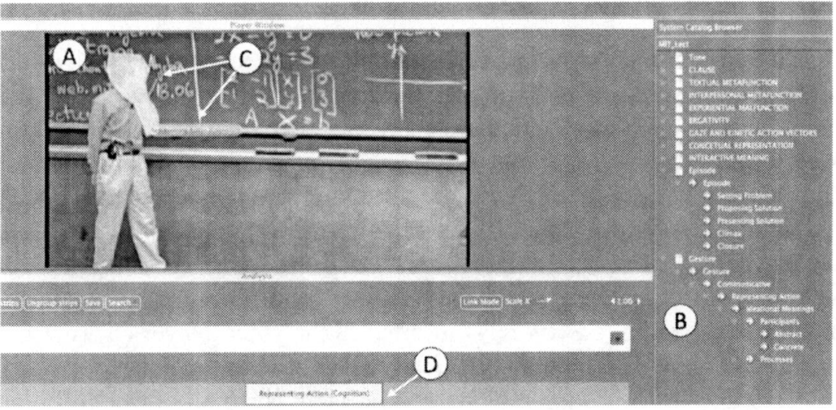

Figure 12.3: Image annotation interface: (A) Image annotation area; (B) Systems Catalogue browser; (C) Created overlays; and (D) Overlay representations in annotation strip

Image annotation is the process of associating user-defined descriptions with regions of image located with 2D coordinates. The image annotation GUI is illustrated in Figure 12.3 where area (A) is the image annotation area; (B) is the Systems Catalogue browser where system choices for "Episode" and "Gesture" are displayed; (C) is a sample overlay for Professor Strang's gesture, which is annotated with the system choice "Representing Action (Cognition)"; and (D) is the overlay representation in the annotation strip which contains system choice "Representing Action (Cognition)". Annotations inserted in the image annotation area (A) automatically appear in the overlay representation area (D).

12.2.3.3 Sound and video annotation GUI

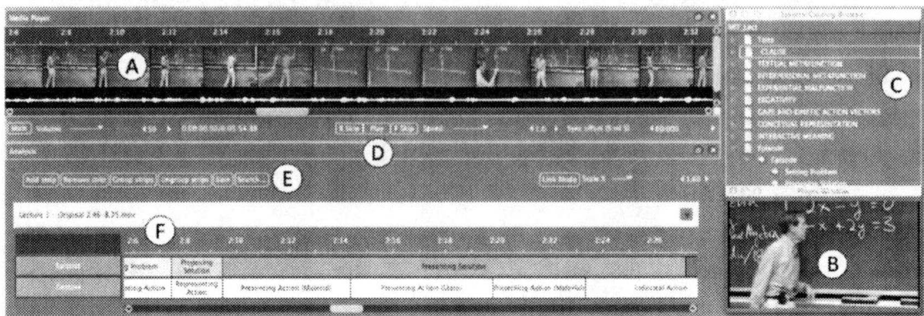

Figure 12.4: Sound and video annotation GUI: (A) Filmstrip and waveform area; (B) Player window; (C) Systems catalogue browser; (D) Playback controls; (E) General controls; and (F) Annotation strip area

Sound and video annotation interfaces are combined into one GUI, since video usually contains both moving pictures and sound streams. From that point of view, one may annotate sound as video with no picture. Figure 12.4 displays the GUI for annotating videos, where area (A) is a filmstrip and waveform view, in this case for Professor Strang's lecture; (B) is the player window for the video; (C) is the Systems Catalogue browser; (D) is the playback controls; (E) is the general controls; and (F) is the annotation strip area where system choices for "Episode" and "Gesture" are displayed as time stamped nodes. Overlays inserted in the video player (B) (not displayed in Figure 12.4) are automatically converted to time-stamped nodes in (F) to display the duration of the overlays (for gesture, for example).

12.2.3.4 Text time stamping GUI

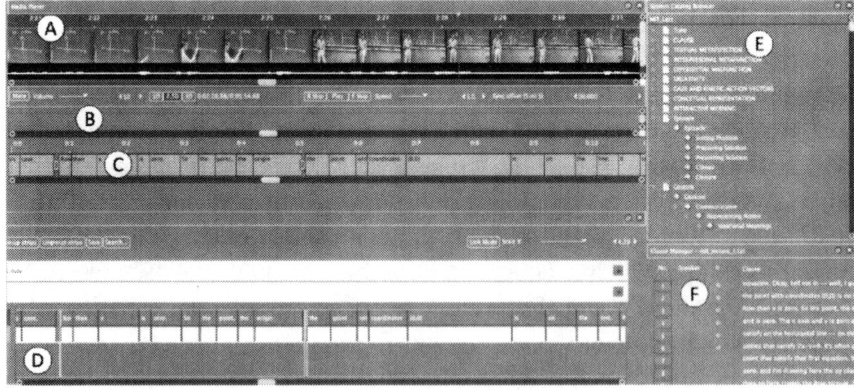

Figure 12.5: Time stamping GUI: (A) Filmstrip area; (B) Clause overlap navigation area; (C) Time stamped clause view; (D) Time stamp table view; (E) Systems Catalogue browser; and (F) Clause editor

The text time stamping GUI is a specially designed interface which relates the linguistic transcript from a dynamically unfolding media (e.g. sound or video) to the dynamics in the source media, creating a link between the coordinates for text annotations and the time stamps for sound. That is, the time-stamping GUI connects both domains (text annotation and time/sound) together, permitting the user to distribute text clauses by assigning time stamps in the temporal domain of the source video. The interface is illustrated in Figure 12.5, where area (A) is the filmstrip visualization area for Professor Strang's lecture; (B) is the strip to visualize and navigate through overlapping clauses (when several people are talking at once, for example); (C) is the strip to view time-stamped clauses transcribed from Professor Strang's lecture; (D) is the annotated clause area where the linguistic analysis of the clauses is coded; (E) is the Systems Catalogue browser; and (F) is the Clause editor which contains the complete transcript.

12.2.4 Inter-relations

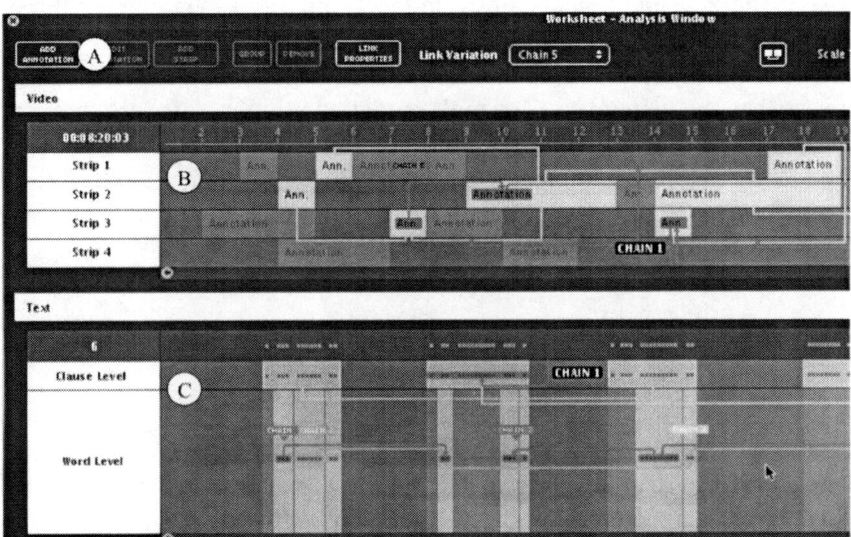

Figure 12.6: Inter-relation GUI (projected mock-up): (A) general controls; (B) inter-relating video annotations; (C) Inter-relating text annotations

Multimodal analysis requires analysis of the relations between annotated instances within and across different media. Therefore, *Semiomix* provides functions to define network-like relationships between annotation units and to annotate those relationships. The relationship is implemented as nested links and chains, which may contain annotation units and/or other groups, and the group itself may be annotated using a system choice and free text annotations. The GUI for creating such groups is illustrated in Figure 12.6 where area (A) is the general controls area; (B) presents an example of inter-related video annotation units; and (C) presents an example of word and clause level inter-relations for text.

12.2.5 Analysis

The GUIs provided by the software enable users to define and code complex descriptions of multimodal phenomena. However, the interpretation of the analysis by simply looking at annotation interfaces is a difficult task without the help of appropriate tools. The software provides following functions to facilitate analysis and understanding of created annotations in terms of searching and exporting for visualisation purposes.

12.2.5.1 Search

Two main principal aspects motivate the design of the search GUI. First, the GUI must provide the ability to locate patterns of interest defined with respect to all types of annotations created in *Semiomix*. Second, we are aware that the general user of multimodal annotation software may not be comfortable using complex programming such as query languages. Therefore, *Semiomix* implements search GUI in What-You-See-Is-What-You-Get (WYSIWYG) manner to define temporal and spatial patterns with respect to:

- Attributes
- Structures
- Time
- Space

The *Attributes* search refers to the systemic and free text annotations; *Structures* search refers to specific relations between annotation units; *Time* search refers to specific temporal patterns; and *Space* search refers to specific spatial patterns. Figure 12.7 illustrates the search GUI, where Area (A) is used to create search entities and enter search conditions related to text; (B) is used to input desired system choices; (C) is used to graphically define structural patterns to search; (D) is used to graphically construct desired temporal relationships; and (E) is used to graphically construct spatial patterns. Graphically defined filters are then automatically translated into machine-understood search queries which are extracted from the database.

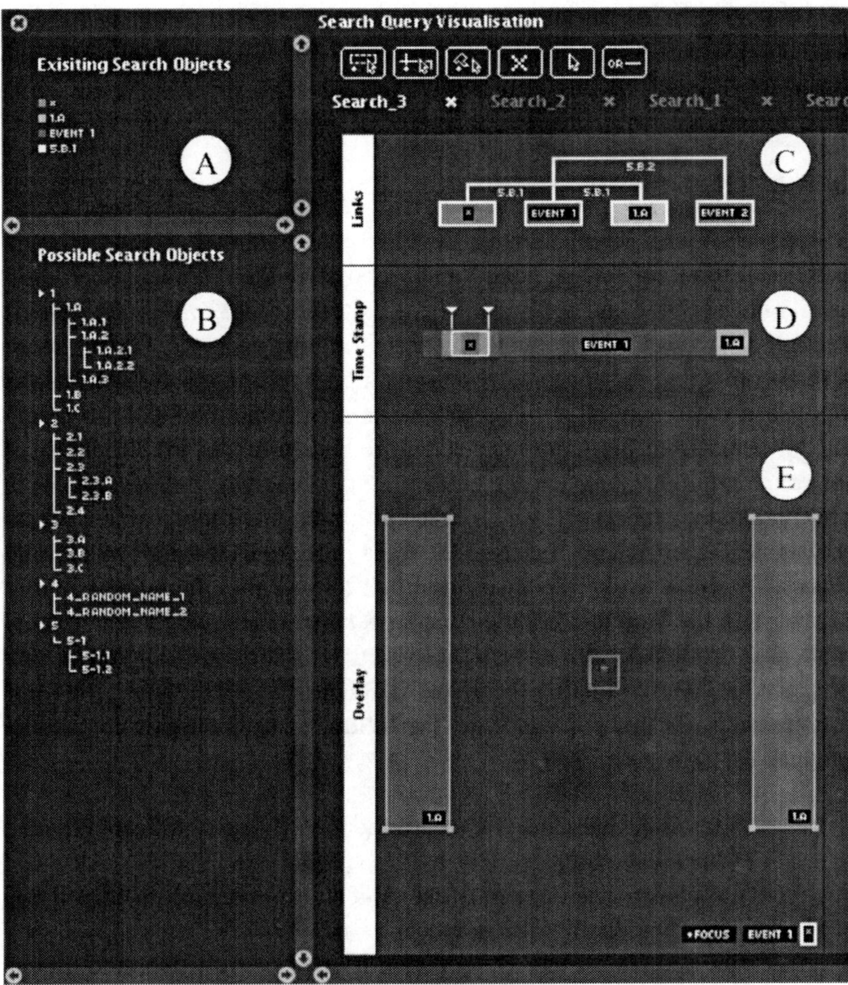

Figure 12.7: Search GUI (projected mock-up): (A) attribute definition area; (B) system choices definition area; (C) structural relationships area; (D) temporal relationships area; (E) spatial relationships area

12.2.5.2 Exporting

Search results are generally delivered to the user by highlighting the matching annotation units in the corresponding GUIs. This, however, may not be enough if quantitative analysis of the annotations is required. The most efficient solution of this problem is enabling the user to export search results in a format which permits the data to be imported into third-party software or frameworks specifically designed for numerical data visualization and analysis, such as, for example, Microsoft Excel for a general user or Matlab or Tulip[3] for the advanced user. This feature brings the power of modern data analysis software packages to multimodal analysis without investing resources into re-implementing similar functions.

12.2.6 Media analytics

Modern computer scientists have developed an extensive palette of computational tools for image, sound and video analysis. Although such tools are highly specific and technical, there are algorithms which are generic enough to enhance the productivity of multimodal analysts. The main criteria for selecting the appropriate computational techniques for multimodal analysis are: (a) general applicability because specific tools are not practical for users from non-computer scientific backgrounds; (b) simplicity of implementation because we are investing our resources in development of multimodal annotation software, not in cutting-edge computer science techniques; and (c) efficiency because the tools must be useful for typical multimodal analysis work. It is also important to note that the human analyst is always in the loop to correct erroneous results which are generated automatically. From that point of view, automatic tools are useful as long as running the tool and correcting the errors takes less time than doing the same job manually. At this point of time, the following technologies are used or planned for *Semiomix*:

- Video shot detection – a technique identifying significant changes in the video
- Audio silence/speech/music classification – a technique identifying intervals of likely silence, speech or music
- Face detection – a technique identifying faces in videos and images
- Tracking – a technique automatically tracking objects in videos
- Optical character recognition – a technique automatically translating texts from raster images into a string of characters
- Basic image enhancement and filtering algorithms.

As illustrated in Figure 12.8, the multiplayer functionality in *Semiomix* permits image processing techniques, in this case optical flow (top video strip) and edge processing (bottom video strip) algorithms to be applied to the original source video (middle video strip) to assist the multimodal analyst. These two image-processing techniques are discussed in the analysis of Professor Strang's mathematics lecture in Section 12.3.3.

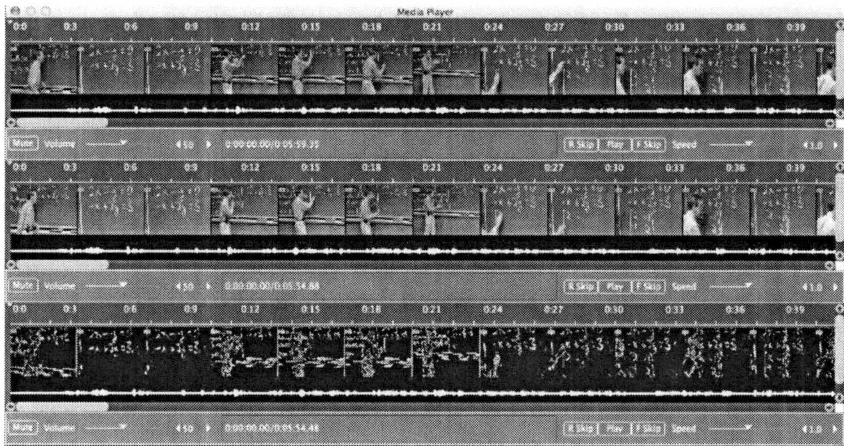

Figure 12.8: Multiplayer functionality

12.3   Gesture and language analysis in the MIT mathematics lecture

In what follows, we present a multimodal analysis of a video segment (2.46 min – 8.35 min) of Professor Gilbert Strang's Lecture 1 in Linear Algebra[4], which was undertaken using the text and video annotation GUIs in *Semiomix*. The focus of the analysis is Professor Strang's use of language and gesture, which combine inter-semiotically to form distinct patterns in relation to different stages of the mathematics lecture. In what follows, the Gesture system and the stages of the lecture are described before the patterns of linguistic and gestural choices are discussed. The multimodal analysis is not exhaustive, but rather it serves to illustrate how the software permits multimodal semantic patterns to be detected in ways which would difficult, if not impossible, without digital tools (O'Halloran *et al.*, 2011; Smith *et al.*, 2011).

12.3.1 Gesture system

Systemic Functional approaches to gesture have classified actions according to their realizations of ideational, interpersonal and textual metafunctional meanings (see, for example, Hood, 2011; Martinec, 2000, 2001, 2004). Martinec (2000) argues that action realizes metafunctional meanings based on formal observable criteria, and he proposes three types of actions with distinctive systems that realize ideational meanings. The three types of actions are *Presenting Action*, *Representing Action* and *Indexical Action*.

Martinec (2000: 243) defines Presenting Action as 'most often used for some practical purpose' and 'communicates non-representational meanings'. For instance, Presenting Action realizes ideational meaning through transitivity processes analogous to language, and as such are analysed as Material, Behavioural, Mental, Verbal and State processes. Representing Actions 'function as a means of representation' and are strongly coded representations. Representing Action realizes ideational meaning through representations of participants, processes and circumstances as well as congruent entities and metaphorical concepts. Indexical Action realizes ideational meaning in relation to the meanings made by the accompanying language. Indexical Action also adds another layer of semantics, such as the representations of importance, receptivity or relations to it, thus realizing interpersonal and textual meanings as well.

Martinec (2000, 2001, 2004) formulates the systems for action which includes movement and proxemics. He explains that 'part of the system of engagement in Presenting Action, for example, has been considered as belonging to proxemics and quite separate from the system of affect. Neither has been previously related to engagement in indexical action' (Martinec, 2001: 144). Nevertheless, Martinec (2001) argues that there are merits in considering action and proxemics together as 'they all express the same broad kind of meaning' (p. 144). This paper draws upon and extends Martinec's (2000, 2001, 2004) approach to gesture and action.

12.3.2 Episode and episodic stages in the mathematics lecture

Professor Strang's mathematics lecture is divided into many smaller teaching units, referred to as Episodes, which consist of a key teaching point he wishes to communicate to the students. An Episode comprises of various Episodic Stages, realized through the meanings made through co-deployment of a repertoire of semiotic resources, in particular language, gesture, movement and blackboard work. The Episodic Stages are colour coded in the annotation strips area (A) in *Semiomix*, along with accompanying gesture choices, which also appear as overlays in the video player (B) in Figure 12.9. The time-stamped linguistic text and the time-stamped tables of linguistic annotations appear in (C) and (D) respectively. In Figure 12.9, the video player indicator (E) shows the actual point of time in the lecture, with the corresponding choices for language and gesture.

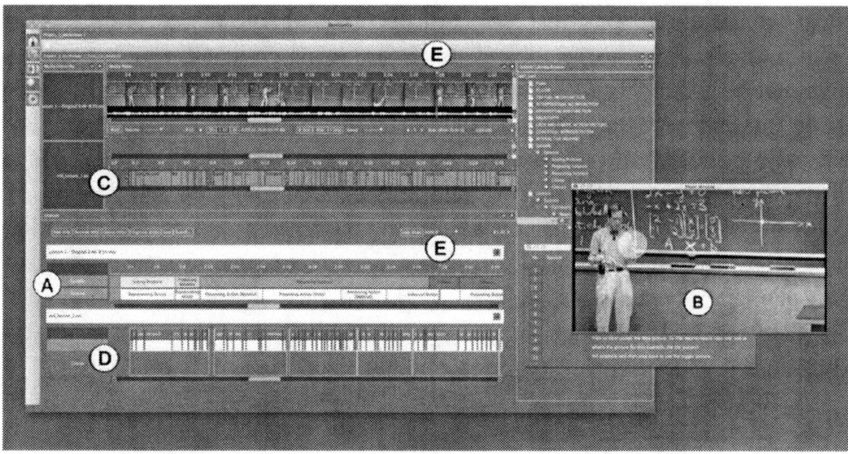

Figure 12.9: Professor Strang's Linear Algebra Lecture 1: (A) annotation strips; (B) player window; (C) time stamped clause view (D) time stamp table view and (E) player indicator

The Episodes begin with the Episodic Stage of *Setting the Problem*. This is where, typically, Professor Strang asks a question to define the problem. In some cases, the Episodic Stage of *Proposing a Solution* follows. This is usually realized as an invitation for the students to help investigate a possible solution to the problem. This stage is characterized linguistically by the use of modality and hedging which realize low power relations. Interpersonal meanings, rather than experiential meanings, are typically foregrounded in the *Proposing a Solution* Episodic Stage.

In the Episodic Stage of *Presenting the Solution*, the teaching point of the Episode is expressed. During this stage, Professor Strang intently works on the solution, usually through board demonstration. In contrast to the previous Episodic Stage, experiential meanings, rather than interpersonal meanings, are foregrounded. The Episodic Stage of *Climax*, where the teaching point is repeated and emphasized, sometimes follows the Episodic Stage of *Presenting the Solution*. Finally, the Episodic Stage of *Closure* marks the end of the teaching Episode, where Professor Strang summarizes the teaching point and often provides a brief intermission before initiating the next Episode.

The Episodes are found to have a generic structure with obligatory and optional Episodic Stages. As observed in Professor Strang's mathematics lecture, the obligatory Episodic Stages are *Setting the Problem*, *Presenting the Solution* and *Closure*. The optional Episodic Stages are *Proposing the Solution* and *Climax*.

In what follows, one teaching Episode from Professor Strang's lecture (4 min 48 sec – 5 min 18 sec)[5] is discussed in more detail, and the meanings made through gesture, language and body movement are highlighted using media analytics tools. In particular, the co-contextualizing relations between language and gesture are explicated (see Lim (2012) for extended discussion of co-contextualizing relations between language and gesture). Following Thibault (2000: 362), it is 'on the basis of co-contextualizing relations that meaning is created'. In this case, the co-contextualizing relations between language and gesture are fundamental to establishing the Episodic Stages in the lecture, which are clearly designed to build the necessary hierarchical knowledge structures in mathematics (O'Halloran, 2007, 2011).

12.3.3 Analysis of an Episode

The Episodic Stage of *Setting the Problem* is instantiated by Professor Strang through his statement 'So I am looking at all the points that satisfy two x minus y equals zero'. Accompanying the linguistic declarative, Professor Strang points at the mathematical symbolism on the board with his entire palm, as displayed in Figure 12.10a, where the gesture is highlighted by the optical flow algorithm which automatically displays patterns of motion of objects, surfaces, and edges using arrows. In this case, the hand gesture is quite marked in relation to the body which remains largely stationary. Pointing with an entire palm like this, rather than with a finger, indicates low specificity (Hood, 2011). Interpersonally, this indexical action of connection realizes low power.

Figure 12.10(a): Optical flow and overlays for gesture and movement analysis: indexical action

Figure 12.10(b): Optical flow and overlays for gesture and movement analysis: representing action cognition

Figure 12.10(c): Optical flow and overlays for gesture and movement analysis: representing action surrender

In the next Episodic Stage of *Proposing a Solution*, Professor Strang dramatically raises both hands with palms facing outwards, as displayed in Figure 12.10(c). This is a representing action, realizing the metaphorical concept of surrender. This is accompanied linguistically with his stammer, 'I, I, I …'. The semiotic choices realize very low power, which is a marked selection for Professor Strang who, by default, has authority over the students. In a sense, the interpersonal meanings realized by his combination of semiotic choices put himself in the position of the learner, attempting to offer a solution to solve the problem. This is a deliberate dramatization, enhanced by body movement as displayed by the optical flow algorithm (see Figure

12.10c), because Professor Strang is fully cognizant of the solution to the question, as demonstrated in the next Episodic Stage. While not an obligatory Episodic Stage, the Episodic Stage of *Proposing a Solution* is observed on a fairly consistent basis throughout Professor Strang's lecture. This Episodic Stage, though often fleeting, serves as an important rapport-building strategy that makes Professor Strang both an engaging and effective teacher.

The shift to the Episodic Stage of *Presenting the Solution* is indicated by Professor Strang's movement forward as he declares 'It is often ...'. This is also co-contextualized through gesture as he points at the problem with his index finger, as displayed by the edge detection algorithm and overlay in Figure 12.11(a). The indexical action of connection, this time realizing high specificity, serves to bring the problem into focus. The interpersonal meanings enacted by his movement and gesture realize high power, which is a sharp contrast to the interpersonal meanings realized in the preceding Episodic Stage.

Figure 12.11(a): Edge detection and overlays for gesture analysis: Indexical Action

Figure 12.11(b): Edge detection and overlays for gesture analysis: Indexical Action

Figure 12.11(c): Edge detection and overlays for gesture analysis: representing Action Horizontal Line

Following this, Professor Strang launches into the discourse of solving the mathematical problem. He signals the beginning of this by three downward beats of his right hand, displayed by the overlay in Figure 12.11(b), as he points to the board with his index finger. This is an Indexical Action that realizes the importance of and draws attention to the solution which he is about to show. This gesture co-contextualizes his evaluative comment of '… good to start with which point on this horizontal line' as an orientation for the solution to the problem which he is about to present on the board.

As mentioned earlier, the discourse of *Presenting the Solution* foregrounds experiential meaning rather than interpersonal meaning. In this mathematics lecture, the ideational content is communicated both linguistically and gesturally. Selections in gesture are made in the Presenting Action of writing on the board and the Representing Action of communicating metaphorical concepts, congruent entities and processes. For instance, the representation of a horizontal line is realized gesturally with the action of a sideward horizontal movement of the hand, as displayed in Figure 12.11(c). Interestingly, the dynamic movement, repeated three times, realizes the linguistic entity of 'horizontal line' as a gestural process. This is an instance of a semiotic metaphor between language and gesture (i.e. a linguistic entity becomes a gestural process), an extension of O'Halloran's (1999a) original conception of semiotic metaphor across language, images and mathematical symbolism, as described in Lim (2012). While the variegated nature of the experiential meanings made in this Episodic Stage through the semiotic selections of language and gesture deserve further analysis, the discussion has focused on interpersonal and textual meanings due to space constraints.

The optional Episodic Stage of *Climax*, displayed in Figure 12.9 (see Video Player Indicator), is realized after the solution has been presented. Professor Strang emphasizes the critical point in the worked solution by exclaiming, 'Zero, zero' as 'the point, the origin ... the point'. The linguistic repetition is co-contextualized with the two punches of his left fist forward, as displayed in the overlay in area (B) in Figure 12.9. These intersemiotic selections signal interpersonal meanings of high power and emphasis. The repetition and dynamic movement draw attention to and accentuate the finality and, perhaps, certainty of the solution presented. As mentioned earlier, not all teaching Episodes in the lesson have this stage. Some Episodes could end rather impassively after the solution is derived. This variety enlivens the lesson and possibly serves to distinguish the more important teaching Episodes from others. This conjecture, however, requires further investigation.

Finally, the Episodic Stage of *Closure* concludes the entire teaching Episode. This is usually realized by a lull, where, sometimes, there is a marked absence of language and dynamic gesture. In this case, there is a movement backwards which co-contextualizes with Professor Strang's declarative, 'It solves that equation'. The retreat allows Professor Strang to recuperate and the students some time to contemplate and reflect on the solution presented. Interpersonally, low power is realized in the Episodic stage of *Closure* and presents opportunities for students to challenge or clarify the solution presented.

Remarkably, the Episode took less than one minute, though some Episodes are longer. Notwithstanding, the consistent patterning of the Episodic stages in the Episodes of Professor Strang's lecture operate to construct an engaging and effective mathematics lesson for the students. For instance, immediately after this Episode, Professor Strang begins another Episodic Stage of *Setting the Problem* by saying, 'Okay, tell me'. This is followed by the Episodic Stage of *Proposing the Solution* with, 'Well, I guess I have to tell you', co-contextualized with a retreat and a dismissive wave of the hand forward. These intersemiotic selections set the stage for the commencement of the next teaching Episode which immediately follows the Episode analysed here.

12.3.4 Structured informality in the orchestration of the lesson

The analysis of gesture and language in the mathematics lecture demonstrates the interplay of experiential, interpersonal and textual meanings to construct a sense of 'structured informality' which may also be found in secondary school classrooms. Lim (2012) and Lim *et al.* (2012) propose that structured informality is constructed through the interplay of multimodal meanings resultant from the effective combination of semiotic resources. A specific combination of semiotic choices is coordinated to construct a participative learning environment for students where explicit display of power dynamics between the teacher and the students are managed. Through specific semiotic choices which function to maintain a didactic structure for learning, other semiotic choices are made to mitigate the hierarchical distance between the teacher and students. This achieves a degree of rapport uncharacteristic of traditional authoritative classrooms.

Structured informality is regularly observed in lessons by highly effective and engaging teachers, particularly when the learners are adolescents or adults. In this multimodal analysis, it is observed that Professor Strang coordinates his selections in language, gesture and movement to realize interpersonal meanings of solidarity and affability, while at the same time, organizing experiential meanings in a highly structured and formal manner, with discernable Episodic Stages and Episodes within the lesson.

Structured informality facilitates the achievement of formal tasks in teaching and learning. While it is common for teachers to attempt to construct structured informality in their lessons, the differing effectiveness usually lies in the personality, pedagogical beliefs of the teachers and the profile of the students. How the teacher orchestrates the delicate combination of semiotic selections to achieve the balance in structured informality ultimately distinguishes an effective and engaging teacher from a lesser one.

12.3.4.1   Achievements and limitations

Due to the current stage of software development, where inter-relational links, search and export functionalities are not yet fully operational in *Semiomix*, it has not been possible to demonstrate exactly how semiotic choices combine in patterns over space and time, in this case for the mathematics lecture. Significantly, however, *Semiomix* contains the facilities to store such data and the next stage of development will involve retrieving and displaying multimodal patterns derived from close empirical analysis undertaken using the software.

Moreover, the multimodal analysis software was complex to conceptualize and design, involving a wide range of research areas which include semiotic data models, raw data projectors for images and video, temporal and spatial reasoning, visual analytics and media analytics. The time taken to assemble a competent (and interested) interdisciplinary team of computer scientists, graphical designers and software developers to design and implement the system infrastructure and the GUIs has meant that many advanced ideas, theories and techniques have not been tested nor implemented in *Semiomix*. For example, the inferential logic operating between systems and system choices cannot be defined in the current software, and the analysis must be exported to visualize patterns in the quantitative data analysis.

Nonetheless, advances have been made, as described here. In addition to the facilities which *Semiomix* provides, graphical visualization tools have been used to convert time-stamped annotations into state-transition diagrams to reveal patterns in how business news networks represent social actors and social interactions in news videos (Podlasov *et al.*, 2012) and teachers' use of space with respect to positioning and the directionality of movement in the classroom (Lim *et al.*, 2012). Interactive visualization functionalities have permitted the analyst to synchronize the state-transition diagrams with the original media file to investigate first-hand the semantic patterns in videos.

Prototype interactive visualizations for viewing systems according to different dimensions (e.g. semiotic resource, metafunction and stratum) and their hierarchical position within those dimensions have also been developed, as displayed in Figure 12.12(a)–(b). The dimensions are colour coded (green, yellow, purple, blue and red) and their associated hierarchies are indicated by concentric circles. The systems (located in the centre of the concentric circles) are automatically positioned by a force-based algorithm (Fruchterman and Reingold, 1991) which places the selected system in the optimal position according to its dimensional and hierarchical classification, indicated by the lines which link the system to different points in the concentric circles. In this way, the user may select a system (e.g. 'Gesture') and see first hand how the system is organized in relation to the overall theoretical framework (e.g. metafunction, stratum and co-contextualizing relations).

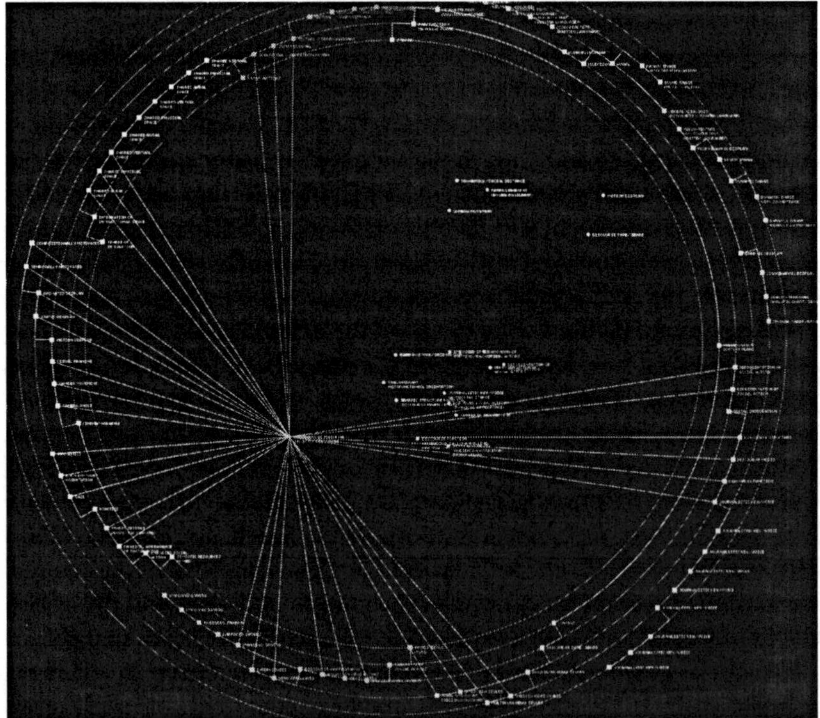

(a) force-based position for System A

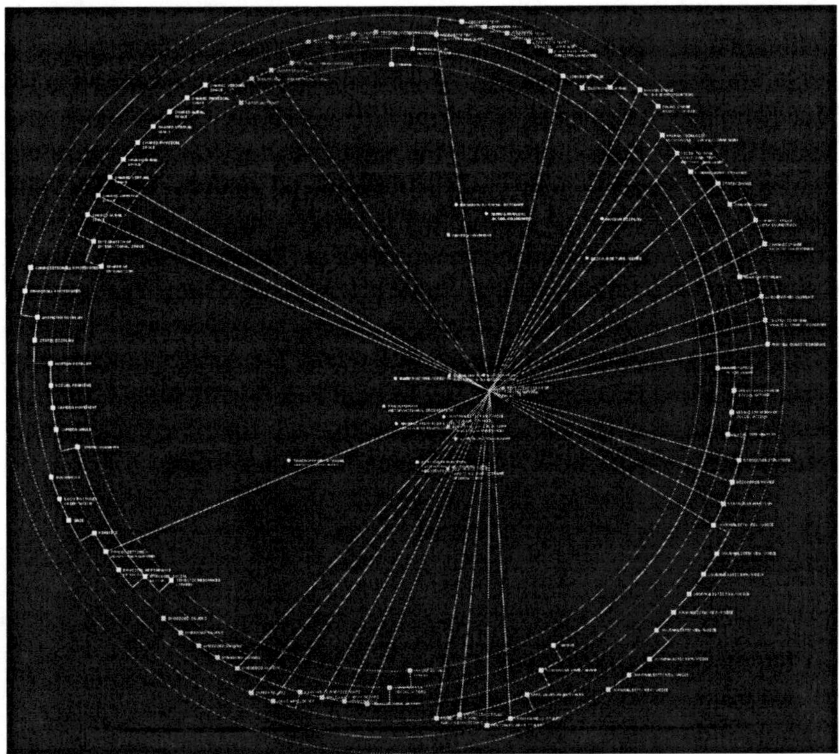

(b) force-based position for System B

Figure 12.12: Interactive visualization for modelling dimensions and hierarchies:

The field of multimodal studies will advance as social scientists work closely with scientists to develop and use interactive media technologies and data analysis software packages because ultimately it is not possible to manage the complexity of multimodal theory and analysis, particularly for dynamic media, without such tools. Interdisciplinary research is essential if we are to understand and address the complex social, political and economic issues arising from the rapid advance of digital technology.

Acknowledgements

This research project was supported by Interactive Digital Media Programme Office (IDMPO) in Singapore under the National Research Foundation (NRF) Interactive Digital Media R&D Program (Grant Number: NRF2007IDM-IDM002-066).

Kay L. O'Halloran was the Principal Investigator for the project in the Multimodal Analysis Lab. Alexey Podlasov (Research Fellow) helped to design, implement and manage the software development process. Alvin Chua (Graphics Designer) designed the GUI interfaces. Christel- Loic Tisse (Senior Research Fellow) proposed the basic design of the software. Victor Lim Fei (PhD student) completed the multimodal analysis. Bradley Smith (Research Fellow) worked on the first prototype version of the software. Other team members included Stefano Fasciani (Research Fellow), Marissa K. L. E (Research Fellow), Sabine Tan (PhD student), Zhang Yiqiong (PhD student) Feng Dezheng (PhD student), Ravi Venkatesh (Research Engineer), Melany Legaspi (Research Assistant), Rohanizah Bte Ali (Laboratory Technician and Management Officer) and the software development team from Dicetek, Singapore. The project succeeded through the close collaboration, commitment and hard work from this interdisciplinary team.

Websites

1.   http://ocw.mit.edu/courses/mathematics/18-06-linear-algebra-spring-2010/
2.   http://ffmpeg.org
3.   http://www.mathworks.com/products/matlab/index.html; http://tulip.labri.fr/TulipDrupal/
4.   http://ocw.mit.edu/courses/mathematics/18-06-linear-algebra-spring-2010/video-lectures/lecture-1-the-geometry-of-linear-equations/
5.   http://www.youtube.com/watch?v=ZK3O402wf1c

References

Baldry, A. P. and Thibault, P. J. (2006a) Multimodal Corpus Linguistics. In G. Thompson and S. Hunston (eds), *System and Corpus: Exploring Connections*, 164–183. London: Equinox.

Baldry, A. P. and Thibault, P. J. (2006b) *Multimodal Transcription and Text Analysis*. London: Equinox.

Bateman, J. (2008) *Multimodality and Genre: A Foundation for the Systematic Analysis of Multimodal Documents*. Hampshire: Palgrave Macmillan.

Bateman, J. (2011) The decomposability of semiotic modes. In K. L. O'Halloran and B. A. Smith (eds) *Multimodal Studies: Exploring Issues and Domains*, 17–38. London and New York: Routledge.

Bateman, J., Delin, J. and Henschel, R. (2007) Mapping the multimodal genres of traditional and electronic newspapers. In T. Royce and W. Bowcher (eds), *New Directions in the Analysis of Multimodal Discourse*, 147–172. Mahwah, NJ: Lawrence Earlbaum Associates.

Bednarek, M. (2010) *The Language of Fictional Television: Drama and Identity*. London and New York: Continuum.

Bednarek, M. and Martin, J. R. (eds). (2010) *New Discourse on Language: Functional Perspectives on Multimodality, Identity, and Affiliation*. London and New York: Continuum.

Caldwell, D. (2010) Making metre mean: Identity and affiliation in the rap music of Kanye West. In M. Bednarek and J. R. Martin (eds), *New Discourse on Language: Functional Perspectives on Multimodality, Identity, and Affiliation*, 59–80. London and New York: Continuum.

Dreyfus, S., Hood, S. and Stenglin, M. (eds) (2011) *Semiotic Margins: Meaning in Multimodalities*. London and New York: Continuum.

Forceville, C. J. and Urios-Aparisi, E. (eds) (2009) *Multimodal Metaphor*. Berlin and New York: Mouton de Gruyter.

Fruchterman, T. M. J. and Reingold, E. M. (1991) Graph drawing by force-directed placement. *Software -Practice and Experience*, 21 (11): 1129–1164.

Halliday, M. A. K. (1978) *Language as Social Semiotic: The Social Interpretation of Language and Meaning*. London: Edward Arnold.

Halliday, M. A. K. and Matthiessen, C. M. I. M. (2004) *An Introduction to Functional Grammar* (3rd edn, revised by C. M. I. M. Matthiessen, ed.). London: Arnold.

Hood, S. (2011) Body language in face-to-face teaching: A focus on textual and interpersonal meaning. In S. Dreyfus, S. Hood and M. Stenglin (eds), *Semiotic Margins: Meaning in Multimodalities*, 31–52. London and New York: Continuum.

Jewitt, C. (ed.). (2009) *Handbook of Multimodal Analysis*. London: Routledge.

Kress, G. and van Leeuwen, T. (2006 [1996]) *Reading Images: The Grammar of Visual Design* (2nd edn). London: Routledge.

Lemke, J. L. (1998) Multiplying meaning: Visual and verbal semiotics in scientific text. In J. R. Martin and R. Veel (eds), *Reading Science: Critical and Functional Perspectives on Discourses of Science*, 87–113. London: Routledge.

Lim, F. V. (2012) *A Systemic Functional Multimodal Discourse Analysis Approach to Pedagogic Discourse*. National University of Singapore, Singapore.

Lim, F. V., O'Halloran, K. L. and Podlasov, A. (2012) Spatial pedagogy: Mapping meanings in the use of classroom space. *Cambridge Journal of Education*, 42 (4): 235–251.

Liu, Y. and O'Halloran, K. L. (2009) Intersemiotic texture: Analyzing cohesive devices between language and images. *Social Semiotics*, 19 (4): 367–387.

Martin, J. R. (2011) Multimodal semiotics: Theoretical challenges. In S. Dreyfus, S. Hood and M. Stenglin (eds), *Semiotic Margins: Meaning in Multimodalities*, 243–270. London: Continuum.

Martinec, R. (2000) Types of processes in action. *Semiotica*, 130 (3/4): 243–268.

Martinec, R. (2001) Interpersonal resources in action. *Semiotica*, 135 (1/4): 117–145.

Martinec, R. (2004) Gestures that co-concur with speech as a systematic resource: The realization of experiential meanings in indexes. *Social Semiotics*, 14 (2): 193–213.

Martinec, R. (2005) A system for image-text relations in new (and old) media. *Visual Communication,* 4 (3): 337–371.

McDonald, E. (2005) Through a glass darkly: A critique of the influence of linguistics on theories of music. *Linguistics and the Human Sciences,* 1 (3): 463–488.

Norris, S. (2004) *Analyzing Multimodal Interaction: A Methodological Framework.* London: Routledge.

O'Halloran, K. L. (1999a) Interdependence, interaction and metaphor in multisemiotic texts. *Social Semiotics* 9 (3): 317–354.

O'Halloran, K. L. (1999b) Towards a systemic functional analysis of multisemiotic mathematics texts. *Semiotica,* 124 (1/2): 1–29.

O'Halloran, K. L. (2005) *Mathematical Discourse: Language, Symbolism and Visual Images.* London and New York: Continuum.

O'Halloran, K. L. (2007) Systemic functional Multimodal Discourse Analysis (SF-MDA) approach to mathematics, grammar and literacy. In A. McCabe, M. O'Donnell and R. Whittaker (eds), *Advances in Language and Education,* 75–100. London and New York: Continuum.

O'Halloran, K. L. (2011) The semantic hyperspace: Accumulating mathematical knowledge across semiotic resources and modes. In F. Christie and K. Maton (eds), *Disciplinarity: Functional Linguistic and Sociological Perspectives,* 217–236. London and New York: Continuum.

O'Halloran, K. L., Podlasov, A., Chua, A. and E, M. K. L. (2012) Interactive Software for Multimodal Analysis. *Visual Communication: Special Issue Multimodal Methodologies,* 11 (3): 352–370.

O'Halloran, K. L. and Smith, B. A. (eds) (2011) *Multimodal Studies: Exploring Issues and Domains.* London and New York: Routledge.

O'Halloran, K. L., Tan, S., Smith, B. A. and Podlasov, A. (2011) Multimodal analysis within an interactive software environment: Critical discourse perspectives. *Critical Discourse Studies,* 8 (2): 109–125.

O'Toole, M. (2011 [1994]) *The Language of Displayed Art* (2nd edn). London and New York: Routledge.

Podlasov, A., Tan, S. and O'Halloran, K. L. (2012) Interactive state-transition diagrams for visualization of multimodal annotation. *Intelligent Data Analysis: An International Journal,* 16 (4): 683–702.

Ravelli, L. J. (2000) Beyond shopping: Constructing the Sydney Olympics in three dimensional text. *Text,* 20 (4): 489–515.

Royce, T. (1998) Intersemiosis on the page: A metafunctional interpretation of composition in the *Economist* magazine. In P. Joret and A. Remael (eds) *Language and Beyond,* 157–176. Amsterdam: Rodopi.

Royce, T. and Bowcher, W. (eds) (2006) *New Directions in the Analysis of Multimodal Discourse.* Hillsdale, NJ: Lawrence Erlbaum Associates.

Scollon, R. (2001) *Mediated Discourse: The Nexus of Practice.* London and New York: Routledge.

Smith, B. A., Tan, S., Podlasov, A. and O'Halloran, K. L. (2011) Analyzing multimodality in an interactive digital environment: Software as metasemiotic tool. *Social Semiotics,* 21 (3): 353–375.

Stenglin, M. (2009) Space Odyssey: Towards a social semiotic model of 3D space. *Visual Communication,* 8 (1): 35–64.

Stenglin, M. (2011) Spaced out: An evolving cartography of a visceral semiotic. In S. H. M. S. S. Dreyfus (ed.), *Semiotic Margins: Meaning in Multimodalities,* 73–100. London: Continuum.

Tan, S. (2009) A systemic functional framework for the analysis of corporate television advertisements. In E. Ventola and A. J. M. Guijjaro (eds), *The World Told and The World Shown: Multisemiotic Issues,* 157–182. Hampshire: Palgrave Macmillan.

Thibault, P. J. (2000) The multimodal transcription of a television advertisement: Theory and practice. In A. P. Baldry (ed.), *Multimodality and Multimediality in the Distance Learning Age,* 311–385. Campobasso, Italy: Palladino Editore.

Unsworth, L. (ed.) (2008) *Multimodal Semiotics: Functional Analysis in Contexts of Education.* London: Continuum.

Unsworth, L. and Cleirigh, C. (2009) Multimodality and reading: The construction of meaning through image-text interaction. In C. Jewitt (ed.) *The Routledge Handbook of Multimodal Research,* 151–163. London and New York: Routledge.

van Leeuwen, T. (1999) *Speech, Music, Sound.* London: Macmillan.

van Leeuwen, T. (2009) Parametric systems: The case of voice quality. In C. Jewitt (ed.), *The Routledge Handbook of Multimodal Analysis,* 68–77. London and New York: Routledge.

Ventola, E. and Moya, J. (eds) (2009) *The World Told and the World Shown: Multisemiotic Issues.* Hampshire: Palgrave Macmillan.

Zappavigna, M. (2010) Visualising logogenesis: Preserving the dynamics of meaning. In S. Dreyfus, S. Hood and M. Stenglin (eds), *Semiotic Margins: Meaning in Multimodalities,* 211–228. London: Continuum.

Zappavigna, M., Cleirigh, C., Dwyer, P. and Martin, J. R. (2010) The coupling of gesture and phonology. In M. Bednarek and J. R. Martin (eds) *New Discourse on Language: Functional Perspectives on Multimodality, Identity, and Affiliation,* 219–236. London and New York: Continuum.

Zhao, S. (2010) Intersemiotic relations as logogenetic patterns: Towards restoration of the time dimension in hypertext description. In M. Bednarek and J. R. Martin (eds), *New Discourse on Language: Functional Perspectives on Multimodality, Identity, and Affiliation,* 195–218. London and New York: Continuum.

Zhao, S. (2011) *Learning through Multimedia Interaction: The Construal of Primary Social Science Knowledge in Web-Based Digital Learning Materials.* Sydney: University of Sydney.

13 Motivated selection in verbal art, 'verbal science', and psychotherapy: When many methods are at one

David G. Butt,[*] Caroline Henderson-Brooks,[†] Alison Moore,[‡] Russell Meares,[§] Joan Haliburn,[¶] Anthony Korner[**] and Roy Eyal[††]

13.1 Introduction

The choices a speaker makes in grammar and in lexis accumulate in ways that are not clear or accessible to the speakers in a sustained interaction, for example, in an hour of interaction between a psychotherapist and a patient. This consistency, that is regularity beyond the typical threshold of human powers for tracking, is familiar to us from the discussion of verbal art: it is part of debate around Jakobson's claims for 'subliminal' patterns (e.g. 1987); and it underlies the cognate theories of organization in verbal art enunciated by Mukařovský (1964, 1977) and Hasan (e.g. 1975, 1985a). So too, in Halliday's concepts of 'prominence' and 'deautomatization' in relation to verbal art (e.g. 1971), such accumulating patterns are a recruitment of the habitual resources in existing forms of language to a non-habitual degree of consistency in their semantic consequences. It is only in this orienting of the choices to a thematic consistency that one can then go on to account for innovation of forms, or novelty. Verbal art rarely involves 'poetic licence'; rather it is a 'consistency of foregrounding' within conventions which needs to be illuminated. Such 'consistency of foregrounding' is a strategy of higher order 'symbolic articulation' for Hasan – evidence that the category 'literature' is not only 'in the eye of the beholder', and

---

[*]   David G. Butt is Associate Professor of Linguistics, Macquarie University, Sydney.

[†]   Dr. Caroline Henderson-Brooks teaches at the University of Western Sydney.

[‡]   Dr. Alison R. Moore teaches at the University of Wollongong, Australia.

[§]   Russell Meares is Professor Emeritus of Psychiatry at Sydney University.

[¶]   Dr. Joan Haliburn is a clinician and practitioner at Westmead, Sydney, Australia.

[**]   Dr. Anthony Korner is a Clinical Senior Lecturer at Westmead, Sydney, Australia.

[††]   Roy Eyal, M.D., is in private practice in Berkeley, California.

not merely in the 'response' of the reader. The 'art' of verbal art, in such an approach, relies on the methods by which the established categories of community practice can be functionally oriented to create that strangeness (the 'making strange') of individuated experience.

Such consistencies are also significant in that they can realize a semantic 'drift' quite distinct from the explicit topic. They can be an index of an 'angle' on the topic, a perspective which is relevant to the affective *and* ideational judgements a person is making moment by moment, albeit unconsciously. In this potential for realizing the *latent choices*, particularly in the grammar of an extended text (Butt, 1988), one can see how similar methods of 'deep reading' (Hasan, p.c.) are demanded across a spectrum of discourse studies, while the emerging results of such readings may reveal distinct conditions of text creation and clearly contrastive dimensions of text structure (i.e. register by register). In this regard, more recently, Halliday has written of a higher order metaphorization in the discourse of sciences (Halliday, mimeo). Halliday sees an analogy between first order meaning and Theme in verbal art on the one hand, and *grammatical metaphor* and 'Theory' in 'verbal science' on the other (mimeo: 6). The analogy appears in the way an ensemble of textual strategies can produce a coherence that is novel and culturally unique – in verbal art, we have a 'thesis' on experience; in science, we are presented with a thesis on nature (and, more latterly, on human interactions with nature, thereby returning science and humanities into a new era of mutual interests).

The methods of discourse analysis are shared by discourse analysts no matter what the form of discourse since the task of holding the instance of text against the meaning potential in the system is common (mimeo: 5), albeit that both the *instance* and the *system* are dynamic phenomena, with semantic vectors and phases. But the organization of verbal art, with its extra level of 'symbolic articulation' (Hasan, 1971; 1975, 1979, 1985a), is an index of the totally metaphoric status of text in verbal art and, hence, of the peculiar contextual conditions that pertain to its creation and reception (Hasan, p.c.). Crucial in this regard is the fact that the author can exercise a form of arbitrary choice over the parameters of the context – at least the 'internal' contexts of verbal art (its subject matter and setting). The internal context is, therefore, also an artefact of the metaphoric imperative in the genres of verbal art.

The issues raised above offer us an opportunity to elaborate why it should be that discourse analysis, along with the functional theories of verbal art and 'verbal science', should be so promising for psychiatrists and others working in psychotherapy. First of all one might suggest, as with research into registerial and linguistic variation more generally, the working world of psychotherapists involves the difficult step of 'turning language back on itself'. As Firth (e.g. 1957: 190) and Halliday (2002 [1988]) have emphasized, this is both a natural and a paradoxical undertaking. In the first place, you accept that there is no basis upon which a metalanguage can be settled outside of the natural languages which must be themselves described (hence, one has to propose 'ad hoc' categories as a positive method, guided by the immediate priorities of research). Second (but following from the first point), there never can be a complete rationale for semiotic categories, and so the 'ineffability of grammatical categories' is inherited from the natural language being described into any language of theoretical description. The latter point means that Saussure's notion of 'valeur' – the central distinguishing concept of a linguistic perspective on the relational complexity of language – affects the analysis twice over: first, in relation to the units being described, and second, in relation to the terms adopted for describing those units. Consequently, we must just do our rational best in managing the relativities of a reflexive stance on linguistic categories and their 'appliability' to any specific research task in question.

The relativities are a dimension of complexity in human transactions with the natural world, of which the transactions are themselves a product of change in that natural order. The relativities cannot be removed by a more formal method or by any 'double blind controlled experiment'. The degrees of complexity are at their apogee when language is the evidence *and* the instrument of intervention in the interpretation of mental health. It is in this challenge that one can see the importance of the notion of register, particularly with the tool of network representation, since we can build a description stratum by stratum, from phonology to context, in which those choices most salient for the research being undertaken can be represented homogeneously in terms of five relations, namely:

1.   OR (choose this or that or….);
2.   AND (choose in specific systems simultaneously);
3.   EITHER or ALL of the choices lead to another system x …;
4.   ONLY IF /WHEN ALL of indicated choices have combined can one then go on to choose in system x;
5.   RE-ENTER/CHOOSE OVER.

[The relations are exemplified in the network of Semantic Solidarity, below].

This is a dramatically effective method for both capturing and naturalizing the complexity of the Saussurean perspective while also being able to set the lens of analysis to the 'depth of field' most efficacious for the research to hand – the researcher must choose 'the semiotic address' and degree of *delicacy* needed in the research much as, when using Google Earth, we all need to adjust 'up and down' and from 'abstract to actual' in order to achieve our bearings and the appropriate detail for material location on earth.

13.2 Latent patterning and discourse analysis

From the research project undertaken by this team (and outlined below), it emerged that the 'semantic drift' of unconscious patterns of meaning making is something that an experienced therapist 'reads off' from the interaction. Furthermore, it seems probable that it is in responding to a bandwidth of latent patterns in the structure of discourse that psychotherapists find the motivation for the semiotic techniques their practice propounds as theory. The practitioners in the 'Conversational Model (CM) of Psychotherapy', in particular, address these semantic responsibilities explicitly and 'full on'. Their motivations, evident from the writings of the developers of CM – Robert Hobson (e.g. 1985) and Russell Meares (2005)[1] – are not linguistic, but rather organized around the critical psychic values of intersubjectivity, quality of relatedness, and the centrality of the 'self' as elucidated by William James (1842–1910). Given these core concepts, it should not be surprising that both the leading practitioner and theorist of the Conversation Model, Russell Meares, and the linguist who developed Systemic Functional Linguistics (SFL), M. A. K. Halliday, have had a collaboration in common – namely, with the psychologist and neuroscientist Colwyn Trevarthen (e.g. 1987). Trevarthen's work on intersubjectivity, between neonates and mothers, has been congruent with, and supportive of, both the CM and Systemic Functional Linguistics. In parallel forms of enquiry, Halliday, Trevarthen and Meares have explored the intricacy of mindfulness as it is created between two people in a profound relationship of reciprocation (viz. child to mother, patient to therapist).

Meares and his research team have specialized in treating the difficult case of Borderline Personality Disorder (BPD). Such patients present with what might be called an 'inert core': as if their commitment to lived experience has been extinguished, or severely compromised (through trauma, for example). A challenge to the psychotherapists is the restoration of animus or aliveness by creating an empathic relationship within which the analogical connections between aspects of living can be created. Crucial to this undertaking is a form of narrative in which memory, reverie, and a new form of meaning potential come together. Such 'coming together' is the aim of the therapist's discourse, producing a new level of insight about the past and an inclination to the possibilities of the future. Discourse in the therapist-patient relationship must be the catalyst of change since it is the resource in which the reciprocation can be created, that is, semiotically.

In many socio-semantic enquiries – therapeutic; literary; philosophical; educational – the initiating move can be sought in what motivates the professional enquiry from the point of view of the specialist, in this case, the therapist. For example, a therapist may be concerned at the degree to which a patient makes herself a background (i.e. gives herself low visibility) in her own discourse. Other motivating issues could be the degree to which a patient projects herself as agentive, or as the experiencer of feelings, or as the 'victim' of inexorable events (of 'happenings', rather than the actions of others, or of herself). Such questions of role allocation and of general textual visibility (of thematic or semantic weight) can be answered by tracking a number of simultaneous but independent choices in a text from clause to clause: for example, by tracking what is *grammatical agent* (if there is one); what is *grammatical subject* (that which can be argued over in a clause of English); and what is marked for *priority* and what for *newsworthiness* (*theme* and *new* respectively, Halliday and Matthiessen, 2004). This four line 'polyphony' of grammatical patterns renders a remarkable display of the moment to moment construction of unconscious meaning by a persona in an interaction (it could be the persona of the patient or of the therapist, or additionally the 'drift' of the dyad as a unit). The meanings are unconscious because (1) they are realized by choices which few people can consciously report; (2) they accumulate and ramify to degrees which even few linguists could monitor (or censor) in real time; (3) they accumulate and ramify to amounts that require considerable reflective and statistical processing, since the rates (bunchings and dispersions of a linguistic phenomenon) and quantities (numbers of actual instances of a relevant linguistic choice) can be salient both independently and, therefore, when combined.

It needs to be emphasized in relation to such textual analysis, with its opportunities for tracking of semantic threads in the discourse, that the meanings emerging in an interaction are *not* outside of the methods of objective science, including the expectations of quantification and prediction (the latter being of a probabilistic kind, centred on the task of settling 'typicalities', whether of patient discourse or of the therapist, or of the interaction between the two). It is reasonable to show how one can codify this linguistic 'polyphony' to bring out related notions of textural prominence and 'instantial weight'. Table 13.1 is one way of reading off the semantic weight of a choice in the context of a clause in a flow of clauses. The scale of five steps in a cline is arbitrary, and slightly at variance with my original proposal (1984) for graphing this change in a text.[2] The tool power lies in the clear separation along a cline of more and less dominating grammatical roles. A text involves the allocation of such roles. As emphasized above, the accumulation of what has been bestowed in the fabric of the text is difficult to monitor in real time, even for linguists. While we can all 'listen for' the lexical allocation of Actor roles, it is harder to simultaneously track the clause complexing (with its latent semantic force and shifts between parataxis/aggregation and hypotaxis/interdependence); and it is harder still to note what has been 'unchosen' – what might have been taken up in the discourse but which has been grammatically neutralized or occluded.

Such measures of interactive 'styles' suggest the potential for semantic profiles to assist in the arguments and evidence for change in a patient's development. One can be concerned with the technique of a therapist; or with the discrimination of efficacious and less efficacious interactional strategies in therapeutic method more generally. Such linguistic evidence could also contribute to measuring the efficacy of therapy as a medical practice (additional to the current methods which include the tracking of time without patients returning to destructive behaviours – e.g. self-harm; illicit drug taking, etc, see Meares *et al.*, 1999). This could be particularly the case if one combines measures of 'instantial weight' with already established textual measures of cohesion and cohesive harmony (see examples offered below). Cohesion and its semantic interpretation in cohesive harmony bear directly upon difficult domains of psychotherapeutic practice. These include the interpretation of 'dissociative' episodes – cases in which the 'fragmentation' of the personality of the patient means that he or she may lose touch with the immediate context and re-experience traumatic events, sometimes with details of other times and events 'fused' with the re-lived trauma. Cohesive chains offer a method for tracking the consistency of texture and of control as a patient exercises better management of the disruptive material (see Janet, 1924; Meares, 2005).

It is just this pattern of allocations that permits us, with the registerial tools of SFL, to follow the profile of bias in political imbroglios, especially in the reporting of war (viz. Lukin, 2006, 2008a, b, 2010; Butt *et al.*, 2004). When it is rational to expect certain topics to arise and certain participants to be involved, as is typical in the case of bias, their absence is palpable (what might be described in recent idiom as a semantic 'elephant in the room'). Whether in this overt form or as the habituation to choices not made by comparison with the actual utterance of a speaker, absent options constitute an implicit order against which the explicit wording takes on its meaning. The poet W. B. Yeats, in an analogy from verbal art, described metre in verse as a 'ghostly voice' against which the rhythm of the specific wording of a poem creates a tension or counterpoint, through unconscious comparison. Such a presence underwrites the 'valeur' of the choices actually made. This is an example of Saussure's distinction between the 'in absentia' and 'in praesentia' in linguistic relations (the axis of alternatives against the axis of elements which must be present together).

13.3 A rhetorical toolbox and the 'Techne' of a therapist

If we take a sample of discourse from therapy, the issues of analytic method and of the differences between registerial consistencies can be exemplified. In the following opening to a 50 minute session with a therapist, many

Table 13.1: Instantial weight

1 Status/	Primary	Hypotactic	Hypot²	Rankshifted	b in r/shifted	R/s in R/s
depth	5	4	3	2	1	0
2 Finiteness	Tense	Modality	Non-finite Pred	Nominalized	Minor	Exclam/Voc
	5	4	3	2	1	0
3 Process	Material	Behavioural	Verbal	Mental	Existential	Relational
	5	4	3	2	1	0
4 Voice	Middle + Domain (Circ/Range)	Middle	Effective (Operative)	Eff (Receptive) + Agent	Eff/Rec -Agent	-Voice
	5	4	3	2	1	0
5 Agent/	X Acts (Med/Actor)	X acts on Y (Agent/Actor)	X is acted upon (Med/Goal)	X is Domain (Range like)	X is Circum (Circ/Inst)	Experiential occluded
Role	5	4	3	2	1	0
6 Subject	X is Subject	Complement	Predicator	Adjunct	Vocative	Occluded
	5	4	3	2	1	0
7 Theme	Marked as Theme: Complement	Adjunct	Predicator	3rd Person	1st/2nd	
	5	4	3	2	1	0
8 News	Marked News (Theme)	News Only	Non-final	Marked Final (e.g. Predicator)	Final Unmarked	Theme only
	5	4	3	2	1	0
9 Person	Realized as 1st	As 2nd	As 3rd (particular)	As 3rd (homophoric)	General Thing/Stuff	No reference

thematic strands and rhetorical motifs from the interaction are set in train. These include the overwhelming character of the patient's recent behaviour: her protestation of disgust and responsibility with respect to her actions (these become explicit, declared topics), and her underlying attempt to position herself as a victim of conditions, and of another therapist (latent and nascent themes, as discussed below).

Table 13.2: Example 1 [R = therapist; C = client/patient]

R:	Sorry for the interruption at the beginning.
C:	It's been a roller coaster for about three weeks. Panic full blown
R:	It really seems that you did something that wasn't your fault, ups and downs…
C:	It just really hard to … take my self … I have to take responsibility. I saw it coming. When I came here I was really pepped up, but I still had enough incentive to understand the situation, but I kind of let it roll, I didn't put the brakes on or anything, and didn't do any of the things that could have helped it from going where it went, you know? I just.. I can't help but blame myself for what happened.
R:	I imagine there was a conflict. …

13.4 The dispersion of linguistic enquiry across strata

Linguistic enquiry, when undertaken as discursive analysis, is simply an interpretation of what is meant when the actual choices of a semantic interaction are viewed against the 'potential' – what might have been said. Establishing the 'potential', or what is to be selected from the actual, are not simple steps. Nevertheless, while conceding the variability of what might be typical in different situations and for different dyads in therapy, pursuing a conventional approach to text analysis produces immediate opportunities for construing the dominant meanings between therapist and patient. This is because an amassing analysis of instance to system changes the depth of field of human interpretation, much as an optical telescope changes human vision by enhancing the process, not by modifying it. The 'conventional approach' also offers semantic motifs and semantic threads which can guide the analyst as to what is salient in the text, and what might be the appropriate ordering of steps of analysis.

By a conventional approach to analysis, we mean taking the strata of language – context; semantics; lexicogrammar; phonology/phonetics – and asking questions which will elucidate how the construction of meaning is dispersed across systems on different strata, as well as how different resources contribute to the ensemble which we take as the 'figure' a person makes. (Consider the 'figura' of semiotics here: namely the figurae of speaking – our turns in the direction of meaning making). Cohesion systems seem paradoxical (Reference; Ellipsis; Substitution; Conjunction; Lexis). They are lexicogrammatical resources for text bonding with exponents *in* the clause, but not *of* clause systems. Yet, like all the systems of form, it is the semantic consequences of selections that one is seeking to represent.

The benefits of the instance (actual) to system (potential) can be seen even at the semantic periphery of a text – at the clause taxis (see Example 2 in Table 13.3).

Table 13.3: Example 2

α	I can't help (1)	
βα		but blame myself (2)
αββ(?)		(for) [[what happened]] (3)

The patient, in undeniable distress, chooses to expand on her role in the chaotic pattern of her recent life in three clauses. The Subject/first person is placed at two grammatical removes from the 'what happened'. The third element is either a group expanding the second clause with an embedded clause at its head, or a projected clause from 'blame'. In either case, the embedding means that there is one more form of grammatical 'insulation' between the 'I' and whatever 'she did'. Furthermore, the happening is not the directly available alternative wording: 'what I did'. By choosing the middle voice (x happened), the personal agency is diminished. In clause 2, the 'blame myself' is first person, but with 'myself' as grammatical Target. This combines the concession of her own guilt with the grammatical role of acted upon or even 'victim' (note the traditional term is the 'accused' or 'accusative' case). In this one first 'cut' of analysis, we can see already how the explicit avowal of self criticism is distanced by the implicit meanings of grammatical organization. The latent choices produce a form of textual counterpoint between guilt and the blaming of others. And, certainly, the unfolding of the text shows that this clause complex is a harbinger of the meanings to come in the generic morphology of the therapy session: the patient moves through disgust with herself to strong claims about the role of others in taking advantage of her obvious illness.

Table 13.4: Transitivity concerning action and blame in opening exchange

Cl ID	Sp	Clause text	Process	Proc type	Agency	Agent	Medium	Range
2_1	C	It's been a roller coaster for about three weeks	be	relational	middle		It [life?]	[Attribute:] a roller coaster
3_1	C	Panic full blown…	none		middle		[Carrier:] ??	[Attribute:] Panic full blown
4_1	R	It really seems [[that you did something [[that wasn't your fault]], ups and downs..]]	do	material	effective	[Actor:] you [C]	[Goal:] did something [[that wasn't your fault]], ups and downs..	
5_1	C	It just really hard [[not to … take myself …]]	be	relational	middle		[Carrier:] It … [[not to … take myself …]]	[Attribute:] really hard
5_2	C	I have to take responsibility	take	material	effective	[Actor:] I [C]	[Goal:] responsibility	
6_1	C	I saw it coming	see	mental	middle		[Senser:] I [C]	[Phenom-enon:] it coming
7_1	C	When I came here	come	material	middle		[Actor:] I [C]	
7_2	C	I was really pepped up	be	relational	middle		[Carrier:] I [C]	[Attribute:] pepped up
7_3	C	but I still had enough inventive [[to understand the situation]]	have	relational	middle		[Carrier:] I [C]	[Attribute] enough incentive [[to understand the situation]]
7_4	C	but I kind of let it roll	roll	material	effective	[Ini-tiator:] I [C]	[Actor]: it [situation?]	
8_1	C	I didn't put the brakes on or anything	put	material	middle		[Actor:] I [C]	[Scope:] the brakes on or anything
9_1	C	And didn't do any of the things [[that could help it from [[going [[where it went]]]]]], you know?	do	material	middle		[Actor:] I [C]	[Scope:] any of the things [[that could help it from [[going [[where it went]]]]]]
10_1		I just						
11_1		I can't help	help	mental	middle		[Senser:] I [C]	
11_2		other than blame myself for [[what happened]]	blame	verbal	effective	[Sayer:] I [C]	[Target:] myself [C]	
12_1	R	I imagine	imagine	mental	middle		[Senser]: I [R]	
12_2	R	there was a conflict	be	existential	middle		[Existent:] a conflict	

13.5 Registerial or generic structure: The shape of the interaction overall

A review of the generic structure of the exchange is crucial in that it allows one to establish the value of a choice or of a pattern of choices. For example, an initial discussion on the efficacy of medication may be an obligatory step with many of the patients in our data; but, while important, the linguistic patterns of such a segment may not be a relevant inclusion in the linguistic measure of change in the reflexive, self evaluation that develops over the 50 minutes of the therapeutic interaction. In the session quoted above, the openings and closing 'Coda' to the therapy were actually tightly linked to the therapeutic conversation overall: the patient offered a parting gift of a book, and set the gift within a vignette of her views on Existentialist writers (specifically on decisions and responsibility). But, nevertheless, the relevance of each step of the session to the linguistic measurement of change ought to be adjudicated, including the comparison of the structure of a session with the typical cycle of therapeutic treatment overall, with its changing priorities and obligatory procedures.

Figure 13.1 draws attention to the decision that might be made to separate openings and closings from the relation building discourse (which constitutes the criterial technique of psychotherapeutic interactions in the Conversational Model).

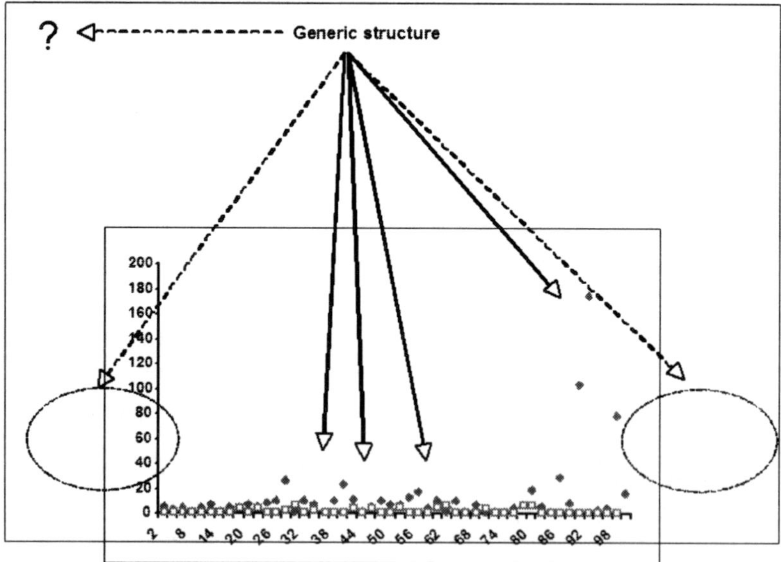

Figure 13.1: Openings and closings

The two ellipses indicate procedural zones (e.g. concerning medication at the outset and, perhaps, appointment dates at the closure). The issue is whether or not qualitative analysis of the texture in the therapeutic session should, or should not, include procedural segments. The answer may be 'yes', if and only if they encompass instances which are marked against what is considered the procedural (or non-discretionary) use of the potential.

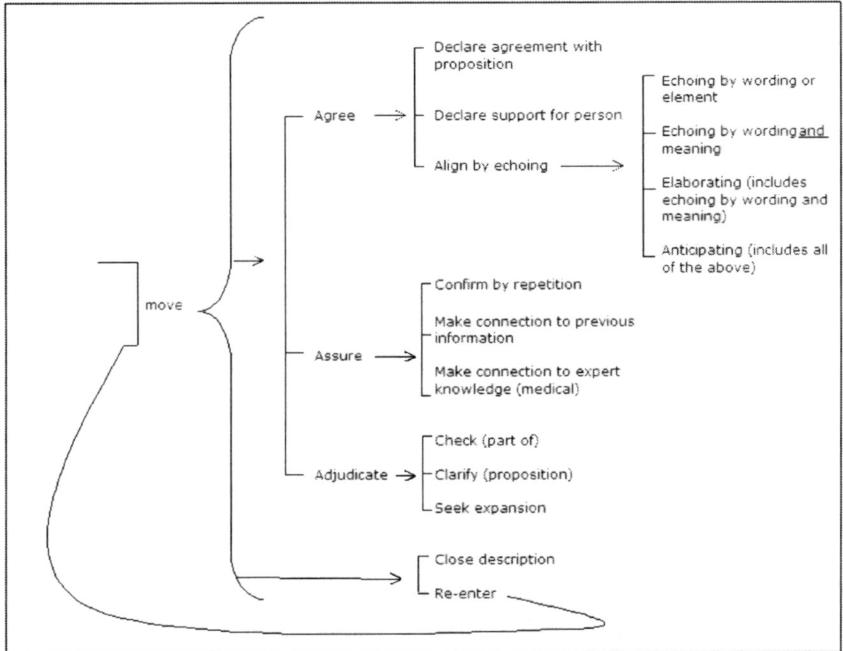

Figure 13.2: Semantics of turn taking

Additional concrete steps of tracking also contribute to the analyst's method by offering co-ordinates in extended discourse. Turn taking, measured here in clauses, can be revealing, in particular when viewed against the general structure of the session (or typical sessions), and when examined in relation to therapist techniques (for example, for establishing the degree to which the process of conversation is shared out). From the theoretical coordinates supplied by the SFL linguistic model, organized as it is by strata, by metafunctions, by ranks, and, ultimately, into systems, we can move into register specific zones of meaning making. For example, a fundamental achievement for a therapist in the CM is to establish an empathic solidarity with the patient in which language is selected with a number of principles as guidance. These include:

- 'using what is given';
- 'using the language of the other' (incorporating and co-creating an idiom that the patient can 'hear' as reflecting his or her immediate experience);
- 'attunement' to indices of positive value in tone and various layers of expression in the patient; and
- 'amplification' of the experience and emotional value implicit in the reactions of the patient.

Amplification, as the word suggests, involves an 'enlargement' of the patient's response to a wider world of actual and imaginable possibilities. It is a response to 'what is most alive' in the patient's expression, and an attempt to open up the 'meaning potential'.

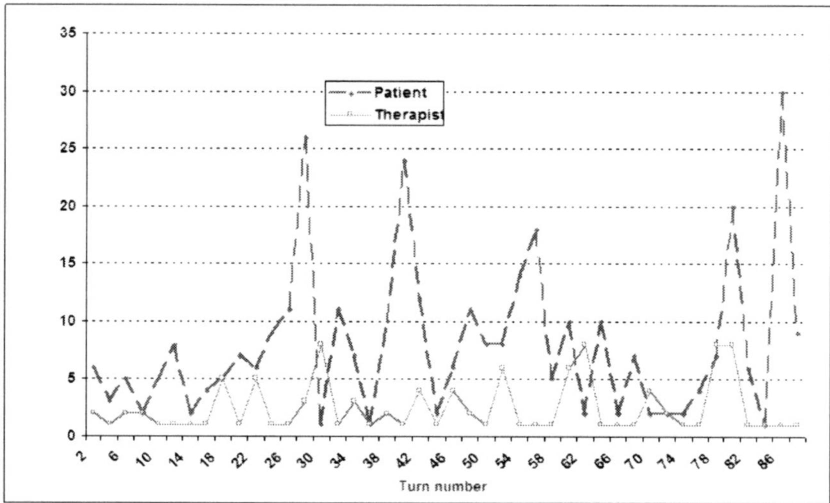

Figure 13.3: Techniques of semantic solidarity

Something of these strategies can be captured in a network at the stratum for empathic solidarity (at least as a first step of broad description). The network works well to characterize how a respondent chooses to reflect back to a speaker that speaker's own preoccupations. These could be evident in the wording, the meaning, or in the enlargement of vision – the dynamic spatialization of a semantic motif created by the patient's discourse. The *and* brace represents the fact that one must choose in both systems (to the right). Essentially, one zone of choices characterizes the reciprocation from the therapist and the other merely offers a stop or re-enter: the 'latter' meaning that new turns in the interaction require alternative descriptions.

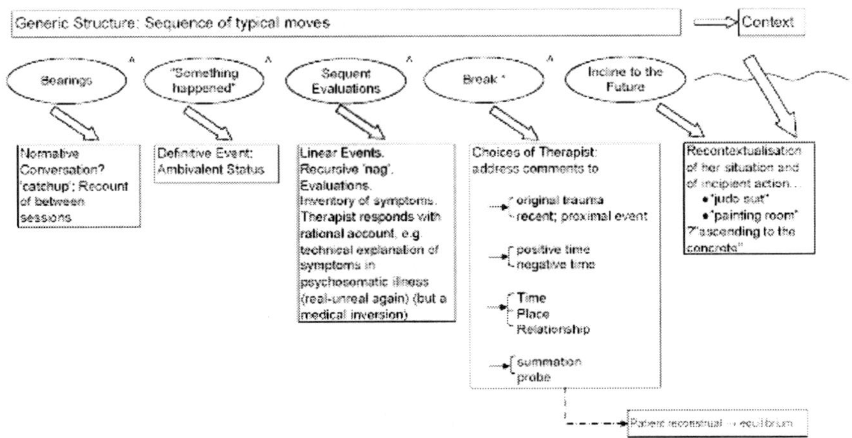

Figure 13.4: Affective cycles: Semantic motifs

Such motifs of perturbation (from patient) and complementation (from therapist) transform the recounts of the patient into multi-dimensional discourses in which an energy of emotion, of reflection, and of imaginative prospection (a plausible vision of living with 'value') can be shared. The 'affective cycle' of the 'roller coaster' session is set out against the 50 minutes of interaction. The patient sets out from her motifs of 'panic full blown' and 'roller coaster' both implying a supervening event rather than personal agency (the patient's own human control). Her attack on herself leads to a collapse into tears and dysfunction (2 + 3). This disordered state becomes more organized as she moves onto the accusations against a previous psychiatrist and her being 'betrayed' (4). A new stage of equilibrium, or catharsis, becomes apparent at the close with the gift giving. The narratological principles of disturbed and restored equilibrium are particularly close to the vector character of the therapeutic session.

An interesting difference may be in the dominance of the interpersonal metafunction (in an 'affective' cycle) by contrast with the ideational dominance in many tools of narrative analysis. Taking Hasan's detailed Generic Structure Potential as an explicit method, one can bring out the degree to which the register of therapy involves breaking out of a singular, 'stimulus entrapped', version of what is possible for one's future (see Butt *et al.*, 2007/2010).[3] Compare the diagram of Affective Cycle to diagrammatic summary of GSP.

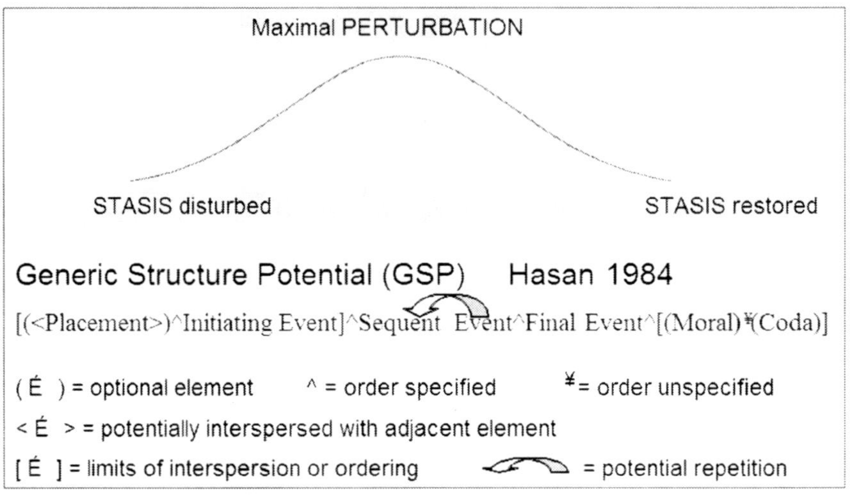

Figure 13.5: Cycles of narrative and of narratology

Each 'move' or Generic Element is motivated by a distinct dimension of the social process – by steps in the 'business to hand' (Greek: 'pragma'). In the description of therapy (above), an overarching or long-term purpose appears to be a fresh inclination to a future freer of the sense of a deadened core that is the chief behavioural sign of Borderline Personality Disorder – the profound mental illness upon which the practitioners of the CM have focused their research. This *inclination is to a future* with an extended value, an extended potential to mean. If language is like Wittgenstein's city, then the inclination is to a future in which all the suburbs are habitable, none shut off or shut down.

Such a breakout into a 'freer', more alive, space is realized only when the interaction finds a way out of an 'aporia' – the conundrum that has entrapped the patient in a loop of hopelessness (viz. aporia – Greek: lack or resources; an impasse of material or semantic impoverishment). Such impasses in our data include the logistical and personal constraints of breaking away from abusive relationships. The domestic and emotional reasons 'to stay' can appear overwhelming; but the reasons lead to a cascade of problems. For example, in the following extract a mother considers her treatment of her own children as the result of the abuse she experiences from her partner (described earlier as like 'acid eating away'). The therapist draws attention to the patient's own agency ('if you stopped him doing that to you', not 'if he stopped doing it to you'). This creates a pathway into a meditation – carefully balanced as it is uttered – in which the patient can envisage a different existence, modalized and in small increments though it may be. Such realistic review of her own situation has its own discourse correlates. Here, the modalization of her memory and judgements and the balanced clausal taxis are part of a grammatical ensemble, a therapeutic music which realizes the feeling that has emerged: change can be envisaged. Therefore, change has already occurred.

Table 13.5: Example 3: 'Blow ups' … 'flow on acid eating away at me'

Therapist:	
1	Ha! … does that mean
2	If you stopped
3	him doing that to you
4	You would do it less to the children?
5	Is that it?
She replies:	
6	well I might feel better about myself
7	Yeah. I might, mm …
8	cause he stopped for a few days –
9	I think
10	it was last week
11	or, I don't know
12	I think
13	there was some abatement
14	and then it just …
15	just for a couple of days
16	as if it was –
17	I don't know
18	maybe it's sort of delusional, escape
19	it was just living and breathing
20	which was just a little bit easier,
21	y'know … erm

13.6 'Disaggregation'

So too, there are numerous ways in which the details of narratorial reports – say of recent disturbing events, and/or past traumatic episodes – can be developed as evidence in the interpretation of states of mind. In the description of Dissociative experience, the emphasis in the literature concerns fragmentation, compartmentalization, depersonalization and disconnection. These suggest a primary move in linguistic analysis which represents the degree of textual cohesion in the patient's recounts, and how that cohesion can be evaluated in the light of the coherence of the emergent discourse. The distinction between cohesion and coherence is important in linguistics: cohesion deals with the resources in the wording for 'stitching' one clause to another and another and so on (Halliday and Hasan, 1976; Hasan, 1984). Coherence, however, assumes a linking of a higher order: a balance in the topics being discussed and in the similarity of things being said about those topics.

By itself, then, cohesion does *not* offer us direct information about what the 'stitching' produces – the fabric or quality of cloth; and whether it will function as a piece of clothing. By combining choices of related lexical tokens (words, but with some specific conditions) and repetitions of grammatical roles (with some specific conditions as 'repetition'), we can produce a map and a measure of semantic bonding across an extended passage of text. There is, then, the opportunity for us to visualize the connectedness of a patient's version of experience, and to offer some measures of how well a topic is developed, and how well it is tied in with other topics, or not.

A confounding factor may be that Dissociation also involves the 'fusion' of traumatic material, with other past events and with 'everyday' reports and recent events. Nevertheless, the three main principles of cohesion – (1) similarity; (2) identity; and (3) the cross-stitching of these two forms of text tokens through repeated grammatical roles – can be evaluated in quantitative and iconic (diagrammatic) forms. A balance in the liaison of similarity and identity can be quantified as Cohesive Harmony (following the work of Hasan, e.g. 1984).

13.7 Fragmentation, and fusion: Lexis and cohesive chains

A straightforward device for tracking the semantic connectedness between words in a text is the cohesive chain. A cohesive chain is built out of similarities. The similarities are based on relationships that are *not* specific to this text but which are carried over to typical uses of the word(s). These chains are built then from 'open system' items (i.e. *not* from a small set of grammatical choices like pronouns, but drawn from the dictionary head words). These are inter-related by their various meanings, especially if they are standard logical relations of equivalence (synonymy), oppositeness (antonymy), class membership (hyponymy) or part to whole (meronymy).

A second form of chain is based on the accumulation of words which 'point' to an identical person or 'thing'. Such words are grammatical items like pronouns and demonstratives, which create threads of identity; and these are specific to the given text: hence Identity Chains.

A third kind of chain figures in this analysis. It is built from explicit declarations of equivalence in the wording of the specific text e.g. and 'the birds, the birds were soldiers ....' In the semantics of this instance of text (a war poem by the poet Wallace Stevens), it is necessary, after this declaration in the text, to construe 'birds' and soldiers together because that equivalence has been legislated by the text itself. The equivalence is only for this instance of text ('birds' and 'soldiers' will *not* carry this relation beyond the text). Consequently we can refer to these chains, following Hasan, as 'Instantial'. They will net in links between terms which are specialized, technical versions of experience (often made explicit in appositions). The instantial chain will also capture metaphoric relations which become significant to the logical skeleton of meanings within a text (as in the 'birds ↔ soldiers' text).

When the tokens (words) in the chains are set against the numbers of the unit of text (i.e. clauses or sentences) in which they occur, we can see the threads of similarity, identity and of metaphoric equivalences (or of technical formulations) laid out in a diagram of the connectedness of words and referential items (pronouns/definite articles) in that text. The chain diagram is 'iconic' (as C. S. Pierce used the term) in that the chains display a resemblance relationship with the 'threading', from word to word, through the text. Such chains offer certain specific quantitative perspectives on the text – viz. the number and relative density or scatter of these cohesive devices, clause by clause. Also, the percentage of words which do *not* contribute to a chain can be ascertained. But such simple quantities will not discriminate sense from nonsense, or either of these from fragmentation and other grades of incoherence.

The issue of fragmentation demands that we introduce another principle, essentially an index of how the 'threads' are themselves interwoven or interacting. Hasan found that she could represent 'chain interaction' by indicating where tokens in two different chains had the 'same' grammatical relationship repeated or 'echoed'. The 'same' grammatical relationship means here that words in two chains serve in the same grammatical roles with respect to each other, at least twice (i.e. their relationship is 'echoed'). The crucial grammatical roles pertain to experiential roles (Actor/Acted upon/...). These interacting tokens (words) take on a new analytical status: Central Tokens. Such 'central tokens' do serve as an index of textual coherence (not merely of 'cohesion'). In fact, there are a number of quantitative relations which can be brought to bear on the question of textual coherence.

These involve the number of central tokens (interacting tokens) *as a proportion of*:

1. the total tokens in the text;
2. the total relevant tokens in a text (i.e. those which enter into a chain); and

3.   the number of peripheral tokens (i.e. those which do **not** enter into any chain).

A further, iconic sign of textuality might be thought of as the bridging or 'step' function resulting from the chain interactions: does the diagram show any chain, or grouping of chains, without a bridge of interaction with other chains? Such 'islands' in cohesive chaining suggest a failure of connectedness, or (depending on the genre) such a segment may be indicative of a leap of analogical thinking, a leap that will be interpreted as a parable or excursus. Such leaps may become retroactively relevant if a case can be made for a leap of imagination (i.e. of similarity without explicit identity through a pronominal chain). It should be noted, however, that analogical leaps are important textual phenomena in many registers (e.g. in sciences, in verbal art, in philosophical arguments, and in joking). So too, analogical connections in discourse are crucial to the Conversational Model (as explicated by Meares, 2005); this follows Vygotsky's emphasis on the value of non-linearity in discourses of self- reflection.

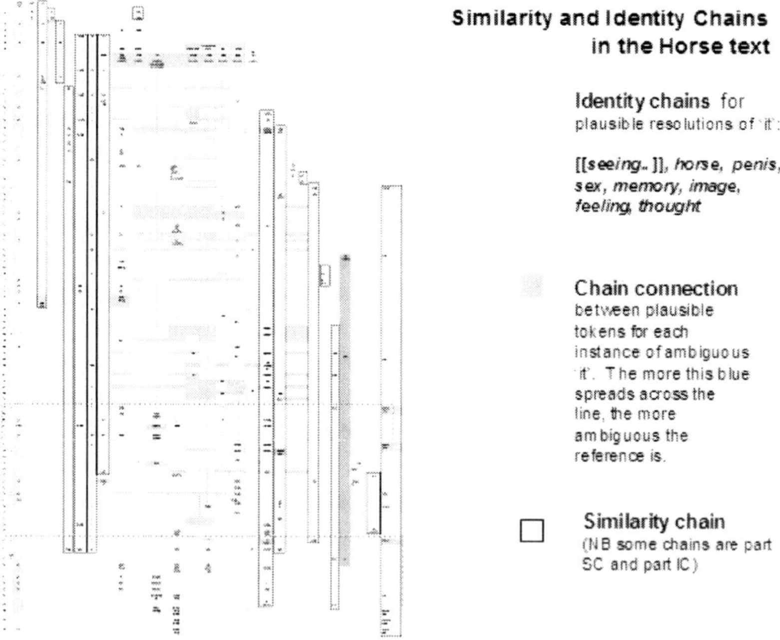

Figure 13.7: Similarity and Identity Chains. See full explanation of this instance and of this method in Butt *et al.* (2007/2010).

Cohesive Harmony was first developed by Hasan in the late 1960s for the measurement of textual explicitness in the recounts of pre-school children (see Hasan, 1985b). This tool can be utilized to test in what ways the texts created by patients can be regarded as fragmenting and disconnected: what might be the basis of the therapist's experience of incoherence and 'zoning out'.

Three clarifications should be stated up front. We are not saying that evidence from the wording of the texts is the only index of how the therapist may judge a patient's language to be dissociative; in fact, quite the opposite: many forms of gestural and contextual cues form a suite with language, or even provide the signal of a person's experience in the absence of any 'wording'. Much of our public behaviour is meaning bearing or 'semiotic' and provides an 'indexical' signal of being. The philosopher-semiotician C. S. Peirce (a co-founder of Pragmatism with William James) used the word 'indexical' for any meaning carried by a natural (not conventional) expression: hence, this would include expressions of pain or disgust, grimacing, etc. after the principle that one can infer the passage of a large person from the nature of the footprint. Our whole breathing apparatus produces indexical signs, many of which migrate to be part of the standardized, conventional repertoire of embodied meanings (viz. Korner, 2010; and Korner, 2012).

A second point is the general relationship between language and states of mind and brain. One can ask: why should language be given such a central role in the interpretation of a psyche and, particularly, in the characterization of any form of mental disorder? There are many points to consider on this issue and many of those have been taken up by Meares and others in the development of the 'Conversational Model' of psychotherapy. One point we would emphasize here is that language 'cuts to the quick' (archaic for the core of our living being) in that it is taken up preconsciously in our formative, earliest relationships with carers. Our taking on of personhood, and the personalization of our brains (Greenfield 2008: e.g. Chapter 1), is continuous with the meanings we take on and with the meanings by which our intersubjectivities are sustained. In this there is a common theory of intersubjectivity across the work of Trevarthen (e.g. 1974 – Conversations with a 2 month old; see also Bullowa, 1979), Meares (2005 – The Metaphor of Play, see endnote 1), and the functional linguistics of Halliday (1975; 2003). We trust that debate around the status of linguistic evidence will be encouraged by the exemplification in this report as well as by other aspects of the debate which have been the basis of related publications (ours and from others like Fine, 2006; Muntigl, 2004). Such traditions of functional interpretation of child language development and of the semantic self help us to envisage a biological drive for human interaction. This is in complete contrast with the Chomskyan assumption of an autonomous (cognitively separate) organ for syntax, or any appeal to 'intention' as an explanation of meaning (viz following Searle, 1969).

13.8 Latent patterning in text

In an unconscious linguistic pattern there is a prima facie case for 'motivated selection' (Jakobson, 1987 (and see Appendix); Tynjanov, 1978; Tynjanov and Jakobson, 1978; see also the useful, critical, discussion in Medvedev, 1985[1928]: 106ff; and the elaboration in Butt and Lukin, 2009). A non-random consistency of textual choices (as set out in the works cited at the outset of this discussion above; see also Butt (1988) for a discussion of the 'implicate order' of non-random selection in text) requires explanation or interpretation: it is potentially an integrating, semantic vector. It is the system turned to a recognizable functional end. Such consistency may be the best evidence one can obtain of 'purpose'. Such a tendency – or consistency of construction in meaning making – is the textual realization of a consistency of mind.

In this line of argumentation, one is using the linguistic expression of the patient as evidence of an orientation to experience which is motivating the latent consistencies in the text. Such motivation, and such linguistic evidence, has then been achieved without any appeal to 'intention' or illocutions (or any other circular method of separating 'superficial' meanings from 'real' meaning). Motivated selections are choices made then in the latent, even covert, organization of a text when such organization is unlikely to be the result of random choices. We claim that such linguistic, semantic, evidence has its place alongside other forms of scientific investigation of the human psyche, that is alongside other forms of clinical report, and as complementary to the insights to be drawn from neuroscience with its dramatically widening potential in brain imaging. [In this respect, we should draw attention to colleagues in the Meares group who have been in the lead of brain imaging research into Borderline Personality Disorder (BPD), amongst other topics: especially Lea Williams (2011) and Kim Felmingham (2011). At the *International Society for the Study of Personality Disorders Congress* (Melbourne, 2011), a forum led by Meares and Haliburn addressed BPD from multiple perspectives: from theoretical, clinical, brain imaging, and linguistic enquiries.]

With the techniques of linguistics for displaying latent patterns in an interaction, the 'techne' of the therapists in the Conversational Model makes a great deal of sense. The therapist is constructing a particular kind of relationship with a patient: it creates a security at the same time that it builds individuation (first called 'alone-together' by Hobson, 1985); it seeks the complementarity of shared subjectivity (explored by Trevarthen, 1974 and demonstrated linguistically by Halliday's language development study, 1975); the empathic techniques involve recognizing and linking with the patient's expressions of concern (*coupling*), sharing (*resonance*), and extending those elements of 'conversation' which have most 'animus', most spark of an engaged mind (*amplification*). In the commitment to an extended mindfulness, one can see that stylistic and therapeutic methods are linked by more than their interpretative methods. Both specializations involve a form of meta-poeisis: a form of making which draws out the incipient, yet to be fully realized and recognized, patterns in meaning. Such patterns of meaning extend our sense of the world by creating shared reflections where previously there may only have been an inchoate, private response.

Notes

1. This reference is to the third edition of Meares' book. The first edition was published in 1992.
2. Presented in a plenary paper, at the Writing to Mean Conference, University of Sydney.
3. The paper was published in 2010. Due to re-scheduling, the volume in which it appears has 2007 on its cover.

References

Bullowa, M. (ed.) (1979) *Before Speech: the beginning of interpersonal communication*. Cambridge: Cambridge University Press.

Butt, D. G. (1988) Randomness, order and the latent patterning of text. In D. Birch and L. M. O'Toole (eds) *Functions of Style*. London: Pinter

Butt, D. G., Lukin, A. and Matthiessen, C. I. M. M. (2004) Grammar as covert operation. In J. Edwards, B. Hawkins and J. R. Martin (eds) Special 9/11 volume of *Discourse and Society*, 15 (2–3): 267–290.

Butt, D. G. and Lukin, A. (2009) Stylistic analysis: construing aesthetic organization. In M. A. K. Halliday and J. J. Webster (eds) *Continuum Companion to Systemic Functional Linguistics*, 190–216. London: Continuum.

Butt, D. G., Moore, A. R., Henderson-Brooks, C., Haliburn, J. and Meares, R. (2007/2010) Dissociation, relatedness, and 'cohesive harmony': A linguistic measure of degrees of 'fragmentation'? *Linguistics and the Human Sciences* 3 (3): 263–293.

Felmingham, K. (2011) *The Impact of Dissociation in Post Traumatic Stress Disorder on Electronic Brain Activity*. Presentation from the Brain Dynamics

Centre (Westmead Hospital, Sydney) at the International Society for the Study of Personality Disorders Congress, Melbourne.

Fine, J. (2006) *Language in Psychiatry: A Handbook of Clinical Practice*. London: Equinox.

Firth, J. R. (1951) Modes of meaning. Essays and studies. In J. R. Firth (ed.) *Papers in Linguistics: 1934–1957*. Oxford: Oxford University Press.

Greenfield, S. (2008) *ID: The Quest for Identity in the 21st Century*. London: Sceptre.

Halliday, M. A. K. (1971) Linguistic function and literary style: an enquiry into the language of William Golding's 'The Inheritors'. In S. Chatman (ed.) *Literary Style: A Symposium*. New York: Oxford University Press.

Halliday, M. A. K. (1975) *Learning How to Mean: Explorations in the Development of Language*. London: Edward Arnold.

Halliday, M. A. K. (2002). On the ineffability of grammatical categories. In J. Webster (ed.) *The Collected Works of M. A. K. Halliday* Vol. 1, 291–322. London and New York: Continuum. (Originally printed in 1988.)

Halliday, M. A. K. (2003). *The Language of Early Childhood*. In J. Webster (ed.) *The Collected Works of M. A. K. Halliday* Vol. 4. London and New York: Continuum.

Halliday, M. A. K. (mimeo). Text, discourse and information: A systemic-functional overview. Plenary talk written for a discourse conference in Shanghai in 2010, and translated into Chinese; and later rewritten as: Some thoughts on text and discourse, information and meaning. Paper delivered to Choice and Text Group, University of Southern Denmark, Institute of Language and Education.

Halliday, M. A. K. and Hasan, R. (1976) *Cohesion in English*. London: Longman.

Halliday, M. A. K. and Matthiessen, C. M. I. M. (2004) *An Introduction to Functional Grammar* (3rd edition). London: Arnold.

Hasan, R. (1971) Rime and reason in literature. In S. Chatman (ed.) *Literary Style: A Symposium*. London: Oxford University Press.

Hasan, R. (1975) The place of stylistics in the study of verbal art. In H. Ringbom (ed.) *Style and Text*. Amsterdam: Skriptor.

Hasan, R. (1979) Workshop Report No. 6: Language in the Study of Literature. In M. A. K. Halliday (ed.) *Working Conference on Language in Education: Report to Participants*. Sydney: University of Sydney.

Hasan, R. (1984) Coherence and cohesive harmony. In J. Flood (ed.) *Understanding Reading Comprehension*, 181–221. Newark, DE: IRA.

Hasan, R. (1985a) *Linguistics, Language and Verbal Art*. Geelong, VIC: Deakin University Press.

Hasan, R. (1985b). Part B. In M. A. K. Halliday and R. Hasan (eds) *Language, Context and Text: Aspects of Language in a Social Semiotic Perspective*. Geelong, VIC.: Deakin University Press.

Hobson, R. F. (1985) *Forms of Feeling: The Heart of Psychotherapy*. New York: Routledge.

Jakobson, R. (ed.) (1987) *Language in Literature*. Cambridge, MA: The Belknap Press of Harvard University Press.

Janet, P. (1924) *Principles of Psychotherapy*. London: George Allen and Unwin.

Korner, A. (2010) Cry and Response. Presentation at the Grand Rounds, Westmead Hospital, Sydney. April 2010.

Lukin, A. (2006) The unseen engineer: linguistic patterning in war discourse. *Linguistics and the Human Sciences* 2(1): 59–87. (ERA: B) [appeared in 2008]).

Lukin, A. (2008a). Journalistic voice, register and contextual configuration: A case study from the Spanish and Argentinian press. In E. Thompson and P. R. R. White (eds) *Communicating Conflict: Multilingual Case Studies of the News Media,* 143–171. London and New York: Continuum.

Lukin, A. (2008b) The explanatory power of the SFL dimensions for the study of news discourse. In C. Wu, C. M. I. M. Matthiessen and M. Herke (eds) *Proceedings of ISFC 35: Voices Around the World* Vol. 1, 106–111. Sydney: The 35th ISFC Organizing Committee. ISBN 978-0-9804447-1-8.

Lukin, A. (2010) 'News' and 'register': a preliminary investigation. In A. Mahboob and N. Knight (eds) *Appliable Linguistics: Texts, Contexts and Meanings,* 92–113. New York and London: Continuum.

Meares, R. (1993) *The Metaphor of Play: Disruption and Restoration in the Borderline Experience.* Northvale, NJ: J. Aronson.

Meares, R., Stevenson, J. and Comerford, A. (1999) Psychotherapy with borderline patients, I: A comparison between treated and untreated cohorts. *Australian and New Zealand Journal of Psychiatry* 33: 467–472.

Medvedev, P. N. (1985 [1928]) *The Formal Method in Literary Scholarship.* Cambridge, MA: Harvard University Press.

Melkonian, D. and Korner, A. (2012) Increasing sensitivity in the measurement of Heart Rate Variability: The method of Non-Stationary RR spectral analysis. *Computer Methods and Programs in Biomedicine,* 108 (1): 53–67.

Mukařovský, J. (1964) Standard language and poetic language. In P. L. Garvin (ed.) *A Prague School Reader on Esthetics, Literary Structure and Style.* Washington, DC: Georgetown University Press.

Mukařovský, J. (1977) *The Word and Verbal Art.* New Haven, CT: Yale University Press.

Muntigl, P. (2004) *Narrative Counselling: Social and Linguistic Processes of Change.* Amsterdam: John Benjamins.

Searle, J. (1969) *Speech Acts: An Essay in the Philosophy of Language.* Cambridge: Cambridge University Press.

Trevarthen, C. (1974) Conversations with a two-month old. *New Scientist,* 2, 230–235.

Trevarthen, C. (1987) Sharing makes sense: Intersubjectivity and the making of an infant's meaning. In R. Steele and T. Threadgold (eds) *Language Topics: Essays in Honour of M. A. K. Halliday,* 177–200. Amsterdam: John Benjamins.

Tynjanov, J. (1978) On Literary Evolution. In L. Matejka and K. Pomorska (eds) *Readings in Russian Poetics: Formalist and Structuralist Views.* Cambridge, MA: MIT Press.

Tynjanov, J. and Jakobson, R. (1978) Problems in the study of literature and language. In L. Matejka and K. Pomorska (eds) *Readings in Russian Poetics: Formalist and Structuralist Views.* Cambridge, MA: MIT Press.

Webster, J.J. (2001) Thumboo's *David.* In C. K. Tong, A. Pakir, Ban Kah Choon and R. B. H. Goh (eds) *Ariels: Departures and Returns. Essays for Edwin Thumboo.* Oxford: Oxford University Press.

Williams, L. (2011) *BPD and brain markers of disconnectedness.* Presentation from the Brain Dynamics Centre (Westmead Hospital, Sydney) at the International Society for the Study of Personality Disorders Congress, Melbourne.

Appendix

Quotes from Jakobson (1987): 'Subliminal Verbal Patterning in Poetry'

'A calculus of probability as well as an accurate comparison of poetic texts with other kinds of verbal messages demonstrates that the striking particularities in the poetic selection, accumulation, juxtaposition, distribution, and exclusion of diverse phonological and grammatical classes cannot be viewed as negligible accidentals governed by the rule of change. Any significant poetic composition, whether it is an improvisation or the fruit of long and painstaking labor, implies a goal-oriented choice of verbal material' (p. 250).

'Phonology and grammar of oral poetry offer a system of complex and elaborated correspondences which come into being, take effect, and are handed down through generations without anyone's cognizance of the rules governing this intricate network. The immediate and spontaneous grasp of effects without rational elicitation of the processes by which they are produced i snot confined to the oral tradition and its transmitters. Intuition may act as the main or, not seldom, even sole designer of the complicated phonological and grammatical structures in the writings of individual poets. Such structures, particularly powerful on the subliminal level, can function without any assistance of logical judgment and patent knowledge both in the poet's creative work and in its perception by the sensitive reader of *Autorenleser* (author's reader), according to an apt coinage by that courageous inquirer into the sound shape of poetry, Eduard Sievers' (p. 261).

14 Systemic Functional Linguistics in the round: Imagining foreign language education for a global world

Heidi Byrnes*

14.1 Introduction

The topic I wish to address in this chapter, 'Systemic functional linguistics in the round: imagining foreign language education for a global world', is the result of interactions with my SFL colleagues in the real world and through their writings. What I learned in both contexts has had considerable effect on my interpretation of a number of vexing issues in foreign language (FL) education in colleges and universities in the United States. More immediately, it has also deeply influenced a comprehensive educational project that I spearheaded in my home department, the German Department at Georgetown University in Washington, DC. Specifically, over a three year period, between 1997 and 2000, the department, a Ph.D. granting department in literary-cultural studies, created an integrated four-year undergraduate curriculum that puts major tenets of SFL into educational practice (Developing Multiple Literacies, 2000).

These three strands of experience coalesce in my proposal in this chapter for explicitly linking FL teaching and SFL. The proposal assumes that key insights in SFL can be translated into the FL environment and lead to effective pedagogical practices in an extended programmatic context. That assumption has been well substantiated in the curricular project of my own department (Pfeiffer and Byrnes, 2009). But the proposal I present here goes further than that: I see the real benefit of a link between FL teaching and learning and SFL in terms of providing an intellectual frame and frame-

---

* Heidi Byrnes is George M. Roth Distinguished Professor of German at Georgetown University.

work for a complex, challenging, and much needed educational effort. Specifically, such framing would inform decisions on how one might model an entire programme's educational vision (Byrnes and Maxim, 2004; Byrnes, 2006c, 2012; Byrnes *et al.*, 2010), how one might develop a curriculum for a particular educational setting (Byrnes *et al.*, 2006), create suitable materials (Byrnes, 2006a), assess whether the envisioned learning outcomes had been attained (Byrnes, 2002a; 2008; Byrnes *et al.*, 2010), and, finally, how one would prepare teachers for this kind of language teaching (Byrnes, 2001, 2011b).

Admittedly, those are high expectations, but to me they are nonetheless realistic for the following reasons. They recognize the power of an elaborated functional theory of language to affect teaching and research practice, where it would replace the non-distinct form-oriented structuralism that amounts to the reigning default theory. They also recognize the power of such a theory to develop a principled approach to more comprehensive issues in educational decision-making, where it would replace endlessly *ad hoc* decisions that, good intentions notwithstanding, cannot bring lasting effects. Finally, they acknowledge the power of a theoretical approach that conceptualizes language in a fashion that speaks to the best spirits in and the fundamental educational ethos of collegiate foreign language cultural studies departments as humanities departments.

So, how might this more encompassing role for a link between SFL and FL studies be accomplished? Importantly, one would not begin with the major conceptual apparatus of SFL as an independent theory of language. Rather, one should begin with educational concerns so as to create a rich understanding of the values, beliefs, and goals of collegiate FL programmes as educational units; one would consider as well the oftentimes disparate expectations on the part of the public *vis-à-vis* collegiate FL teaching and learning; and, finally, one should begin with a sympathetic appreciation of the affordances but also the weaknesses and frustrations, not to mention severe limitations, collegiate FL departments encounter as they strive to offer quality programmes.

What about the values, beliefs, and goals that one can rightly associate with collegiate foreign language programmes? What does the public expect of them? What frustrations, needs, and limitations characterize them? How would these aspects, the goals and the limitations, influence a proposal of the kind I have in mind? How would the proposed project differ from what is already 'out there'? What sort of focus would distinguish it? What would need to happen for the short term, what might be long-term considerations? And what might be the long-term consequences of such a project if all went right – for applied linguistics, for second language acquisition research, and ultimately for how teaching and learning languages is being talked about, not by specialists, but by learners or, even more broadly, by the general public (see MLA, 2007)?

I pose this set of questions not with the intention of answering each of them. Rather, I raise them in order to circumscribe the educational concerns that are at issue and then to claim an assured and assertive presence for SFL in FL education. Accordingly, I will begin with a global characterization of the educational situation of collegiate FL departments, particularly in the United States, though I have observed it as well in other parts of the world. I will follow that up with a closer look at the imperatives and foci that govern FL teaching and learning in specific programmes. By way of anticipating where this will take us, an overarching theme is that of 'development'. How can we, how should we, how must we imagine the nature of instructed multiple language development by adults in light of pressing educational mandates for collegiate FL learning, and, in linked thought, how can, how should, how must SFL guide and inform that kind of imagining?

I will provide some thoughts on how such questions might play themselves out in two areas of educational activity: (1) in modelling educational goals in relation to language and content/culture learning; and (2) in developing curricula for specific educational settings. Three other critical areas, namely outcomes assessment, materials development, and teacher education will run along only implicitly although I consider them to be indispensable areas of attention in the work of FL programmes. I will conclude by placing my proposal in the larger context of possible developments in SFL as well as in applied linguistics in general.

14.2 Positioning collegiate foreign language education in the world

I begin with a broad characterization of how collegiate FL education is now positioned.

1. The teaching and learning of foreign languages takes place in a globalized educational environment. At present that environment is dominated by English language teaching and learning. But precisely because English now has that role, the position of other languages alongside English, the so called LOTEs, deserves careful thought. Demands for professional-level competencies, something like multiple cultural literacies, exist for many of these languages

and cultural areas. How an entire educational system can intelligently negotiate these multiple demands and not see them as mutually exclusive is an enormous challenge – and not merely in the obvious sense that it is impossible to teach all the languages that should be taught. As I will argue, the challenge goes much deeper – and precisely there lies also the opportunity for SFL's relationship to FL teaching.

2.   It is an open secret that the dominant paradigm for FL educational activities is unable to meet the complex demands made of contemporary language education. Specifically, communicative language teaching is insufficient in terms of the underlying assumptions about language that it tends to project, in terms of the language learning goals it has put forward, whether by design or by default, and the pedagogical actions it has helped popularize (Byrnes, 2002b, 2006, 2007, 2012; Byrnes and Maxim, 2004; Byrnes *et al.*, 2010). That set of insufficiencies is bolstered further by a concurrent SLA research enterprise,which takes a strong interactionist, psycholinguistically-focused, language processing-oriented stance, thereby virtually assuring that the complex nexus of *learning and knowing in a language* (through a language and with a language in its cultural context) does not enter scholarly discussion (see Doughty and Long, 2003, for representative publications).

If that analysis is correct, the critical question is this: What kind of theoretically motivated talking about language teaching and learning is needed to dislodge these two reigning discourses of educational and research practice in applied linguistics?

3.   Answering that question in favour of SFL, the direction I have advocated, will not be a straightforward matter of simply 'applying' existing SFL constructs to FL educational contexts. Rather, a viable link between FL education and SFL begins with a detailed understanding of the particular dynamics of that educational setting, something like a situated educational needs analysis (see Byrnes *et al.*, 2010). On that basis one can endeavour to translate existing insights in SFL into now well circumscribed institutional–educational themes and topics. Such efforts should, on the one hand, contribute to further clarification and targeted specification of the existing conceptual apparatus in SFL; on the other hand they should also spur SFL's own development in line with the foregrounded FL educational concerns.

14.3 Towards an educational–institutional needs analysis for foreign language teaching and learning

In this section, then, I want to explore at some level of detail, selected aspects of such an institutionally situated needs analysis for FL teaching and learning.

My first point is so obvious as to run the risk of sounding trite: FL learning is about learning an FL, usually on the part of adults; it is not mother tongue learning by children. In other words, at least from a strategic standpoint, it is justified to highlight the differences between those two forms of language learning rather than their undeniable similarities (for the latter, see Halliday, 2007a). The most obvious difference is that FL learners already possess, to varying degrees, a semiotic system with which they have been making sense of the world around them and which they have used to interact with others (Halliday and Matthiessen, 1999). Just how that affects the learning process itself, whether those effects are better or even at all well described in terms of positive or negative 'transfer' or 'interference' or, yet more starkly, as an inherent inability on the part of adults to learn the FL to high levels of ability, is not the most immediate concern. Rather, given what we know about the relationship between meaning-making and languages – and SFL theorizing has enabled us to know this with considerable clarity – the issue is that adult FL learners will have to learn how to mean with and through the new language alongside their mother tongue (Halliday, 2004b; Matthiessen, 2006, 2009). That implies, first and foremost, that they will have to gain access to the meaning-making resources the language makes available in its particular lexicogrammar, a task and challenge that is quite distinct from learning the 'grammatics' of that language (see Halliday 1973, 1975, 1993, 1996, 1999, 2004a and b). And they will have to do so in a setting that cannot possibly provide the rich occasions and, indeed, needs and desires in the real sense for engaged meaning-making that otherwise drive language use as a social activity.

In light of that undeniable fact, what countermoves at all levels of educative action can be launched to facilitate the **need** for engaged and invested meaning-making on the part of learners and to facilitate as well the **potential** for experiencing grammar as a meaning-making resource, rather than as formal inventory, particularly a formal inventory deceptively described in terms of sentence-level rules? Would it be possible to harness for this enormous learning feat an ability that adult learners do have, though surely to differing degrees, namely the ability to create an entirely semiotic world of meaning through texts which, of course, have embedded in them social realities, including the need of social actors to communicate? If that possibility can be contemplated, how might it shape an FL programme?

Only slightly less obvious is my second point. While FL learning takes place at all educational levels, **at the college level** it faces two tasks at the opposite end of the spectrum: the need to support very advanced learning, surely an overriding societal educational goal; and the need to assure that even beginning learners receive effective instruction that might potentially lead to advanced levels of ability.

(a) At the advanced end of the spectrum, college FL programmes must enable learners to attain the kind of **professional- or academic-level, advanced language abilities or L2 literacies** that are increasingly in demand in a global world (Byrnes, 2004). They have this task even in countries, such as China or most European countries, that, unlike the United States, firmly integrate FL learning into the curricula of primary and secondary education.

- A first and by no means frivolous question is therefore: What is the nature of advanced level abilities? A quick look at FL education practice and also the scholarly literature shows astoundingly amateurish, if not to say educationally unusable, responses to that question (Byrnes, 2002c, 2011).
- Assuming that we would, at some point, know more about advanced instructed L2 abilities, an obvious second question pertains to how we might foster their development through educational activity (Crane, 2006).
- A third, yet more probing question is this: What acquisitional preconditions would have to exist at all levels of a programme for the development of such advanced abilities to become a real possibility for the majority of learners and not merely the 'gifted' few? Importantly, can we state those preconditions in meaning-oriented **and** in lexicogrammatical terms? And what would be their interrelationship so as to capture **language developmental factors** (Byrnes, 2006c; 2009, 2014 in press)?

Let me comment a bit more on this last issue: By now an argument can be made that one of the reasons why communicative language teaching has created something like its own glass ceiling might lie in the fact that the meaning-making resources that it tends to lay before learners present an insufficiently broad foundation for the challenging task of advanced language learning in a classroom setting. Specifically, it affords neither the **need** to acquire certain lexicogrammatical resources in order to mean certain things nor the multiple **opportunities** for their carefully linked deployment in all modalities that are known to be necessary for a gradual increase in the ease of their nuanced situation-appropriate use (Byrnes *et al.*, 2010).

(b) At the other end of the spectrum FL departments must competently meet the demands of **beginning levels of instruction,** for the simple reason that the pre-collegiate educational system encounters limits in the number of languages that can be accommodated in the normal school day and year. That fact relegates to tertiary education the teaching of those languages that were left out earlier on. Assuming that some language learning did take place in the K–12 environment, instructional programmes need to recognize the special potential of third language learning.

- Are there aspects of third language teaching and learning that might facilitate **that** project? Would it be possible to infuse an entire programmatic and pedagogical approach with them? Might they also be able to circumvent the oftentimes impracticable creation of separate tracks beyond the beginning level? Let me venture a preliminary response: Perhaps one way to harness the advantages of third language learning would be through a heightened meta-awareness of the nature of language by creating opportunities for taking a kind of intellectual-affective-aesthetic pleasure in language as a meaning-making system. I would like to propose that, for literate adults, this might be one of the most powerful ways to motivate, in the agentive sense of the word, continued FL development, an approach to learning that subsumes and yet exceeds the attraction of merely being able to 'communicate' because it enables the learner to imagine a desirable possible future self (Dörnyei, 2009a; also Byrnes, 2011).

Behind these two broad areas stands a stark reality for any language programme: Time is of the essence! FL learning at the college level, no matter how generously it might be conceived, has available to it a distressingly short number of years within which to enable adult learners to acquire the kinds of advanced literacies that society increasingly demands. In short, matters of efficiency and effectiveness are an inescapable part of the calculus – and that does not in any way mean that one is beholden to an industrial production model for learning.

On the contrary; we know this: Even if we had all the time in the world, certain abilities do not miraculously and on their own come about (Christie, 1989; Halliday, 1993, 2007b, c, d; Schleppegrell, 2004; Christie and Derewianka, 2008). We also know that no statements about fixed acquisitional sequences proffered by psycholinguistically driven research offer substantive insights about the kind of language development that is here at issue. For one thing, their notions of acquisition have next to no connection to the ethos and culture of FL literary-cultural studies department. For another, the research itself shows serious shortcomings even if one were to subscribe to a cognitivist, psycholinguistic model for language learning.

In other words, assuming that time is of the essence, assuming, furthermore, that issues of efficiency and effectiveness are valid, how can FL development be conceptualized in terms of efficiency of acquisition towards the ability to mean something worth meaning?

At the risk of entering hostile territory I would like to press the issue further yet by introducing the provocative notion of 'benchmarks' for language development, a particularly 'toxic term' in academic discussions about language learning.

By benchmarking I mean some substantiated, principled, and evidence-based sense of what it is reasonable to expect learners to be able to do under the condition that we have provided for them the best possible programmatic and pedagogical scaffolding we know so that they can develop the linked capacity **to mean in and with and through the language that is being learned**.

Setting out that agenda is not a way to resurrect the tired and ill-advised notion of 'best methods' that we should slavishly follow, perhaps not even 'best practices' we should adopt if we want to succeed. Nor does such 'benchmarking' deny the fact that there will always be substantial variation among learners in terms of their learning outcomes, even when they experience the same instruction. However, without any sense of what is a reasonable and what is a quite unreasonable expectation for learning outcomes in a particular educational setting, any talk of what in fact was achieved or not, but should have been achieved, is, deep down, uninterpretable and uninformative, therefore unhelpful, perhaps even offensive and downright dangerous for educational decision-making.

In fact, in a seemingly contradictory way, 'benchmarking' acknowledges the fact that what is 'efficient' and what is 'effective' in language learning is quite relative. But it is relative in relationship to a frame of reference, not endlessly relative on its own terms. Indeed, our aversion to grappling seriously with the nature of instructed language development – the real way to embrace benchmarking – has created some strange bedfellows. For example, the often distressingly meagre learning outcomes reported for much of US language learning become self-fulfilling prophecies, not because we have expected too little of our learners, but because we have provided them with too little curricular and pedagogical scaffolding to know what otherwise might have been appropriate learning outcomes. In light of that serious shortcoming, the oft-repeated notion that adult language learning is really a 'too little–too late' deficitary project makes all too much and deeply troubling sense. When both phenomena (the meagreness of actual outcomes and the undeniable need for better learning outcomes) are then robed in highly valued theoretical garments, such as the critical period hypothesis or the input and interaction hypothesis, professional discussion that might embrace advancedness as a viable project is essentially held hostage. At the other end of the spectrum, the learning outcomes implied in the much acclaimed report by the Modern Language Association in the United States (2007) about higher education FL learning are just as distressingly off the mark inasmuch as they demand of FL learners what few native language users are able to accomplish. I will return to this topic once more in conjunction with the topic of curriculum development. For now I phrase the issue in the following terms:

- Is it possible to present principled general proposals about learning development that sit somewhere along the continuum between all too meagre learning outcomes and successful learning outcomes relative to a particular instructional level, where such proposals build on a general model of adult FL literacy development and are connected to a general model of the ontogenesis of knowledge as well as a general model of language development in the sense of 'learning how to mean' (see in particular (Halliday, 2007d: 354–355).

Among many favourable consequences of well-considered statements of reasonable learning outcomes would be this: learning outcomes would no longer be nearly recklessly left up to chance – or to study abroad! Rather, as research regarding syntactic development as development in meaning-making in a textual environment indicates, such learning is indeed possible across a cohort of learners (see Chapter 8 in Byrnes *et al.*, 2010; also Ryshina-Pankova, 2010; Byrnes, 2011a). Remarkably, in this literacy-focused curriculum, oral language abilities also developed in unexpectedly rapid fashion (Norris and Pfeiffer, 2003).

I conclude this section by returning to two of the four areas I identified earlier on as core educational activities that any programme will have to consider: (1) how we might clarify educational goals, and (2) how we might create a curricular progression, but now with the understanding that statements of reasonable educational goals statements and, on that basis, thoughtful proposals for a curricular sequence are not a luxury but a necessity if we are to move forward in FL education. At the same time, that strong affirmation clearly recognizes the formidable challenges to faculty and programmes this conclusion entails and the near-absence of curricular thinking (Byrnes, 1998).

What might explain this counter-productive and deeply unsatisfactory situation? I refer to three intersecting and, at times countervailing dynamics:

1. Even when faculty and entire departments are willing to engage in curricular thinking, they have few resources on which they might draw, not least because their own educational background has provided them with precious little relevant knowledge and expertise in the area.

2. With a bit of guidance faculty members in literary cultural studies, the majority of tenure lines in FL departments, who are neither applied linguists and certainly not systemicists, can develop a level of sophistication that is sufficient to enable an entire group to gradually develop a self-sustaining discourse community of practice. The creation of such a bedrock of assumptions that can be developed further is important because the complex issues arising in the creation and affirmation of educational goals and in the creation and maintenance of a curriculum cannot possibly be gotten 'right' the first time around. On the contrary, curriculum and pedagogy are always works in progress in need of further revision, or, actually more correctly, suitable for and hospitable to further revision as the faculty community of practice becomes more and more knowledgeable about the nature of instructed learning development. But a first step does have to be taken: Without initial proposals there will be no revisions – and therefore no benefits, neither for the faculty nor for the students in a programme.

3. With good leadership by key faculty members the project can, in relatively quick order, develop a facilitating dynamic all of itself. This is so because an invigorated culture of teaching and learning, coupled with favourable learning outcomes, creates its own momentum, affirmation of long-held, though often incompletely articulated beliefs and values, and intellectual excitement in one's professional practice (Byrnes, 2001).

14.4 Creating educational goals in collegiate FL cultural studies programmes

As constituted in the United States, collegiate foreign language departments have over the last 2–3 decades become literary-cultural studies departments, that is, they have expanded their content interests from narrowly conceived national canonical literature departments to broadly conceived cultural studies departments (Byrnes, 2002b). While the relationship to the study of their respective languages has been ambivalent all along, the recent cultural turn has made an already burdened relationship downright problematic. On the literature side it has privileged a highly theorized notion of culture and text that, quite ironically, has moved further and further away from engagement with those texts and attributes intellectual merit primarily to various interpretive theories – Marxist, feminist, psychological, queer, post-structuralist, hermeneutic, and the like. Concurrently, on the language side, communicative language teaching and its goals, not to mention its entire conceptual apparatus, has created an alien and alienating world of language teaching that is far removed from the literary-cultural interests of the department – quite literally another discourse world. As I once observed quite casually: To my accomplished colleagues in literary cultural studies the dominant shibboleths of the FL studies field of 'input' and 'output' are quite off-putting.

The consequences of this kind of complementary schismogenesis, to use Bateson's term, are starkly obvious even with a minimalist description. FL departments labour under a debilitating bifurcation between so called 'language' courses for the first 2–4 semesters and so called 'content' courses of various literary-cultural foci for the remaining time of the undergraduate programme. Another way to describe the scene would be in terms of content-indifferent language courses and language-indifferent content courses, with only token continuity between these two separate worlds (Byrnes and Maxim, 2004). As a result, learners have to create their own coherence in their courses of study. Worse yet, faculty power rests with the literary cultural scholars whose professional background includes only the most rudimentary education in language teaching and learning, compelling them to fall back on little more than received folk wisdom about what is good language teaching and appropriate learner development. And here the original sin of the enterprise takes on near tragic dimensions: On one hand faculty expect high levels of grammatical and lexical accuracy, fluency, and complexity of their students, who oftentimes have experienced only very short periods of study; on the other hand, they want these same learners to engage in nuanced reading, discussing, and writing about literary texts in ways that would honour many a native user of the language.

In a recent, unusually bluntly worded report 'Foreign languages and higher education: New structures for a changed world', the Modern Language Association (2007), the largest humanities professional association in the United States, has therefore concluded that this bifurcated programme model in nearly all FL departments must be overcome, to be replaced with a 'more coherent curriculum in which language, culture, and literature are taught as a continuous whole' (2007: 237). It is difficult not to agree with that sentiment. However, it is also difficult to see how the educational goals put forward in the report, namely translingual and transcultural competence, can possibly be attained in departments that are so unable to see their work in literary cultural studies as fundamentally language-based, more precisely foreign language-based, with all the consequences that entails.

There is little need to elaborate on the resulting educational dilemma. But, putting a positive spin on matters, there is then also little need to argue in support of the change that I have advocated in this chapter, namely that core tenets of systemic functional linguistics could provide an unusually advantageous path towards intellectual wholeness on the part of FL departments in terms of their educational vision and goals. The following points are no more than a general trajectory of development on the part of the entire faculty:

The integrative task before departments is to recognize that the entire language system, not just its words, expresses culture, thereby providing a window for understanding a culture in terms of the topics or content it treats in all manner of texts, written and otherwise. That makes *how* the language system does so through its lexicogrammatical resources and their particular forms of deployment in the range of oral and written texts the intellectually intriguing question to be put before a faculty group. Fortunately, it appears that just such a textual focus, more than anything else, can enable the literature faculty to imagine themselves as linking the foreign language studies field and SFL (Byrnes, 2001; Byrnes *et al.*, 2006). Not surprisingly, for my own colleagues, that kind of reflective engagement with textual knowing became particularly plausible through the construct of genre. Genre became a way of demonstrating how language and culture, knowing and meaning, text and context, text and co-text, use and meaning might be integrated *in educational settings*, not only in the outside world. Here they found it possible to start exploring *how* texts differ in their forms of realization when they accomplish more one goal than another, to examine how similar goals, both large and small, can be accomplished differently in different linguistic and cultural contexts, and how that might differ across times. Gradually that enabled them to understand what Bazerman and Prior (2004: 3) have well summarized when they say: 'These questions focus on *what texts do* and *how texts mean* rather than *what texts mean*'. Of course, what texts mean will continue to be of paramount interest in a foreign language literary cultural studies department, but a focus on the *how* can provide the 'aha' moment necessary for setting in motion the process of linking meaning and knowing in languaging.

14.5 Towards developing a curriculum

But that is only the first half of the story. The second half is taken up by the task of specifying a developmental path through a professionally informed statement about the educational experiences learners should encounter in order to develop towards high levels of FL capacities, that is, a curriculum. It stands to reason that, if FL departments have had great difficulty envisioning a conceptually integrated field, they have been even more challenged to imagine a vertical curricular integration. That challenge begins with something as basic as imagining the beginning and a reasonable end point for an educational programme. As previously stated, what is 'reasonable' is knowable only after a series of articulated proposals have been made about valued possible outcomes for each instructional level of a programme and all of them put together, after one has made a concerted effort to realize them through the educative process, and then, in a last step, has assessed the learning outcomes *in light of the proposal* (Pfeiffer and Byrnes, 2009).

Just as a new understanding of textual meaning-making was crucial, so a new kind of understanding of the nature of curriculum, and therefore curriculum development, turned out to be a way of engaging my faculty colleagues in the department. All too often curriculum is understood in normative fashion, following a simplistic means–end model. By contrast, the noted British curriculum specialist Stenhouse (1975) defines a curriculum as 'an attempt to communicate the essential principles and features of an educational proposal in such a form that it is open to critical scrutiny and capable of effective translation into practice' (p. 4). That means that informed practitioners first imagine a curriculum as a possibility of worthwhile or valued forms of knowledge and then find ways of studying the experience of putting it into place through instruction. Both aspects require much collaborative talk and much collaborative action. Our faculty group came to summarize this formative experience by recognizing that it was in the doing of curriculum development and instruction that we gained increasingly sophisticated forms of educational knowing.

Such an understanding of curriculum in time also enabled the next conceptual move, namely an increasing appreciation for and increasingly fine-grained understanding of the nature of the relevant forces during language development and their complex interplay over extended periods of language learning. Specifically, if the semiotic meaning-making nature of language is to be implicated in adult FL learning and development – and that claim is at the heart of linking content and FL learning within a literacy orientation – these contours must make it possible to project a two-way link: one that spells out how the meaning-making potential of learners' available linguistic resources bolsters their capacity to learn the FL as a formal system, and a second one that investigates how linguistic resources enable learners to expand their FL meaning-making capacities, particularly in extended texts (Byrnes, 2002a).

To restate the obvious, such a fluid, energy-laden, dynamic interplay must be imagined as occurring along an entire curricular pathway in line with Clare Painter's (1996) insight: 'there is a symbiotic relation between learning through language [the content] and developing language itself ... it involves actualizing the semiotic systems of knowledge and language into text and continuously reinterpreting the systems on the basis of new experiences in texts' (1996: 80–81). A study that I have recently published investigated that phenomenon through a closer look at the relationship of syntactic abilities and textual abilities via the concept of grammatical metaphor, by observing development in both areas longitudinally (see Byrnes, 2009).

Let me conclude this discussion of the task of curriculum development like this: Once texts, or more specifically textual genres, have come to be understood as central to the educational enterprise, are there ways in which the central task of any curriculum development, namely selection and sequencing of educational experiences – here text-based educational experiences – can be motivated in a principled way in order to come up with the desired curricular proposal? In the experience of the Georgetown German Department three continua proved particularly useful. SFL scholars, of course, will immediately recognize their proximity to SFL thinking: the oral–written continuum, a semiotic continuum, and a generic continuum.

The oral–written continuum makes it possible to array texts in terms of Michael Halliday's felicitous distinction of the two types of complexity of spoken and written discourse and their attendant different ways of meaning: 'speech as spun out, flowing, choreographic, oriented towards events ... Process-like, intricate, with meanings related serially; writing as dense, structured, crystalline, oriented toward things (entities, objectified processes), product-like, tight, with meanings related as components' (2002: 350).

The semiotic continuum is built on the assumption that there is a movement in semiosis, from more 'congruent' forms to more 'non-congruent' or 'metaphorical' forms. Importantly, this shift is both a linguistic and a meaning-making phenomenon, whereby congruent semiosis retains a relatively direct line to experience, while non-congruent semiosis makes that connection more indirect, therefore a site for potential additional meaning-making (cf. Halliday, 1994: xix). It is here that the enormous power of grammatical metaphor comes into play; it is most readily grasped when it is realized through nominalizations, especially deverbal and deadjectival nominalizations, but of course is realized in numerous other ways throughout the system (Byrnes, 2009; Ryshina-Pankova and Byrnes, 2013).

Finally, genres are an accessible way of imagining a curricular progression so as to facilitate language learning. Their central quality is, of course, that they instantiate registerial bundles into staged, goal-oriented language-based activity types (see, among others, Jones *et al.*, 1989; Rothery, 1989, 1996; Martin, 1993, 1999, 2002, 2009; Matthiessen, 1993, 2006; Macken-Horarik, 1996; Martin and Rose, 2003, 2008; Coffin, 2006). Another way of staging genres across a curriculum is inspired by Jim Gee, the noted American discourse and literacy scholar, who distinguishes between the primary discourses of non-specialized everyday life and the secondary discourses of public life in the wider community, particularly institutional, professional, and academic life (2002). In a nice extra touch, one can array these discourses in line with Bakhtin's notion of dialogicality in diverse genres (1981, 1986). Here the continuum would move from the overt dialogicality of the utterance as prototypically occurring in conversations and, by implication, more oral forms of writing, to the covert dialogicality of intratextual aspects of coherence and cohesion, and, even further, into various forms of intertextual reference (Wertsch, 2006).

Considering all three continua provides a decision-making framework that is at once specific enough to be useful and flexible enough to be adaptable and open to local choices. For our curriculum they might be summarized like this:

1. The curriculum begins with narrative genres that focus on the verbal system, the heart of what SFL refers to as congruent semiosis, which builds up the major features of the transitivity system – participants, processes and circumstances – in real-life situations and reaches towards complex clause structures and their potential for building up logical relationships (Teruya, 2006; Ryshina-Pankova, 2010).

2. The next stage are genres that move towards non-congruent or metaphorical realizations of the world in public life but still primarily involve human participants in their relationships to societal issues and values, particularly through the nominalization processes afforded by GM (Byrnes, 2009; Ryshina-Pankova and Byrnes, 2013); and

3. Finally, the bulk of the programme focuses on diverse academic and institutional genres that feature both human and abstract actors in created textual spaces, while expanding the kinds of verbal processes, chunks, collocations, and phrasal stems necessary for further enhancing already competent GM use in different general and disciplinary and content areas (Byrnes *et al.*, 2006; Crane, 2006; Rinner and Weigert, 2006).

What has been created in this fashion is a proposal for *a language-based approach to language learning and teaching* across an extended curricular sequence that will integrate content and language learning towards cross-cultural literacies. At the same time, it constitutes a proposal for how one might both imagine and foster instructed language development. Even though I will not be able to address either of these crucial topics, I trust that readers will have no difficulty seeing its potential for a principled pedagogy as well as for beneficial forms of assessment (Byrnes, 2002; Matthiessen *et al.*, 1992).

14.6 Concluding reflections

Systemic-functional linguistics has quite correctly been identified as a theory of language that is nearly unique for its interest in receiving inspiration from 'societal' problems to be solved, from 'questions' being asked, and from the 'demands' this raises for theory construction. It has also become known as an education-friendly theory, not in the simple sense, but in that it has recognized and theorized the enormous influence of educational activity on language development for individual and societal language use, for knowing and for being. It has done so by considering the relation between education and language development on the part of the individual and education and language development in terms of the system language.

I can think of few tasks in the contemporary world that constitute such a deep challenge for societies as does the task of enabling people to become linguistically multicompetent citizens of their countries and of the world. Accepting the consequences of that configuration will no doubt severely challenge our disciplinary thinking, indeed our academic positioning and posturing in our disciplines inasmuch as they will require a rededication to a public orientation for our scholarship. Thus, Martin Bygate (2004), a past president of the International Association for Applied Linguistics, a few years back observed that the gradual emergence of the field of applied linguistics as a generic discipline has created two major challenges in the relationship between the academy and the lay community: (1) the challenge of identifying and studying issues held to be problems by those outside the academy; and (2) the challenge of clarifying the nature of the contributions of research to those real world problems. In a similar vein, Lourdes Ortega (2005) underscored that what we know and believe about L2 learning and teaching does matter, most particularly in educational contexts, 'because the stakes are high for many groups of people who need formal instruction in a language other than their mother tongue (or tongues) in order to have access to basic educational and societal rights' (2005: 319). Finally, from the standpoint of assessment, too, research has generally not advanced assessment models that respond to the educative needs of foreign language educational contexts, precisely because it has not offered a principled way of addressing what language development would mean in an instructed setting (see Norris and Ortega, 2000, 2003; Norris, 2006).

History does not repeat itself. But in preparing this chapter I was struck by the parallel between the current moment and a moment in the history of SFL theorizing and practice that occurred in the 1980s and 1990s. At that time, the societal problem was the need to enhance literacy teaching and learning across all sectors of schooling in Australia. The move by SFL researchers like James Martin, Frances Christie, Caroline Coffin, Mary Macken-Horarik, Susan Hood and Joan Rothery, among others, to apply SFL insights to that issue had important consequences on both sides. On the education side, it allowed teachers to come to see grammar as a meaning-making resource in language, thereby enabling them to help their students to deploy those resources in oral and written texts. On the side of SFL theorizing it led to ever greater specification of the construct of genre, as a textual unit that connected a certain text type with a situation type, that is, with a context of situation within a context of culture.

In a similar vein, I suggest that a critical current societal problem is that of assuring a kind of multiliterate capacity. I chose collegiate foreign language departments as a particularly revealing site for understanding the nature of that 'problem' and I proposed that one might learn to grapple with it, in theory, research and educational practice, through the overarching construct of 'instructed foreign language development', an issue that is of paramount importance in a global, multicultural and multilingual world, where development will encompass the simultaneous acquisition of both literary cultural content and language (Byrnes, 2013). What makes this challenge so potent is that few notions in applied linguistics, in SLA research, in educational, and in societal practice are as central as the notion of ontogenetic development through schooling. What makes it potent as well is that a multi-perspectival language-cum-literary cultural-knowledge development in an instructed setting is also one of the least understood areas despite the fact that its specification touches the core of the field's identity, values and beliefs.

To the extent that SFL could help specify what a truly functionally oriented way of understanding the simultaneous development of language abilities and cultural literacy in an instructed setting is all about, what it can be all about, and what it must be all about, it would contribute to reshaping central educational activities. I leave it to SFL scholars to imagine as well how the very activities that I am proposing might also stretch SFL constructs into new conceptual territory, thereby benefiting an intellectual house that has, for many of us, become our intellectual home.

References

Developing multiple literacies: A curriculum renewal project of the German Department at Georgetown University, 1997–2000. (2000) http://www1.georgetown.edu/departments/german/programs/undergraduate/curriculum/.

Bakhtin, M. M. (1981) *The Dialogic Imagination. Four Essays by M. M. Bakhtin*. M. Holquist (ed.) Austin, TX: University of Texas Press.

Bakhtin, M. M. (1986) The problem of speech genres. In C. Emerson and M. Holquist (eds) *M. M. Bakhtin. Speech Genres and Other Late Essays*, 60–102. Austin, TX: University of Texas Press.

Bazerman, C. and Prior, P. (2004) Introduction. In C. Bazerman and P. Prior (eds) *What Writing Does and How It Does It. An Introduction to Analyzing Texts and Textual Practices*, 1–10. Mahwah, NJ: Lawrence Erlbaum.

Bygate, M. (2004) Some trends in applied linguistics: Towards a generic view. *AILA Review* 17: 6–22.

Byrnes, H. (1998) Constructing curricula in collegiate foreign language departments. In H. Byrnes (ed.) *Learning Foreign and Second Languages: Perspectives in Research and Scholarship*, 262–295. New York: Modern Language Association.

Byrnes, H. (2001) Reconsidering graduate students' education as teachers: It takes a department! *Modern Language Journal* 85: 512–530.

Byrnes, H. (2002a) The role of task and task-based assessment in a content-oriented collegiate FL curriculum. *Language Testing* 19: 419–437.

Byrnes, H. (2002b) The cultural turn in foreign language departments. Challenge and opportunity. *Profession 2002*: 114–129.

Byrnes, H. (2002c) Toward academic-level foreign language abilities: Reconsidering foundational assumptions, expanding pedagogical options. In B. L. Leaver and B. Shekhtman (eds) *Developing Professional-level Language Proficiency*, 34–58. Cambridge: Cambridge University Press.

Byrnes, H. (2006a) A semiotic perspective on culture and foreign language teaching: Implications for collegiate materials development. In V. Galloway and B. Cothran (eds) *Language and Culture out of Bounds: Discipline-blurred Perspectives on the Foreign Language Classroom*, 37–66. Boston, MA: Heinle Thomson.

Byrnes, H. (ed.) (2006b) Perspectives: Interrogating communicative competence as a framework for collegiate foreign language study. *Modern Language Journal* 90: 244–266.

Byrnes, H. (2006c) What kind of resource is language and why does it matter for advanced language learning? An introduction. In H. Byrnes (ed.) *Advanced Language Learning: The Contribution of Halliday and Vygotsky*, 1–28. London: Continuum.

Byrnes, H. (2007) Language acquisition and language learning. In D. Nicholls (ed.) *Introduction to Scholarship in Modern Languages and Literatures* (3rd edn), 48–69. New York: Modern Language Association.

Byrnes, H. (2008) Assessing content and language. In E. Shohamy (ed.) *Language Testing and Assessment* Vol. 7, 37–52. Berlin: Springer-Kluwer Academic Publishers.

Byrnes, H. (2009) Emergent L2 German writing ability in a curricular context: A longitudinal study of grammatical metaphor. *Linguistics and Education* 20: 50–66.

Byrnes, H. (2011a) Beyond writing as language learning or content learning: Construing foreign language writing as meaning-making. In R. M. Manchón (ed.) *Learning-to-Write and Writing-to-Learn in an Additional Language*, 137–157. Philadelphia, PA/Amsterdam: John Benjamins.

Byrnes, H. (2011b) Reconsidering graduate students' education as scholar-teachers: Mind your language! In H. W. Allen and H. H. Maxim (eds) *Educating the Future Foreign Language Professoriate for the 21st Century*, 17–42. Boston, MA: Heinle Cengage Learning.

Byrnes, H. (2012) Of frameworks and the goals of collegiate foreign language education: Critical reflections. *Applied Linguistics Review* 3: 1–24.

Byrnes, H. (2013) Renting language in the ownership society. Reflections on language and language learning in a multilingual world. In J. Arnold and T. Murphey (eds) *Meaningful Action. Earl Stevick's Influence on Language Teaching*, 216–234. Cambridge: Cambridge University Press.

Byrnes, H. (2014, in press) Theorizing language development at the intersection of 'task' and L2 writing: Reconsidering complexity. In H. Byrnes and R. M. Manchón (eds) *Task-based Language Learning: Insights from and for L2 Writing*. Philadelphia, PA/Amsterdam: John Benjamins.

Byrnes, H. and Maxim, H. H. (2004) Introduction: Creating sites for collegiate advanced foreign language learning. In H. Byrnes and H. H. Maxim (eds) *Advanced Language Learning: A Challenge to College Programs*, vii–xv. Boston, MA: Heinle Thomson.

Byrnes, H., Crane, C., Maxim, H. H. and Sprang, K. A. (2006) Taking text to task: Issues and choices in curriculum construction. *ITL: International Journal of Applied Linguistics* 152: 85–110.

Byrnes, H., Maxim, H. H. and Norris, J. M. (2010) Realizing advanced L2 writing development in collegiate FL education: Curricular design, pedagogy, assessment. *Modern Language Journal 94* S-1[Monograph].

Christie, F. (1989) Language development in education. In R. Hasan and J. R. Martin (eds) *Language Development: Learning Language, Learning Culture*, 152–198. Norwood, NJ: Ablex.

Christie, F. and Derewianka, B. (2008) *School Discourse: Learning to Write across the Years of Schooling*. London: Continuum.

Coffin, C. (2006) *Historical Discourse: The Language of Time, Cause and Evaluation*. London: Continuum.

Crane, C. (2006) Modelling a genre-based foreign language curriculum: Staging advanced L2 learning. In H. Byrnes (ed.) *Advanced Language Learning: The Contribution of Halliday and Vygotsky*, 227–245. London: Continuum.

Crane, C., Liamkina, O. and Ryshina-Pankova, M. (2004) Fostering advanced level language abilities in foreign language graduate programs: Applications of genre theory. In H. Byrnes and H. H. Maxim (eds) *Advanced Foreign Language Learning: A Challenge to College Programs*, 150–177. Boston, MA: Heinle-Thomson.

Doughty, C. J. and Long, M. H. (eds) (2003) *The Handbook of Second Language Acquisition.* Malden, MA: Blackwell.

Dörnyei, Z. (2009) The L2 motivational self system. In Z. Dörnyei and E. Ushioda (eds) *Motivation, Language Identity and the L2 Self,* 9–42. Bristol: Multilingual Matters.

Gee, J. P. (2002) Literacies, identities, and discourses. In M. J. Schleppegrell and M. Cecilia Colombi (eds) *Developing Advanced Literacy in First and Second Languages: Meaning with Power,* 159–175. Mahwah, NJ: Lawrence Erlbaum.

Halliday, M. A. K. (1973) *Explorations in the Functions of Language. Explorations in Language Study.* London: Edward Arnold.

Halliday, M. A. K. (1975). *Learning How to Mean: Explorations in the Development of Language.* London: Edward Arnold.

Halliday, M. A. K. (1993) Towards a language-based theory of learning. *Linguistics and Education* 5: 93–116.

Halliday, M. A. K. (1994) *An Introduction to Functional Grammar* (2nd edn). London: Edward Arnold.

Halliday, M. A. K. (1996) On grammar and grammatics. In R. Hasan, C. Cloran and D. G. Butt (eds) *Functional Descriptions: Theory in Practice,* 1–38. Philadelphia, PA/Amsterdam: John Benjamins.

Halliday, M. A. K. (1999) Grammar and the construction of educational knowledge. In R. Berry, B. Asker, K. Hyland and M. Lam (eds) *Language Analysis, Description and Pedagogy,* 70–87. Hong Kong: Language Centre, The Hong Kong University of Science & Technology and Department of English, Lingnan University.

Halliday, M. A. K. (2002) Spoken and written modes of meaning. In J. J. Webster (ed.) *On Grammar,* 323–351. London: Continuum.

Halliday, M. A. K. (2004a) On grammar as the driving force from primary to higher-order consciousness. In G. Williams and A. Lukin (eds) *The Development of Language: Functional Perspectives on Species and Individuals,* 15–44. London: Continuum.

Halliday, M. A. K. (2004b) Three aspects of children's language development: Learning language, learning through language, learning about language (1980). In J. J. Webster (ed.) *The Language of Early Childhood,* 308–326. London: Continuum.

Halliday, M. A. K. (2007a) Is learning a second language like learning a first language all over again? (1978). In J. J. Webster (ed.) *Language and Education,* 174–193. London: Continuum.

Halliday, M. A. K. (2007b) *Language and Education.* J. J. Webster (ed.) (Vol. 9). London: Continuum.

Halliday, M. A. K. (2007c) A language development approach to education (1994). In J. J. Webster (ed.) *Language and Education,* 368–382. London: Continuum.

Halliday, M. A. K. (2007d) On the concept of 'educational linguistics' (1990). In J. J. Webster (ed.) *Language and Education,* 354–367. London: Continuum.

Halliday, M. A. K. and Matthiessen, C. M. I. M. (1999) *Construing Experience through Meaning: A Language-Based Approach to Cognition.* London/New York: Continuum.

Hasan, R. and Martin, J. R. (eds) (1989) *Language Development: Learning Language, Learning Culture.* Norwood, NJ: Ablex.

Jones, J., Gollin, S., Drury, H. and Economou, D. (1989) Systemic-functional linguistics and its application to the TESOL curriculum. In R. Hasan and J. R. Martin (eds) *Language Development: Learning Language, Learning Culture,* 257–328. Norwood, NJ: Ablex.

Macken-Horarik, M. (1996) Literacy and learning across the curriculum: Towards a model of register for secondary school teachers. In R. Hasan and G. Williams (eds) *Literacy in Society,* 232–278. London: Longman.

Martin, J. R. (1993) Genre and literacy – modeling context in educational linguistics. *Annual Review of Applied Linguistics* 13: 141–172.

Martin, J. R. (1999) Mentoring semogenesis: 'Genre-based' literacy pedagogy. In F. Christie (ed.) *Pedagogy and the Shaping of Consciousness: Linguistic and Social Processes,* 123–155. London: Cassell.

Martin, J. R. (2002) Writing history: Construing time and value in discourses of the past. In M. J. Schleppegrell and M. C. Colombi (eds) *Developing Advanced Literacy in First and Second Languages: Meaning with Power,* 87–118. Mahwah, NJ: Lawrence Erlbaum.

Martin, J. R. (2009) Genre and language learning: A social semiotic perspective. *Linguistics and Education* 20: 10–21.

Martin, J. R. and Rose, D. (2003) *Working with Discourse: Meaning beyond the Clause.* London: Continuum.

Martin, J. R. and Rose, D. (2008) *Genre Relations: Mapping Culture.* London: Equinox.

Matthiessen, C. M. I. M. (1993) Register in the round: Diversity in a unified theory of register analysis. In M. Ghadessy (ed.) *Register Analysis: Theory and Practice,* 221–292. London: Pinter.

Matthiessen, C. M. I. M. (2006) Educating for advanced foreign language capacities: Exploring the meaning-making resources of languages systemic-functionally. In H. Byrnes (ed.) *Advanced Language Learning: The Contribution of Halliday and Vygotsky,* 31–57. London: Continuum.

Matthiessen, C. M. I. M. (2009) Meaning in the making: Meaning potential emerging from acts of meaning. *Language Learning, 59-Suppl. 1*: 206–229.

Matthiessen, C., Slade, D. and Macken, M. (1992) Language in context: A new model for evaluating student writing. *Linguistics and Education* 4: 173–193.

MLA Ad Hoc Committee on Foreign Languages (2007) Foreign languages and higher education: New structures for a changed world. *Profession* 2007: 234–245.

Norris, J. M. (2006) Assessing advanced foreign language learning and learners: From measurement constructs to educational uses. In H. Byrnes, H. Weger-Guntharp and K. Sprang (eds) *Educating for Advanced Foreign Language Capacities: Constructs, Curriculum, Instruction, Assessment,* 167–187. Washington, DC: Georgetown University Press.

Norris, J. M. and Ortega, L. (2000) Effectiveness of L2 instruction: A research synthesis and quantitative meta-analysis. *Language Learning* 50: 417–528.

Norris, J. M. and Ortega, L. (2003) Defining and measuring SLA. In C. Doughty and M. H. Long (eds) *Handbook of Second Language Acquisition,* 716–761. London: Blackwell.

Norris, J. M. and Pfeiffer, P. C. (2003) Exploring the use and usefulness of ACTFL oral proficiency ratings and standards in college foreign language departments. *Foreign Language Annals* 36: 572–581.

Ortega, L. (2005) For what and for whom is our research? The ethical as transformative lens in instructed SLA. *Modern Language Journal* 89: 427–443.

Painter, C. (1996) The development of language as a resource for thinking: A linguistic view of learning. In R. Hasan and G. Williams (eds) *Literacy and Society*, 50–85. London: Longman.

Pfeiffer, P. C. and Byrnes, H. (2009) Curriculum, learning, and the identity of majors: A case study of program outcomes evaluation. In J. M. Norris, J. McE. Davis, C. Sinicrope and Y. Watanabe (eds) *Toward Useful Program Evaluation in College Foreign Language Education*, 183–208. Honolulu, HI: National Foreign Language Resource Center Monograph series.

Rinner, S. and Weigert, A. (2006) From sports to the EU economy: Integrating curricula through genre-based content courses. In H. Byrnes and H. H. Maxim (eds) *Advanced Language Learning: A Challenge to College Programs*, 136–151. Boston, MA: Heinle Thomson.

Rothery, J. (1989) Learning about language. In R. Hasan and J. R. Martin (eds) *Language Development: Learning Language, Learning Culture*, 199–256. Norwood, NJ: Ablex.

Rothery, J. (1996) Making changes: Developing an educational linguistics. In R. Hasan and G. Williams (eds) *Literacy in Society*, 86–123. London: Longman.

Ryshina-Pankova, M. (2010) Towards mastering the discourses of reasoning: Use of grammatical metaphor at advanced levels of foreign language acquisition. *Modern Language Journal* 92: 181–197.

Ryshina-Pankova, M. and Byrnes, H. (2013) Writing as learning to know: Tracing knowledge construction in L2 German compositions. *Journal of Second Language Writing* 22: 179–197.

Schleppegrell, M. J. (2004) *The Language of Schooling: A Functional Linguistics Perspective*. Mahwah, NJ: Lawrence Erlbaum.

Stenhouse, L. (1975) *An Introduction to Curriculum Research and Development*. London: Heinemann.

Teruya, K. (2006) Grammar as a resource for the construction of language logic for advanced language learning in Japanese. In H. Byrnes (ed.) *Advanced Language Learning: The Contribution of Halliday and Vygotsky*, 109–133. London: Continuum.

Wertsch, J. V. (2006) Generalized collective dialogue and advanced foreign language capacities. In H. Byrnes (ed.) *Advanced Language Learning: The Contribution of Halliday and Vygotsky*, 58–71. London: Continuum.

15 Systemic Functional Linguistics and Corpus Linguistics: Interconnections and current state

Mick O'Donnell[*]

15.1 Introduction

Both Corpus Linguistics (CL) and Systemic Functional Linguistics (SFL) came into being as disciplines in the early 1960s, and have both developed strongly in the intervening years. In the 50 years that the two linguistic disciplines have co-existed, it is only recently that the two disciplines have started to have much to do with each other. While there have been anecdotal connections throughout their history, SFL has not been at the centre of CL, nor has CL been taken seriously within SFL, until recently.

This chapter will explore some of the reasons for the lack of interaction between these two disciplines. We will first outline the history of CL to provide some background to the subsequent discussion as to why CL has not made much use of SFL. We will then discuss why SFL has not made much use of CL.

In the final section, we will discuss ways in which SFL and CL are currently beginning to profit from each other, and ways in which the tools and methodology of corpus linguistics still need to be developed in order to fully support the needs of a sociological oriented theory such as SFL.

15.2 The evolution of Corpus Linguistics

15.2.1 Studies using non-digital corpora

It was really with the introduction of computers that CL as a discipline became a reality, but the use of corpora to study language by no means

* Mick O'Donnell is a lecturer in English Studies at the Universidad Autónoma de Madrid, Spain.

began with the computer. As early as the thirteenth century, monks were compiling concordances of the Christian bible by hand, indexing the occurrence of all non-function words.[1] During the 1950s, J. R. Firth investigated collocation in text, which required hand-counting of word co-occurrences in a collection of texts (Firth, 1957).

At this time, others were compiling corpora as resources to help in the description of English grammar, first by C. C. Fries (Fries, 1952), based on a 250,000-word corpus of recorded telephone conversations. During the 1960s, a team led by Randolph Quirk collected a one million word corpus which was used to develop 'The Survey of English Usage' (Quirk, 1968). This corpus, originally on paper, was used to inform the study of English grammar, and led to a number of well-known grammar reference works, including *A Comprehensive Grammar of the English Language* (Quirk *et al.*, 1985).

15.2.2 Studies using unannotated computational corpora

As access to computers became more widespread, corpus texts were entered on computers, which allowed the processing power of the computer to replace manual work.

During the 1960s, researchers at Brown University created a one million word digitalized corpus of standard American English, called the *Brown corpus*, which they used for various statistical studies of English (Kucera and Francis, 1967). This corpus lacked any tagging at all, and thus their findings consisted of reports such as word frequencies, etc.

Also during the 1960s, John Sinclair, later director of the COBUILD project, was involved in a UK-government funded project (funded by OSTI) to explore collocation patterns. His team constructed a 135,000 word corpus of spoken conversation transcripts, and used computer programs to search for collocational patterns of specified terms (see Sinclair *et al.*, 2004, first printed 1970). This was reportedly the first electronic corpus of spoken language (Krishnamurthy, 2004: xiv).

During the 1970s, a computational corpus of British English was established by a team led by Geoffrey Leech at Lancaster University, and from 1977, the corpus was taken over and extended by a group led by Stig Johansson at the University of Oslo in Norway. The corpus is now called the Lancaster-Oslo/Bergen (*LOB*) corpus. Again, the text was not tagged at that time, except for marking headings, quoted material, etc.

In the late 1970s, Quirk's 'Survey of English usage' corpus was digitalized by a group at Lund University in Sweden, and rebranded as the 'London-Lund corpus', which is still in use today.

Unannotated digital corpora such as these provide the basis for automatic concordance studies, whereby occurrences of particular terms can be returned, along with the preceding and following context (often in 'KWIC' tables – Keyword in Context).

For the most part, an unannotated corpus supports the study of the patterning of particular words. For instance, the researcher can find all instances of the word 'after', and classify the particular lexical environments in which the term occurs.

The use of unannotated corpora does permit some level of grammatical study, where such studies can be defined in terms of words. For instance, to check the prevalence of clausal negation in a particular corpus, one can search for sentences containing 'not' vs. sentences without this word. Note however that without more linguistic information, mistakes will be made, for instance, sentences such as 'John but not Mary arrived.' include 'not', but are not instances of clausal negation.

Wildcard matching can also be used to perform grammatical analysis of the corpus. For instance, the pattern '*ing' will match mostly gerund verbs, but note that it will also match nouns such as 'swing', 'ring', 'netting', etc. Grammatical studies using such patterns consequently need some level of human filtering to eliminate false matches, which on a large corpus, can be time consuming. Also, the types of grammatical phenomena which can be identified using such patterns is quite limited (e.g. distinguishing third-person singular verbs by a final '-s' fails because plural nouns usually end with the same pattern (e.g. 'runs')).

15.2.3 Studies based on POS-tagged corpora

During the 1970s, some of the existing untagged corpora were tagged, at least with part-of-speech (POS) information, providing word classes (noun, verb, etc.) and inflectional information. The Brown corpus was tagged using one of the earliest POS taggers, called 'TAGGIT' (Greene and Rubin, 1971), with only 70% of tags assigned correctly, which were corrected manually (over several years) using a text editor. During the 1980s, the LOB corpus was also POS-tagged, with their tagger providing around 95% accuracy. More recently, larger corpora have been POS tagged, such as the British National Corpus (BNC), containing 100 million words (Leech *et al.*, 1998). Taggers these days can achieve up to 98% accuracy on the right sort of text.

POS-tagging in a large corpus greatly increases the range of studies that can be reliably performed. Many syntactic features can be expressed in terms of POS patterns. For instance, a search specification '[vb*] [v?n*]' (any form of the verb 'be' followed by any participle verb) will match 90% of English passive clauses, and allowing for one intervening token will capture 7% more of the cases.[2] The occurrence of grammatical systems such as finiteness, modality, tense, aspect and polarity can be queried in the corpus with a reasonable degree of certainty. A standard approach is to retrieve all matches to a specified search query, and eliminate the false matches. An examination of a small sample of the text itself can be used to estimate the percentage of cases which were missed by the automatic search.

In this way, one can perform certain types of linguistic studies, using large corpora to guarantee that the results are reasonably significant.

It is worth mentioning here *WordSmith* (Scott, 2004), which is a tool for searching in a tagged corpora (and in untagged corpora also). Probably more corpus studies have been done with this software than with any other software. The *WordSmith* website lists almost 350 publications which have used *WordSmith* for the research, and this is certainly only a fraction of the actual total.[3]

15.2.4 Syntactically parsed corpora

Syntactic parsers for English have existed since the 1960s, although the early ones could not handle the majority of sentences that occur in real text, and even those it parsed were often given an incorrect parse.

In the 1980s, some parsers (for phrase structure grammar) were producing better results, with large sets of rules and lexicons, written by grammarians. Some corpora were automatically tagged with syntactic structure (NP ^VP, etc.), and then humans manually edited the tagging where wrong. During the early 1990s, the *Cobuild* corpus (collected in a project directed by John Sinclair) was syntactically annotated by a team at the University of Helsinki, using such a rule-based parser.

In the mid-1980s, statistical parsers were coming into use, parsers which, given a parsed corpus (a treebank), could derive their own model of the language. Then, the parser could be used to parse previously unseen texts, getting higher rates of accuracy than the parsers using human-constructed grammars/lexicons.

However, it was only in the last few years that parsers have produced results reliable enough to be used without much human editing, e.g. the Stanford Parser (Klein and Manning, 2003), the Charniak parser (Charniak, 2000), and the Collins parser (Collins, 1999). While mistakes are still made, purely automatic parsing can be applied to large corpora (100s of millions of words), and such a large set of parses can be used for many valuable studies, even with the errors.

15.2.5 Semantically parsed corpora

While within SFL, 'semantics' refers to all of ideational, interpersonal and textual meaning, in the general CL community (and related communities), 'semantics' refers to just ideational semantics: the ontological classes of entities and processes, and the semantic relations between them.

There has been substantial work in the last 10 years on the task of semantic tagging of text, particularly in relation to what is called 'the semantic web'. The idea here is that if each noun phrase in a text is tagged by a semantic class, then web search need not be restricted to searching for words; we can search for concepts instead. We should then be able to find matches to search queries even when web pages do not contain the exact words of our search query: 'doctor' could match 'medic', 'healthcare professional' and 'surgeon', etc.

Semantic tagging usually requires a large semantic dictionary. The most widely used is *WordNet*,[4] for English, and versions exist for many other languages. Polysemy is a major problem, with words such as 'bank' corresponding to several meanings. So one of the basic processes involves *word sense disambiguation*: looking at the words around each word to try and resolve which sense was intended.

Today, semantic tagging of nouns is reasonably robust. However, work on tagging verbs, adjectives, etc. is still in early days.

More ambitious work tries to discover the semantic structure of sentences: how each sentence breaks down into processes, participants and circumstances, and the function labels for each participant.

Probably the most advanced work in this field has made use of FrameNet, a large database providing the semantic dependencies (valencies) for around 10,000 word senses. This resource is based on the work of Charles Fillmore's Frame Semantics (e.g. Fillmore, 1976).

Various semantic parsers have been produced using this resource, perhaps the best known being Gildea and Jurafsky (2002). Note however that reliability of semantic parsing is nowhere near as high as syntactic parsing, and they are currently not suitable for annotating text corpora without a large degree of human post-editing.

15.2.6 Summary

In summary, the history of corpus linguistics has been one of continual advancement in abstraction: initially only dealing with words, POS tagging was added and then syntactic annotation, and more recently, semantic annotation has been added. Each advancement has led to an increase in what the corpus linguist can do with the corpus.

15.3   SFL connections with Corpus Linguistics

Halliday has long been an advocate of using corpus linguistics within SFL, e.g.:

> The study of grammatical frequencies is not, I think, some kind of optional extra: such quantitative patterns are a feature of the lexicogrammaticalisation of meaning, the process by which meaning potential becomes selectively without a limit. The project cannot be other than a corpus project. (Halliday, 2006: 299)

However, the connections between SFL and corpus linguistics before the current century were largely anecdotal. For instance, J. R. Firth, whose study of a non-digital corpus was mentioned above, happened to be the (unofficial) supervisor of Halliday's dissertation, and the main influence on his work.

Another coincidental connection was C. C. Fries, who has been attributed with writing the first corpus-informed grammar. He was the father of Peter Fries, who has been a central figure in Systemic Linguistics, particularly through his contribution to the area of thematic development (e.g. Fries, 1983). C. C. Fries himself however had no connection with SFL.

Quirk, the force behind the 'Survey of English usage' corpus, was responsible for Halliday getting his position as head of Linguistics at University College London. Quirk was not a Firthian, although he took undergraduate classes from him (Quirk, 2002: 241–223).

Perhaps the strongest connection between SFL and CL were through John Sinclair and Cobuild. Sinclair and Halliday were close colleagues. Sinclair was taught by Halliday when Halliday was a lecturer in Edinburgh around 1960. Sinclair was then a fellow teacher with Halliday at Edinburgh University in the early 1960s, and when Sinclair started his OSTI project into collocation, Halliday was a consultant on the design of the project, and was also on the Steering committee of the project (Sinclair *et al.*, 2004: 2).

Later, Halliday was again a consultant on the Cobuild project. In 1991, he spent a few months visiting the Cobuild project offices at Birmingham University. Working with a Cobuild researcher, Zoe James, they explored grammatical patterns using the 18 million words then held in Cobuild's written text section. Halliday states that the major consideration in deciding what to explore was that the phenomena of interest had to be clearly identifiable in the corpus (see Halliday, 2004: 146), and lacking even part-of-speech tagging, this was a difficult problem. Because they could come up with mechanical means for identifying clausal polarity and primary tense with a reasonable degree of accuracy, they settled on exploring these structures.

Interpreting Halliday's influence on Sinclair, we should note that Sinclair was more a neo-Firthian than Hallidayan. The classes Sinclair took with Halliday were before Halliday released his Scale and Category grammar, the precursor to Systemic Grammar. So most of what Sinclair received from Halliday was an exposure to the Firthian approach to language. This is confirmed by comments from one of the Cobuild crew in 2004:

> the neo-Firthian orientation which Birmingham work embodies is based on a commitment to a contextual theory of meaning and the study of authentic language rather than the invented sentences of the 'armchair' linguist. (http://www.hh.se/shl/Engelska/Paddy. htm, November 2004)

The starting point for Sinclair's use of corpora was to explore lexical collocation, which was continuing Firth's earlier work in this area, reported above. Sinclair, in an interview (Teubert, 2004), does make clear that Halliday's work in this area was also influential. Halliday's own work in collocation was published as 'Lexis as a linguistic level' (Halliday, 1966).

Lexis in Halliday's work played a decreasing role in later years, while for Sinclair, lexis was central, and his work focused on lexical patterns in text (with the exception of his work in the 1970s on dialogue).

However, apart from producing dictionaries, the Cobuild project moved towards producing corpus-informed reference grammars. The Collins-Cobuild English grammar (Sinclair, 1990) itself shows some influence from SFL, although it is largely a traditional grammar of the Greenbaum and Quirk variety (cf. Greenbaum and Quirk, 1990). However, some aspects are influenced by SFL, for instance, they use the term 'group' rather than 'phrase', and the book groups structures together based on similarity of what they do, rather than similarity of form (Sinclair, 1990: v). Susan Hunston says that the Pattern Grammar work (e.g. Hunston and Francis, 2000), which was developed within the project, was influenced by SFL:

> If you look at the meaning groups in the pattern grammar books you see traces of assumptions about relevant classes of words, e.g. process types, that can be traced back to Halliday. (Hunston, 2011, personal communication)

Apart from the above connections, inter-relation between SFL and CL were relatively minor until the current century. As will be discussed below, a number of small-corpus studies were done, but were intended on the whole for an SFL audience, not for the CL community.

In the next section, we will discuss why SFL has had little input to CL, and vice versa.

15.4   Why SFL and CL have had little to do with each other

Why have SFL and CL had so little to do with each other until recently? We will look at this question from both sides: why CL has made little use of SFL, and why SFL has until recently ignored CL.

15.4.1 Why CL has made little use of SFL

Corpus Linguistics has been for the most part concerned with using large bodies of text to verify hypotheses about language. The richer the annotation of the text (in both quality and quantity), the better the hypotheses that can be explored. Initially, one million words was considered 'large', although today many corpora contain hundreds of millions of words, or more.

Corpus linguists as a whole are not partisan to any particular linguistic theory: they will use whatever resources are available to achieve their goal of analysing language. When POS tagging was made available by computational linguists, CL leaped on this resource for their own use. As new and improved forms of syntactic analysis have been developed, corpus linguists have made use of them.

Unfortunately, for reasons to be explored below, until recently, none of the techniques for automatic text analysis were informed by SFL. While a subset of corpus linguists may have preferred to work in an SFL environment, the lack of SFL-informed language analysis tools for large corpora made this impossible. CL used those tools which were available.

Force of community history: Related to this point here, the way that corpus technology developed biased the way that corpus linguists in general looked at text. In the 1960s, when only untagged words were available to them, they started looking at words, because that is all that could be done at that point. Those interested in patterns above the word (meaning, discourse, etc.) were forced to find alternative means to find answers to their research questions, and thus (with exceptions) did not become corpus linguists.

This word-based focus has continued to influence CL even today: words and their distribution remains the single most central focus within CL, if one judges by the range of papers at any of the CL conferences, and also from the wide use of WordSmith and similar tools.

The introduction of POS and syntactic tagging allowed more focus on grammar, but the CL's historical orientation towards words remains. One of the greatest advances in CL in recent years, Sketch Engine (Kilgarriff and Tugwell, 2001), applies the power of syntactic parsing to large corpora, but the final goal is still to describe individual words.

15.4.2 Why SFL has made little use of large corpora

The main reasons SFL has made little use of large corpora are just those stated above: it has proved difficult to automatically annotate the kinds of patterns Systemicists are interested in exploring, and thus SFL researchers have not (until recently) been able to use large corpora to answer their research questions.

SFL is fundamentally concerned with language as a social semiotic system, as a means we use to function in social contexts. It is not primarily concerned, as some other linguistic theories are, with explaining how language is structured.

To better link language to the social context, the grammar of an SFL architecture is more abstract ('semantic') than in the post-Chomskian approaches. A basic maxim of Halliday's approach is that language has evolved in the expression of meaning, and we can thus expect the grammar of the language to reflect the way meanings are organized (cf. Halliday, 1978: 22). And since language means in different ways (ideational, interpersonal and textual meaning), SFL proposes a grammar which is multi-layered, each layer related to a particular kind of meaning (usually simplified as: Transitivity, Mood and Theme).

Because of its functional complexity and higher level of semantic abstraction, reliable automatic parsers for Systemic Grammar have not as yet manifested, which means that linguistic studies involving Systemic Grammar need to be based on manually annotated corpora.

Additionally, SFL research rarely stops at the grammar: semantics is an important interface between grammar and the context of language use, and semantics in an SFL model is far more extensive than the semantics in most other theories, taking in what others call pragmatics and discourse analysis as well.

As a result, most linguistic studies in SFL are not concerned with simple lexical or structural concerns. They usually concern how meanings are made in context, or how meanings are expressed differently in different social contexts.

Meanwhile, the tools of corpus linguistics have only been able to produce sequences of words, perhaps their POS tag, and more recently, syntactic information from a very structuralist (non-functional) approach. The information contained in annotated corpora of these kinds does not generally support research into most of the questions SFL practitioners are interested in.

To exemplify, Ruqaiya Hasan's work in the 1970s and 1980s, extending on Basil Bernstein's work, concerned the different strategies that mothers used to interact with their young children (cf. Hasan, 1986; Hasan and

Cloran, 1990). In one part of this work, the focus is on the language used by the mother to regulate the behaviour of the child (e.g., threats, appeals, warnings, etc.), and how the mother's choice of strategy may correlate with their social class.

So, the basic unit of focus here is the act of regulation, which may be realized through a number of speech functions (questions, statements, commands, etc.), and these in turn can be realized in various grammatical expressions.

For this kind of study, automatic recognition of these regulation strategies is close to impossible. Some basic structures may be recognized by lexical patterns (e.g. *if you* ... *I will/won't* ...), but the sheer range of possible realizations of each regulation strategy makes automatic recognition of these categories difficult.

So, in summary, the kind of resources that CL offers (POS-tagging, structuralist syntactic tagging, etc.) have not in general supported the kinds of studies most SFL researchers are interested in.

Having said all the above, we should be aware that this is not a total answer. Halliday and James' study of English tense demonstrated that large corpora can be used to verify SFL hypotheses.

More importantly, we should mention here the work of Doug Biber describing the differences between various registers (1988; 1995). It is significant that the major work using corpora to describe spoken and written registers was not produced by a systemicist. Biber showed that this sort of study was possible with corpus technology, yet until recently, little work was done to replicate this work from an SFL perspective.

15.5 SFL and small corpus studies

Because of the reasons discussed above, few systemic linguists were involved in corpus research on large corpora. Instead, those who did study language through corpora opted for a different approach: the use of small corpora, which have the following advantages:

1. Not limited to the tags provided with the corpus: With manual annotation, the researcher is not limited to the categories provided in the supplied corpus, and are thus free to develop their own categories, regardless of the fact that it is difficult to automate the recognition of these categories. Halliday (2004: 146) talks about the 'triviality trap': 'the easier a thing is to recognize, the less it is worthwhile recognizing it'. We can use POS tagging to discover some patterns in text, but the patterns which are more revealing

about our social context require deeper analysis, such as offered by SFL. I like to compare the use of large pre-annotated corpora to the man who lost his watch in a dark alley, but is searching for it out on the street, because there is more light there. The more interesting patterns in text are not out in the open, not visible under the flood-light of POS-tagged corpora. Rather, we need to go into the darker alleys to find them. And for this, we need to carry our own light, a torch, and manual annotation allows us to move into the darkness.

2. Not limited to the text-types included in the corpus: Another problem of large corpora studies is that the large corpora may not contain the kinds of texts that you are interested in studying. If one is exploring the language of blogs, or of email, the BNC is not a good choice, as it does not contain these text-types. If one is exploring a particular text-type, or the language of a particular kind of writer/speaker, then often the existing corpora will not contain the texts one needs. In such cases, collecting your own corpus is necessary.

3. Not limited to the metadata supplied with the corpus: Large corpora often have good metadata associated to the texts (register, country of collection, etc.), but in many cases the variables that a researcher may wish to study may be missing, e.g. if one is interested in studying linguistic differences in gender, the British National Corpus would not be adequate since it does not provide gender of author in its metadata.

So, given these limitations, those in SFL interested in using corpora to verify their theories against real texts have generally resorted to collecting texts themselves to best support the topic of their investigation, and manually annotated the corpus with a coding scheme they develop themselves.

Because manual annotation is slow, the size of corpora in these studies is generally quite small, often less than 50,000 words.

Given that SFL-oriented corpus studies have been generally restricted to small studies, this section explores the nature of these studies until recently.

15.5.1 Small studies using text editors and spreadsheets

Linguists have performed studies on small corpora since before the computer manifested, reading through printed text for instances of a phenomenon, and counting them. In the 1980s, with the spreading availability of desktop computers, linguists started to use the computer to help them organize their studies. At the most basic, this may have consisted of using a text editor to collect segments of text of interest. More recently, spreadsheet programmes such as Microsoft Excel have been used to organize the data, one column for the text of interest, and other columns to record features of the text, contextual information, etc.

One example of such a study in the 1980s was Guenter Plum's study of contextual conditioning of grammatical choice, realized through a study of a small corpus of 53,000 words of transcribed spoken narrative-like texts (see Plum, 1988).

At much the same time, Suzanne Eggins taped a series of dinner conversations with her friends, and transcribed the conversations. This corpus served as the basis of her study of casual conversation (Eggins, 1990).

While the use of text editors and spreadsheets helped linguists organise their data to a degree, these tools are not designed for linguistic studies and thus offer limited help for such studies. In particular, such studies typically involve collecting only the segments of text that are of interest (e.g. passive clauses), removing the text from its original context.

15.5.2 Small studies using text annotation tools

The spread of accessible computing also brought with it the implementation of software specifically designed for studying text. Probably the earliest software for manual annotation of this kind was the *NUDIST* system (Richards and Richards, 1981), principally designed for sociological studies over sets of documents, but useful for linguistic studies as well. This system started off as an academic system, but has spread in use, and is now the basis of a company with 30 employees (the product is currently called *NVIVO*). *NUDIST* has not been that widely used within linguistics, possibly because it is commercial, and also possibly because it is not directly aimed at linguists.

In the early 1990s, I was working on a Fujitsu-funded project in relation to automatic discourse analysis (see Matthiessen *et al.*, 1991), using SFL. Part of the project involved the development of a parser for Systemic Grammar. To help us focus the development of the grammar on just those structures which were likely to occur in the type of texts we were dealing with (computer manuals), we needed a small corpus of such texts having each clause tagged with the clause-level features from the grammar. I thus developed a tool which could load in a system network (the NIGEL grammar as developed by Christian Matthiessen as part of the PENMAN project, cf. Mann and Matthiessen, 1985), and present each sentence of a text in turn, allowing the user to then walk through the system network, assigning features to the clause. This software was eventually released as *Systemic Coder* (O'Donnell, 1995), and for 10 years was fairly widely used in the SFL community for small corpus annotation. The software allowed the user to provide their own coding scheme for the annotation.

At about the same time, Jonathan Webster developed *Functional Grammar Processor* (FGP), a tool for manual analysis of the function structure of clauses in terms of Transitivity, Mood or Theme (Webster, 1994). The software ran within a word processor (Borland Sprint on IBM-PCs). The software allowed the analysis to be saved as a Prolog database, which could then be studied statistically if the analyst had basic programming skills.

Soon after, two other coding tools were developed within the SFL community, *SysFan*[5] (Wu Canzong and Christian Matthiessen) and *Systemics* (O'Halloran and Judd, 2002). The tools allowed the user to annotate texts both functionally and in terms of features.

These four tools allowed SFL researchers to annotate small corpora with semantic and grammatical categories which are beyond the ability of computers to automatically recognize (sometimes called computer-assisted manual annotation, or CAMA). This has allowed linguists to begin to study systematically the relationship between phenomena previously beyond reach, although with smaller corpora than can be used for studies based on machine-annotated corpora.

Some of the small corpus studies performed with *Systemic Coder* include that of instructional texts (Hartley and Paris, 1996; Bielsa and Delin, 2001), grammatical metaphor (McGowan, 1997), lexical semantics (Sharoff, 2005) and reference (Fontaine, 2007). One notable study was that reported in Neumann (2003), comparing the linguistic differences (in terms of SFL) between English and German travel guides. She manually coded a range of clause systems, including process type, modality, mood, circumstantiation, voice and theme. Her corpus contained around 75,000 words, of which she comments: 'the corpus size chosen for the present study is the maximum that can be handled by one annotator' (2003: 88).

SysFan has also been used for some corpus studies, most particularly by Annabelle Lukin within the project 'Reporting war: Mapping meaning and the potential for bias in the news' (e.g. Lukin, 2006), and the 'SPIRT' project (e.g. Matthiessen *et al.*, 2005).

Because *Systemic Coder* was limited to dealing with one text at a time, and analysing the text at a single layer, in 2007 I introduced *UAM CorpusTool* (O'Donnell, 2008), a total reimplementation of Coder based on the idea that the user provides a corpus (a set of documents) and specifies a number of analysis layers (e.g. Context, Speech Function, Grammar, Appraisal, etc.). The extra power of a system which deals with multiple files analysed at multiple levels allows for far more complex small corpus studies. This tool is now fairly widely used in the SFL community, and is starting to be used in the CL community.

15.6 Recent advances: SFL with large corpora

In recent years, there have been various efforts towards automatic recognition of various aspects of SFL. To a degree, this has become possible due to the increasing robustness of syntactic parsers. While these parsers provide a fairly structural analysis, this syntactic analysis can be used as a basis to automatically recognize more meaningful patterns in the text. For instance, once basic syntactic functions such as Subject, Object, Adjunct, etc. are recognized, it is easier to assign participant roles (Actor, Sensor, etc.) and also to identify thematic elements.

I will mention here two systems which use parsing towards different aspects of SFL. First, Honnibal and Curran (2007) developed a system that converted the Penn treebank (4.5 million words of English all syntactically analysed and manually-corrected) into an SFL format. Their system produced layers for transitivity, mood, theme, and taxis (clause complexing). While only applied to a treebank, the importance of this system is it could equally be applied to the output of a structural parser, meaning that SFL style analyses could be derived from previously unseen English corpora.

O'Donnell extended UAM CorpusTool (mentioned above) to incorporate the Stanford parser (Klein and Manning, 2003), allowing each English text in the user's corpus to be parsed, producing a NP^VP style parse for each sentence. This parse is then converted to what might be called an SFL-informed Quirk/Greenbaum style grammar (function structure only in terms of Subject, Predicator, Object, Adjunct, etc. but features from a system network corresponding to transitivity, mood, tense, aspect, modality, polarity, etc.).

These two systems, and others, will be discussed below, where we discuss the state of the art in SFL analysis of large corpora.

15.6.1 Mood, Tense, Aspect, Modality

Clause structure in terms of Subject, Object, Adjunct, etc. is often provided by the existing structural parsers, or can be easily derived from the output. For instance, the Stanford parser provides the following dependency analysis of 'He said that he liked you':

```
nsubj(said-2, He-1)
```

```
complm(liked-5, that-3)
nsubj(liked-5, he-4)
ccomp(said-2, liked-5)
dobj(liked-5, you-6)
```

SFL Mood structure differs slightly from traditional analysis (e.g. Complement rather than Object, etc.), but it is simple to translate between these naming variants.

The sequencing of clause functions, along with other information in the parse, can be used to provide the feature selections from a mood network (e.g. Finite before Subject suggests `yes-no-question`).

Tense/Aspect features can also be readily identified from the syntactic parse (and even from simpler POS-tagged data). This was done in the work of Honnibal and Curran (2007) and is also done by UAM CorpusTool.

Modality in the limited sense of modal auxiliaries is provided by UAM CorpusTool, and easily located in any POS-tagged corpora. Recently, the 'autocode' feature of UAM CorpusTool (which allows you to create segments based on concordance matches) has been used to identify all verbal, adverbial, and adjectival tokens expressing modality in a 500,000 word corpus.

15.6.2 Process types and participant roles

While there have been various attempts at producing a parser for systemic grammars, none have been produced that work to any degree on previously unseen text, and thus these systems are not useful for annotating large corpora.

What has been more successful has been building on top of the existing structural parsers, adding a component to convert the output of these parsers into an SFL representation.

In regards to transitivity, Honnibal and Curran (2007) decided that the resources needed to distinguish process types were lacking at that time, so simply distinguished Participant, Process and Circumstance:

> Distinguishing process types requires a word sense disambiguated corpus and a word sense sensitive process type lexicon. While there is a significant intersection between the Penn Treebank and the Semcor word sense disambiguated corpus, there is currently no suitable process type lexicon. Consequently, Participants have not been subtyped. The Process is simply the verb phrase, while the Subject and Complements are Participants. (Honnibal and Curran, 2007: 93)

While UAM CorpusTool does not provide participant role labels, each clause is classified according to its process type, and this classification is reasonably robust, with around 90% accuracy. Clauses are classified as material (ergative vs. transitive), mental, verbal or relational. The system simplifies the identification of relational processes by including only those verbs that do not passivise ('be', 'have', 'seem', 'appear', 'become' and attributive perceptual verbs such as 'feel', 'look', etc).

This system uses a process-type categorized lexicon of English verbs, including 9,200 senses. Where a verb occurs under more than one process type, currently one is assigned using a lookup table of most frequent classification, or if none is provided, at random. While the nature of the complements in the clause could be used to improve this process, it has not currently been implemented.

This approach has been used to grammatically annotate user-provided corpora up to a million words (over this, the system becomes too slow to be usable). It is useful for rapid profiling of text types. For instance, a quick study of a 31,000 word corpus of editorials and front-page news (FPN), with no manual annotation apart from document type, produced the results shown in Table 15.1. The table shows the percentage of clauses which take the particular process type, showing that front-page news articles are significantly more likely to quote people than editorials, while editorials contain far more relational information.

Table 15.1: Use of process types over two text types

	Editorials	*FPN*
Material-clause	60.5%	61.6%
Mental-clause	9.9%	8.9%
Verbal-clause	5.5%	15.7%
Relational-clause	24.1%	13.8%

It is worth noting here the existence of Amy Neale's 'Process Type Database', a spreadsheet providing process type classification (in terms of Fawcett's SFL) of 5,400 verb senses.[6] This might be used in future systems for process type classification of Fawcett's dialect of SFL.

15.6.3 Theme

To automatically identify the thematic elements of a sentence or clause presumes knowledge of syntactic function and structure. Once one has a working syntactic parser, identification of theme is not that difficult. Usually, the first occurring Adjunct, Subject, or Complement at the beginning of the clause will be the topical theme, skipping over Adjuncts which can be classified as interpersonal or textual themes. Textual themes are conjunctions, or a small set of conjunctive Adjuncts, such as 'in consequence', etc. Interpersonal themes are usually adverbs, or prepositional phrases, and a dictionary of the most common would allow these to be identified in most cases.

Honnibal and Curran (2007), mentioned above, identified textual, interpersonal and topical themes in their processing using similar methods.

A group based at the Technical University of Darmstadt, including Elke Teich and Sabine Bartsch, have in recent years developed software to automate theme classification (see Schwarz *et al.*, 2008). They parse texts using the Stanford parser, and apply a number of rules to extract out the topical theme of each clause within the sentences. From a trial on a small corpus of 209 academic abstracts, roughly 82% of all themes were correctly identified. Some of their problems stem from the fact that the parser itself does not always produce the correct parse.

A group at Saarland University (Neumann and Hansen-Schirra, forthcoming) automatically annotated a 1 million word parallel corpus of English and German in terms of grammatical functions, (e.g. Subject, Object, Adjunct, etc.), and then queried the corpus to see how often each grammatical function occurred first in a sentence, assuming that the first occurring grammatical function was the theme. In this way they could explore how theme choices varied over a range of distinct registers, and between English and German texts.

15.6.4 Appraisal Analysis

Appraisal Analysis (Martin and White, 2005) has often been regarded as one of the hardest areas of SFL to automate. The argument is that the appraisal value of a phrase is often very context dependent. For instance, 'good' can in some contexts be an instance of judgement:propriety (as in *He was a good boy.*), or of appreciation as in *It's a good wine*, or it may not even be appraisal if used in contexts like *It's a good seven miles to the hotel.* While generally a positive appraisal token, it can be negative in contexts such as: *This wine is not good.* Invoked appraisal is even more problematic: for instance, the statement *He was the kind of bloke who drives a BMW* could be a positive or negative appraisal, depending on what you expect the speaker's attitude to the well-off to be.

However, some efforts have been made to automate appraisal annotation. As with many issues in computational linguistics, most think that it is too difficult, that we will never achieve 100%, so why bother. Some bright sparks see the challenge and attempt to see how well they can do, even if it is only a 20% solution.

Whitelaw *et al.* (2005) set themselves the challenge of identifying adjectival appraisals in film reviews. They initially manually identified 1,329 'appraisal groups' (adjectives with associated premodifiers, e.g. 'not very good') which appeared in this type of text, and manually assigned them an appraisal category. They then took a corpus of film reviews and located instances of the previously identified and coded appraisal groups.

I note that this work was not intended for Appraisal annotation of a corpus, but rather to identify sufficient appraisal tokens to be able to classify the review as positive or negative. That being the case, they did not intend to identify all appraisal tokens in the texts.

Bloom *et al.* (2007) extended this work, extending the adjective lexicon, and also adding a set of admire-type and judgement verbs (2007: 280).

Sano (2011) describes work to build a dictionary of over 8,500 Japanese words expressing attitude.[7] Where particular lexis is ambiguous in terms of their appraisal value, the words around that word were used to identify which sense was intended. He then applied this technique to a 6 million word sub-corpus from the Balanced Corpus of Contemporary Written Japanese, identifying 81,756 appraisal tokens and their appraisal class.

15.6.5 Summary

So, while during most of the history of CL, SFL has not made extensive use of large corpora, recently this has begun to change. One study currently under way involves 500 essays (around 500,000 words) of learner English, using automatic parsing to produce a grammar layer of annotation (to see what the students do at each level of proficiency) and also manually annotating errors in the texts (to see what the students are still struggling with) (see O'Donnell *et al.*, 2009).

15.7 Looking forward

So, SFL and CL are starting to come together, with automatic annotation of large corpora in terms of transitivity, mood, theme and appraisal information, both in terms of function structure and features. However, there are several dimensions of SFL which still need to be addressed.

15.7.1 Discourse semantics

Discourse semantics (e.g. Martin and Rose, 2007; Halliday and Hasan, 1989) involves the analysis of text using a set of different semantic analyses, such as ideational structuring, thematic progression, identity chains, cohesion, generic structure, rhetorical structure, etc.

As mentioned in Section 15.2.5 above, semantic analysis of text in terms of its ideational structure (identifying processes, participants and circumstances) is still at an early stage, but there is some work in this area from a non-Systemic perspective. However, work with the FrameNet resources may be translatable to an SFL-compatible analysis system.

One resource is required before most areas of discourse semantics can be automated, and this is reference resolution: ability to identify where nominal groups and pronouns are referring to earlier-mentioned entities, etc. Fortunately, reference resolution is becoming reasonably robust at least for English, and to a lesser degree for other languages. For instance, the Stanford CoreNLP software[8] tags nominal groups which co-refer.

This resource is invaluable for automating Martin's identity chaining and for recognition of several types of cohesion in Halliday and Hasan's approach (reference, ellipsis, nominal substitution, some aspects of lexical cohesion, etc.). Reference resolution also increases the power of automatic appraisal analysis, e.g. seeing how particular participants are appraised throughout a discourse. Automatic identification of Thematic Progression (where does the new theme derive from in the prior text) will also benefit from reference resolution. With reference resolution, we can also track how particular participants in the text are construed in terms of transitivity roles (as an Actor, Sayer, Sensor, etc.)

Another resource that is invaluable is Wordnet, which provides not only synonym information, also provides superordinate-subordinate relations, meronymy (part-whole relations), and antonyms. This resource is particular valuable for identification of instances of lexical cohesion, or of lexical chains.

15.7.2 Dialogue

Many systemicists are interested in dialogue modelling: analysis of multi-participant dialogue in terms of moves, exchanges, turns, frames, etc. While tools exist for the manual annotation of dialogue (both in terms of audio files or transcripts), there is little in the way of automatic analysis of dialogue, and for manual annotation, there is nothing available for a particularly SFL approach to dialogue.

In 2011, a project led by Ana Linares and Rachel Whittaker at the Universidad Autónoma de Madrid has been using UAM CorpusTool to automatically segment transcripts of dialogue into turns (using the automatic paragraph segmentation feature), and tagging these turns by the speaker, using the 'autocode' feature. It is left up to the user to manually identify moves.

Future work would provide automatic treatment of dialogue, identifying turns, moves, exchanges, etc. in transcripts of discourse.

15.7.3 Multimodality

Also changing is the nature of the text we examine. An increased interest in the multimodal structure of the page, of video, etc., has called for software which helps in the analyses of these texts. Some multimodal annotation tools have started to appear (e.g. *MCA*, see Baldry and Taylor, 2004; and *Semiomix*, see O'Halloran *et al.*, 2011), although these are early days in the story of such tools. In 2008, I introduced a tool called *UAM ImageTool* to support the manual annotation of images,[9] although this offers only bare functionality: tagging of segments of an image, and search to retrieve these (e.g. find all 'eye' in female/Asian faces). O'Halloran's *Semiomix* offers fairly comprehensive annotation of image and video, and allows for separate annotation of text or audio language within the video or image.

15.8 Conclusions

This chapter has explored the limited interaction between CL and SFL. I argued that CL has made limited use of SFL because the categories of SFL are not easily computed, and that SFL has made limited use of large corpus studies for the same reason. As a consequence, SFL has turned to small corpus studies (manual annotation) as a means to verify linguistic hypotheses, and to build descriptions.

However, over the last few years, this has started to change, with automation of areas such as transitivity, theme and appraisal being in early stages, and promises of automation in many areas of discourse semantics are on the horizon.

The history of corpus linguistics has been a movement of increasing automation of the linguist's work (e.g. from manually scanning through a text for instances, replaced by the use of a corpus search facilities).

One tool which will lead us further into the future is machine learning, whereby the computer is presented with a manually coded corpus, and from this information, the system derives a model which allows it to annotate new text. Because such systems are rarely perfect, the human then intervenes to correct errors made by the machine (hopefully less work than doing all the coding themselves).

As we steer into the twenty-first century, we can start to conceptualize that an ideal corpus tool is not one where the linguist's time is spent annotating text and managing corpora. Rather, the ideal system would allow the linguist to present the tool with a hypothesis, and be given in return the evidence (instances and statistics) for or against the hypothesis.

Notes

1.   See http://encyclopedia.farlex.com/concordance.
2.   Figures derived from a sample over a million word corpus held by the author.
3.   See: http://www.lexically.net/wordsmith/corpus_linguistics_links/papers_using_wordsmith.htm
4.   http://wordnet.princeton.edu/
5.   http://www.ling.mq.edu.au/nlp/resource/AnalysisTools/SysAm/SysFan/Contents.htm
6.   Available from: http://www.itri.brighton.ac.uk/~Amy.Neale/
7.   The dictionary is available from http://www.gsk.or.jp/index_e.html.
8.   http://nlp.stanford.edu/software/corenlp.shtml
9.   http://www.wagsoft.com/ImageTool/index.html

References

Baldry, A. and Taylor, C. (2004) Multimodal concordancing and subtitles with MCA. In A. Partington, J. Morley and L. Haarman (eds) *Corpora and Discourse*, 57–70. Bern: Peter Lang.

Biber, D. (1988) *Variation across Speech and Writing*. Cambridge: Cambridge University Press.

Biber, D. (1995) *Dimensions of Register Variation: a Cross-Linguistic Comparison.* Cambridge: Cambridge University Press.

Bloom, K., Stein, S. and Argamon, S. (2007) Appraisal extraction for news opinion analysis at NTCIR-6. *Proceedings of NTCIR-6 Workshop Meeting*, May 15–18, 2007, Tokyo, Japan.

Charniak, E. (2000) A maximum-entropy-inspired parser. *NAACL'00* 132–139.

Collins, M. (1999) *Head-Driven Statistical Models for Natural Language Parsing.* Ph.D. Dissertation, University of Pennsylvania.

Eggins, S. (1990) *Conversational Structure: A Systemic-Functional Analysis of Interpersonal and Logical Meaning in Multiparty Sustained Talk*, Ph.D. Thesis, Department of Linguistics, University of Sydney.

Fillmore, C. J. (1976) Frame semantics and the nature of language. In *Annals of the New York Academy of Sciences: Conference on the Origin and Development of Language and Speech*, Volume 280: 20–32.

Firth, J. R. (1957) Modes of meaning. In J. R. Firth (ed.) *Papers in Linguistics,* 190–215. London: Oxford University Press.

Fontaine, L. (2007) The variability of referring expressions: an alternative perspective on the noun phrase in English. In D. Coleman, W. Sullivan and A. Lommel (eds) *LACUS Forum XXXIII – Variation,* 159–170. Houston TX: LACUS.

Fries, C.C. (1952) *The Structure of English: An Introduction to the Construction of English Sentences.* New York: Harcourt Brace.

Fries, P. (1983) On the status of Theme in English: arguments from discourse. In P. Janos and E. Soezer (eds) *Micro and Macro Connexity of Texts,* 116–152. Hamburg: Helmut Buske Verlag.

Gildea, D. and Jurafsky, D. (2002) Automatic labeling of semantic roles. *Computational Linguistics* 28(3): 245–288.

Greenbaum, S. and Quirk, R. (1990) *A Student's Grammar of the English Language.* London: Addison Wesley.

Greene, B. B. and Rubin, G. M. (1971) *Automatic Grammatical Tagging of English.* Technical report, Department of Linguistics, Brown University, Providence, Rhode Island.

Halliday, M. A. K. and James, Z. L. (1993) A quantitative study of polarity and primary tense in the English finite clause. In J. M. Sinclair, M. Hoey and G. Fox (eds) *Techniques of Description: Spoken and Written Discourse,* 32–66. London: Routledge.

Halliday, M. A. K. (1966) Lexis as a linguistic level. In C. E. Bazell, J. C. Catford, M. A. K. Halliday and R. Robins (eds) *In Memory of J. R. Firth,* 150–161. London: Longman.

Halliday, M. A. K. (1978) *Language as Social Semiotic: The Social Interpretation of Language and Meaning.* London: Edward Arnold.

Halliday, M. A. K. (2004) Quantitative studies and probabilities in grammar. In J. J. Webster (ed.) *Computational and Quantitative Studies* (Collected Works of M. A. K. Halliday Vol. 6), 130–156. London: Continuum.

Halliday, M. A. K. (2006) Afterwords. In G. Thompson and S. Hunston (eds) *System and Corpus: Exploring Connections,* 293–299. London: Equinox.

Halliday, M. A. K. and Hasan, R. (1989) *Language, Context and Text: Aspects of Language in a Social Semiotic Perspective* (2nd edn). Oxford: Oxford University Press.

Hartley, A. and Paris, C. (1996) Two sources of control over the generation of software instructions. *Proceedings of the 34th Annual Meeting of the Association for Computational Linguistics,* 192–199.

Hasan, R. (1986) The ontogenesis of ideology: an interpretation of mother-child talk. In T. Threadgold, E. Grosz, G. Kress and M. A. K. Halliday (eds) *Semiotics – Language – Ideology,* 125–146. Sydney: Sydney Studies in Society and Culture.

Hasan, R. and Cloran, C. (1990) A sociolinguistic study of everyday talk between mothers and children. In M. A. K. Halliday, J. Gibbons and H. Nicholas (eds) *Learning, Keeping, and Using Language* Vol.1, 67–100. Amsterdam and Philadelphia, PA: Benjamins.

Honnibal, M. and Curran, J. R. (2007) Creating a systemic functional grammar corpus from the Penn Treebank. *Proceedings of the ACL 2007 Workshop on Deep Linguistic Processing (DLP),* 89–96.

Hunston, S. and Francis, G. (2000) *Pattern Grammar: A Corpus-driven Approach to the Lexical Grammar of English*. Amsterdam: Benjamins.

Kilgarriff, A. and Tugwell, D. (2001) WORD SKETCH: Extraction and display of significant collocations for lexicography. *Proceedings of the ACL workshop on COLLOCATION: Computational Extraction, Analysis and Exploitation, 32–38*. Toulouse, July.

Klein, D. and Manning, C. (2003) Fast exact inference with a factored model for natural language parsing. *Advances in Neural Information Processing Systems, 15 (NIPS 2002), 3–10*. Cambridge, MA: MIT Press.

Krishnamurthy, R. (2004) Editor's preface. In J. Sinclair, S. Jones, R. Daley (eds) *English Collocation Studies: The OSTI Report*, viii–xv. London: Continuum.

Kucera, H. and Francis, W. (1967) *Computational Analysis of Present-day American English*. Providence, RI: Brown University Press.

Leech, G., Garside, R., and Bryant, M. (1994) CLAWS4: The tagging of the British National Corpus. *Proceedings of the 15th International Conference on Computational Linguistics* (COLING 94), 622–628. Japan: Kyoto.

Lukin, A. (2006) What is media 'bias'? A case study of Aljazeera's reporting of the Iraq war. *Journal of Policing, Intelligence and Counter-Terrorism* Vol. 1, 65–80.

Matthiessen, C. M. I. M. (1985) The systemic framework in text generation: Nigel. In J. Benson and W. Greaves (eds) *Systemic Perspectives on Discourse*, 96–118. Norwood, NJ: Ablex.

Matthiessen, C. M. I. M., Lukin, A., Butt, D., Clereigh, C., and Nesbitt, C. (2005) A case study of multistratal analysis. *Australian Review of Applied Linguistics* 19: 123–150.

Martin, J. R. and Rose, D. (2007) *Working with Discourse – Meaning beyond the Clause*. London: Continuum.

Martin, J. R. and White, P. R. R. (2005) *The Language of Evaluation, Appraisal in English*. London & New York: Palgrave Macmillan.

Matthiessen, C M. I. M., O'Donnell, M. and Zeng, L. (1991) Discourse analysis and the need for functionally complex grammars in parsing. *Proceedings of the Second Japan-Australia Joint Symposium on Natural Language Processing*, 274–293. October 2–5, 1991, Kyushu Institute of Technology, Iizuka City, Japan.

McGowan, U. (1997) Metaphor and congruence in the media: Barriers for international students of Economics and Commerce. *Prospect: A Journal of Australian TESO* 12 (1): 20–34.

Murcia Bielsa, S. and Delin, J. (2001) Expressing the notion of purpose in English and Spanish instructions. *Functions of Language* 8 (1): 79–108.

Neumann, S. (2003) Exploitation of an SFL-annotated multilingual register corpus. In A. Abeillé, S. Hansen-Schirra and H. Uszkoreit (eds) *Proceedings of the 4th International Workshop on Linguistically Interpreted Corpora* (LINC-03), 85–92. Budapest, Ungarn.

Neumann, S. and Hansen-Schirra, S. (forthcoming) Exploiting the incomparability of comparable corpora for contrastive linguistics and translation studies. In R. Rapp, S. Sharoff and P. Zweigenbaum (eds) *BUCC: Building and Using Comparable Corpora*. Heidelberg: Springer.

O'Donnell, M. (1995) From corpus to codings: Semi-automating the acquisition of linguistic features. In *Proceedings of the AAAI Spring Symposium on Empirical Methods in Discourse Interpretation and Generation*, Stanford University, California, March, 27–29.

O'Donnell, M. (2008) Demonstration of the UAM CorpusTool for text and image annotation. *Proceedings of the ACL-08:HLT Demo Session (Companion Volume)*, 13–16. Columbus, OH, June 2008. Association for Computational Linguistics.

O'Donnell, M., Murcia, S., García, R., Molina, C., Rollinson, P., MacDonald, P., Stuart, K. and Boquera, M. (2009) Exploring the proficiency of English learners: The TREACLE project. *Proceedings of the Fifth Corpus Linguistics Conference*, Liverpool. (http://ucrel.lancs.ac.uk/publications/cl2009/).

O'Halloran, K. L. and Judd, K. (2002) Systemics 1.0. Singapore: Singapore University Press.

O'Halloran, K. L., Tan, S., Smith, B. A. and Podlasov, A. (2011). Multimodal analysis within an interactive software environment: Critical discourse perspectives. *Critical Discourse Studies* 8 (2): 109–125.

Plum, G. (1988) *Text and Contextual Conditioning in Spoken English: A Genre-based Approach*. Ph.D. Dissertation. Linguistics Department, University of Sydney.

Quirk, R. (1968) The survey of English usage. In R. Quirk (ed.) *Essays on the English Language: Medieval and Modern*, 70–87. London: Longman.

Quirk, R. (2002) Randolph Quirk. In E. K. Brownand and V. Law (eds) *Linguistics in Britain: Personal Histories*, 239–248. London: Wiley-Blackwell.

Quirk, R., Greenbaum, S., Leech, G. and Svartvik, J. (1985) *A Comprehensive Grammar of the English Language*. Harlow: Longman.

Richards, L. and Richards, T. (1981) NUDIST: a computer assisted technique for thematic analysis of unstructured data. *La Trobe Working Papers in Sociology*, no. 59.

Sano, M. (2011) Reconstructing English system of ATTITUDE for the application to Japanese: An exploration for the construction of a Japanese dictionary of appraisal. Paper presented at the 38th International Systemic Functional Congress, Lisbon.

Schwarz, L., Bartsch, S., Eckart, R. and Teich, E. (2008) Theme Annotator: A rule-based approach to automatic Theme-Rheme identification. *Proceedings of the 9th Conference on Natural Language Processing (KONVENS 2008)*, 15–26. Berlin, New York: Mouton de Gruyter.

Scott, M. (2004) *WordSmith Tools version 4*. Oxford: Oxford University Press.

Sinclair, J., Jones, S. and Daley, R. (1970) *English Lexical Studies, Report to OSTI on Project C/LP/08*; Dept of English, Birmingham University.

Sharoff, S. (2005) How to handle lexical semantics in SFL: A corpus study of purposes for using size adjectives. In S. Hunston and G. Thompson (eds) *Systemic Linguistics and Corpus*, 184–205. London: Equinox.

Sinclair, J., Jones, S. and Daley, R. (2004) *English Collocation Studies: The OSTI Report*. R. Krishnamurthy (ed.). London: Continuum. Reprinted from Sinclair, J., Jones, S. and Daley, R. (1970) *English Lexical Studies. Report to OSTI on Project C/LP/08*, Department of English, University of Birmingham.

Sinclair, J. (ed.) (1990) *Collins Cobuild – English Grammar*. London: HarperCollins.

Teubert, W. (2004) Interview with John Sinclair. In J. Sinclair, S. Jones and R. Daley (eds) *English Collocation Studies: The OSTI Report*, xvii–xxix. London: Continuum.

Webster, J. (1994) Building a Windows-based bilingual functional semantic processor. *Proceedings of the 15th conference on Computational linguistics (COLING)* Vol. 2, 71–75.

Whitelaw, C., Garg, N. and Argamon, S. (2005) Using appraisal groups for sentiment analysis. *Proceedings of the 14th ACM International Conference on Information and Knowledge Management* 625–631.

16 Systemic Functional Theory and Cyberspace

Eija Ventola[*]

16.1 Introduction: Cyberspace and Systemic Functional Linguistics (SFL)

This chapter analyses the nature of the Cyberspace presence and actions of Systemic Functional Linguistics (SFL). Cyberspace uses the Internet as its medium. The term 'cyberspace' is attributed to the science fiction author, William Gibson. Here, in this chapter, Cyberspace refers to *the platform for creating knowledge and interaction,* and the Internet is the medium by which it is virtually transmitted. So, as far as this chapter is concerned, Cyberspace is described as: (1) reaching a wide audience, which is 'not tied to geographic location'; and (2) enabling numerous ways of interacting.

The following questions arise:

(a) What is the nature of the presence of SF-theory in Cyberspace and its use for internal communication?

(b) How successful are we in using Cyberspace for external communication to enhance SF knowledge to outsiders, to brand and to market SF-theory?

(c) Is it time to take steps towards realizing a 'Global Virtual Systemic Functional University'?

These issues are discussed with reference to SF-teaching/learning possibilities on the internet, and the ways in which people might use this medium for interconnecting and working together.

---

[*] Professor Eija Ventola is a member of Academia Scientiarum Fennica who teaches Business and Corporate Communication at Aalto University, School of Business.

16.2 (a) What is the nature of SFL's presence in Cyberspace?

What is the actual nature of the presence and use of SFL in Cyberspace? The main function of Cyberspace is to create a space in which users can interact and exchange ideas. So how much of this kind of activity related to SFL – including E-mail lists and postings – is taking place on the Internet?

Typically **E-mail lists** work for internal communication within a group. Lists are open only for those who join in, but once you have joined, then you can send messages to members in the group. When Cyberspace opened up, the SFL-community responded enthusiastically and several, some geographically-oriented, some interest-oriented, mailing lists were established (http://www.isfla.org/Systemics/Lists/index.html). The idea was that the Europeans would interact through a list called 'Sysfling' and the 'Down Under' systemicists would use 'Sysfunc' (http://listserv.uts.edu.au/mailman/listinfo/sys-func). Other lists were established, too, such as 'The SFL New Researchers' Network', which was intended to serve the needs of those who were not yet initiated to the theory but learning it. All who have joined any of the SFL-lists have probably found them a beneficial source for new books, new research, conference information, etc. But there are problems involved in maintaining such lists. E-mail lists can easily become 'drowsy'. For example, The SFL New Researchers' Network (http://www.cf.ac.uk/encap/fontaine/sfl/) is no longer active, and directs one to Sysfling, which itself has been incorporated into 'Sysfunc'. Keeping participation active is a real challenge within any scientific community.

Although the SFL community can consider itself fortunate to have relatively many, very active members who voluntarily maintain both the international and more local networking, it is obvious that without proper organizational support and funding such lists will eventually fall prey to the limits of voluntary 'human manpower'. Many of the active maintainers of lists have their normal work duties and private lives that limit the time they may devote to supporting online SFL-activities. The need for manpower and resources to maintain communication links on the Internet is a matter which needs to be addressed by the ISFLA – the International Systemic Linguistic Association. Unfortunately, the resources for maintaining effective Internet-based communication are limited.

16.3 (b) How successfully do we use Cyberspace for promoting SFL?

Although not highly regarded in academic circles as an acceptable source of information, Wikipedia has succeeded in its overall function of freely distributing information in Cyberspace globally. It often functions as an initial source, whose information needs to be further verified from other sources. Thus, for SFL-theory and practice it would be **most beneficial** to use Wikipedia as a means for providing accurate information on SFL and promoting the theory to newcomers.

When I searched the internet for hits related to 'systemic functional grammar' and 'systemic functional linguistics', what I found (27.6.2009) was the following explanation at Wikipedia:

(1)

> **'Systemic functional grammar (SFG) or systemic functional linguistics (SFL) is** a model of grammar developed by <u>Michael Halliday</u> in the 1960s.[1] It is part of a broad social <u>semiotic</u> approach to language called <u>systemic linguistics</u>. The term 'systemic' refers to the view of language as 'a network of systems, or interrelated sets of options for making meaning';[2] The term 'functional' indicates that the approach is concerned with <u>meaning</u>, as opposed to <u>formal grammar</u>, which focuses on <u>word classes</u> such as nouns and verbs, typically without reference beyond the clause. ... (http://en.wikipedia.org/wiki/Systemic_functional_grammar, 27.6.2009)

More recently, when I returned to Wikipedia, I found that the explanation for SF-grammar and SF-linguistics has been expanded to include 'Influences' and 'Basic tenets'. Also, whereas the previous 2009-version of the Wikipedia page listed under 'See also' and 'Other significant systemic functional grammarians', only Robin Fawcett – with a link leading nowhere; and James R. Martin, whose link led to his home page, the 2011-version included Ruqaiya Hasan (without a link), and Sue Wharton (with a link to her home page). Two years on, apparently little had changed in terms of the information provided.

Below is an extract of some of the discussion that took place between July 2007–May 2009 about the contents about SFL on Wikipedia:

(3)

> The jargon issue is not a problem restricted to this page. It is a very recurrent problem throughout the theory. I guess there must be a way to *demetaphorize* the theory for the uninitiated... I think this article works OK at the moment. At least some focus should be on expanding the article rather than clarifying existing information. <u>Narssarssuaq</u> 09:10, 11 July 2007 (UTC)
>
> **It's not what *I'd* call 'OK'; it's appalling. I intend to remove the link to 'Word grammar', which is so far off the mark it's not funny.** <u>Tony</u> 11:07, 27 August 2007 (UTC)

OK, it's not OK. <u>Narssarssuaq</u> 14:51, 27 August 2007 (UTC)

...

I've had a go at expanding and clarifying the article. ... The section on the ideational metafunction needs attention – **I only have information on the experiential part of it and don't know what is meant by the logical metafunction.** The stuff about Chomsky and instantiations back-feeded by instantiations (WTF?) also needs clarifying and referencing. ... <u>Snookerfran</u> (<u>talk</u>) 14:45, 30 July 2008 (UTC)

...

Hi there. I've done a quick copy-edit of the lead. May I suggest that we:

gather more folk around this task;

create a list of items that might well be linked, eventually, and stubs created (*lexis* and 'lexicogrammar' are two I see in the lead); and

decide which variety of English this should be in.

I'd go for AusEng, since Halliday has done just about all of his major work as foundation professor of linguistics at the <u>University of Sydney</u>, and *is now happily retired adjacent to a long sunny beach north of here.* But it's no big deal. Comments? **<u>Tony</u> (<u>talk</u>) <u>01:48, 15 August 2008 (UTC)</u>**

Thanks for putting those requests out; it'd be fantastic if we could get more people to help. Australian English is fine by me - .... A few other general thoughts: 1. At the moment, it's unclear how the metafunctions relate to the semantic, phonological, and lexicogrammatical strata. This will need explaining. 2. The metafunctions section should probably be called 'theory', and there should probably be a 'history' section first. 3. The metafunctions section will need a full rewrite; what I put down there is very rushed. 4. The last two sections also need a rewrite. ... – *<u>snookerfran</u>* (<u>talk</u>) 14:32, 15 August 2008 (UTC)

OK Fran ... I'll need to think carefully about the metafunctions section; **I have time at the moment to brush up again with IFG3 (2004).** Is that the edition you have? You sound like a professional linguist; I'm only an amateur, but a serious one. **I've never formally studied SFG, but was close friends with two of Halliday's doctoral students.** (http://en.wikipedia.org/wiki/Talk:Systemic_functional_grammar)

The only addition to the above discussion is the last posting on the list, done in 2011: 'Fran, please let me know if you're around WP. Tony (talk) 03:30, 5 February 2011 (UTC)'.

According to a *Helsingin Sanomat* (the main newspaper in Finland, 4.5.2011, p. A 16), the Finnish Wikipedia is updated by 2,074 persons, many of whom are young, like a 23-year-old writer interviewed for the newspaper article. Many of these updaters according to the interviewee are not active, and very often he admitted to be the only active updater of many themes. The same seems to be the case of the SFL-page in the Wikipedia as far as the frequency and the expertise of updating the page is concerned. Being a close friend to Halliday's doctoral students hardly qualifies one to be the expert on external communication on SF-theory: *'I'm only an amateur, but a serious one. I've never formally studied SFG, but was close friends with two of Halliday's doctoral students.'* Surely the SFL-community should not leave these enthusiastic Wikipedia writers on their own, but find the time to support them and use the marketing and branding value that a good Wikipedia page can freely offer to the SFL-community. At the very least, the SFL-community should link the Wikipedia page properly with the official SFL-internet site of ISFLA: http://www.isfla.org, which also incorporates information about its sub-associations. The ISFLA site is a valuable source for information both the theory and applications. Examples of many SFL-studies and research reports are posted at http://www.isfla.org/Systemics/.

The SFL community has to consider both the internal and external aspects of communication. By Internal I mean looking into how we can conveniently and efficiently use Cyberspace and the Internet to facilitate cooperation among SFL linguists. By External, I am referring to how we meet the needs of those interested outsiders who are searching for information about SFL and possible co-operation with the SFL-practitioners.

Here, I propose the establishment of an internationally reviewed *SFL-Internet Journal* and a reviewed *SFL-Internet E-Book Series* on ISFLA-pages. For a modest fee, full-versions of publications could be made available for download and/or printing. Also, examples of analyses based on SF-theory could be made available. Some of the work could be based on already existing text books (provided the copyrights/licences could be negotiated).

16.4 (c) Steps towards realizing a 'Global Virtual Systemic Functional University' – a true possibility?

As I suggested in my plenary talk at the 31st International Systemic Functional Congress in Kyoto, Japan, 2004, I propose developing and organizing *a global virtual systemic-functional university* – web based learning environment. Our goal would be to offer full professional training in the field of SFL, social semiotics, multimodality and multisemiotics.

We have so many enthusiastic practitioners of SF-theory around the world who are doing excellent work both in teaching as well as in conducting research that it seems a shame that not more people are able to benefit from the work of these members of the community, especially when the technology is there to link us all as a community of learners and researchers. Live-video-conferencing-debates on particular issues could be arranged, some perhaps with such simple, inexpensive technologies as Skype, some using more advanced technologies. Perhaps a special SFL-video-conferencing channel and platform could be established. While time differences would present a challenge to participating in some video-events, still such hindrances could be overcome by establishing a video portal where the talks from various events could be maintained. Many universities actually offer such open, globally accessible, video portals (see e.g. http://video.helsinki.fi/).

A very famous portal that could also function as a model for building up a SF-portal is the TED-portal, which had its beginnings at a conference called *Technology, Entertainment and Design,* in 1984 (see http://www.ted. com/pages/about). This is an interdisciplinary enterprise that brings various professionals together, but also allows outsiders to follow their events via the Internet. The mission statement declares TED to be 'a global community, which welcomes people from every discipline and culture who seek a deeper understanding of the world.' TED has 'two annual conferences – the TED Conference in Long Beach and Palm Springs each spring, and the TED Global conference in Edinburgh UK each summer – TED includes the award-winning TED Talks video site, the Open Translation Project and TED Conversations, the inspiring TED Fellows and TEDx programs, and the annual TED Prize.' TED is a nonprofit enterprise (http://www.ted.com/pages/about), with such sponsors as Blackberry, Coca Cola, Goldman Sachs, Gucci, Johnson and Johnson, etc. (see http://www.ted.com/pages/about). TED organizes a variety of events, including social spaces, lunchtime salons, conversation breaks, evening events, workshops, innovation lab spaces, pre-conference activities, etc. (see http://partners.ted.com/conferences/opportunities.php). The press site of TED (http://partners.ted.com/press/) states: 'By combining the principles of 'radical openness' and of 'leveraging the power of ideas to change the world,' TED is in the process of creating something brand new. I would go so far as to argue that it's creating a new Harvard – the first new top-prestige education brand in more than 100 years. Fast Company, September 1, 2010 (see also http://www.fastcompany.com/)

The TED community offers a model to the SFL-community.

There is evidence that SLF is moving in the right direction. For the first time in the history of systemic-functional congresses, the plenaries of the 37th congress, held in Vancouver in 2010, were put on the web for everyone to watch and appreciate, e.g. Michael Halliday's talk can be watched at: http://www.youtube.com/watch?v=nC-blhaIUCk. The webcast was sponsored by the Irving K Barber Learning Centre.

16.5 Conclusion

This chapter has focused on the nature of the SFL-presence in Cyberspace as mediated via the Internet. It has looked at the kind of information that exists on SF-theory and practice in Cyberspace and what kind of SFL-teaching/learning/research possibilities are available in Cyperspace. The discussion prompts a recommendation for the global unification of teaching and research of SFL, and consideration for how we might better address the challenges that face the SF-community in the 21st century in Cyberspace. The SFL community, as an academic community, needs to consider how to better interact with others, and how to improve its public image. It is not just enough to discuss the research and the work we do among those who are already familiar with SFL-theory, but it is also important to introduce the theory and its applications to the wider audience in Cyberspace who might not know about SFL. We can also organize video-conferencing-chats around particular themes. The dissemination of information in languages other than English could be organized in a similar fashion as the translation of TED talks and information, which have resulted in 20,039 translations of the TED talks into 82 different languages by 5,853 translators by 12 July 2011 (see http://www.ted.com/OpenTranslationProject where the Nokia sponsored project is described as 'one of the most comprehensive attempts by a major media platform to subtitle and index online video content. It's also a groundbreaking effort in the public, professional use of volunteer translation').

We all need 'dreams', and some of those dreams are more realizable than others, and some will require extensive co-operation and organization. In Tokyo in 2004 I asked: What stops us from creating a global web based learning environment – the Global Virtual Systemic-Functional University? Almost a decade has passed. We have perhaps not taken seriously the necessary steps to enhance this possibility of creating a truly global SFL learning and research community.

The whole educational field is currently debating such questions as: What are the challenges of adding emerging technologies or tools to the classroom and what can we do to improve integration of traditional classroom with online experience and other uses of Web-based technology? What are the software and hardware issues? Does the traditional classroom provide sufficient learning experience? Does the use of Web-based technology improve or hinder the learning process?

We need to guarantee free and open access to SFL-theory and practice (some experimentation has been made with free conferences, free courses and free publications) as well as find a balance between what is free and what will require fees to cover costs. But we also need to make our needs known to those who might be in the position of sponsoring our work and interests in developing a global, virtual SF-university. This means looking after our public relations.

This chapter began with the Wikipedia's definition of 'cyberspace' and it will close with the Wikipedia definition of 'public relations', to encourage us to promote our work and our public image among the possible sponsors for our work and other parties interested in our work. The Wikipedia writes about the function of public relations: 'Public relations is used to build rapport with employees, customers, investors, voters, or the general public. Almost any organization that has a stake in how it is portrayed in the public arena employs some level of public relations.' Further, Wikipedia states that the increasing use of various technologies helps the processes of 'democratization and 'demysticication of subjects' (http://en.wikipedia.org/wiki/Public_relations). Similarly, SFL-theory and its community will benefit from both of these processes when the global, virtual SFL-university becomes reality.

References

This chapter has used electronic references only, mentioned in the text, the access of which all have been checked on 13 July 2011.

Index

CPSIA information can be obtained at www.ICGtesting.com
Printed in the USA
BVOW03*0213070414

349204BV00001B/2/P